CW00922158

CICERO

IX

LCL 198

CICERO

PRO LEGE MANILIA
PRO CAECINA · PRO CLUENTIO
PRO RABIRIO PERDUELLIONIS

WITH AN ENGLISH TRANSLATION BY

H. GROSE HODGE

HARVARD UNIVERSITY PRESS
CAMBRIDGE, MASSACHUSETTS
LONDON, ENGLAND

First published 1927

LOEB CLASSICAL LIBRARY® is a registered trademark
of the President and Fellows of Harvard College

ISBN 978-0-674-99218-4

*Printed on acid-free paper and bound by
The Maple-Vail Book Manufacturing Group*

CONTENTS

PREFATORY NOTE   vii

SHORT BIBLIOGRAPHY   viii

SUMMARY OF EVENTS   ix

SPEECH ON THE APPOINTMENT OF GNAEUS
    POMPEIUS

    Introduction   2
    Text and Translation   14

SPEECH IN DEFENCE OF AULUS CAECINA

    Introduction   86
    Text and Translation   96

SPEECH IN DEFENCE OF AULUS CLUENTIUS
    HABITUS

    Introduction   208
    Text and Translation   222

SPEECH IN DEFENCE OF GAIUS RABIRIUS
    CHARGED WITH HIGH TREASON

    Introduction   444
    Text and Translation   452

INDEX   493

PREFATORY NOTE

IT may fairly be claimed that no four speeches of
Cicero surpass in interest those contained in this
volume : the rhetorical splendour of the *De imperio*,
the legal and antiquarian lore of the *Pro Caecina*,
the dramatic story and impassioned pleading of
the *Pro Cluentio* and the historical significance
of the *Pro Rabirio*—all this, coupled with the fact
that the second and fourth of these speeches
do not appear to have been translated into English
before, has made the translator's task particularly
attractive.

In translating the *De imperio* I have followed the
text, and am chiefly indebted to the edition, of
J. R. Nicol. In the *Pro Caecina* I followed
Baiter's text and gained some useful information
from Long's edition. In the *Pro Cluentio* I followed
Faussett's text, based on that of Classen, and
owe much to his and to Peterson's edition. In the
Pro Rabirio I followed Heitland's text, based
on that of Kayser, and am greatly indebted to
his exhaustive edition. Deviations from these
texts have been pointed out in the footnotes.
On historical questions I have throughout consulted
Mommsen.

I should like also to express my thanks to Mr.
W. H. Moresby, C.B.E., barrister-at-law of the

PREFATORY NOTE

Inner Temple, who has helped me in questions involving technical legal phraseology ; and to Mr. Harold Hodge, barrister-at-law of the Middle Temple and formerly editor of the *Saturday Review*, who, in addition to reading the proofs of this volume, has contributed some valuable suggestions.

H. G. H.

SUMMARY OF EVENTS REFERRED TO IN
THE FOUR SPEECHES

Civil

B.C.
133. Tribunate and murder of Ti. Gracchus.

123. Tribunate of G. Gracchus : institution of equestrian jurors.
121. Murder of G. Gracchus.

106. Birth of Cicero and Pompeius. Proposal to restore the law courts to the Senate. Lex Servilia of Caepio.

100. Birth of Julius Caesar. Marius consul for the sixth time.
Death of Saturninus and Glaucia.
Failure of the *Leges Appuleias*.

Military

B.C.
133. The province of Asia formed by bequest of the kingdom of Pergamus to Rome.

120. Birth of Mithridates VI.

102. Marius defeats the Teutons at Aquae Sextiae.
101. Marius defeats the Cimbri at Vercellae.

SUMMARY OF EVENTS

Civil	Military
B.C.	B.C.
99. Condemnation of Sextus Titius.	
91. Attempt of Drusus to reform the Senate: proposal to punish (retrospectively) corrupt jurors. Murder of Drusus.	91. Outbreak of the Social War.
	89. Pompeius serves under his father.
88. Consulship of Sulla and Q. Pompeius Rufus.	88. First Mithridatic War: massacre of 80,000 Romans.
	87. Sulla sails to Greece.
	86. Victory of Chaeronea.
	85. Victory of Orchomenus.
	84. End of first Mithridatic War. Murena left in charge of Asia.
	83. Sulla returns to Italy: Pompeius raises troops to support him.
82. Sulla dictator: proscription of the Marians. *Leges Corneliae*: law courts transferred from Equestrians to Senate; degradation of tribunate. Oppianicus at Larinum. Disfranchisement of Volaterrae.	82. Second Mithridatic War.
81. Cicero called to the Bar.	81. Pompeius recovers Sicily from the Marians. Pompeius in Africa: his first triumph.

x

SUMMARY OF EVENTS

Civil	*Military*
B.C.	B.C.
	80. Revolt of Sertorius in Spain.
79. Cicero defends the woman of Arretium against Sulla.	
78. Attempted revolution of Lepidus.	
	77. Pompeius, appointed to command against Sertorius, marches through Gaul into Spain.
76. Cicero quaestor.	
75. *Lex Aurelia* of Cotta : partial restoration of the tribunate.	75. Bithynia bequeathed to Rome. Mithridates in treaty with Sertorius.
74. Cicero defends Scamander. Trial of Oppianicus. " iudicium Iunianum."	74. Third Mithridatic War. Antonius commissioned against the Pirates. Mithridates besieges Cyzicus.
74-66. Propaganda by Quinctius : various jurors put on trial.	
	73. Lucullus relieves Cyzicus. The Slave War.
72. Death of Oppianicus.	72. Defeat of Mithridates at Cabira and flight to Armenia. Murder of Sertorius ends war in Spain.
	71. Death of Spartacus and end of Slave War. Triumph of Pompeius.

SUMMARY OF EVENTS

Civil	*Military*
B.C.	B.C.
70. Consulship of Pompeius and Crassus: restoration of the tribunate and division of the law courts between Senate, Equestrians, and *Tribuni aerarii*.	70. Lucullus declares war on Armenia.
Gellius and Lentulus censors.	
69. Cicero curule aedile. Trial of Caecina.	69. Victory of Tigranocerta.
	68. Retreat of Lucullus from Artaxata.
67. Cicero elected praetor.	67. Retreat of Lucullus to Pontus. Defeat of Ziela: recovery of Mithridates.
	Lex Gabinia. Pompeius exterminates piracy in 49 days.
66. Cicero *Pro lege Manilia.*	66. *Lex Manilia.* Pompeius appointed to command in Asia.
Trial of Cluentius.	
63. Cicero consul.	
Agrarian law of Rullus proposed and rejected.	
Trial of Rabirius for High Treason.	

THE SPEECH OF MARCUS TULLIUS CICERO ON THE APPOINTMENT OF GNAEUS POMPEIUS

INTRODUCTION

§ 1. THE destruction of Carthage left Rome free to become the mistress of the world. She had had to fight her way step by step for the sovereignty of Italy and for every stage which she advanced beyond it ; and to fight still harder for her very existence against her great rival in the West. But once that rivalry was no longer to be feared, she was free to turn her attention to the East ; and in the course of the next fifty years she conquered, absorbed, and even inherited wide dominions in Greece and Asia.

This period of imperial expansion coincided with the supremacy at Rome of the Senate, a narrow, aristocratic oligarchy which, though admirably fitted to pilot the Republic through a time of national danger, failed to resist the effects of comparative security and the temptations involved in a world-wide empire ; while troubles at home and abroad diverted the attention of the central government from responsibilities which were perhaps hardly realized. There were efforts at reform ; but the reformers could not look beyond Italy : Gaius Gracchus deliberately sacrificed the provinces to the greed of the new, plutocratic class by whose elevation he strove to check the power of the Senate ; and the plight of the provincials, ground between the upper

2

and the nether millstone of the governor and the tax-farmer, was an unhappy one indeed.

The provincial governor during the later years of the Republic was not, as under the Empire, a trained civil servant, but a successful politician. He looked forward during his political career to the command of a province as a means whereby to pay his debts and to live in comfort after his return: to many, such a career was impossible as well as unattractive without this prospect; and Cicero himself, whose humanity had won him the love of the provincials when quaestor in Sicily, and who was profoundly shocked by the cruelty and rapacity of a man like Verres, shows in the present speech that he still regards Asia as primarily a gold-mine.

While the provincial governor regarded it as a perquisite of his office to despoil his province, its complete exploitation was due to the system which placed the collection of provincial taxes in the hands of private individuals. The financiers and business men, who constituted the Equestrian order, secured at an auction held in Rome the right to farm the taxes of Asia; and the large staff of agents maintained for the purpose in the province, while supported by all the resources of Rome, were responsible only to the " company " which employed them. The sole object of such a company was to extract the uttermost farthing from the provincials.

It was to their governor that the provincials should have been able to look for redress; but his private interests made it probable that he would connive at the misdeeds of the tax-farmers in return for their silence about his own. So that it was only by a formal trial at Rome that either could be

brought to book. But both safeguarded themselves
by methods of extortion sufficiently thorough to
provide them with an ample surplus wherewith to
bribe the jury, whose members at this time were
mostly drawn from the Senatorial and Equestrian
orders—that is to say, it consisted of men who,
whether they hoped to be provincial governors
themselves or had money invested in the farming
of the revenues, were ready enough to give their
support to the governor or the tax-farmer in return
for a share in the spoils of the world ; while little
sympathy was to be expected from the Roman people
as a whole who had no interest to spare for the
condition of the provinces and an increasing need for
their riches.

Under this vicious system and without hope of
redress, the condition of the provinces was well nigh
desperate : Cicero himself provides abundant evidence both of their misery and of its cause. It may
be that, as an advocate, he was taking on the com-
plexion of his cause ; but as an Equestrian by
birth and a Senator by elevation, he was as much
prejudiced one way as another, and there is no
reason to doubt the truth of his admission in this
speech that " words can hardly express the hatred
felt against us by foreign nations, owing to the
wanton and outrageous conduct of those whom of
late years we have sent them as governors."

§ 2. In these circumstances the provincials of Asia
were ready to look in any direction for a saviour ;
and it is not surprising that they believed they
had found one in the brilliant and ambitious king
of Pontus. Mithridates VI., despite a veneer of
Hellenism, was a thorough oriental save only for the

energy and tenacity with which he pushed his schemes of aggrandizement and which brought him within a little of overthrowing the power of Rome in Asia.

The first collision occurred in 92 B.C. Aggression and intrigue had by this time placed most of Asia Minor under the control of Mithridates ; but when he planted his nominee on the throne of Cappadocia, the buffer state between his territory and that of Roman Cilicia, Lucius Sulla, the governor, with a small force succeeded in ejecting the usurper and putting Ariobarzanes in his place. But no sooner had Sulla left for Italy than Mithridates drove Ariobarzanes into exile, restored his nominee to the kingdom of Cappadocia, and supplanted the king of Bithynia with another more useful to himself.

Ariobarzanes appealed to Rome and a struggle became inevitable. But Mithridates was prepared for it : in 91 B.C. with a vast army he swept away the resistance of the Romans, overwhelmed the province of Asia, and, not content with putting to death by torture the chief Roman official, Manius Aquilius, he ordered the massacre, on a single day of 88 B.C., of every Italian in Asia Minor : the groaning provincials were avenged at last. But such a vengeance was Mithridates' greatest mistake, for it was more than even the supineness of the Roman Senate could overlook and it meant that the Mithridatic war must be fought to a finish. Sulla was the one man for the task ; and leaving Italy to his enemies he crossed with a small army to Greece, where, by 85 B.C., he defeated the hosts of Mithridates in two pitched battles. Next year he dictated the terms of peace in Asia ; but he could no longer delay

5

his return, and the final punishment of Mithridates was postponed.

The end of this first campaign left Mithridates in a position not much worse than he was in at the beginning, and he set himself at once, under cover of peace, to recapture lost ground. The so-called second Mithridatic war was not of his choosing : he contented himself with inflicting a heavy defeat upon Murena who had rashly attacked him, and Sulla at once recalled his lieutenant. The peace was renewed in 81 B.C., leaving Mithridates free to continue his preparations for the final struggle in conjunction with his son-in-law Tigranes, king of Armenia.

§ 3. On the death in 75 B.C. of the king of Bithynia, his kingdom passed, in accordance with his will, to Rome, whose territory was thus advanced still nearer to the frontiers of Pontus ; and Mithridates, seeing Rome already occupied by the war with Sertorius in Spain, took this opportunity to declare war and immediately overran Bithynia. Sulla was dead : Lucius Lucullus was appointed to the command in Asia and a brilliant campaign followed. Mithridates barely escaped from before Cyzicus with the remnant of his army : his fleet, largely manned by Romans from the camp of Sertorius, was intercepted on its way to Italy and sunk ; and after his utter defeat at the battle of Cabira in 72 B.C. he fled for refuge to Armenia and remained, little more than a prisoner, at the court of Tigranes. Lucullus spent the next three years in reorganizing Asia; but this could never be done securely till Armenia was dealt with also. Accordingly he demanded the surrender of Mithridates : Tigranes refused and, in 69 B.C., Lucullus

6

crossed the Euphrates. He won a brilliant and overwhelming victory at Tigranocerta and started out to finish the campaign by an attack on Artaxata, the capital of Armenia.

But he had tempted Fortune too far : his strict discipline had made him unpopular with his troops and his reforms in Asia had brought him into collision with the tax-farmers. As a result he now found himself hampered by intrigues at home and threatened with a mutiny in the field. He turned to retreat ; and though he conducted his retirement with credit and even with success, it had its inevitable consequences in a war against orientals. Tigranes, whose cause had but lately seemed hopeless, yielded to the influence of Mithridates and took the offensive with renewed vigour and resources ; and when at last Lucullus made his way back to Pontus in 67 B.C., he found that the army which he had left there under a lieutenant had been annihilated at Ziela and that a successor had already been sent from Rome to take his place. Glabrio, indeed, refused to take over the command, but Lucullus was rendered powerless by the mutinous temper of his soldiers to prevent the undoing of all that eight years' campaigning had achieved ; and when both he and Glabrio were finally superseded in 66 B.C., the position in Asia Minor was much what it had been when he first took the field in 74 B.C.

§ 4. Gnaeus Pompeius, who was now invested with the supreme command in Asia, was already established as the favourite general of the Roman people by a series of victories more appreciated if less deserved than those of Lucullus. Born, like Cicero, in 106 B.C., he served at the age of seventeen in his father's

army against Cinna. On Sulla's return to Italy in 83 B.C. he joined him with an army which he had raised on his own authority. Sulla then commissioned him to crush the survivors of the Marian party in Sicily and Africa, his success being rewarded by a triumph in 81 B.C. After Sulla's death in 78 B.C. he came forward as the champion of the Senate against the attempted revolution of Lepidus, which he crushed at Mutina in 77 B.C., insisting on being appointed, as a reward for his services, to the command of the war against Sertorius in Spain in the following year. He was far from successful; and it was only by the assassination of Sertorius in 72 B.C. that he was enabled to win an easy, if belated, victory. Returning to Italy in 71 B.C. at the head of his army, he found the rising of the gladiators almost at an end through the efforts of Crassus, who, just before the arrival of Pompeius, defeated them in a decisive battle ; but having the good fortune to fall in with the main body of fugitives, he cut it to pieces and then wrote to the Senate proclaiming himself the hero of the Slave War.

He now proposed himself as a candidate for the consulship, and although he was rendered ineligible for it alike by his age and by his absence from Rome he was too much loved by the people and feared by the Senate to be in any danger of failure. And so, though a simple Equestrian, he entered Rome in triumph for the second time on the last day of 71 B.C. and on the first day of the new year took office as consul with Crassus as his colleague. Rome was at his feet ; and he used his power to undo the work of Sulla, restoring among other things the position of the Equestrian order in the courts and their

control of the revenues of Asia. His year of office ended, he retired into private life.

§ 5. But once again his country's extremity proved the opportunity which Pompeius needed. The Mediterranean Sea was swarming with pirates whose numbers and daring had so much increased during the recent troublous times that the communications of the entire civilized world were interrupted : the coastal cities, even of Italy, were constantly subject to attack; and, worst of all, the populace of Rome, dependent upon imported corn, was threatened with starvation. The people turned to their idol ; and in 67 B.C. the Gabinian Law, which conferred almost unlimited powers and resources upon Pompeius for the extermination of piracy, was carried with acclamation despite the foreboding of the Senate. Popular confidence was not misplaced : in three months his powers of organization and leadership and, not least important, his clemency enabled him to clear the pirates from the seas and from their innumerable strongholds along the coasts.

§ 6. His task performed, the victorious general lingered in Cilicia, while at Rome the name of Pompeius was on every lip : his victories formed a brilliant contrast with the disasters which, in the same year, had befallen Lucullus in Asia ; the long dreaded power of the pirates had been abolished in three months, while eight years' campaigning had left that of Mithridates unimpaired. The remedy seemed obvious ; and in 66 B.C. the necessary bill was proposed by G. Manilius [a] : Pompeius was to be invested with the supreme command, with unlimited resources,

[a] From the name of its proposer the law came to be known as the Lex Manilia : hence the alternative title to this speech.

and without restriction of time or place. The grateful
Equestrians, the adoring populace were clamouring
for its ratification : only the Senate, seeing in
Pompeius one of many future masters, held aloof ;
and Cicero, wishing to make his first appearance on
the political platform in the most popular, and
therefore the most profitable, of causes, lent his
eloquence to support the Manilian proposal.

§ 7. There is every indication that the present
speech was intended by Cicero to be the best that
his utmost endeavour could make it. The occasion on
which it was delivered marked a turning-point both
in his own fortunes and in those of his country ; and
the orator, then in the prime of life and elated by
his recent election to the praetorship, was eager to
crown his eloquence with political as well as with
forensic success. We have no reason to doubt that
his speech was enthusiastically received, and he tells
us himself that he was satisfied with it ; while one
modern critic considers that " the orator expresses
himself with studious moderation and in a dis-
passionate and dignified tone." [a]

But this verdict is not likely to be the general one.
Compared with the other speeches contained in this
volume, the *De imperio*, despite all its cleverness, its
rhetoric, and its gorgeous display of superlatives,
must seem artificial and even tawdry : it lacks the
subtlety and variety of the *Pro Caecina*, the absorbing
interest and the personal enthusiasm of the *Pro
Cluentio*. Despite the protestation of his concluding
words, we feel that Cicero was endeavouring to
conceal from his audience, and even from himself,
his true motives in making this speech—a desire at

[a] See Cicero, *Orator* § 101, and J. E. Sandys' note, *ib.*

once to embellish his reputation and to secure his
future by ranging himself from the first moment of
his political career on the side of Pompeius, to
whom the people looked then, and the Senate were
presently to look, as their champion ; and by
supporting a measure which was destined—though
the orator little suspected it—to make Pompeius
master of Senate and people alike, until such time
as a greater than Pompeius should sweep away
the political power of them both.

Analysis of the Speech

§§ 1-5. On this my first appearance on the public
platform[a] I am fortunate in having the merits of
Pompeius as my theme. The situation in Asia is
one that calls for his appointment.

§§ 6-19. First, *the nature of the war* involves both
your honour and your interests. Remember Mithridates' atrocities and that he is still unpunished
despite the efforts of our generals. He has devoted
an interval of peace to preparing an attack upon
Rome in concert with her other enemies. You
cannot overlook his conduct to your citizens and your
allies. No wonder that they unite to demand the
appointment of Pompeius. You must defend so
rich a province even from a feeling of insecurity
which is sufficient by itself to destroy your revenues
and which is now amply justified. Moreover, you
cannot sacrifice the business interests of so many
private citizens without loss to the whole state, as
you learned in the first Mithridatic war.

[a] Cicero, recently elected praetor, thus acquired for the first
time the right of submitting questions to the people (*agere cum
populo*).

§§ 20-26. Second, *the magnitude of the war* must not be underestimated. I recognize with gratitude the successes of Lucullus; but they left Mithridates still alive, able to recuperate his fortunes in Armenia and ultimately to turn upon our war-weary troops and inflict a disaster upon them. Lucullus was recalled —and so the situation remains at this moment.

§§ 27-35. Lastly, *the choice of a general* should not be difficult: Pompeius alone possesses the requisite experience and ability, as witness his campaigns by land and sea. Rome was at the mercy of the pirates, who were everywhere victorious till Pompeius exterminated them with amazing speed and thoroughness.

§§ 36-48. Pompeius has moral as well as military qualities: there are no scandals in his army. The allies, generally the chief sufferers from your soldiers, are glad to provide his troops with quarters; nor does he allow any form of self-indulgence to hamper his movements. His character commands as much admiration abroad as does his versatile ability at home. Another asset is his prestige: his reputation has accomplished much already, and this alone saved Asia at the recent crisis. His success against the pirates was a purely personal one. Again, if I dare say so, he has the luck of most great generals and we may at least hope that it will never desert him.

§§ 49-50. Such is the general whom Providence has given you for a war of this nature and this magnitude. He is already on the scene of action: all you have to do is to appoint him.

§§ 51-58. This measure is opposed by two distinguished men; but it is facts, not personalities. that should influence you. As for Hortensius, he

opposed the Gabinian Law: what would have happened had you followed his advice? That was a time of unparalleled humiliation for us at sea, for we could not protect our own coasts against the pirates, let alone our allies; and so, despite Hortensius, supreme command was given to Pompeius and our sovereignty at once restored. It is merely petty to oppose the appointment of Gabinius as lieutenant to Pompeius: he has an especial claim to the position and there is ample precedent for it. I will see that the question is referred to the Senate.

§§ 59-64. As for Catulus, greatly as I respect his qualities, he is over-cautious and fears " an innovation "—though no such thing is actually proposed. Catulus has been the first to approve of Pompeius's career, which has been a series of innovations unprovided for by our constitution and unprecedented in our history. Our opponents have the country against them and it is they, not the country, who have been proved wrong.

§§ 65-68. Pompeius has the character as well as the ability needed for a campaign in Asia, where the outrageous conduct of our officers has made us justly hated; and experienced men like Hortensius and Catulus know that self-control is an necessary to our generals as strategy. The vilest abuses can only be checked by giving Pompeius a free hand, and I am supported in this opinion by men as eminent as my opponents.

§ 69. Good luck, then, to your proposal, Manilius: you have the country at your back. For myself, I pledge you my whole-hearted support—not that I hope to profit thereby, but because I consider it a patriotic duty.

M. TULLI CICERONIS DE IMPERIO CN.
POMPEI AD QUIRITES ORATIO

1 I. Quamquam mihi semper frequens conspectus
vester multo iucundissimus, hic autem locus ad
agendum amplissimus, ad dicendum ornatissimus est
visus, Quirites, tamen hoc aditu laudis, qui semper
optimo cuique maxime patuit, non mea me voluntas
adhuc, sed vitae meae rationes ab ineunte aetate
susceptae prohibuerunt. Nam cum antea per aetatem nondum huius auctoritatem loci attingere
auderem statueremque nihil huc nisi perfectum ingenio, elaboratum industria adferri oportere, omne
meum tempus amicorum temporibus transmittendum
2 putavi. Ita neque hic locus vacuus umquam fuit ab
iis, qui vestram causam defenderent, et meus labor
in privatorum periculis caste integreque versatus ex
vestro iudicio fructum est amplissimum consecutus.
Nam cum propter dilationem comitiorum ter praetor

ᵃ *Quirites* signifies the Roman People in their civil
capacity.
ᵇ The title *Pro lege Manilia* has no ancient authority.
ᶜ Praetors were elected by the Comitia Centuriata. Cicero
received the votes of all the centuries and was thus elected
first: the voting for the other vacancies was still going on
when the interruption (probably by violence) took place.

THE SPEECH ADDRESSED TO HIS FELLOW - CITIZENS[a] BY MARCUS TULLIUS CICERO ON THE APPOINTMENT OF GNAEUS POMPEIUS[b]

I. Although it has at all times given me an especial 1
pleasure to behold your crowded assembly, and
this place in particular has seemed to me to afford
the amplest scope for action, the fairest stage for
eloquence, none the less, fellow-citizens, this approach
to fame, which the best have ever found most widely
open, has hitherto been barred to me, not certainly
by any wish of mine, but by that scheme of life
which, from my earliest years, I had laid down
for myself. For previously, seeing that I was debarred by my youth from aspiring to this proud
position and was resolved to bring here nothing but
the mature outcome of my talent, the finished
product of my industry, I considered that my every
hour should be devoted to my friends in their hours
of peril. And so, while this platform has never been 2
without fit champions of your cause, the disinterested
and blameless employment of my labours in private
lawsuits has been crowned by the dignity which
your verdict has conferred. For when, owing to the
postponement of the elections,[c] my name was thrice
proclaimed as heading the poll for the praetorship

15

primus centuriis cunctis renuntiatus sum, facile intellexi, Quirites, et quid de me iudicaretis et quid aliis praescriberetis. Nunc cum et auctoritatis in me tantum sit, quantum vos honoribus mandandis esse voluistis, et ad agendum facultatis tantum, quantum homini vigilanti ex forensi usu prope cotidiana dicendi exercitatio potuit adferre, certe et, si quid auctoritatis in me est, apud eos utar, qui eam mihi dederunt, et, si quid in dicendo consequi possum, iis ostendam potissimum, qui ei quoque rei fructum suo iudicio

3 tribuendum esse duxerunt. Atque illud in primis mihi laetandum iure esse video, quod in hac insolita mihi ex hoc loco ratione dicendi causa talis oblata est, in qua oratio deesse nemini possit. Dicendum est enim de Cn. Pompei singulari eximiaque virtute ; huius autem orationis difficilius est exitum quam principium invenire. Ita mihi non tam copia quam modus in dicendo quaerendus est.

4 II. Atque ut inde oratio mea proficiscatur, unde haec omnis causa ducitur, bellum grave et periculosum vestris vectigalibus ac sociis a duobus potentissimis regibus infertur, Mithridate et Tigrane, quorum alter relictus, alter lacessitus occasionem sibi ad occupandam Asiam oblatam esse arbitratur. Equitibus Romanis, honestissimis viris, adferuntur ex Asia cotidie litterae, quorum magnae res aguntur in vestris vectigalibus exercendis occupatae ; qui ad

---

a i.e. the Roman province of Asia, which at this time consisted of Phrygia, Mysia, Caria, and Lydia.

by the vote of each century in turn, I could not fail
to understand, gentlemen, what verdict you were
passing upon myself, and what course you were
recommending to others. And now, since I possess
such a measure of influence as, by conferring office
upon me, you have intended should be mine, and
such a degree of skill in public speaking as an almost
daily practice in pleading can bestow through his
experience in the courts upon one anxious to learn,
then assuredly any influence that may be mine I
will exercise among those to whom I owe it, and
any attainments I can achieve as an orator I will
display most chiefly to those whose verdict has
pronounced that oratory, too, is deserving of reward.
And I realize that I am especially entitled to con- 3
gratulate myself upon the fact, that, unaccustomed
as I am to the style of oratory that becomes this
platform, the cause I have to plead is such as could
leave no one at a loss for words. For it is mine to
speak of the unique and extraordinary merits of
Gnaeus Pompeius, and a speech upon that topic is
harder to end than to begin ; so that my task as a
speaker lies in the search not for material but for
moderation.

II. To start, then, with the cause that is respon- 4
sible for the whole situation—a serious and dangerous
war is being waged against your tributaries and your
allies by two mighty kings, Mithridates and Tigranes,
who are led, the one by his impunity, the other by
his exasperation, to suppose that an opportunity is
offered them to lay hold on Asia.[a] Every day letters
arrive from Asia for my good friends the Roman
knights who are concerned for the great sums they
have invested in the farming of your revenues ; and

17

me pro necessitudine, quae mihi est cum illo ordine,
causam rei publicae periculaque rerum suarum de-
5 tulerunt : Bithyniae, quae nunc vestra provincia
est, vicos exustos esse complures, regnum Ariobar-
zanis, quod finitimum est vestris vectigalibus, totum
esse in hostium potestate ; L. Lucullum magnis
rebus gestis ab eo bello discedere ; huic qui succes-
serit, non satis esse paratum ad tantum bellum
administrandum ; unum ab omnibus sociis et civibus
ad id bellum imperatorem deposci atque expeti,
eundem hunc unum ab hostibus metui, praeterea
neminem.

6 Causa quae sit, videtis : nunc, quid agendum sit,
considerate. Primum mihi videtur de genere belli,
deinde de magnitudine, tum de imperatore deligendo
esse dicendum.

Genus est belli eius modi, quod maxime vestros
animos excitare atque inflammare ad persequendi
studium debeat ; in quo agitur populi Romani gloria
quae vobis a maioribus cum magna in omnibus rebus,
tum summa in re militari tradita est ; agitur salus
sociorum atque amicorum, pro qua multa maiores
vestri magna et gravia bella gesserunt ; aguntur
certissima populi Romani vectigalia et maxima,
quibus amissis et pacis ornamenta et subsidia belli
requiretis ; aguntur bona multorum civium, quibus
est a vobis et ipsorum et rei publicae causa con-
7 sulendum.   III. Et quoniam semper appetentes

on the strength of my close connexion with that order they have represented to me the position of the public interests and the danger of their private fortunes : how that in Bithynia,[a] now a province of 5 yours, many villages have been burnt to the ground ; the kingdom of Aziobarzanes which borders on your tributary states, is entirely in the hands of the enemy ; Lucius Lucullus, despite great achievements, is retiring from the campaign ; his successor is not adequately equipped for the conduct of so great a war : one man is universally desired and demanded by citizens and allies alike as the commander for this war ; one and the same commander is feared by the enemy, and they fear none but him.

You see what the situation is : now consider what 6 is to be done. I think it best to deal first with the nature of the war, next with its magnitude and lastly with the choice of a commander.

The nature of the war is such as is most calculated to rouse and fire your hearts with the determination to carry it through ; for it involves the glory of Rome, which has come down to you from your forefathers great in everything but greatest of all in war : it involves the safety of your allies and friends, in whose defence your forefathers undertook many great and serious wars : it involves the most assured and the most considerable sources of the public revenue, the loss of which would cause you to look in vain for the ornaments of peace or the munitions of war : it involves the property of many citizens whose interests you are bound to consult both for their own sake and for that of the commonwealth. III. And since you have ever been, beyond 7

---

[a] Bithynia was bequeathed to Rome in 75 B.C.

gloriae praeter ceteras gentes atque avidi laudis
fuistis, delenda est vobis illa macula Mithridatico
bello superiore concepta, quae penitus iam insedit
ac nimis inveteravit in populi Romani nomine, quod
is, qui uno die tota in Asia, tot in civitatibus, uno
nuntio atque una significatione litterarum cives Romanos necandos trucidandosque denotavit, non modo
adhuc poenam nullam suo dignam scelere suscepit,
sed ab illo tempore annum iam tertium et vicesimum
regnat, et ita regnat, ut se non Ponti neque Cappadociae latebris occultare velit, sed emergere ex patrio
regno atque in vestris vectigalibus, hoc est in Asiae
8 luce, versari. Etenim adhuc ita nostri cum illo rege
contenderunt imperatores, ut ab illo insignia vic-
toriae, non victoriam reportarent. Triumphavit L.
Sulla, triumphavit L. Murena de Mithridate, duo
fortissimi viri et summi imperatores, sed ita trium-
pharunt, ut ille pulsus superatusque regnaret. Verum
tamen illis imperatoribus laus est tribuenda, quod
egerunt, venia danda, quod reliquerunt, propterea
quod ab eo bello Sullam in Italiam res publica,
Murenam Sulla revocavit.

9   IV. Mithridates autem omne reliquum tempus non
ad oblivionem veteris belli, sed ad comparationem
novi contulit ; qui postea, cum maximas aedificasset
ornassetque classes exercitusque permagnos, quibus-
cumque ex gentibus potuisset, comparasset et se
Bosporanis, finitimis suis, bellum inferre simularet,

other nations, seekers after glory and greedy of renown, I call upon you to wipe out that stain incurred in the first Mithridatic war which is now so deeply ingrained and has so long been left upon the honour of the Roman people ; in that he who, upon a single day throughout the whole of Asia and in many states, by a single message and by one dispatch marked out our citizens for butchery and slaughter, has hitherto not only failed to pay any penalty adequate to his crime but has remained on the throne for two-and-twenty years from that date, a king who is not content with lurking in the fastnesses of Pontus or Cappadocia but issues out from his hereditary kingdom and flaunts himself in your tributary states, aye, for all Asia to behold. For 8 hitherto our generals have maintained the conflict with this monarch in such a way as to bring home the trappings of victory over him, not victory itself. One triumph over Mithridates was celebrated by Lucius Sulla and another triumph by Lucius Murena, brave men and great generals both, but their triumphs left Mithridates beaten and conquered—yet still upon his throne ! None the less those generals deserve praise for what they did, pardon for what they left undone, since both were recalled to Italy from the war, Sulla by a crisis at home and Murena by Sulla.

IV. Mithridates, however, devoted all the period 9 which followed not to effacing the memory of the late war but to preparing for a new one. For thereupon he built and fitted out mighty fleets and raised enormous armies from whatever nations he could under pretence of attacking his neighbours on the Bosphorus, and sent envoys as far as Spain with

usque in Hispaniam legatos ac litteras misit ad eos
duces, quibuscum tum bellum gerebamus, ut, cum
duobus in locis disiunctissimis maximeque diversis
uno consilio a binis hostium copiis bellum terra
marique gereretur, vos ancipiti contentione districti
10 de imperio dimicaretis. Sed tamen alterius partis
periculum, Sertorianae atque Hispaniensis, quae
multo plus firmamenti ac roboris habebat, Cn.
Pompei divino consilio ac singulari virtute depulsum
est ; in altera parte ita res a L. Lucullo, summo viro,
est administrata, ut initia illa rerum gestarum magna
atque praeclara non felicitati eius, sed virtuti, haec
autem extrema, quae nuper acciderunt, non culpae,
sed fortunae tribuenda esse videantur. Sed de
Lucullo dicam alio loco, et ita dicam, Quirites, ut
neque vera laus ei detracta oratione mea neque falsa
11 adficta esse videatur ; de vestri imperii dignitate atque
gloria, quoniam is est exorsus orationis meae, videte
quem vobis animum suscipiendum putetis.

V. Maiores nostri saepe mercatoribus aut navi-
culariis nostris iniuriosius tractatis bella gesserunt ;
vos tot milibus civium Romanorum uno nuntio atque
uno tempore necatis quo tandem animo esse debetis ?
Legati quod erant appellati superbius, Corinthum
patres vestri, totius Graeciae lumen, exstinctum esse
voluerunt ; vos eum regem inultum esse patiemini,
qui legatum populi Romani consularem vinculis ac
verberibus atque omni supplicio excruciatum necavit ? Illi libertatem imminutam civium Romano-

---

ᵃ *i.e.* Sertorius : see Introduction, § 4.
ᵇ Against the Illyrian pirates, 229 B.C.
ᶜ In 146 B.C.
ᵈ Manius Aquilius.

letters to the general with whom we were then at war,[a] in order that the war by land and sea might be conducted by two hostile armies acting in concert on two fronts at the opposite ends of the earth, and that you might have to fight for your supremacy with the distraction of a twofold attack. But the 10 danger in the West from Sertorius in Spain, which was much the more serious and substantial, was removed by the inspired strategy and extraordinary valour of Gnaeus Pompeius ; while on the Eastern front the conduct of the campaign by that fine general, Lucius Lucullus, suggests that the great and glorious achievements with which it began were due more to his good qualities than to his good luck, and the recent events with which it ended to no fault of his but to ill-fortune. As for Lucullus, I will speak of him anon, and when I do so you will see that no word of mine, gentlemen, either robs him of his true glory or flatters him with false. As for the honour 11 and glory of your empire, since that was the theme with which my speech began, consider with what feelings it should inspire you.

V. Our forefathers often undertook wars to defend our merchants or ship-masters against any high-handed treatment :[b] what, then, should be your feelings when, by a single order and at a single moment, so many thousands of Roman citizens have been put to death ? Because their envoys had been somewhat disrespectfully addressed, your ancestors decided on the extinction of Corinth,[c] the light of Greece : will you allow to go unpunished the king who imprisoned, scourged, and put to death by every kind of torture a Roman envoy[d] of consular rank ? They would not brook any restriction on the liberty

rum non tulerunt ; vos ereptam vitam neglegetis ?
Ius legationis verbo violatum illi persecuti sunt ; vos
legatum omni supplicio interfectum relinquetis ?
12 Videte, ne, ut illis pulcherrimum fuit tantam vobis
imperii gloriam tradere, sic vobis turpissimum sit id,
quod accepistis, tueri et conservare non posse.

Quid ? quod salus sociorum summum in periculum
ac discrimen vocatur, quo tandem animo ferre debetis ?   Regno est expulsus Ariobarzanes rex, socius
populi Romani atque amicus ; imminent duo reges
toti Asiae non solum vobis inimicissimi, sed etiam
vestris sociis atque amicis ; civitates autem omnes
cuncta Asia atque Graecia vestrum auxilium ex-
spectare propter periculi magnitudinem coguntur ;
imperatorem a vobis certum deposcere, cum praesertim vos alium miseritis, neque audent neque se id
13 facere sine summo periculo posse arbitrantur. Vident
et sentiunt hoc idem, quod vos, unum virum esse, in
quo summa sint omnia, et eum propter esse, quo
etiam carent aegrius ; cuius adventu ipso atque
nomine, tametsi ille ad maritimum bellum venerit,
tamen impetus hostium repressos esse intellegunt ac
retardatos.   Hi vos, quoniam libere loqui non licet,
taciti rogant, ut se quoque, sicut ceterarum provinciarum socios, dignos existimetis, quorum salutem tali
viro commendetis, atque hoc etiam magis, quod
ceteros in provinciam eius modi homines cum imperio
mittimus, ut, etiam si ab hoste defendant, tamen

---

^a *e.g.* by the Achaean League which insulted the Roman
envoys, 147 B.C.
^b *i.e.* Glabrio.

of Roman citizens : will you pass over the loss of
their lives ? They avenged the verbal infringement
of an envoy's privilege : *a* will you leave unnoticed the death by every kind of torture of your
envoy ? See to it that, as it was the proudest 12
achievement of your forefathers to bequeath to you
so glorious an empire, so it be not your deepest
shame to be powerless to protect and maintain that
heritage.

Again, when your allies' safety is in a perilous
and critical position, what, pray, should be your
feelings ? King Ariobarzanes, the ally and friend
of Rome, has been driven from his kingdom :
Asia is threatened by two kings who are the sworn
enemies of your allies and friends as well as of yourselves ; and it is to you that every state in Greece
and Asia is, by the magnitude of its peril, forced to
look for help : to demand from you one particular
general (especially as you have sent someone else *b*)
they neither dare nor do they think that they
could do so without extreme danger. They see and 13
feel, even as you do yourselves, that there is one
man who possesses in all respects the highest qualifications and that he is near at hand, wherefore
they are the sorrier to be without him : the fact of
his arrival, his reputation alone, although it is for a
naval war that he has come, they feel to have
checked and restrained the onslaughts of their foes.
They, then, debarred from speaking openly, mutely
beseech you to regard them, like your allies in other
provinces, as worthy that their safety should be
entrusted to this great man, and all the more because
the usual governors whom we send to administer the
province are of a type that makes their arrival in an

ipsorum adventus in urbes sociorum non multum ab
hostili expugnatione differant. Hunc audiebant antea,
nunc praesentem vident tanta temperantia, tanta
mansuetudine, tanta humanitate, ut ii beatissimi esse
videantur, apud quos ille diutissime commoretur.

14 VI. Quare, si propter socios nulla ipsi iniuria
lacessiti maiores nostri cum Antiocho, cum Philippo,
cum Aetolis, cum Poenis bella gesserunt, quanto vos
studio convenit iniuriis provocatos sociorum salutem
una cum imperii vestri dignitate defendere, praesertim cum de maximis vestris vectigalibus agatur ?
Nam ceterarum provinciarum vectigalia, Quirites,
tanta sunt, ut iis ad ipsas provincias tutandas vix
contenti esse possimus, Asia vero tam opima est ac
fertilis, ut et ubertate agrorum et varietate fructuum
et magnitudine pastionis et multitudine earum rerum,
quae exportantur, facile omnibus terris antecellat.
Itaque haec vobis provincia, Quirites, si et belli
utilitatem et pacis dignitatem retinere vultis, non
modo a calamitate, sed etiam a metu calamitatis est
15 defendenda. Nam in ceteris rebus cum venit calamitas, tum detrimentum accipitur ; at in vectigalibus
non solum adventus mali, sed etiam metus ipse adfert
calamitatem. Nam cum hostium copiae non longe
absunt, etiam si irruptio nulla facta est, tamen
pecuaria relinquitur agri cultura deseritur merca-
torum navigatio conquiescit. Ita neque ex portu
neque ex decumis neque ex scriptura vectigal con-

---

allied city differ but little from an assault by the
enemy, even though they defend it from the enemy
himself ; whereas this man, as formerly they heard
and now see with their eyes, is so moderate, so
merciful, and so humane that those are accounted
the most fortunate in whose midst his stay is most
prolonged.

VI. If then it was for their allies' sake that 14
our forefathers, though unprovoked by any injury to
themselves, waged war with Antiochus, with Philip,
with the Aetolian League *a* and with Carthage,*b*
how great should be your zeal, when challenged by
injury, to defend at one and the same time the
safety of your allies and the honour of your empire,
especially when your chief sources of revenue are
involved ! For while the revenues of our other
provinces, gentlemen, are barely sufficient to make
it worth our while to defend them, Asia is so rich
and fertile as easily to surpass all other countries in
the productiveness of her soil, the variety of her
crops, the extent of her pastures and the volume
of her exports. This province, gentlemen, if you
wish to retain what makes either war possible or
peace honourable, it is your duty to defend not only
from disaster but from fear of disaster. For in most 15
cases it is at the moment when disaster occurs that
loss is sustained ; but in the case of revenue it is
not only the occurrence of a calamity but the
mere dread that brings disaster ; for when the
enemy's forces are near at hand, even though they
have not crossed the frontier, the pastures are
deserted, the fields left untilled and the sea-borne
trade comes to an end. Consequently neither from
customs duties, tithes nor grazing dues can the

servari potest ; quare saepe totius anni fructus uno
rumore periculi atque uno belli terrore amittitur.
16 Quo tandem igitur animo esse existimatis aut eos,
qui vectigalia nobis pensitant, aut eos, qui exercent
atque exigunt, cum duo reges cum maximis copiis
propter adsint ? cum una excursio equitatus perbrevi
tempore totius anni vectigal auferre possit ? cum
publicani familias maximas, quas in saltibus habent,
quas in agris, quas in portubus atque custodiis, magno
periculo se habere arbitrentur ? Putatisne vos illis
rebus frui posse, nisi eos, qui vobis fructui sunt,
conservaritis, non solum, ut ante dixi, calamitate,
sed etiam calamitatis formidine liberatos ?

17 VII. Ac ne illud quidem vobis neglegendum est,
quod mihi ego extremum proposueram, cum essem
de belli genere dicturus, quod ad multorum bona
civium Romanorum pertinet ; quorum vobis pro
vestra sapientia, Quirites, habenda est ratio diligenter. Nam et publicani, homines honestissimi
atque ornatissimi, suas rationes et copias in illam
provinciam contulerunt, quorum ipsorum per se res
et fortunae vobis curae esse debent. Etenim, si
vectigalia nervos esse rei publicae semper duximus,
eum certe ordinem, qui exercet illa, firmamentum
18 ceterorum ordinum recte esse dicemus. Deinde ex
ceteris ordinibus homines gnavi atque industrii par-

revenues be maintained ; and so a single rumour of danger, a single alarm of war, often means the loss of a whole year's income. What, pray, do you 16 suppose to be the state of mind either of those who pay us the taxes or of those who farm and collect them, when two kings with mighty armies are near at hand ; when a single cavalry raid can in an instant carry off the revenue of a whole year ; when the tax-farmers feel that there is the gravest risk in keeping the large staffs which they maintain on the pastures and the corn lands, at the harbours and the coastguard stations ? Do you imagine that you can enjoy these advantages unless you preserve those from whom you derive them and keep them free not only, as I said before, from disaster but from fear of disaster ?

VII. There is still another point which, when 17 starting out to discuss the nature of the war, I decided to keep to the end—a point of which you must not lose sight : I mean the fact that there are many Roman citizens whose property is affected by this war ; and wise men like yourselves know that their interests demand your careful consideration. For in the first place the honourable and distinguished men who farm our revenues have transferred their business and their resources to that province, and their interests and fortunes ought, on personal grounds, to be your concern. For if we have always held that our revenues are the sinews of the common-wealth, then we shall assuredly be right in saying that the class which farms those revenues is the mainstay of the other classes. Moreover, of those 18 other classes there are men of energy and industry who are some of them personally engaged in business

tim ipsi in Asia negotiantur, quibus vos absentibus
consulere debetis, partim eorum in ea provincia
pecunias magnas collocatas habent. Est igitur
humanitatis vestrae magnum numerum eorum
civium calamitate prohibere, sapientiae videre multorum civium calamitatem a re publica seiunctam esse
non posse. Etenim primum illud parvi refert, nos
publicanis amissis[1] vectigalia postea victoria recuperare ; neque enim isdem redimendi facultas erit
propter calamitatem neque aliis voluntas propter
19 timorem. Deinde, quod nos eadem Asia atque
idem iste Mithridates initio belli Asiatici docuit, id
quidem certe calamitate docti memoria retinere debemus. Nam tum, cum in Asia res magnas permulti
amiserant, scimus Romae solutione impedita fidem
concidisse. Non enim possunt una in civitate multi
rem ac fortunas amittere, ut non plures secum in
eandem trahant calamitatem. A quo periculo prohibete rem publicam et mihi credite, id quod ipsi
videtis, haec fides atque haec ratio pecuniarum, quae
Romae, quae in foro versatur, implicata est cum illis
pecuniis Asiaticis et cohaeret ; ruere illa non possunt,
ut haec non eodem labefacta motu concidant. Quare
videte, num dubitandum vobis sit omni studio ad id
bellum incumbere, in quo gloria nominis vestri, salus
sociorum, vectigalia maxima, fortunae plurimorum
civium coniunctae cum re publica defendantur.

[1] amissis *codd.* : omissis *Müller.*

[a] See Introduction, § 1.
[b] In 88 B.C.; see Introduction, § 2.

in Asia, and you ought to consult their interests in their absence ; while others of them have vast sums invested in that province. Your humanity therefore enjoins that you should save this large body of citizens from ruin, and your wisdom shows you that the State cannot but be involved in the ruin of many of its citizens. For in the first place the subsequent recovery of our taxes through victory makes but little difference once the tax-farmers are lost ; for the individuals in question will lack the power to buy the contract *a* owing to their ruin and any others the inclination owing to their fear. In the second 19 place we ought assuredly to remember the lesson which we learned from this same Mithridates at the beginning of the Asiatic war, since we were taught it through disaster. For, coinciding with the loss by many people of large fortunes in Asia, we know that there was a collapse of credit at Rome owing to suspension of payment.*b* It is, indeed, impossible for many individuals in a single State to lose their property and fortunes without involving still greater numbers in their own ruin. Do you defend the commonwealth from this danger ; and believe me when I tell you—what you see for yourselves—that this system of credit and finance which operates at Rome, in the Forum, is bound up in, and depends on capital invested in Asia ; the loss of the one inevitably undermines the other and causes its collapse. Bethink you, therefore, whether you should hesitate to throw yourselves with the utmost enthusiasm into a war to defend the honour of your name, the well-being of your allies, the most important of your revenues and—a thing in which the commonwealth is closely concerned—the fortunes of so many citizens.

20 VIII. Quoniam de genere belli dixi, nunc de
magnitudine pauca dicam. Potest enim hoc dici,
belli genus esse ita necessarium, ut sit gerendum,
non esse ita magnum, ut sit pertimescendum. In
quo maxime laborandum est, ne forte ea vobis, quae
diligentissime providenda sunt, contemnenda esse
videantur. Atque ut omnes intellegant me L.
Lucullo tantum impertire laudis, quantum forti viro
et sapienti homini et magno imperatori debeatur,
dico eius adventu maximas Mithridati copias omnibus
rebus ornatas atque instructas fuisse, urbemque
Asiae clarissimam nobisque amicissimam Cyziceno-
rum obsessam esse ab ipso rege maxima multitudine
et oppugnatam vehementissime, quam L. Lucullus
virtute, assiduitate, consilio summis obsidionis peri-
21 culis liberavit ; ab eodem imperatore classem magnam et ornatam, quae ducibus Sertorianis ad Italiam
studio atque odio[1] inflammata raperetur, superatam
esse atque depressam ; magnas hostium praeterea
copias multis proeliis esse deletas patefactumque
nostris legionibus esse Pontum, qui antea populo
Romano ex omni aditu clausus fuisset ; Sinopen
atque Amisum, quibus in oppidis erant domicilia
regis, omnibus rebus ornatas ac refertas ceterasque
urbes Ponti et Cappadociae permultas uno aditu
adventuque esse captas ; regem spoliatum regno
patrio atque avito ad alios se reges atque ad alias

[1] atque odio *H* : *om. cett.*

VIII. Having spoken about the nature of the war, 20
I will now say a few words about its magnitude.
For it may be urged that while the war is by its
nature so necessary that we must engage in it, it is
not of such magnitude that we need greatly fear it ;
and in this connexion my chief task lies in persuading
you not to underestimate those facts for which you
need to make most careful provision. Now in order
to make it plain that I ascribe to Lucius Lucullus
that meed of praise which is due to a gallant soldier,
a wise man and a great general, I assert that at the
time of his arrival the forces at the disposal of
Mithridates were enormous, furnished and equipped
in every respect ; that the king in person with a
mighty host had laid siege to Cyzicus, the most
distinguished and loyal city in Asia, and had made
furious assaults upon it ; and that Lucius Lucullus,
by his valour, perseverance, and skill, relieved the
same from the desperate perils of the siege. By 2
this same general also the mighty and well-equipped
fleet which, under Sertorian leadership and fired
with all the zeal of resentment, was bearing down
upon Italy, was defeated and sunk ; moreover, in
the course of many battles he annihilated great
hosts of the enemy and opened a way for our legions
into Pontus, every approach to which had hitherto
been closed to the Roman people. Sinope and
Amisus, which contained the king's palaces and
were filled to overflowing with every kind of provision, as well as countless other cities of Pontus and
Cappadocia, capitulated to him on his mere approach
and arrival ; while the king, stripped of the kingdom
that had been his father's and grandfather's before
him, betook himself as a suppliant to foreign courts

33

CICERO

gentes supplicem contulisse ; atque haec omnia salvis
populi Romani sociis atque integris vectigalibus esse
gesta. Satis opinor haec esse laudis, atque ita,
Quirites, ut hoc vos intellegatis, a nullo istorum, qui
huic obtrectant legi atque causae, L. Lucullum
similiter ex hoc loco esse laudatum.

22   IX. Requiretur fortasse nunc, quem ad modum,
cum haec ita sint, reliquum possit magnum esse
bellum. Cognoscite, Quirites ; non enim hoc sine
causa quaeri videtur. Primum ex suo regno sic
Mithridates profugit, ut ex eodem Ponto Medea illa
quondam profugisse dicitur, quam praedicant in fuga
fratris sui membra in iis locis, qua se parens *per*-
sequeretur, dissipavisse, ut eorum collectio dispersa
maerorque patrius celeritatem persequendi retar-
daret. Sic Mithridates fugiens maximam vim auri
atque argenti pulcherrimarumque rerum omnium,
quas et a maioribus acceperat et ipse bello superiore
ex tota Asia direptas in suum regnum congesserat,
in Ponto omnem reliquit. Haec dum nostri colligunt
omnia diligentius, rex ipse e manibus effugit. Ita
illum in persequendi studio maeror, hos laetitia
23 tardavit. Hunc in illo timore et fuga Tigranes, rex
Armenius, excepit diffidentemque rebus suis con-
firmavit et adflictum erexit perditumque recreavit.
Cuius in regnum posteaquam L. Lucullus cum exercitu venit, plures etiam gentes contra imperatorem
nostrum concitatae sunt. Erat enim metus iniectus

---

* Father of Medea.

and foreign nations; and all this was accomplished without danger to the allies of Rome or loss to her revenues. This, I imagine, is praise enough and such as will satisfy you, gentlemen, that no like eulogy has been passed upon Lucullus from this platform by any of those who take exception to the measure which I advocate.

IX. Perhaps I shall now be asked: " How, in 22 view of all this, can what is left of the war be of any magnitude ? " Let me tell you, gentlemen, for the question appears not unreasonable. In the first place the flight of Mithridates from his kingdom reminds us of the way in which Medea in the legend fled long ago from that same Pontus : the story goes that in her flight she scattered the limbs of her brother along the track which her father would follow in pursuit, in order that his pursuit might be checked by a father's grief as he collected the scattered remains. In the same way Mithridates left behind him in Pontus as he fled the whole of his vast store of gold and silver and all his treasures— both those which he had inherited and those which he had himself accumulated in his kingdom as the spoils of all Asia taken during the former war. While our soldiers were too carefully engaged in collecting all this, the king himself slipped through their hands. And so, in the eagerness of pursuit, Aeetes *a* was delayed by his sorrow, our troops by their joy. Mithridates meanwhile, a panic-stricken 23 fugitive, found a welcome with Tigranes, king of Armenia, who comforted his despair, raised his drooping spirits and restored his ruined fortunes. On the arrival of Lucullus and his troops in Armenia, yet other nations rose against our general ; for fear

35

iis nationibus, quas numquam populus Romanus
neque lacessendas bello neque temptandas putavit;
erat etiam alia gravis atque vehemens opinio, quae
animos gentium barbararum pervaserat, fani locuple-
tissimi et religiosissimi diripiendi causa in eas oras
nostrum esse exercitum adductum. Ita nationes
multae atque magnae novo quodam terrore ac metu
concitabantur. Noster autem exercitus tametsi
urbem ex Tigranis regno ceperat et proeliis usus erat
secundis, tamen nimia longinquitate locorum ac
24 desiderio suorum commovebatur. Hic iam plura non
dicam; fuit enim illud extremum, ut ex iis locis a
militibus nostris reditus magis maturus quam pro-
gressio longior quaereretur. Mithridates autem et
suam manum iam confirmarat,[1] et magnis adventiciis
auxiliis multorum regum et nationum iuvabatur.
Nam hoc fere sic fieri solere accepimus, ut regum
adflictae fortunae facile multorum opes adliciant ad
misericordiam, maximeque eorum, qui aut reges sunt
aut vivunt in regno, ut iis nomen regale magnum et
25 sanctum esse videatur. Itaque tantum victus efficere
potuit, quantum incolumis numquam est ausus optare.
Nam cum se in regnum suum recepisset, non fuit eo
contentus, quod ei praeter spem acciderat, ut illam,
posteaquam pulsus erat, terram umquam attingeret,
sed in exercitum nostrum clarum atque victorem impetum fecit. Sinite hoc loco, Quirites, sicut poetae
solent, qui res Romanas scribunt, praeterire me
nostram calamitatem, quae tanta fuit, ut eam ad

---

[1] et eorum, qui se ex ipsius regno collegerant *codd.*:
del. Benecke.

had fallen upon those peoples whom Rome had never intended to attack in war or even to disturb: besides which, a strong and fanatical belief had become general among the barbarous nations that our army had been directed to those regions in order to loot a very wealthy and much-venerated temple. In this way many great peoples were roused to action by a new feeling of terror and alarm. Our own army, moreover, despite their capture of a city from the kingdom of Tigranes and their successes in battle, began to feel the extreme remoteness of their position and to long for home. Now I do not 24 propose to say more about that: for the end of it was that our soldiers were more anxious for an early return from these regions than for a further advance. Mithridates meanwhile had rallied his own following and was aided by large bodies of foreign auxiliaries from many kings and peoples. For we recognize how very generally it happens that the fallen fortunes of kings easily attract the pity of many able to help them, and especially of those who are either kings themselves or the dwellers in a kingdom, as they are likely to hold the name of king in the greatest awe and veneration. The result was that 25 he seemed able to accomplish more after his defeat than ever he dared hope before it. For on his return to his kingdom, not satisfied at having, beyond all his hopes, reached that land once more after being driven out of it, he attacked our army, despite its reputation and its victories. At this point, gentlemen, allow me to use the licence customary with poets writing of Roman history and to pass over our disaster, of which the magnitude was such that it was no messenger from the battle

aures imperatoris non ex proelio nuntius, sed ex
26 sermone rumor adferret. Hic in illo ipso malo
gravissimaque belli offensione L. Lucullus, qui tamen
aliqua ex parte iis incommodis mederi fortasse
potuisset, vestro iussu coactus, quod imperii diu-
turnitati modum statuendum vetere exemplo puta-
vistis, partem militum, qui iam stipendiis confectis
erant, dimisit, partem M'. Glabrioni tradidit. Multa
praetereo consulto ; sed ea vos coniectura perspicite,
quantum illud bellum factum putetis, quod coniungant
reges potentissimi, renovent agitatae nationes, sus-
cipiant integrae gentes, novus imperator noster
accipiat vetere exercitu pulso.
27 X. Satis mihi multa verba fecisse videor, quare
esset hoc bellum genere ipso necessarium, magnitudine periculosum ; restat, ut de imperatore ad id
bellum deligendo ac tantis rebus praeficiendo dicendum esse videatur.

Utinam, Quirites, virorum fortium atque inno-
centium copiam tantam haberetis, ut haec vobis
deliberatio difficilis esset, quemnam potissimum tantis
rebus ac tanto bello praeficiendum putaretis ! Nunc
vero cum sit unus Cn. Pompeius, qui non modo eorum
hominum, qui nunc sunt, gloriam, sed etiam anti-
quitatis memoriam virtute superarit, quae res est,
quae cuiusquam animum in hac causa dubium facere
28 possit ? Ego enim sic existimo, in summo imperatore
quattuor has res inesse oportere, scientiam rei militaris, virtutem, auctoritatem, felicitatem. Quis igitur
hoc homine scientior umquam aut fuit aut esse

but the rumour of the countryside which brought the tidings of it to the general's ears. Here in the 26 very hour of disaster and of a most serious reverse, because you thought that, out of deference to old precedent, some limit should be set to his long tenure of command, Lucullus—a man who might perhaps have been able in some measure to repair these losses—was by your orders compelled to disband a part of his troops, who had served their time, and to hand over a part to Manius Glabrio. There is much that I leave out on purpose : you must supply the omission for yourselves and realize what magnitude this war must have attained when it is waged in concert by two most powerful kings, renewed by tribes in ferment, taken up by fresh nations and entrusted, after the defeat of the old army, to a new Roman general.

X. I think I have said enough to show why this 27 war is by its nature necessary and in its magnitude dangerous : it remains, I think, to speak of the choice of a general to direct the war and of his appointment to a command of such importance.

I only wish, gentlemen, that you had so large a supply of brave and upright men as to make it difficult for you now to decide whom to put in charge of these great issues and of this great war ! But as it is, since Gnaeus Pompeius stands alone as one whose merit has surpassed in glory not only his contemporaries but even the annals of the past, what consideration exists such as to cause anyone to hesitate at this juncture ? For I consider that 28 a perfect general must possess four attributes— knowledge of warfare, ability, prestige, and luck. Who, then, ever possessed or had reason to possess

debuit ? qui e ludo atque pueritiae disciplinis, bello maximo atque acerrimis hostibus, ad patris exercitum atque in militiae disciplinam profectus est ; qui extrema pueritia miles in exercitu fuit summi imperatoris, ineunte adulescentia maximi ipse exercitus imperator ; qui saepius cum hoste conflixit, quam quisquam cum inimico concertavit, plura bella gessit quam ceteri legerunt, plures provincias confecit quam alii concupiverunt ; cuius adulescentia ad scientiam rei militaris non alienis praeceptis, sed suis imperiis, non offensionibus belli, sed victoriis, non stipendiis, sed triumphis est erudita. Quod denique genus esse belli potest, in quo illum non exercuerit fortuna rei publicae ? Civile, Africanum, Transalpinum, Hispaniense,[1] servile, navale bellum, varia et diversa genera et bellorum et hostium non solum gesta ab hoc uno, sed etiam confecta nullam rem esse declarant in usu positam militari, quae huius viri scientiam fugere possit.

29 XI. Iam vero virtuti Cn. Pompei quae potest oratio par inveniri ? Quid est, quod quisquam aut illo dignum aut vobis novum aut cuiquam inauditum possit adferre ? Neque enim illae sunt solae virtutes imperatoriae, quae vulgo existimantur, labor in negotiis, fortitudo in periculis, industria in agendo, celeritas in conficiendo, consilium in providendo, quae

---

[1] mixtum ex civilibus atque ex bellicosissimis nationibus *del. Bloch. These words are not contained* in toto *by any of the best* MSS. *and are probably a gloss.*

---

^a *i.e.* in the Marsian war, 89 and 88 B.C.
^b The war against the pirates, 67 B.C.

more knowledge of warfare than Pompeius—a man who left school and the studies of boyhood to join his father's army and study war in a serious campaign against formidable foes[a]; who when hardly more than a boy served as a soldier in an army commanded by a great general, and in early manhood was himself a general in command of a large army; who has done battle more often with his country's enemies than any other man has quarrelled with his own, fought more campaigns than other men have read of, discharged more public offices than other men have coveted; who, in his youth, learned the lessons of warfare not from the instructions of others but from the commands he held himself, not by reverses in war but by victories, not through campaigns but through triumphs? In short, what manner of warfare can there be in which the vicissitudes of his country have not afforded him experience? The civil war, the wars in Africa, Transalpine Gaul and Spain, the Slave war and the Naval war,[b] wars different in type and locality and against foes as different, not only carried on by himself unaided but carried to a conclusion, make it manifest that there is no item within the sphere of military experience which can be beyond the knowledge of Pompeius.

XI. Moreover, to the ability of Gnaeus Pompeius 29 what words can be found to do justice? What tribute can anyone pay other than what would be unworthy of him, stale to you and familiar to everybody? For the qualities proper to a general are not only those which are commonly supposed to be so— application to duty, courage in danger, thoroughness in operation, rapidity in execution, wisdom in

tanta sunt in hoc uno, quanta in omnibus reliquis imperatoribus, quos aut vidimus aut audivimus, non
30 fuerunt. Testis est Italia, quam ille ipse victor L. Sulla huius virtute et subsidio confessus est liberatam ; testis est Sicilia, quam multis undique cinctam periculis non terrore belli, sed consilii celeritate explicavit ; testis est Africa, quae magnis oppressa hostium copiis eorum ipsorum sanguine redundavit ; testis est Gallia, per quam legionibus nostris iter in Hispaniam Gallorum internicione patefactum est ; testis est Hispania, quae saepissime plurimos hostes ab hoc superatos prostratosque conspexit ; testis est iterum et saepius Italia, quae cum servili bello taetro periculosoque premeretur, ab hoc auxilium absente expetivit, quod bellum exspectatione eius attenuatum atque imminutum est, adventu sublatum ac sepul-
31 tum ; testes nunc vero iam omnes sunt orae atque omnes exterae gentes ac nationes, denique maria omnia cum universa, tum in singulis oris omnes sinus atque portus. Quis enim toto mari locus per hos annos aut tam firmum habuit praesidium, ut tutus esset, aut tam fuit abditus, ut lateret ? Quis navigavit, qui non se aut mortis aut servitutis periculo committeret, cum aut hieme aut referto praedonum mari navigaret ? Hoc tantum bellum, tam turpe, tam vetus, tam late divisum atque dis-

---

a In 83 B.C.

b In 81 B.C., when Pompeius recovered Sicily from the Marian general Carbo.

c In 81 B.C., when Pompeius defeated at Utica a combination between the Marian generals and the king of Numidia.

d In 76 B.C., when he cleared from the passes of the Alps the Gauls who supported Sertorius.

e In 72 B.C. he ended the war against Sertorius.

42

strategy—qualities which are possessed in greater measure by Pompeius alone than by all other generals whom we have seen or heard of. Italy *a* is my witness, 30 which, as the great conqueror, Lucius Sulla himself admitted, was set free by the able co-operation of Pompeius. Sicily *b* is my witness, which, beset on every side with numerous perils, was released not by the terror of his arms but by the swiftness of his strategy. Africa *c* is my witness, which, overwhelmed by great hosts of the enemy, was drenched with the blood of the same. Gaul *d* is my witness, through which a way was opened into Spain *d* for our legions by the utter destruction of the Gauls. Spain *e* is my witness, which many a time beheld countless foes by him conquered and laid low. Italy *f* is my witness again and again, which, when in the throes of the shameful and perilous Slave war, sought aid from him though far away and saw that war reduced and brought low by the expectation of his coming, dead and buried on his arrival. Nay, every region is my 31 witness and every foreign nation and people, and lastly every sea,*g* both in its whole expanse and in the separate creeks and harbours of its coasts. For what position on the whole sea-board during those years was either so strongly defended as to be secure or so well hidden as to escape notice ? Who sailed the seas without exposing himself to the risk either of death or of slavery, sailing as he did either in the winter or when the sea was infested with pirates ? Who ever supposed that a war of such dimensions, so inglorious and so long-standing, so widespread and

f In 71 B.C. he defeated Spartacus.
g In 67 B.C. he destroyed the pirates. For this and the rest of his career see Introduction, § 4.

CICERO

persum quis umquam arbitraretur aut ab omnibus
imperatoribus uno anno aut omnibus annis ab uno
32 imperatore confici posse ?   Quam provinciam tenui-
stis a praedonibus liberam per hosce annos ? quod
vectigal vobis tutum fuit ? quem socium defendistis ?
cui praesidio classibus vestris fuistis ? quam multas
existimatis insulas esse desertas, quam multas aut
metu relictas aut a praedonibus captas urbes esse
sociorum ?

   XII. Sed quid ego longinqua commemoro ?   Fuit
hoc quondam, fuit proprium populi Romani, longe a
domo bellare et propugnaculis imperii sociorum fortunas, non sua tecta defendere.   Sociis ego nostris
mare per hos annos clausum fuisse dicam, cum exercitus vestri numquam a Brundisio nisi hieme summa
transmiserint ?   Qui ad vos ab exteris nationibus
venirent, captos querar, cum legati populi Romani
redempti sint ?   Mercatoribus tutum mare non fuisse
dicam, cum duodecim secures in praedonum potes-
33 tatem pervenerint ?   Cnidum aut Colophonem aut
Samum, nobilissimas urbes, innumerabilesque alias
captas esse commemorem, cum vestros portus atque
eos portus, quibus vitam ac spiritum ducitis, in
praedonum fuisse potestate sciatis ?   An vero ignoratis portum Caietae celeberrimum ac plenissimum
navium inspectante praetore a praedonibus esse
direptum, ex Miseno autem eius ipsius liberos, qui
cum praedonibus antea ibi bellum gesserat, a prae-

---

[a] Probably Marcus Antonius, the orator (see the *Pro
Cluentio*, § 140), who defeated the pirates in 103 B.C. and
whose daughter (*liberi!*) was kidnapped and held to
ransom.

44

so extensive, could be brought to an end either by any number of generals in a single year or by a single general in any number of years ? What 32 province did you keep free from the pirates during those years ? What source of revenue was secure for you ? What ally did you protect ? To whom did your navy prove a defence ? How many islands do you suppose were deserted, how many of your allies' cities either abandoned through fear or captured by the pirates ?

XII. But why do I remind you of events in distant places ? Time was, long since, when it was Rome's peculiar boast that the wars she fought were far from home and that the outposts of her empire were defending the prosperity of her allies, not the homes of her own citizens. Need I mention that the sea during those wars was closed to our allies, when your own armies never made the crossing from Brundisium save in the depth of winter ? Need I lament the capture of envoys on their way to Rome from foreign countries, when ransom has been paid for the ambassadors of Rome ? Need I mention that the sea was unsafe for merchantmen, when twelve lictors have fallen into the hands of pirates ? Need I 33 record the capture of the noble cities of Cnidus and Colophon and Samos and of countless others, when you well know that your own harbours and those, too, through which you draw the very breath of your life, have been in the hands of the pirates ? Are you indeed unaware that the famous port of Caieta, when crowded with shipping, was plundered by the pirates under the eyes of the praetor, and that from Misenum the children of the very man who had previously fought there against the pirates[a] were

donibus esse sublatos? Nam quid ego Ostiense
incommodum atque illam labem atque ignominiam
rei publicae querar, cum prope inspectantibus vobis
classis ea, cui consul populi Romani praepositus esset,
a praedonibus capta atque oppressa est? Pro di
immortales! tantamne unius hominis incredibilis ac
divina virtus tam brevi tempore lucem adferre rei
publicae potuit, ut vos, qui modo ante ostium
Tiberinum classem hostium videbatis, nunc nullam
intra Oceani ostium praedonum navem esse audiatis?
34 Atque haec qua celeritate gesta sint, quamquam
videtis, tamen a me in dicendo praetereunda non
sunt. Quis enim umquam aut obeundi negotii aut
consequendi quaestus studio tam brevi tempore tot
loca adire, tantos cursus conficere potuit, quam
celeriter Cn. Pompeio duce tanti belli impetus navigavit? qui nondum tempestivo ad navigandum mari
Siciliam adiit, Africam exploravit, in Sardiniam cum
classe venit atque haec tria frumentaria subsidia rei
publicae firmissimis praesidiis classibusque munivit.
35 Inde cum se in Italiam recepisset, duabus Hispaniis
et Gallia Transalpina praesidiis ac navibus confirmata,
missis item in oram Illyrici maris et in Achaiam
omnemque Graeciam navibus Italiae duo maria
maximis classibus firmissimisque praesidiis adornavit,
ipse autem ut Brundisio profectus est, undequin-
quagesimo die totam ad imperium populi Romani
Ciliciam adiunxit; omnes, qui ubique praedones
fuerunt, partim capti interfectique sunt, partim unius
huius se imperio ac potestati dediderunt. Idem

kidnapped by the pirates ? Why should I lament
the reverse at Ostium, that shameful blot upon our
commonwealth, when almost before your own eyes
the very fleet which had been entrusted to the
command of a Roman consul was captured and
destroyed by the pirates ? Great Heavens ! Is it
possible that the incredible, the superhuman genius
of a single man has in so short a time illumined the
darkness which beset his country, that you, who but
lately saw with your eyes a hostile fleet before the
Port of Tiber, now hear the news that there is not
a pirate ship within the Portal of Ocean ? The 34
rapidity with which this feat was accomplished you
all know, but I cannot omit to mention it in my
speech. For who, however eager for the transaction
of business or the pursuit of gain, has ever succeeded
in visiting so many places in so short a time or in
accomplishing such long journeys at the same speed
with which, under the leadership of Pompeius, that
mighty armament swept over the seas ? Pompeius,
though the sea was still unfit for navigation, visited
Sicily, explored Africa, sailed to Sardinia and, by
means of strong garrisons and fleets, made secure
those three sources of our country's corn supply.
After that he returned to Italy, secured the two 35
provinces of Spain together with Transalpine Gaul,
dispatched ships to the coast of the Illyrian Sea, to
Achaea and the whole of Greece, and so provided
the two seas of Italy with mighty fleets and strong
garrisons ; while he himself, within forty-nine days
of starting from Brundisium, added all Cilicia to
the Roman Empire. All the pirates, wherever they
were, were either captured and put to death or they
surrendered to his power and authority and to his

47

Cretensibus, cum ad eum usque in Pamphyliam
legatos deprecatoresque misissent, spem deditionis
non ademit obsidesque imperavit. Ita tantum bellum, tam diuturnum, tam longe lateque dispersum,
quo bello omnes gentes ac nationes premebantur,
Cn. Pompeius extrema hieme apparavit, ineunte vere
suscepit, media aestate confecit.

36   XIII. Est haec divina atque incredibilis virtus
imperatoris. Quid? ceterae, quas paulo ante commemorare coeperam, quantae atque quam multae
sunt! Non enim bellandi virtus solum in summo ac
perfecto imperatore quaerenda est, sed multae sunt
artes eximiae huius administrae comitesque virtutis.
Ac primum quanta innocentia debent esse imperatores! quanta deinde in omnibus rebus temperantia!
quanta fide, quanta facilitate, quanto ingenio, quanta
humanitate! quae breviter qualia sint in Cn. Pompeio
consideremus. Summa enim omnia sunt, Quirites,
sed ea magis ex aliorum contentione quam ipsa per sese
37 cognosci atque intellegi possunt. Quem enim imperatorem possumus ullo in numero putare, cuius in
exercitu centuriatus veneant atque venierint? Quid
hunc hominem magnum aut amplum de re publica
cogitare, qui pecuniam ex aerario depromptam ad
bellum administrandum aut propter cupiditatem
provinciae magistratibus diviserit aut propter avaritiam Romae in quaestu reliquerit? Vestra admur-

alone. Again, when the pirates of Crete sent envoys to him as far as Pamphylia to plead their cause, he did not rob them of the hope that he would accept their surrender but demanded hostages. And so this war, so great and so protracted, so far and so widely extended, a war which pressed so heavily upon all nations and peoples, was by Gnaeus Pompeius organized at the end of winter, started at the beginning of spring, and finished by the middle of summer.

XIII. Such is his superhuman and unbelievable 36 genius as a commander. As for his other qualities of which I began to speak a little while since, how great and how numerous they are! For in a general of the highest and most perfect type we must not look for military genius alone. For there are many notable qualities which support and go with it. First, how great is the integrity needed by a general; and again, what self-control in every department; what trustworthiness, what condescension; what a brain and what a heart! Let us briefly review these qualities as they are found in Gnaeus Pompeius. For they are all to be found in him, gentlemen, and in the highest degree, though they may be recognized and appreciated better when contrasted with those of other men than when regarded simply by themselves. For what general can we hold in any sort of esteem 37 when in his army the appointment of centurions is for sale and has been sold? How can we attribute a great and lofty conception of patriotism to the sort of man who has been induced, by his ambition to become a governor, to divide among the magistrates the money issued to him from the treasury for the conduct of a campaign or, by his avarice, to leave it on interest at

muratio facit, Quirites, ut agnoscere videamini, qui
haec fecerint ; ego autem nomino neminem ; quare
irasci mihi nemo poterit, nisi qui ante de se voluerit
confiteri. Itaque propter hanc avaritiam impera-
torum quantas calamitates, quocumque ventum sit,
38 nostri exercitus ferant, quis ignorat ? Itinera quae
per hosce annos in Italia per agros atque oppida
civium Romanorum nostri imperatores fecerint, recordamini ; tum facilius statuetis, quid apud exteras
nationes fieri existimetis. Utrum plures arbitramini
per hosce annos militum vestrorum armis hostium
urbes an hibernis sociorum civitates esse deletas ?
Neque enim potest exercitum is continere imperator,
qui se ipse non continet, neque severus esse in iudicando, qui alios in se severos esse iudices non vult.
39 Hic miramur hunc hominem tantum excellere ceteris,
cuius legiones sic in Asiam pervenerint, ut non modo
manus tanti exercitus, sed ne vestigium quidem cuiquam pacato nocuisse dicatur ? Iam vero quem ad
modum milites hibernent, cotidie sermones ac litterae
perferuntur ; non modo ut sumptum faciat in militem
nemini vis adfertur, sed ne cupienti quidem cuiquam
permittitur. Hiemis enim, non avaritiae perfugium
maiores nostri in sociorum atque amicorum tectis
esse voluerunt.
40 XIV. Age vero, ceteris in rebus qua ille sit temperantia, considerate. Unde illam tantam celeritatem

Rome ? Your groans, gentlemen, show that you recognize the men who have done these things : for my part, I mention no names, so that no one can feel resentment against me unless he would admit that the cap fits. Who then does not know how great is the ruin which, owing to this avarice on the part of our generals, is caused by our armies in every place to which they go ? Think of the tours which 38 of late years our generals have made in Italy itself through the lands and the towns of Roman citizens, and then you will more easily judge what, it seems, are their practices among foreign peoples. Which do you think have been more frequently destroyed during late years—the cities of your enemies by your soldiers' arms or the territories of your friends by their winter quarters ? No commander can control an army who does not control himself, nor can he be a strict judge if he is unwilling that others should judge him strictly. Are we surprised, then, 39 to find Pompeius so far superior to other commanders, when they tell of his arrival in Asia with his legions that no one who had laid down his arms suffered injury either from any act of violence done by that great army or even from its passage ? And further, the way in which our soldiers behave in winter quarters is shown by the tidings and the letters which reach us daily : so far from any man being compelled to incur expense on a soldier's account, no man is allowed to do so even if he would. For our forefathers desired that the roofs of their allies and friends should be a shelter against the winter, not a refuge for avarice.

XIV. And further, consider the moderation which 40 he displays in other ways as well. Where do you

et tam incredibilem cursum inventum putatis ? Non
enim illum eximia vis remigum aut ars inaudita quaedam gubernandi aut venti aliqui novi tam celeriter
in ultimas terras pertulerunt, sed eae res, quae
ceteros remorari solent, non retardarunt ; non
avaritia ab instituto cursu ad praedam aliquam
devocavit, non libido ad voluptatem, non amoenitas
ad delectationem, non nobilitas urbis ad cognitionem,
non denique labor ipse ad quietem ; postremo signa
et tabulas ceteraque ornamenta Graecorum oppidorum, quae ceteri tollenda esse arbitrantur, ea sibi
41 ille ne visenda quidem existimavit. Itaque omnes
nunc in iis locis Cn. Pompeium sicut aliquem non ex
hac urbe missum, sed de caelo delapsum intuentur ;
nunc denique incipiunt credere fuisse homines
Romanos hac quondam continentia, quod iam
nationibus exteris incredibile ac falso memoriae
proditum videbatur ; nunc imperii vestri splendor
illis gentibus lucem adferre coepit : nunc intellegunt
non sine causa maiores suos tum, cum ea temperantia
magistratus habebamus, servire populo Romano quam
imperare aliis maluisse. Iam vero ita faciles aditus
ad eum privatorum, ita liberae querimoniae de aliorum iniuriis esse dicuntur, ut is, qui dignitate prin-
cipibus excellit, facilitate infimis par esse videa-
42 tur. Iam quantum consilio, quantum dicendi gravitate et copia valeat, in quo ipso inest quaedam
dignitas imperatoria, vos, Quirites, hoc ipso ex loco

suppose he found the secret of that great rapidity of
his, that amazing speed of movement ? For it was
not in his case the unusual strength of his oarsmen or
any undiscovered secret of navigation or some new
wind that bore him so swiftly to the ends of the
earth : it was rather that those things which delay
most other men did not keep him back. Avarice
did not entice him from his appointed course to
plunder of any kind, nor appetite to indulgence, nor
pleasant prospects to enjoyment, nor the fame of
any city to sight-seeing, nor, indeed, even toil to the
taking of rest ; and finally, the statues and pictures
and other treasures of Greek towns which most men
think themselves entitled to carry off, he did not
think fit even to look at. Now, therefore, everyone 41
in those regions regards Gnaeus Pompeius not as an
emissary from this city but as an angel from heaven :
now at last they begin to believe that there once
existed Romans of like self-control, though foreign
nations were beginning to think such a thing incredible, a mere mistaken legend : now does the
brightness of your empire begin to shed the light of
hope upon those races : now they begin to realize
that their forefathers were not without reason in
preferring, at a time when we had magistrates of
like moderation, to serve Rome rather than to rule
others. Moreover, it is said that he is so easy of
access to ordinary people, so open to hear their
complaints of wrongs done them by others, that he
whose greatness surpasses that of princes appears in
accessibility the equal of the lowest. His powers in 42
counsel, the weight and eloquence of his oratory,
which is characterized by the dignity appropriate to
a commander, you have often had occasion, gentle-

saepe cognovistis. Fidem vero eius quantam inter
socios existimari putatis, quam hostes omnes omnium
generum sanctissimam iudicarint? Humanitate iam
tanta est, ut difficile dictu sit, utrum hostes magis
virtutem eius pugnantes timuerint an mansuetudinem
victi dilexerint. Et quisquam dubitabit, quin huic
hoc tantum bellum transmittendum sit, qui ad omnia
nostrae memoriae bella conficienda divino quodam
consilio natus esse videatur?

43   XV. Et quoniam auctoritas quoque in bellis admini-
strandis multum atque in imperio militari valet, certe
nemini dubium est, quin ea re idem ille imperator
plurimum possit. Vehementer autem pertinere ad
bella administranda, quid hostes, quid socii de imperatoribus nostris existiment, quis ignorat, cum
sciamus homines in tantis rebus, ut aut contemnant
aut metuant aut oderint aut ament, opinione non
minus et fama quam aliqua ratione certa com-
moveri? Quod igitur nomen umquam in orbe terrarum clarius fuit? cuius res gestae pares? de quo
homine vos, id quod maxime facit auctoritatem, tanta
44 et tam praeclara iudicia fecistis? An vero ullam
usquam esse oram tam desertam putatis, quo non
illius diei fama pervaserit, cum universus populus
Romanus referto foro completisque omnibus templis,
ex quibus hic locus conspici potest, unum sibi ad
commune omnium gentium bellum Cn. Pompeium
imperatorem depoposcit? Itaque, ut plura non

men, to judge for yourselves in this very place. As
for his word of honour, how greatly, think you, must
it be valued by his allies, when all his enemies, of
whatever race, have adjudged it inviolable? Then,
too, such is his humanity that it were hard to say
whether his enemies have more feared his valour
when fighting against him or welcomed his clemency
when vanquished. And will any man hesitate to
transfer the conduct of this great war to the man
who seems to have been sent into the world by
Providence to bring to a conclusion all the wars of
our time?

XV. Now prestige also is of great importance in 43
the conduct of wars and in the exercise of a military
command; and no one doubts, I am sure, that the
commander I have mentioned is pre-eminent in this
direction too. Who, indeed, is unaware how enor-
mously important to the conduct of a campaign is
the opinion held about our generals by the enemy
and by the allies? For we know that in such crises
people are led to feel fear or scorn, love or hatred,
by fancy and rumour as much as by any process of
reasoning. What name, then, in the whole world
has ever been more famous? Whose achievements
are comparable to his? On whom beside have you
ever bestowed that which above all else confers
prestige, namely, such great and signal proofs of
your esteem? Think you indeed that there was 44
anywhere a coast so desolate that no tidings reached
it of that great day on which the entire Roman
People, thronging into the Forum and filling every
temple that commands a view of this platform,
demanded the appointment of Gnaeus Pompeius
alone to be their general in a world-war? And so,

dicam neque aliorum exemplis confirmem, quantum auctoritas[1] valeat in bello, ab eodem Cn. Pompeio omnium rerum egregiarum exempla sumantur ; qui quo die a vobis maritimo bello praepositus est imperator, tanta repente vilitas annonae ex summa inopia et caritate rei frumentariae consecuta est unius hominis spe ac nomine, quantum vix ex summa ubertate agrorum diuturna pax efficere potuisset.

45 Iam accepta in Ponto calamitate ex eo proelio, de quo vos paulo ante invitus admonui, cum socii pertimuissent, hostium opes animique crevissent, satis firmum praesidium provincia non haberet, amisissetis Asiam, Quirites, nisi ad ipsum discrimen eius temporis divinitus Cn. Pompeium ad eas regiones fortuna populi Romani attulisset.   Huius adventus et Mithridatem insolita inflammatum victoria continuit et Tigranem magnis copiis minitantem Asiae retardavit. Et quisquam dubitabit, quid virtute perfecturus sit, qui tantum auctoritate perfecerit, aut quam facile imperio atque exercitu socios et vectigalia conservaturus sit, qui ipso nomine ac rumore defenderit ?

46 XVI. Age vero illa res quantam declarat eiusdem hominis apud hostes populi Romani auctoritatem, quod ex locis tam longinquis tamque diversis tam brevi tempore omnes huic se uni dediderunt ! quod Cretensium legati, cum in eorum insula noster imperator exercitusque esset, ad Cn. Pompeium in

---

[1] auctoritas *H, Angelius* : huius auctoritas *cett.*

---

[a] *i.e.* Quintus Metellus, with whom Pompeius had an undignified quarrel over this incident.

without going on to prove by the examples of other men how great is the influence of prestige in war, let me quote Pompeius once again as an example of every form of distinction : on the day on which you appointed him to take command in the Naval war, his name alone and the hopes which it inspired caused a sudden fall in the price of wheat, after a time of extreme dearth and scarcity in the corn supply, to as low a level as could possibly have been reached after a long period of peace and agricultural prosperity. And now, after the disaster in Pontus 45 resulting from the battle to which I reluctantly referred a short time ago, since our allies were panic-stricken, the enemy fortified in resource and resolution, and the province possessed of no adequate garrison, you would have lost Asia, gentlemen, unless, at the critical moment, the good fortune of Rome had providentially directed Gnaeus Pompeius to the spot. His arrival restrained Mithridates, who was elated by the unusual experience of victory, and checked Tigranes, who was threatening Asia with great forces. Who, then, will be found to doubt what his valour will accomplish when his prestige has accomplished so much, or how easily he will secure the safety of our allies and our revenues by the armies under his command when he has secured their defence merely by the reputation of his name ? XVI. Again, how great is the prestige of Pompeius 46 among the enemies of Rome is shown by the fact that within so short a space of time, he alone received the surrender of them all, coming as they did from regions so distant and so far apart ; moreover, although there was a Roman general with his army in Crete,[a] to find Pompeius the Cretan envoys went

ultimas prope terras venerunt eique se omnes
Cretensium civitates dedere velle dixerunt ! Quid ?
idem iste Mithridates nonne ad eundem Cn. Pompeium legatum usque in Hispaniam misit ? eum,
quem Pompeius legatum semper iudicavit, ii, quibus
erat molestum ad eum potissimum esse missum,
speculatorem quam legatum iudicari maluerunt.
Potestis igitur iam constituere, Quirites, hanc
auctoritatem multis postea rebus gestis magnisque
vestris iudiciis amplificatam quantum apud illos
reges, quantum apud exteras nationes valituram
esse existimetis.

47 Reliquum est, ut de felicitate, quam praestare de
se ipso nemo potest, meminisse et commemorare de
altero possumus, sicut aequum est homines de
potestate deorum, timide et pauca dicamus. Ego
enim sic existimo, Maximo, Marcello, Scipioni, Mario
et ceteris magnis imperatoribus non solum propter
virtutem, sed etiam propter fortunam saepius imperia
mandata atque exercitus esse commissos. Fuit enim
profecto quibusdam summis viris quaedam ad ampli-
tudinem et ad gloriam et ad res magnas bene
gerendas divinitus adiuncta fortuna. De huius autem
hominis felicitate, de quo nunc agimus, hac utar
moderatione dicendi, non ut in illius potestate fortunam positam esse dicam, sed ut praeterita meminisse, reliqua sperare videamur, ne aut invisa dis
immortalibus oratio nostra aut ingrata esse videatur.

48 Itaque non sum praedicaturus, quantas ille res domi

ᵃ Quintus Fabius Cunctator, who saved Rome from
Hannibal ; Marcus Claudius Marcellus, the conqueror of
Syracuse in 212 B.C.; Scipio Aemilianus the younger, who
destroyed Carthage in 146 B.C. and Numantia in 133 B.C. ;
Gaius Marius, who defeated Jugurtha in 106 B.C. and the
Cimbri and Teutones in 101 B.C.

almost to the ends of the earth, and said that it was to him that all the states of Crete wished to make their surrender. What? Did not this very Mithridates send an envoy to Spain, once more to Gnaeus Pompeius? (For as an envoy Pompeius always regarded him; though people who were annoyed at his being sent expressly to Pompeius chose to regard him as a spy rather than an envoy.) And so you are now in a position to make up your minds how great, think you, will be the effect upon the kings in question, how great upon foreign nations, of a prestige like this, heightened by many subsequent achievements and by signal proofs of your esteem.

It remains for me to speak—though guardedly and **47** briefly, as is fitting when men discuss a prerogative of the gods—on the subject of good luck, which no man may claim as his own, but which we may remember and record in the case of another. For in my opinion Quintus Fabius the Great, Marcellus, Scipio, Marius,[a] and other great generals were entrusted with commands and armies not only because of their merits but not infrequently because of their good fortune. For some great men have undoubtedly been helped to the attainment of honour, glory, and success, by a kind of Heaven-sent fortune. And as for the good luck of the man whom we are now discussing, I shall speak of it with such reserve as to convey the impression that, without claiming good fortune as his prerogative, I am both mindful of the past and hopeful for the future, and to avoid appearing by what I say either to show ingratitude or to cause offence to the immortal gods. And so I do **48** not intend to proclaim his great achievements in

militiae, terra marique, quantaque felicitate gesserit,
ut eius semper voluntatibus non modo cives adsen-
serint, socii obtemperarint, hostes oboedierint, sed
etiam venti tempestatesque obsecundarint; hoc
brevissime dicam, neminem umquam tam impuden-
tem fuisse, qui ab dis immortalibus tot et tantas res
tacitus auderet optare, quot et quantas di immortales
ad Cn. Pompeium detulerunt. Quod ut illi proprium
ac perpetuum sit, Quirites, cum communis salutis
atque imperii, tum ipsius hominis causa, sicuti facitis,
velle et optare debetis.

49   Quare cum et bellum sit ita necessarium, ut neglegi
non possit, ita magnum, ut accuratissime sit administrandum, et cum ei imperatorem praeficere possitis,
in quo sit eximia belli scientia, singularis virtus, clarissima auctoritas, egregia fortuna, dubitatis, Quirites,
quin hoc tantum boni, quod vobis a dis immortalibus
oblatum et datum est, in rem publicam conservandam
50 atque   amplificandam   conferatis?   XVII.   Quodsi
Romae Cn. Pompeius privatus esset hoc tempore,
tamen ad tantum bellum is erat deligendus atque
mittendus; nunc cum ad ceteras summas utilitates
haec quoque opportunitas adiungatur, ut in iis ipsis
locis adsit, ut habeat exercitum, ut ab iis, qui habent,
accipere statim possit, quid exspectamus? aut cur
non ducibus dis immortalibus eidem, cui cetera
summa cum salute rei publicae commissa sunt, hoc
quoque bellum regium committamus?

peace and war, by land and sea, nor the great good luck that has attended them, in that his wishes have always secured the assent of his fellow-citizens, the acceptance of his allies, the obedience of his enemies, and even the compliance of wind and weather ; but this I will briefly assert, that no one has ever been so presumptuous that he dared hope in his heart for such great and such constant favours from Heaven as those which Heaven has bestowed upon Gnaeus Pompeius. That this good luck may always and especially be his, gentlemen, should be, as it is, your earnest hope, both for his own sake and equally for the sake of our commonwealth and our empire.

Wherefore, since this war is both of such import- 49
ance that it cannot be neglected and of such magnitude that it must be conducted with the utmost care ; and since you have it in your power to put in command of it one who possesses remarkable knowledge of warfare, exceptional capacity, brilliant prestige, and unusual good fortune, do you hesitate, gentlemen, to employ for the protection and advancement of the State, this great blessing which Heaven has bestowed and conferred upon you ? XVII. If, indeed, Pompeius were at this time in 50
Rome and a private citizen, you would still be bound to select him and send him to this great war. But as it is, when his other great qualifications are coupled with the advantage that he is on the very spot, that he has an army of his own, and that he can immediately take over other armies from those that have them, what are we waiting for ? Why should we not follow the guidance of Heaven and entrust this Mithridatic war as well to the same man to whom other issues have been entrusted to the great advantage of the State ?

51 At enim vir clarissimus, amantissimus rei publicae,
vestris beneficiis amplissimis adfectus, Q. Catulus,
itemque summis ornamentis honoris, fortunae, virtutis, ingenii praeditus, Q. Hortensius, ab hac ratione
dissentiunt. Quorum ego auctoritatem apud vos
multis locis plurimum valuisse et valere oportere
confiteor ; sed in hac causa, tametsi cognoscetis
auctoritates contrarias virorum fortissimorum et
clarissimorum, tamen omissis auctoritatibus ipsa re ac
ratione exquirere possumus veritatem, atque hoc
facilius, quod ea omnia, quae a me adhuc dicta sunt,
idem isti vera esse concedunt, et necessarium bellum
esse et magnum et in uno Cn. Pompeio summa esse
52 omnia. Quid igitur ait Hortensius ? Si uni omnia
tribuenda sint, dignissimum esse Pompeium, sed ad
unum tamen omnia deferri non oportere. Obsolevit
iam ista oratio, re multo magis quam verbis refutata.
Nam tu idem, Q. Hortensi, multa pro tua summa
copia ac singulari facultate dicendi et in senatu contra
virum fortem, A. Gabinium, graviter ornateque
dixisti, cum is de uno imperatore contra praedones
constituendo legem promulgasset, et ex hoc ipso loco
53 permulta item contra eam legem verba fecisti. Quid ?
tum, per deos immortales, si plus apud populum
Romanum auctoritas tua quam ipsius populi Romani
salus et vera causa valuisset, hodie hanc gloriam
atque hoc orbis terrae imperium teneremus ? An tibi

---

a Quintus Hortensius was Cicero's great rival as an orator
and pleader. They appeared on opposite sides at the trial
of Verres, 70 B.C., after which Cicero was acknowledged to
be supreme.

But it will be said that this view is opposed by no **51** less distinguished a patriot than Quintus Catulus, who enjoys the most honourable proofs of your esteem, and, moreover, by a man endowed with the highest gifts of position and fortune, character and intellect, Quintus Hortensius.[a] I admit that the opinion of those men has had on many occasions and ought to have the greatest weight with you ; but in the case before us, although you will find that the opinions of some brave and illustrious men are ranged against me, we can set opinions on one side and arrive at the truth by a consideration of the actual facts, and the more easily because even my opponents admit the truth of all that I have said hitherto, namely, that the war is a necessary one and a great one, and that Pompeius alone is possessed of all the highest qualifications. What then says Hortensius ? **52** That if one man is to be put in supreme command, the right man is Pompeius ; but that supreme command ought not to be given to one man. That line of argument is now out of date, refuted not so much by words as by the event. For it was you yourself, Quintus Hortensius, who, with all your consummate eloquence and unrivalled fluency, both denounced that courageous man, Aulus Gabinius, in a weighty and brilliant speech before the Senate, when he had introduced a measure for the appointment of a single commander against the pirates ; and also from this platform you spoke at length against the same measure. Now I ask you in Heaven's **53** name—if on that occasion the Roman People had thought more of your opinion than of their own welfare and their true interests, should we to-day be in possession of our present glory and our world-

tum imperium hoc esse videbatur, cum populi Romani legati, quaestores praetoresque capiebantur, cum ex omnibus provinciis commeatu et privato et publico prohibebamur, cum ita clausa nobis erant maria omnia, ut neque privatam rem transmarinam neque publicam iam obire possemus ?

54 XVIII. Quae civitas antea umquam fuit non dico Atheniensium, quae satis late quondam mare tenuisse dicitur, non Carthaginiensium, qui permultum classe ac maritimis rebus valuerunt, non Rhodiorum, quorum usque ad nostram memoriam disciplina navalis et gloria remansit, quae civitas, inquam, antea tam tenuis, quae tam parva insula fuit, quae non portus suos et agros et aliquam partem regionis atque orae maritimae per se ipsa defenderet ? At hercule aliquot annos continuos ante legem Gabiniam ille populus Romanus, cuius usque ad nostram memoriam nomen invictum in navalibus pugnis permanserit, magna ac multo maxima parte non modo utilitatis, sed dignitatis atque imperii caruit ; 55 nos, quorum maiores Antiochum regem classe Persemque superarunt omnibusque navalibus pugnis Carthaginienses, homines in maritimis rebus exercitatissimos paratissimosque, vicerunt, ii nullo in loco iam praedonibus pares esse poteramus ; nos, qui antea non modo Italiam tutam habebamus, sed omnes socios in ultimis oris auctoritate nostri imperii

wide empire? Or could our empire be said to have existed at a time when Roman envoys, quaestors, and praetors were taken prisoners; when we were debarred from communication both private and public with any one of our provinces; when every sea was so completely closed to us that we were actually unable to transact either our private or our public business overseas?

XVIII. Was there ever a state in times past—I 54 do not mean Athens, whose sea power is said to have been quite extensive, nor Carthage, strong as she was in her navy and in sea-warfare, nor Rhodes, the skill and reputation of whose seamen has survived to our own times—but was there ever in the past, I say, a state so weak, an island so small as to be unable by her own resources to defend her own harbours, her fields and a portion of the sea and of the coast? And yet it is an absolute fact that for some years consecutively before the law of Gabinius the great People of Rome, who down to our own times kept their reputation as invincible on the sea, were deprived of a great, nay, of much the greatest part of what belonged not only to their interests but also to their position as an imperial power. We, whose forefathers overcame at 55 sea King Antiochus and Perses,ᵃ who defeated in every naval engagement a people so experienced and so well equipped in naval requirements as the Carthaginians, we, I say, were on no occasion able to hold our own against the pirates. We who in former days, besides keeping the whole of Italy safe, were able to guarantee the safety of all our allies in the farthest coasts by the prestige of our empire—

ᵃ Antiochus was defeated in 190 B.C. and Perses in 168.

salvos praestare poteramus, tum, cum insula Delos
tam procul a nobis in Aegaeo mari posita, quo omnes
undique cum mercibus atque oneribus commeabant,
referta divitiis, parva, sine muro, nihil timebat,
idem non modo provinciis atque oris Italiae maritimis
ac portubus nostris, sed etiam Appia iam via care-
bamus ; et iis temporibus non pudebat magistratus
populi Romani in hunc ipsum locum escendere, cum
eum nobis maiores nostri exuviis nauticis et classium
56 spoliis ornatum reliquissent ! XIX. Bono te animo
tum, Q. Hortensi, populus Romanus et ceteros, qui
erant in eadem sententia, dicere existimavit ea, quae
sentiebatis ; sed tamen in salute communi idem
populus Romanus dolori suo maluit quam auctoritati
vestrae obtemperare. Itaque una lex, unus vir, unus
annus non modo nos illa miseria ac turpitudine
liberavit, sed etiam effecit, ut aliquando vere videremur omnibus gentibus ac nationibus terra marique
57 imperare. Quo mihi etiam indignius videtur ob-
trectatum esse adhuc, Gabinio dicam anne Pompeio
an utrique, id quod est verius, ne legaretur A.
Gabinius Cn. Pompeio expetenti ac postulanti.
Utrum ille, qui postulat ad tantum bellum legatum,
quem velit, idoneus non est qui impetret, cum ceteri

---

^a Delos owed its commercial importance to its situation as
a "half-way house" between Europe and Asia, its excellent
harbour and the security offered by its temple. It became
still more important when Corinth was destroyed by the
Romans in 146 B.C.
^b The Rostrum was so called because it was adorned
with the "beaks" of ships captured in the war against
Antium in 338 B.C.
^c Gabinius, as the proposer of the Lex Gabinia to which,
as the Lex Manilia had not yet been passed, Pompeius owed

in the days when, for instance, the island of Delos,[a] though set so far away from Rome in the Aegean sea, and visited by all men from every country with their merchandise and their cargoes, packed though the island was with riches, small though it was and defenceless, had nothing to fear—we, I repeat, were kept from making use not only of our provinces, the sea-coasts of Italy and our own harbours, but even of the Appian Way ! And yet at such a time the magistrates of Rome were not ashamed to mount this very platform, though our forefathers had left it to us adorned with naval trophies and the spoils of conquered fleets ![b] XIX. The Roman People realized 56 your good intentions, Quintus Hortensius, and those of others who supported your view, in expressing your sentiments ; but that did not prevent this same Roman People from being guided by their own resentment rather than by your opinion where the common weal was at stake. And the result was that one law, one man, and one year not only set you free from that distress and that reproach, but also brought it to pass that you seemed at last in very truth to be holding empire over all nations and peoples by land and sea. And this in my opinion 57 makes still more ungracious the opposition which has hitherto been offered (whether to spite Gabinius or Pompeius, or, as is nearer the truth, both of them) to the urgent request of Pompeius that Gabinius should serve as his lieutenant.[c] Is it that he who demands to have the man of his choice as his lieutenant for this great war is not a fit person to gain his request, though other generals have, in order to

his *imperium*, was debarred by law from holding any office created by his own proposal.

ad expilandos socios diripiendasque provincias, quos
voluerunt, legatos eduxerint, an ipse, cuius lege salus
ac dignitas populo Romano atque omnibus gentibus
constituta est, expers esse debet gloriae eius imperatoris atque eius exercitus, qui consilio ipsius ac
58 periculo est constitutus? An C. Falcidius, Q.
Metellus, Q. Caelius Latiniensis, Cn. Lentulus, quos
omnes honoris causa nomino, cum tribuni plebi
fuissent, anno proximo legati esse potuerunt; in
uno Gabinio sunt tam diligentes, qui in hoc bello,
quod lege Gabinia geritur, in hoc imperatore atque
exercitu, quem per vos ipse constituit, etiam prae-
cipuo iure esse deberet? De quo legando consules
spero ad senatum relaturos. Qui si dubitabunt aut
gravabuntur, ego me profiteor relaturum; neque me
impediet cuiusquam inimicum edictum, quo minus
vobis fretus vestrum ius beneficiumque defendam,
neque praeter intercessionem quicquam audiam, de
qua, ut arbitror, isti ipsi, qui minantur, etiam atque
etiam, quid liceat, considerabunt. Mea quidem
sententia, Quirites, unus A. Gabinius belli maritimi
rerumque gestarum Cn. Pompeio socius ascribitur,
propterea quod alter uni illud bellum suscipiendum
vestris suffragiis detulit, alter delatum susceptumque
confecit.

59 XX. Reliquum est, ut de Q. Catuli auctoritate et

---

* As praetor, Cicero had the right to bring a motion
before the Senate; but this was subject to the veto of an
equal or superior magistrate.

pillage the allies and despoil the provinces, taken
with them as their lieutenants those whom they have
chosen ; or that the very man by whose law the
safety and honour of the Roman People and of all
nations was established, ought himself to have no
share in the glory of the general and the army sent
into the field by his advice and at his peril ? Or 58
again, while Gaius Falcidius, Quintus Metellus,
Quintus Caelius Latinensis and Gnaeus Lentulus
(all of whom I mention with respect) were able to
serve as lieutenants to a general the year after they
had been tribunes of the people, is such scruple to
be shown only with regard to Gabinius, who, in the
case of this war which is carried on under the Gabinian
law, and of this general and army which, through
your vote, he sent into the field himself, was even
entitled to special privilege ? I hope that the
consuls will bring the question of his appointment
before the Senate : if they hesitate or demur, I
protest that I will do so myself ; [a] and neither shall I
be prevented by the malicious ruling of any magistrate from maintaining, in reliance upon your
support, the right and privilege conferred by you,
nor will I brook any interference save a veto ; and
the very tribunes who threaten to apply it will, I
think, reflect more than once how far they may go.
In my personal opinion, gentlemen, Aulus Gabinius
alone is associated with Pompeius in the achievements of the Maritime war ; in that the one, by
means of your vote, entrusted to a single commander
the conduct of that war and the other brought to
a conclusion the war whose conduct had been entrusted to him.

XX. It remains, I think, that I should speak of the 59

sententia dicendum esse videatur. Qui cum ex vobis
quaereret, si in uno Cn. Pompeio omnia poneretis, si
quid eo factum esset, in quo spem essetis habituri,
cepit magnum suae virtutis fructum ac dignitatis,
cum omnes una prope voce in eo ipso vos spem
habituros esse dixistis. Etenim talis est vir, ut nulla
res tanta sit ac tam difficilis, quam ille non et consilio
regere et integritate tueri et virtute conficere possit.
Sed in hoc ipso ab eo vehementissime dissentio, quod,
quo minus certa est hominum ac minus diuturna vita,
hoc magis res publica, dum per deos immortales licet,
frui debet summi viri vita atque virtute.

60   At enim ne quid novi fiat contra exempla atque
instituta maiorum.   Non dicam hoc loco maiores
nostros semper in pace consuetudini, in bello utilitati
paruisse, semper ad novos casus temporum novorum
consiliorum rationes accommodasse, non dicam duo
bella maxima, Punicum atque Hispaniense, ab uno
imperatore esse confecta duasque urbes potentissi-
mas, quae huic imperio maxime minitabantur,
Carthaginem atque Numantiam, ab eodem Scipione
esse deletas ; non commemorabo nuper ita vobis
patribusque vestris esse visum, ut in uno C. Mario
spes imperii poneretur, ut idem cum Iugurtha, idem
cum Cimbris, idem cum Teutonis bellum admini-
61 straret ; in ipso Cn. Pompeio, in quo novi constitui

---

opinion expressed by Quintus Catulus. When he asked you on whom you would set your hopes if anything should happen to Gnaeus Pompeius, in the event of your staking everything upon him, he received a great tribute to his own high character and position when almost with one accord you all asserted that you would set your hopes upon himself. For he is indeed a man of such capacity that, whatever were the magnitude or the difficulty of an undertaking, his wisdom could direct it, his uprightness secure it and his ability bring it to a conclusion. But in this particular instance I most vehemently disagree with him; because the more uncertain and the more ephemeral human life is, the greater is the obligation upon the State to take advantage of the ability of a great man during his lifetime while Heaven allows it.

But, I am told, " Let no innovation be made 60 contrary to usage and the principles of our forefathers." I forbear to mention here that our forefathers always bowed to precedent in peace but to expediency in war, always meeting fresh emergencies with fresh developments of policy : I forbear to mention that two mighty wars, those against Carthage and against Spain, were brought to an end by a single commander and that the two most powerful cities, Carthage and Numantia, which more than any others constituted a menace to our empire, were both alike destroyed by Scipio.[a] I forbear to remind you that, more recently, you and your fathers decided that the hopes of this empire should be reposed in Gaius Marius alone, and that he should direct successive wars against Jugurtha, the Cimbrians, and the Teutons. As for Gnaeus Pompeius, in whose case 61 Quintus Catulus desires that no new precedent should

nihil vult Q. Catulus, quam multa sint nova summa
Q. Catuli voluntate constituta, recordamini.

XXI. Quid tam novum quam adulescentulum
privatum exercitum difficili rei publicae tempore
conficere ? confecit. Huic praeesse ? praefuit. Rem
optime ductu suo gerere ? gessit. Quid tam praeter
consuetudinem quam homini peradulescenti, cuius
aetas a senatorio gradu longe abesset, imperium
atque exercitum dari, Siciliam permitti atque Africam
bellumque in ea provincia administrandum ? Fuit
in his provinciis singulari innocentia, gravitate, virtute, bellum in Africa maximum confecit, victorem
exercitum deportavit. Quid vero tam inauditum
quam equitem Romanum triumphare ? At eam
quoque rem populus Romanus non modo vidit, sed
omnium etiam studio visendam et concelebrandam
62 putavit. Quid tam inusitatum, quam ut, cum duo
consules clarissimi fortissimique essent, eques Romanus ad bellum maximum formidolosissimumque
pro consule mitteretur ? missus est. Quo quidem
tempore cum esset non nemo in senatu, qui diceret
" non oportere mitti hominem privatum pro consule,"
L. Philippus dixisse dicitur " non se illum sua sententia pro consule, sed pro consulibus mittere."
Tanta in eo rei publicae bene gerendae spes con-
stituebatur, ut duorum consulum munus unius adulescentis virtuti committeretur   Quid tam singulare
72

be established, call to mind how many new precedents have already been established in his case with the entire approval of Quintus Catulus.

XXI. What so novel as that a mere youth, holding no office, should raise an army at a time of crisis in the State ? Yet he did raise one. Or that he should command it ? Yet he did command it. Or that he should achieve a great success under his own direction ? Yet he did achieve it. What so contrary to custom as that one who was little more than a youth and far too young to hold senatorial rank should be given a military command and be entrusted with the province of Sicily and Africa and the conduct of a campaign there ? He displayed in the performance of these duties remarkable integrity, dignity and capacity : the campaign in Africa, a very serious one, he brought to an end and led his army home victorious. What, indeed, so unheard of as that a Roman knight should hold a triumph ? Yet even that the Roman People not merely witnessed but thought fit to attend, and to join in celebrating it with universal enthusiasm. What so un- 62 precedented as that, though there were available two distinguished and valiant consuls, a Roman knight should be sent in place of a consul to a great and perilous war ? Yet he was sent. And on that occasion, though there were not a few in the Senate who said it was not right to send a private citizen in the place of a consul, Lucius Philippus is said to have remarked : " I give my vote to send him not in place of a consul but in place of both consuls ! " So great were the hopes reposed in him of a successful administration, that the function of two consuls was entrusted to the capacity of one youth. What so

quam ut ex senatus consulto legibus solutus consul
ante fieret quam ullum alium magistratum per leges
capere licuisset? quid tam incredibile, quam ut
iterum eques Romanus ex senatus consulto trium-
pharet? Quae in omnibus hominibus nova post
hominum memoriam constituta sunt, ea tam multa
non sunt quam haec, quae in hoc uno homine vidimus.

63 Atque haec tot exempla tanta ac tam nova profecta
sunt in eundem hominem a Q. Catuli atque a ceterorum eiusdem dignitatis amplissimorum hominum
auctoritate.

XXII. Quare videant, ne sit periniquum et non
ferendum illorum auctoritatem de Cn. Pompei dignitate a vobis comprobatam semper esse, vestrum ab
illis de eodem homine iudicium populique Romani
auctoritatem improbari, praesertim cum iam suo iure
populus Romanus in hoc homine suam auctoritatem
vel contra omnes, qui dissentiunt, possit defendere,
propterea quod isdem istis reclamantibus vos unum
illum ex omnibus delegistis, quem bello praedonum

64 praeponeretis. Hoc si vos temere fecistis et rei
publicae parum consuluistis, recte isti studia vestra
suis consiliis regere conantur; sin autem vos plus
tum in re publica vidistis, vos iis repugnantibus per
vosmet ipsos dignitatem huic imperio, salutem orbi
terrarum attulistis, aliquando isti principes et sibi et

unparalleled as that he should be exempted from the laws by a decree of the Senate and be made a consul before he would have been entitled by the laws to hold any lower office ? What so incredible as that a second triumph should be awarded by a decree of the Senate to a Roman knight ? All the departures from precedent which, since history began, have been made in individual cases, are less in number than these which our own eyes have seen in the case of this one individual. And all these important **63** and striking innovations were brought about in favour of Pompeius on the initiative of Quintus Catulus and the other honourable men of the same rank.

XXII. Let them beware therefore lest it be unjust and unendurable that, as concerns the high deserts of Gnaeus Pompeius, their authoritative judgement has been approved by you, but that your judgement about the same man and the authority of the Roman People should be disapproved by them— and that, too, when now in the case of Pompeius the Roman People is able of its own right to defend its own authority against all the world, inasmuch as, despite the outcry raised by the same people then as now, you chose Pompeius as the one man above all others whom to invest with the conduct of the Pirate war. If you did this inadvisedly **64** and with too little care for the interests of the country, those men are right in trying to temper your enthusiasm by their counsel ; but if it was you, rather, who at that time had a clear eye for the needs of the country, you who, in their despite and by yourselves alone, brought honour to our empire and safety to the world, these great ones should at last

75

ceteris populi Romani universi auctoritati parendum
esse fateantur.

Atque in hoc bello Asiatico et regio non solum
militaris illa virtus, quae est in Cn. Pompeio singularis,
sed aliae quoque virtutes animi magnae et multae
requiruntur. Difficile est in Asia, Cilicia, Syria
regnisque interiorum nationum ita versari nostrum
imperatorem, ut nihil aliud nisi de hoste ac de laude
cogitet. Deinde, etiam si qui sunt pudore ac temperantia moderatiores, tamen eos esse tales propter
multitudinem cupidorum hominum nemo arbitratur.
65 Difficile est dictu, Quirites, quanto in odio simus apud
exteras nationes propter eorum, quos ad eas per hos
annos cum imperio misimus, libidines et iniurias.
Quod enim fanum putatis in illis terris nostris magistratibus religiosum, quam civitatem sanctam, quam
domum satis clausam ac munitam fuisse ? Urbes
iam locupletes et copiosae requiruntur, quibus causa
66 belli propter diripiendi cupiditatem inferatur. Libenter haec coram cum Q. Catulo et Q. Hortensio,
summis et clarissimis viris, disputarem ; noverunt
enim sociorum vulnera, vident eorum calamitates,
querimonias audiunt. Pro sociis vos contra hostes
exercitum mittere putatis an hostium simulatione
contra socios atque amicos ? Quae civitas est in
Asia, quae non modo imperatoris aut legati, sed unius
tribuni militum animos ac spiritus capere possit ?

* A Roman official when travelling through his province
was attended by a retinue proportionate to his rank : the
retinue, as well as the official, had to be entertained by the
provincials.

admit that they and all other men must bow to the authority of the Roman People.

Moreover, in this war against an Asiatic monarch, not only those military qualities are needed which are so peculiarly to be found in Gnaeus Pompeius, but other great and numerous moral qualities as well. It is difficult for a general of ours to be engaged in Asia, Cilicia, and Syria and the kingdoms of the interior without entertaining a thought save of the enemy and of glory. Again, even though there be those to whom a sense of decency and self-control teaches some degree of moderation, no one credits them with such qualities owing to the rapacity of so many others. Words cannot express, 65 gentlemen, how bitterly we are hated among foreign nations owing to the wanton and outrageous conduct of the men whom of late years we have sent to govern them. For in those countries what temple do you suppose has been held sacred by our officers, what state inviolable, what home sufficiently guarded by its closed doors ? Why, they look about for rich and flourishing cities that they may find an occasion of a war against them to satisfy their lust for plunder. I would gladly discuss the matter personally with 66 eminent and distinguished men like Quintus Catulus and Quintus Hortensius ; for they know the sufferings of our allies, they see their ruin and they hear their groans. Do you imagine that when you send an army, it is to defend our allies and attack the enemy —or to use the enemy as an excuse for attacking your allies and friends ? What state in Asia is sufficient to contain the arrogance and insolence of one military tribune, not to say of a general or his lieutenant ? [a]

XXIII. Quare, etiam si quem habetis, qui collatis signis exercitus regios superare posse videatur, tamen, nisi erit idem, qui se a pecuniis sociorum, qui ab eorum coniugibus ac liberis, qui ab ornamentis fanorum atque oppidorum, qui ab auro gazaque regia manus, oculos, animum cohibere possit, non erit idoneus, qui ad bellum Asiaticum regiumque mit-

67 tatur. Ecquam putatis civitatem pacatam fuisse, quae locuples sit, ecquam esse locupletem, quae istis pacata esse videatur ? Ora maritima, Quirites, Cn. Pompeium non solum propter rei militaris gloriam, sed etiam propter animi continentiam requisivit. Videbat enim praetores locupletari quotannis pecunia publica praeter paucos, neque nos quicquam aliud adsequi classium nomine, nisi ut detrimentis accipiendis maiore adfici turpitudine videremur. Nunc qua cupiditate homines in provincias et quibus iacturis, quibus condicionibus proficiscantur, ignorant videlicet isti, qui ad unum deferenda omnia esse non arbitrantur. Quasi vero Cn. Pompeium non cum suis virtutibus, tum etiam alienis vitiis magnum esse

68 videamus. Quare nolite dubitare, quin huic uni credatis omnia, qui inter tot annos unus inventus sit, quem socii in urbes suas cum exercitu venisse gaudeant.

Quodsi auctoritatibus hanc causam, Quirites, confirmandam putatis, est vobis auctor vir bellorum

---

a Pacata is a sarcastic euphemism: the provincial governor never thought a state was sufficiently reduced until he had stripped it bare. *Istis* (" yonder men ") is rhetorical, as though the speaker were pointing to his opponents.

XXIII. Wherefore, even if you possess a general who seems capable of vanquishing the royal army in a pitched battle, still, unless he be also capable of withholding his hands, his eyes, his thoughts from the wealth of our allies, from their wives and children, from the adornments of temples and of cities, from the gold and treasure of kings, he will not be a suitable man to be sent to the war against an Asiatic monarch. Do you imagine that any state has been **67** " pacified " and still remains wealthy, that any state is wealthy and seems to some men " pacified " *a* ? The coastal regions, gentlemen, were led to ask for the appointment of Gnaeus Pompeius not only by his reputation as a soldier but also by his power of self-control ; for they saw that the governors, all but a few, were making fortunes every year out of the public funds, and that we were achieving nothing by our so-called fleets save that we seemed by our defeats to be incurring yet deeper disgrace. The avarice that to-day inspires a governor's departure for his province, the sacrifices and the bargaining that it entails, are, it would seem, unknown to those who think that supreme command ought not to be given to one man : as though indeed it were not obvious that Pompeius owes his greatness not to his own merits alone but also to the demerits of other men. Then hesitate **68** no longer to entrust supreme command to this one man, the only general found in all these years whose allies rejoice to receive him and his army into their cities.

But if you think, gentlemen, that my cause needs the support of authority, you have the authority of one who is thoroughly experienced in all manner of

omnium maximarumque rerum peritissimus, P.
Servilius, cuius tantae res gestae terra marique ex-
stiterunt, ut, cum de bello deliberetis, auctor vobis
gravior esse nemo debeat ; est C. Curio, summis
vestris beneficiis maximisque rebus gestis, summo
ingenio et prudentia praeditus, est Cn. Lentulus, in
quo omnes pro amplissimis vestris honoribus summum
consilium, summam gravitatem esse cognovistis, est
C. Cassius, integritate, virtute, constantia singulari.
Quare videte, horumne auctoritatibus illorum ora-
tioni, qui dissentiunt, respondere posse videamur.

69 XXIV. Quae cum ita sint, C. Manili, primum istam
tuam et legem et voluntatem et sententiam laudo
vehementissimeque comprobo ; deinde te hortor, ut
auctore populo Romano maneas in sententia neve
cuiusquam vim aut minas pertimescas. Primum in
te satis esse animi perseverantiaeque arbitror ;
deinde, cum tantam multitudinem cum tanto studio
adesse videamus, quantam iterum nunc in eodem
homine praeficiendo videmus, quid est, quod aut de
re aut de perficiendi facultate dubitemus ? Ego
autem, quicquid est in me studii, consilii, laboris,
ingenii, quicquid hoc beneficio populi Romani atque
hac potestate praetoria, quicquid auctoritate, fide

wars and important affairs, even Publius Servilius, whose achievements by land and sea are so conspicuously great that no man's authority ought to carry greater weight with you when deliberating on a question of war. You have the authority of Gaius Curio, raised by your favour to the highest offices, distinguished at once by his splendid achievements and by his consummate ability and foresight. You have the authority of Gnaeus Lentulus, in whom you have all had occasion to appreciate, as befitting the high offices which you have bestowed upon him, the highest degree of wisdom and dignity ; and of Gaius Cassius, who is so remarkable for the uprightness, the nobility, and the firmness of his character. Behold, then, what answer the authority of these men enables us to make to the arguments of those who oppose us !

XXIV. Since this is so, Gaius Manilius, in the first 69 place I applaud and most heartily commend this your law, your purpose and your proposal ; and in the second I exhort you, with the authority of the Roman People behind you, to stand by that proposal undeterred by the violence or the threats of any man. In the first place I realize that you possess in yourself enough of spirit and of resolution, and in the second, seeing how great and enthusiastic is this multitude which we here behold assembled a second time to confer a fresh appointment on Pompeius, what doubt can we entertain either of the proposal itself or of our ability to carry it through ? For my own part, whatever of devotion, wisdom, energy, or talent I possess, whatever I can achieve by virtue of the praetorship which the favour of the Roman People has conferred upon me, or by virtue of my

constantia possum, id omne ad hanc rem conficiendam
70 tibi et populo Romano polliceor ac defero ; testorque
omnes deos, et eos maxime, qui huic loco temploque
praesident, qui omnium mentes eorum, qui ad rem
publicam adeunt, maxime perspiciunt, me hoc neque
rogatu facere cuiusquam, neque quo Cn. Pompei
gratiam mihi per hanc causam conciliari putem,
neque quo mihi ex cuiusquam amplitudine aut praesidia periculis aut adiumenta honoribus quaeram,
propterea quod pericula facile, ut hominem praestare
oportet, innocentia tecti repellemus, honorem autem
neque ab uno neque ex hoc loco, sed eadem illa nostra
laboriosissima ratione vitae, si vestra voluntas feret,
71 consequemur.   Quam ob rem, quicquid in hac causa
mihi susceptum est, Quirites, id ego omne me rei
publicae causa suscepisse confirmo, tantumque abest,
ut aliquam mihi bonam gratiam quaesisse videar, ut
multas me etiam simultates partim obscuras, partim
apertas intellegam mihi non necessarias, vobis non
inutiles suscepisse.   Sed ego me hoc honore praeditum, tantis vestris beneficiis adfectum statui, Quirites, vestram voluntatem et rei publicae dignitatem
et salutem provinciarum atque sociorum meis omnibus
commodis et rationibus praeferre oportere.

own influence, loyalty, and determination, all this I promise and devote to you and to the Roman People for the achievement of our purpose ; and I call all 70 the gods to witness—most especially the guardians of this hallowed spot who clearly see into the hearts of all who enter upon public life—that I am acting thus neither in deference to any man's request nor with any idea of winning for myself by my support of this cause the favour of Gnaeus Pompeius, nor in the hope of gaining for myself from any man's high position either protection from dangers or aids to advancement ; for dangers, so far as a man may guarantee, I shall readily repel in the security of innocence, and advancement will come to me, if such is your good pleasure, not through the favour of any one man nor through speeches delivered from this platform, but as the reward of a life now as ever devoted to hard work. Wherefore any effort I may 71 have made in this cause, gentlemen, I protest has been made in the cause of my country ; and far from seeming to have sought any popularity for myself, I am aware of having even incurred many enmities, some overt and some secret, which I might have avoided, though not without some detriment to you. But I have made up my mind that, invested as I am with this high office and enjoying the great reward of your goodwill, it is my duty to place your wishes, the honour of the State, and the well-being of our provinces and allies above any advantages and interests of my own.

THE SPEECH OF MARCUS TULLIUS CICERO IN DEFENCE OF AULUS CAECINA

INTRODUCTION

The facts in Caecina's [a] case are briefly as follows:

§ 1. Marcus Fulcinius, on his marriage to Caesennia, invested her dowry in the purchase of an estate, and, shortly before his death, bought some more land adjoining it. By his will his wife inherited a life-interest in his property conjointly with the heir, their son. But the son died, and the terms of his will made it necessary for his heir, Publius Caesennius, to put the inheritance up for auction in detail. At this sale Caesennia decided to invest the money she inherited from her son in buying the land, formerly her husband's, which adjoined her own estate, and she commissioned Aebutius to act for her. Caesennia took possession of this land, let it, and shortly afterwards died, making Aulus Caecina her heir, and leaving a small sum to Aebutius. Aebutius challenged Caecina's qualification to be heir and claimed the land as his own. As a usual preliminary to settling the question, Caecina agreed to meet Aebutius on the land in dispute and submit to formal " ejection " from it ; but on arrival he was prevented from entering and driven away by the threats of Aebutius and his armed followers. Accordingly he applied for and obtained an injunction ordering Aebutius to

---

[a] The *i* appears, from the best authorities, to be short.

restore him. Aebutius denied liability: a wager[a] was made raising the issue and " Recoverers "[b] were appointed to try it.

§ 2. The arguments of Aebutius's counsel, as reconstructed from this speech, and Cicero's reply to them on behalf of Caecina, may be tabulated as follows :

ARGUMENT OF PISO	REPLY OF CICERO
1. Caecina was not " ejected " but excluded : he had not entered on the estate.	1. This is a quibble : the two things are the same.
2. No " force " was really used : no one was hurt.	2. Force, in the legal sense, means any extra-legal means of redress.
3. (i.) The injunction specifies possession. (ii.) Caecina was not in possession.	3. (i.) Yes, the ordinary injunction ; but not this one which deals with " armed men." (ii.) *a.* Caesennia had possession through her life interest : Caecina, as her heir, inherited her possession. *b.* Caecina had personally taken possession by entering on and receiving rent for the land. *c.* Aebutius had recognized him as possessor of the estate both by serving him with a formal notice about it and by agreeing to a formal ejection of Caecina.
4. Caecina was not the owner, and had no more right to possession than any adventurer.	4. The whole story of the land shows it was Caecina's : Aebutius's witnesses prove nothing but the original sale and purchase.

[a] See Introduction, § 7 A.

[b] See Introduction, § 7 D.

INTRODUCTION

ARGUMENT OF PISO	REPLY OF CICERO
5. Caecina, as being a Volaterran, was disqualified from inheriting.	5. (i.) Citizenship, like freedom, cannot be taken away.
	(ii.) Sulla's law hedges on the point.
	(iii.) Volaterrae was only reduced to the status of Ariminum, whose citizens retained their rights of inheritance.

§ 3. From the fact that the court, after two hearings of the case, was unable to come to a decision, it would appear that the case admitted of considerable doubt, and we need not take too seriously the reasons which Cicero suggests for the postponement of the verdict. The facts were mostly admitted by both sides : the real issue was a legal one. Nor is it easier for us than it was for the court to decide the rights and wrongs of the case, for we do not know the exact state of Roman law in the days of Cicero. On the whole it would appear that later jurisprudence, at all events, upheld the definitions of " ejection " and " force " by which he answered his opponent's first two arguments, as set forth in the preceding section. His view of Sulla's law (the terms of which we do not possess) and of the formal saving clause which it contained appears to be pressed too far ; but his answer generally to Piso's fifth argument is sound and was probably convincing. With the fourth argument he hardly deals at all : it is the third argument—the question of possession—upon which modern critics are least in agreement and which may well have been responsible for the hesitation of the court.

§ 4. French critics tend to uphold Cicero's view of

the matter : there were two distinct and different injunctions, distinctly and differently worded. The
first, or " ordinary " injunction, dealing simply with
forcible ejection, specified that the petitioner for
restoration must have had flawless possession at the
time of his ejection : in the second, which dealt with
forcible ejection by armed men, no mention of
possession is made. Possession is therefore an irrelevant question in Caecina's case.

To this the German critics, generally, reply that
Cicero's argument was a false interpretation, if not a
false statement, of the terms of the two injunctions ;
and that—as we know to have been the case in
Ulpian's time—possession was required in both injunctions alike.

The probability is, not so much that Cicero was
misquoting the actual terms of the second injunction,
as distorting the sense of the first ; the point of
which was not that the petitioner must have been in
possession : that was assumed as obvious ; but that
his possession must have been flawless. Possession
was assumed also by the second injunction, but as it
need not be flawless, it was not expressly mentioned.
Mr. Roby [a] thinks, therefore, that " Cicero adroitly
in the interest of his client siezed on the apparent
difference in the wording of the two injunctions,"
and laid a false emphasis on the clause in the " ordinary " injunction which specifies possession and on
its absence from the second injunction ; whereas the
mere fact of possession is unimportant in the first
and assumed in the second.

§ 5. Cicero's pleading appears, however, not to have
failed in its effect upon those to whom it was originally

[a] H. J. Roby, *Roman Private Law*, vol. ii. Appendix.

addressed ; for it is probable, though not certain, that he won his case. We know at all events that he remained on good terms with Caecina, who, in subsequent correspondence between them,[a] styles himself his old client ; and we know, too, that Cicero was proud of the speech which he made on this occasion.[b]

§ 6. Whether or no the speech was successful, he had good cause to be proud ; for in it " Cicéron apporte une connaissance profonde du droit. Il discute en maître les termes du texte dont on veut se servir contre lui. Il prouve en suite, avec finesse, que la lettre et le sens de la loi sont en faveur de la cause dont il s'est chargé. Il saisit enfin l'occasion que lui fournit Pison de sortir d'une argumentation pleine d'intérêt, mais un peu trop technique, pour s'élever à de nobles considérations sur la liberté et le droit de cité. Son éloquence s'épanche alors librement sur des sujets qu'il affectionne. Discussions minutieuses, mouvements oratoires, plaisanterie fine, pathétique, Cicéron met tout en œuvre pour faire triompher son client et nous donne ainsi une haute idée de ce que devaient être, dans l'antiquité romaine, les débats judiciaires. Mais il y a, dans ce discours, plus que de la science, de l'habilité, de l'éloquence ; un amour véritable pour la justice et pour le droit s'y révèle à toutes les pages et il résulte de la lecture de ce plaidoyer une émotion pénétrante qui fait que Cicéron gagne encore sa cause devant la postérité, comme il a dû la gagner devant les récupérateurs." [c]

Those who feel that such praise is more enthusiastic

[a] Cic. *Ad Fam.* vi. 5-9.   [b] Cic. *Orator*, xxix. § 102.
[c] Armand Gasquy, *Cicéron jurisconsulte*, pp. 255, 256.

than discriminating will none the less appreciate the exceptional interest of the *Pro Caecina* to the student of Roman law and antiquities; and will at all events be unlikely to cavil at such measure of praise as Cicero, in referring to this speech, bestowed upon himself: "res involutas definiendo explicavimus, ius civile laudavimus, verba ambigua distinximus." [a]

§ 7. NOTE ON THE PROCEDURE IN THE *Pro Caecina*

A. SPONSIO was the earliest and therefore the most sacred method of making any agreement between citizens, of whatever nature. One party put a question to the other (beginning *spondesne?* do you pledge yourself?) as to whether he undertook the obligation in question. The other replied *spondeo*, I do; and the agreement was completed.

At law, any case might be tried on a *sponsio*, which became a sort of wager. One party would "pledge himself" to pay a certain sum to his opponent if or unless (*sive nive*, § 65) his side of the case were found to be true. This sum might be the actual penalty to the loser of the case or a mere formality

A *sponsio* was the proper procedure when, as in the present case, a man desired to deny his liability to an injunction. Aebutius would make a formal promise to pay a certain sum "*nisi restitisset . . .*" "if he had not restored . . ."

B. POSSESSIO, possession, is defined by Mr. Roby as "occupation either by yourself or by someone else for you, with the intention to hold as of right for

[a] Cicero, *Orator*, xxix. § 102.

yourself." It is distinct from absolute ownership, *dominium*, on the one hand, and, on the other, from usufruct or life-interest, which gave only the right to occupy and to enjoy the " use and fruits " of whatever was subject to the usufruct.

C. The INTERDICTUM or injunction was a " police order " designed to safeguard possession. Anybody who thought that his right as a possessor had been infringed might apply to the praetor to issue an injunction in his favour, ordering the person named as defendant to do something or to refrain from doing it or to restore what he had taken from the plaintiff's possession.

In the present case, the procedure, after an ordinary ejection, would have been for the praetor to issue in Caecina's favour against Aebutius the " ordinary " injunction *de vi*, dealing merely with ejection by force, in the following terms : *unde tu, Sexte Aebuti, aut familia, aut procurator tuus, Aulum Caecinam aut familiam aut procuratorem illius, hoc in anno vi deiecisti, cum ille possideret, quod nec vi nec clam nec precario a te possideret, eo restituas* (" that you, Sextus Aebutius, or your servants or your agent, do restore Aulus Caecina, his servants or his agent, to the place whence you have in this year ejected[a] him by force, he being in possession, without having gained it from you by force or stealth or request) ".

But because Aebutius actually employed armed men and real violence, Caecina obtained from the

---

[a] An adequate translation of the word *deicere* has proved often difficult, and sometimes (as in §§ 38 and 50) impossible : no single word in English fits all the contexts. It has therefore seemed best to use the words " eject " and " drive out " as alternatives.

praetor the *interdictum de vi armata*, dealing with ejection by force of arms, which ran as follows : *unde tu, Sexte Aebuti, aut familia aut procurator tuus Aulum Caecinam, aut familiam, aut procuratorem illius, vi hominibus coactis armatisve deiecisti, eo restituas* (" that you, Sextus Aebutius, or your servants or your agent do restore Aulus Caecina, his servants or his agents, to the place whence you have ejected him by force through men collected together and armed ").

Wishing to deny his liability to comply with this injunction, Aebutius had the alternative either of submitting to arbitration or of entering into a wager (*sponsio*) with Caecina which would raise the issue. He chose the latter course, and " recoverers " (*recuperatores*) were appointed to try the case.

D. RECUPERATORES or " recoverers " were originally persons nominated by the *praetor peregrinus* to settle informally disputes arising between citizens and non-citizens : their presence in this case is probably due to the fact that Caecina's claim to be a citizen was disputed. They were probably three in number.

ANALYSIS OF THE SPEECH

(Chapter i.) Aebutius originally put himself in the wrong, though perhaps not at a disadvantage, by using an admittedly ultra-legal degree of force in ejecting Caecina. (ii.) The failure of the court hitherto to condemn him must be due either to a false impression that the legal issues are highly complicated or to an improper reluctance (iii.) to disgrace

him. But he has brought it on himself : there is no other way of dealing with him.

(iv.) This case arises out of the widowed Caesennia's inheritance; (v.) the management of which Aebutius contrived to get into his own hands : (vi.) in particular, he acted as her agent in the purchase of an estate. When she died, she made Caecina her heir and left Aebutius a trifling legacy. (vii.) Not content with this, Aebutius denied Caecina's claim to be her heir and said that the estate in question was his own. Caecina decided to raise the issue by submitting to formal " ejection by force " from the estate ; but when he went there by agreement, (viii.) Aebutius threatened to kill him if he advanced and twice made a murderous attack on him when he tried to do so. He therefore fled and applied for an injunction. (ix.) Aebutius's illegal violence is attested by his own witnesses, (x.) all except the last—the notorious perjurer, Staienus.

(xi.) Such being the facts, what form of redress is open to me ? (xii.) Dare you say that there is none ? An action for assault is useless to me : (xiii.) so is procedure by any injunction other than the present one. Your argument is a mere quibble : (xiv.) I was ejected—whether just before or just after entering makes no difference. To say that actual physical force was not used (xv.) is equally disingenuous. (xvi.) Force in the legal sense was used in plenty.

(xvii.) A merely literal interpretation makes nonsense of the injunction (xviii.) or of any other combination of words. It is the spirit that matters, (xix.) as is shown by precedent. Examine the injunction (xx.) phrase by phrase : the terms employed —" servants," " agent," (xxi.) " collecting together,"

" armed men "—(xxii.) are all meant to be widely interpreted.

(xxiii.) You object to my quoting the Legal Authorities (xxiv.) but they are of the highest value : (xxv.) to disparage them is to disparage the Law, (xxvi.) the mainstay of our civilization, (xxvii.) against lawlessness like that of Aebutius. My particular authority is too honoured a name for you to asperse ; (xxviii.) and the lawyer you yourself quote has admitted to me that I have on my side even the letter of the law (xxix.) on which you challenge me. Caecina *was* ejected—though not necessarily from the estate in question.

(xxx.) The fact is that each expression in the injunction is a general one—not least the expression " whence " which was designed to cover my case, (xxxi.) as you know well enough. The question of possession is irrelevant, (xxxii.) for it is not mentioned in this particular injunction.

(xxxiii.) As for Caecina's alleged inability to inherit, as being a Volaterran and therefore disfranchised, citizenship is something that cannot be taken from anyone. (xxxiv.) Instances quoted to contradict this prove on examination to be false analogies. (xxxv.) Besides, no attempt was made to disfranchise Volaterra completely. To deny Caecina's citizenship would be dangerous as well as absurd.

(xxxvi.) Every point raised by my opponent has been answered : Caecina is both morally and legally in the right.

95

M. TULLI CICERONIS PRO
A. CAECINA ORATIO

1   I. Si quantum in agro locisque desertis audacia potest, tantum in foro atque in iudiciis impudentia valeret, non minus nunc in caussa cederet A. Caecina Sex. Aebutii impudentiae quam tum in vi facienda cessit audaciae. Verum et illud considerati hominis esse putavit, qua de re iure disceptari oporteret, armis non contendere ; et hoc constantis, quicum vi et armis certare noluisset, eum iure iudicioque 2 superare. Ac mihi quidem quum audax praecipue fuisse videtur Aebutius in convocandis hominibus et armandis, tum impudens in iudicio, non solum quod in iudicium venire ausus est, nam id quidem tametsi improbe fit in aperta re, tamen malitia est iam usitatum, sed quod non dubitavit id ipsum quod arguitur confiteri : nisi forte hoc rationis habuit, quoniam, si facta vis esset moribus, superior in possessione retinenda non fuisset ; quia contra ius moremque facta sit, A. Caecinam cum amicis metu perterritum profugisse ; nunc quoque in iudicio, si

THE SPEECH OF M. TULLIUS CICERO IN DEFENCE OF AULIUS CAECINA

I. If effrontery were as potent before a tribunal 1
of justice as recklessness is effective in the lonely
country-side, Aulus Caecina would have as little chance
in the conduct of his case to-day against the effrontery
of Sextus Aebutius as once he had in the employment
of force against his audacity. However he considered that while circumspection forbade him to
contend with arms over an issue which ought to be
decided at law, resolution also bade him overcome
by a legal process one against whom he declined to
fight with armed violence. Personally I consider 2
Aebutius to have displayed both conspicuous audacity
in collecting and arming his followers and also
effrontery in his legal proceedings, not only in daring
to take such proceedings (for though the obvious
nature of the case made even this a wrong thing to
do, such conduct is common enough on the part of a
rogue), but in not hesitating openly to admit the very
point we seek to prove ; unless indeed his idea was
this, that—whereas previously had he used the
customary amount of force, he would have been at
no advantage when it came to retaining possession
—because he used a degree of force contrary to law
and custom, Aulus Caecina and his friends fled in a
panic : so, too, at the present time and in these pro-

caussa more institutoque omnium defendatur, nos
inferiores in agendo non futuros ; sin a consuetudine
recedatur, se quo impudentius egerit hoc superiorem
discessurum. Quasi vero aut idem possit in iudicio
improbitas quod in vi confidentia, aut nos non eo
libentius tum audaciae cesserimus quo nunc im-
3 pudentiae facilius obsisteremus. Itaque longe alia
ratione, recuperatores, ad agendam caussam hac
actione venio atque initio veneram. Tum enim
nostrae caussae spes erat posita in defensione mea,
nunc in confessione adversarii ; tum in nostris, nunc
vero in illorum testibus : de quibus ego antea labora-
bam, ne, si improbi essent, falsi aliquid dicerent, si
probi existimarentur, quod dixissent probarent, nunc
sum animo aequissimo. Si enim sunt viri boni, me
adiuvant, quum id iurati dicunt quod ego iniuratus
insimulo. Sin autem minus idonei, me non laedunt ;
quum iis sive creditur, creditur hoc ipsum quod nos
arguimus, sive fides non habetur, de adversarii
testium fide derogatur.

4   II. Verum tamen quum illorum actionem caussae
considero, non video quid impudentius dici possit ;
quum autem vestram in iudicando dubitationem,
vereor ne id quod videntur impudenter fecisse astute
et callide fecerint. Nam si negassent vim hominibus
armatis esse factam, facile honestissimis testibus in

---

* See Introduction, § 7 D.
⁵ See Introduction, § 3.

ceedings, if his defence were to follow universal
custom and usage, we should be at no disadvantage
in conducting our case, whereas, should precedent
be abandoned, the more outrageous his conduct, the
greater would be his advantage in the end. As if
indeed dishonesty were as efficient in a court of
justice as is impudence in an affair of violence ; and
as if we did not yield the more gladly to his audacity
on that occasion in order the more easily to withstand
his effrontery on this ! And so, gentlemen, my plans 3
for the conduct of my case in these proceedings are
very far different from what they were originally[a] ;
for then the success of our case rested upon my
powers in defence, now it rests on the admissions of
my adversary : then I was relying upon our witnesses,
but now upon theirs. These witnesses of theirs at
one time caused me anxiety : if they were dishonest,
they might lie ; if they succeeded in passing for
honest, what they said might be believed. Now I
am completely happy about them : if they are good
men, they help my case by saying on their oath what
I, not on my oath, merely suggest ; and if they are
not so satisfactory, they do my case no harm : for
if the court believes them, it believes the very point
we seek to prove ; and if it does not credit them, then
my opponent's witnesses are discredited.

II. When, however, I consider my opponent's 4
conduct of the case, I cannot imagine anything more
outrageous ; though when I consider your hesitation
to pronounce judgement[b] I am afraid that their
apparently outrageous conduct may have been a
shrewd and clever move. For had they denied the
employment of force through armed men, they would
have been easily and incontrovertibly met by unim-

99

re perspicua tenerentur ; sin confessi essent, et id
quod nullo tempore iure fieri potest, tamen ab se iure
factum esse defenderent, sperarunt, id quod assecuti
sunt, se iniecturos vobis caussam deliberandi et
iudicandi iustam moram ac religionem ; simul illud,
quod indignissimum est, futurum arbitrati sunt, ut
in hac caussa non de improbitate Sex. Aebutii, sed
5 de iure civili iudicium fieri videretur. Qua in re si
mihi esset unius A. Caecinae caussa agenda, profiterer
satis idoneum esse me defensorem, propterea quod
fidem meam diligentiamque praestarem, quae quum
sunt in actore caussae, nihil est in re praesertim
aperta ac simplici quod excellens ingenium requiratur.
Sed quum de eo mihi iure dicendum sit quod pertineat
ad omnes, quod constitutum sit a maioribus, conser-
vatum usque ad hoc tempus, quo sublato non solum
pars aliqua iuris deminuta, sed etiam vis ea quae iuri
maxime est adversaria iudicio confirmata esse videatur,
video summi ingenii caussam esse, non ut id demon-
stretur quod ante oculos est, sed ne, si quis vobis error
in tanta re sit obiectus, omnes potius me arbitrentur
caussae quam vos religioni vestrae defuisse.

6   Quamquam ego mihi sic persuadeo, recuperatores,
non vos tam propter iuris obscuram dubiamque
rationem bis iam de eadem caussa dubitasse, quam,
quod videtur ad summam illius existimationem hoc

---

peachable evidence : but should they admit the fact
and then put forward the defence that what can
never be done lawfully was on that occasion lawfully
done by themselves, they hoped—and their hopes
were realized—that they would give you ground for
deliberation and make you feel a legitimate scruple
about deciding the case at once. And they further
reckoned that—scandalous though it is that it should
be so—the point at issue in this trial would appear
to be, not the depravity of Sextus Aebutius, but a
point of law. Now if in this trial I had to maintain **5**
the cause of Aulus Calcina and of no one else, I should
profess myself sufficiently qualified to defend it as
guaranteeing honesty and effort on my part : given
these qualities in counsel, there is no cause for exceptional ability, especially in so plain and simple a
matter. But since I have to speak about the Law,
which affects us all, which was established by our
forefathers and has been preserved even to this day,
the overthrow of which would not merely impair our
rights in some respect but would seem to be lending
the support of a legal decision to the use of force,
which is the absolute antithesis of law ; I realize that
the case demands the highest ability, not to prove
what a mere glance can see, but to prevent everyone
supposing, should you be induced to take up a false
position on so important a question, that it is rather
I who have betrayed my cause than you your con-
sciences.

I am, however, persuaded, gentlemen,[a] that your **6**
reason for having twice shown yourselves reluctant
to decide the same case was not any ambiguity or
doubt you may have felt about the law, but the fact
that this trial, seeming to strike at the very root of

iudicium pertinere, moram ad condemnandum acqui-
sisse, simul et illi spatium ad sese colligendum dedisse.
Quod quoniam iam in consuetudinem venit, et id viri
boni, vestri similes, in iudicando faciunt, reprehen-
dendum fortasse minus, querendum vero magis etiam
videtur, ideo quod omnia iudicia aut distrahendarum
controversiarum, aut puniendorum maleficiorum caussa
reperta sunt ; quorum alterum levius est, propterea
quod et minus laedit, et persaepe disceptatore
domestico diiudicatur ; alterum est vehementissi-
mum, quod et ad graviores res pertinet, et non
honorariam operam amici, sed severitatem iudicis ac
7 vim requirit. Quod est gravius et cuius rei caussa
maxime iudicia constituta sunt, id iam mala consuetudine dissolutum est. Nam ut quaeque res est
turpissima, sic maxime et maturissime vindicanda
est : at de eadem hac, quia existimationis periculum
est, tardissime iudicatur. III. Qui igitur convenit,
quae caussa fuerit ad constituendum iudicium,
eandem moram esse ad iudicandum ? Si quis, quod
spopondit, qua in re verbo se obligavit uno, id non
facit, maturo iudicio, sine ulla religione iudicis con-
demnatur : qui per tutelam aut societatem aut rem
mandatam aut fiduciae rationem fraudavit quempiam, in eo, quo delictum maius est, eo poena est
8 tardior. " Est enim turpe iudicium."—Ex facto
quidem turpi.[1] Videte igitur quam inique accidat,

<hr>

[1] turpi *Baiter* : turpe *codd.*

<hr>

[a] The single word was *spondeo*, "I pledge myself."

the defendant's honour, induced you to postpone
your condemnation and so give him time to get
his case together. This practice, which is becoming
customary and is followed by honest men like yourselves when acting as judges, seems perhaps less
reprehensible, though actually more deplorable, just
because all legal processes are designed either for
the settlement of disputes or the punishment of
wrongdoing. Of these functions the former is the
less serious, as it inflicts less suffering and is often
determined by private arbitration ; whereas the
latter is drastic in the extreme, dealing as it does with
grave matters and calling, not for the informal
assistance of a friend, but for the stern and trench-
ant action of a judge. And now the weightier 7
function, the chief purpose for which our courts
exist, is abrogated by this evil practice. For the
more heinous the offence, the greater and the
speedier should be the retribution. But that is precisely the case which, because it imperils a man's
honour, is the slowest to be decided. III. How can
it, then, be right that the very cause responsible for
bringing the courts of justice into being should also
be responsible for delay in passing judgement ? In
a case of solemn contract, he who does not perform
an obligation which he has taken upon himself by
pronouncing a single word,[a] is promptly condemned
without any scruple on the part of the judge. But
in the case of fraud arising over a wardship, a partner-
ship, an informal contract, or the return of a security,
the slowness of the punishment is proportionate to
the gravity of the offence. " Yes," you say, " for 8
the sentence involves infamy." Of course, because
it is passed upon infamous conduct. How unfairly

quia res indigna sit, ideo turpem existimationem
sequi ; quia turpis existimatio sequatur, ideo rem
indignam non vindicari.

Ac si qui mihi hoc iudex recuperatorve dicat :
" Potuisti enim leniore actione confligere : potuisti
ad tuum ius faciliore et commodiore iudicio pervenire ; quare aut muta actionem, aut noli mihi instare
ut iudicem ; " tamen is aut timidior videatur quam
fortem, aut cupidior quam sapientem iudicem esse
aequum est, si aut mihi praescribat quemadmodum
meum ius persequar, aut ipse id quod ad se delatum
sit non audeat iudicare. Etenim si praetor, is qui
iudicia dat, numquam petitori praestituit qua actione
illum uti velit, videte quam iniquum sit constituta
iam re, iudicem quid agi potuerit aut quid possit,
9 non quid actum sit, quaerere. Verumtamen nimiae
vestrae benignitati pareremus, si alia ratione ius
nostrum recuperare possemus. Nunc vero quis est
qui aut vim hominibus armatis factam relinqui putet
oportere, aut eius rei leniorem actionem nobis aliquam demonstrare possit ? Ex quo genere peccati,
ut illi clamitant, vel iniuriarum vel capitis iudicia
constituta sunt, in eo potestis atrocitatem nostram
reprehendere, quum videatis nihil aliud actum nisi
possessionem per interdictum esse repetitam ?

IV. Verum sive vos existimationis illius periculum,

---

* See Introduction, § 7 D.
♦ Part of the praetor's duty was to decide whether an
action should be heard, and when.

it comes about, then, that whereas dishonour is the penalty for evil conduct, that very conduct should remain unpunished just because dishonour is its penalty!

And if any judge or assessor[a] were to say to me : " But you might have brought your action by a less stringent process : you might have secured your rights by an easier and more convenient form of trial ; so either adopt a different process or do not press me to pronounce judgement," he would none the less seem either more nervous than a resolute judge ought to be or more presumptuous than a wise one ; for either he is lacking in the courage to try the case himself or he is seeking to prescribe the method which I am to employ in pursuing my rights. For if the praetor,[b] he who gives leave to bring an action, never prescribes to a claimant what form of action he wishes him to employ, how unfair it is that, when that leave has definitely been obtained, the judge should consider not the line that is being taken but that which may be or might have been taken! None the less we should gladly take advantage of your excessive kindness, if it were possible for us to recover our rights by any other process. But in the circumstances, is there anyone who either supposes that violence through armed men ought to go unpunished, or can inform us of any less stringent process for dealing with it ? When the offence is one of those to which, as our opponents are so fond of asserting, a charge of assault is proper or even a capital charge, can you accuse us of vindictiveness when you see that all we ask is to recover possession through the praetor's injunction ?

IV. But whether it is the danger to which the

sive iuris dubitatio tardiores fecit adhuc ad iudicandum, alterius rei caussam vosmetipsi iam vobis
saepius prolato iudicio sustulistis, alterius ego vobis
hodierno die caussam profecto auferam, ne diutius de
controversia nostra ac de communi iure dubitetis.
10 Et si forte videbor altius initium rei demonstrandae
petisse quam me ratio iuris et ius de quo iudicium
est, et natura caussae coegerit, quaeso ut ignoscatis.
Non enim minus laborat A. Caecina ne summo iure
egisse, quam ne certum ius non obtinuisse videatur.

    M. Fulcinius fuit, recuperatores, e municipio Tar-
quiniensi, qui et domi suae cum primis honestus
existimatus est, et Romae argentariam non ignobilem
fecit. Is habuit in matrimonio Caesenniam eodem
e municipio, summo loco natam et probatissimam
feminam, sicut et vivus ipse multis rebus ostendit et
11 in morte sua testamento declaravit. Huic Caesenniae fundum in agro Tarquiniensi vendidit temporibus illis difficillimis solutionis. Quum uteretur dote
uxoris numerata, quo mulieri esset res cautior,
curavit ut in eo fundo dos collocaretur. Aliquanto
post iam argentaria dissoluta, Fulcinius huic fundo
uxoris continentia quaedam praedia atque adiuncta
mercatur. Moritur Fulcinius : multa enim quae
sunt in re, quia remota sunt a caussa, praetermittam:
testamento facit heredem quem habebat e Caesennia

---

* *i.e.* in the time of Sulla.

defendant's honour is exposed or your uncertainty
on a point of law which has made you hitherto
reluctant to deliver judgement—as to the former,
you have yourselves removed it by your frequent
adjournments of the case ; all grounds for the latter
I will this very day remove forthwith, leaving you
no further ground for hesitation about either the
issue between us or the general right. And if you **10**
should think that I am going further back in tracing
the origins of the case than I am obliged to do by
the principle of law involved, the point of law under
dispute or the nature of the case, I crave your indulgence. For my client is as anxious not to seem
to be pressing his rights to the uttermost as he is not
to fail in obtaining the rights that are manifestly his.

There was one M. Fulcinius, gentlemen, a native
of Tarquinii, who in his native place enjoyed an
eminently honourable reputation and at Rome had
a considerable business as a banker. He was married
to Caesennia, a lady from the same township, of
honourable family and approved character, as he
made known in many ways during her life and after
his death declared by his will. To this Caesennia he **11**
sold an estate in the districts of Tarquinii during
those times of financial stringency,[a] and as he was
using the cash which had comprised his wife's dowry,
he took the precaution of charging the dowry on the
farm in order to give her, as a woman, better security
for it. Some time afterwards Fulcinius gave up his
banking business and bought some land in continua-
tion of and next to this estate of his wife's. Fulcinius died—I will pass over many points in the story
because they are unconnected with this case—and
in his will made his son by Caesennia his heir, subject

filium : usum et fructum omnium bonorum suorum
12 Caesenniae legat ut frueretur una cum filio. Magnus
honos viri iucundus mulieri fuisset, si diuturnum esse
licuisset. Frueretur enim bonis cum eo quem suis
bonis heredem esse cupiebat, et ex quo maximum
fructum ipsa capiebat. Sed hunc fructum mature
fortuna ademit. Nam brevi tempore M. Fulcinius
adolescens mortuus est : heredem P. Caesennium
fecit : uxori grande pondus argenti matrique partem
maiorem bonorum legavit. Itaque in partem
mulieres vocatae sunt.

13 V. Quum esset haec auctio hereditaria constituta,
Aebutius iste, qui iamdiu Caesenniae viduitate ac
solitudine aleretur, ac se in eius familiaritatem in-
sinuasset hac ratione, ut cum aliquo suo compendio
negotia mulieris si qua acciderent controversiasque
susciperet, versabatur eo quoque tempore in his
rationibus auctionis et partitionis, atque etiam se
ipse inferebat et intrudebat et in eam opinionem
Caesenniam adducebat, ut mulier imperita nihil
putaret agi callide posse ubi non adesset Aebutius.
14 Quam personam iam ex quotidiana cognoscitis vita,
recuperatores, mulierum assentatoris, cognitoris
viduarum, defensoris nimium litigiosi, cogniti ad
Regiam,[1] inepti ac stulti inter viros, inter mulieres
periti iuris et callidi, hanc personam imponite
Aebutio ; is enim Caesenniae fuit Aebutius. Ne

---

[1] contriti ad Regiam *Baiter*.

---

[a] At such an auction the heir sold so much of the estate
as was necessary to enable him to discharge the legacies
subject to which he had inherited the whole estate (*uni-
versitas*).

[b] A colonnade (βασιλική) in the Forum, apparently a
common resort of disreputable characters.

to a life interest on her part in all his property, to be
exercised conjointly with her son. She would have 12
appreciated this great honour done her by her
husband could it have been hers for long ; for she
would have been sharing her interest in his property
with the son whom she hoped would be the heir to
her own, and who was her greatest interest in life.
But of this interest Fate deprived her prematurely ;
for in a short time the young Marcus Fulcinius died,
making Publius Caesennius his heir, subject to the
payment of a large sum of money to his wife and the
greater part of his property to his mother. In these
circumstances the two women were notified to take
their shares.

V. It was decided to sell by auction [a] the property 13
thus bequeathed : whereupon Aebutius there, who
had long been battening upon Caesennia's lonely
and widowed situation, and had insinuated himself
into her confidence through his system of undertaking on her behalf, with some advantage to himself,
any business or dispute that might arise, was also
engaged at this particular time over this matter of
selling and dividing the estate, obtruding himself
and pushing himself forward and inducing Caesennia
to believe that a woman's inexperience was incapable
of conducting a good business transaction without
the presence of Aebutius. The character which you 14
know from your daily experience, gentlemen, to
belong to a flatterer of women, a widows' champion,
a litigious attorney, a frequenter of the Basilica,[b]
a clumsy fool among men but a shrewd and clever
lawyer among women—such is the character which
you should ascribe to Aebutius, for such did he prove
himself to Caesennia. Perhaps you may ask : " Was

forte quaeratis, num propinquus ? nihil alienius.
Amicus aut a patre aut a viro traditus ? nihil minus.
Quis igitur ? ille, ille, quem supra deformavi, volun-
tarius amicus mulieris, non necessitudine aliqua, sed
ficto officio simulataque sedulitate coniunctus, magis
opportuna opera nonnumquam quam aliquando fideli.
15 Quum esset, ut dicere institueram, constituta auctio
Romae, suadebant amici cognatique Caesenniae, id
quod ipsi quoque mulieri veniebat in mentem,
quoniam potestas esset emendi fundum illum Fulci-
nianum, qui fundo eius antiquo continens esset,
nullam esse rationem amittere eiusmodi occasionem,
quum ei praesertim pecunia ex partitione deberetur ;
nusquam posse eam melius collocari. Itaque hoc
mulier facere constituit : mandat ut fundum sibi
emat. Cui tandem ? cui putatis ? An non in
mentem vobis venit omnibus illius hoc munus esse ad
omnia mulieris negotia parati, sine quo nihil satis
caute, nihil satis callide posset agi ? Recte attenditis. Aebutio negotium datur.
16 VI. Adest ad tabulam, licetur Aebutius ; deter-
rentur emptores multi, partim gratia Caesenniae,
partim etiam pretio. Fundus addicitur Aebutio :
pecuniam argentario promittit Aebutius : quo testimonio nunc vir optimus utitur sibi emptum esse ;
quasi vero aut nos ei negemus addictum, aut tum

<hr />

^a Literally, the board to which an announcement of the
auction was affixed.
^b The banker kept a written record of the transactions
and, at the conclusion of the sale, received and disbursed all
payments due.

he a relation of hers ? " Far from it. " An old friend
of her father's or her husband's ? " No one less so.
" Who was he, then ? " Why, the very man whose
portrait I have just given you, the lady's self-con-
stituted friend, connected with her by no tie of
relationship but by obtrusive kindnesses and feigned
good offices and by services which, occasionally
undertaken in duty to her, were more often bene-
ficial to himself. When, as I had begun to say, it 15
was settled to hold the auction at Rome, Caesennia's
friends and relations began to persuade her (and the
same idea was occurring to her independently) that
as she had the chance to buy the estate which had
belonged to M. Fulcinius and which adjoined her
own original farm, there was no reason to let such an
opportunity slip, especially as money was owing to
her from the division of the property, which could
not be better invested. This therefore she decided
to do : she gave a commission to buy the farm to—
whom indeed ? Whom do you think ? Does it not
occur to every one of you that this was essentially
the business of the man who was ready to undertake
all the lady's business, without whom no adequate
foresight or shrewdness was possible ? You are
right. The business was entrusted to Aebutius.

VI. Aebutius attends at the sale.[a] He does the 16
bidding. Many purchasers are deterred, some by
consideration for Caesennia, some too, by the value
of the property. The estate is knocked down to
Aebutius. Aebutius promises the money to the
banker[b]—a fact which our worthy friend is now
using as evidence that he bought the estate for himself. As if indeed we denied that it was knocked
down to him ! Or as if anyone doubted at the time

quisquam fuerit qui dubitaret quin emeretur Caesenniae ; quum id plerique scirent, omnes fere audissent, qui non audisset, is[1] coniectura assequi posset, quum pecunia Caesenniae ex illa hereditate deberetur, eam porro in praediis collocari maxime expediret, essent autem praedia, quae mulieri maxime convenirent, ea venirent, liceretur is, quem Caesenniae dare operam nemo miraretur, sibi emere nemo posset

17 suspicari. Hac emptione facta, pecunia solvitur a Caesennia ; cuius rei putat iste rationem reddi non posse, quod ipse tabulas averterit ; se autem habere argentarii tabulas, in quibus sibi expensa pecunia lata sit acceptaque relata : quasi id aliter fieri oportuerit. Quum omnia ita facta essent, quemadmodum nos defendimus, Caesennia fundum possedit locavitque ; neque ita multo post A. Caecinae nupsit. Ut in pauca conferam, testamento facto mulier moritur. Facit heredem ex deunce et semuncia Caecinam, ex duabus sextulis M. Fulcinium, libertum superioris viri, Aebutio sextulam aspergit. Hanc sextulam illa mercedem isti esse voluit assiduitatis et molestiae, si quam ceperat. Iste autem hac sextula se ansam retinere omnium controversiarum putat.

18 VII. Iam principio ausus est dicere non posse heredem esse Caesenniae Caecinam ; quod is de-

---

[1] qui non audisset, is *om. codd. suppl. Baiter.*

---

that it was being purchased for Caesennia ; since most people knew it, everyone had heard it, and anyone who had not heard it might have guessed it, inasmuch as money was owing to Caesennia under this will, as far the best investment for this money would be in land, as the particular land which was much best suited to the lady's needs was for sale, as the bidder was one whom no one was ever surprised to find acting for Caesennia and as no one could suppose he was making the purchase for himself. For the purchase thus concluded the money was 17 found by Caesennia, though our friend calculates that no record of the transaction can be produced because he himself has made away with the account books, while retaining in his own possession the banker's book in which the price was entered on the debit side of his account and then carried over to the credit side. As if any other procedure would have been correct ! After the conclusion of the whole affair in the manner I have maintained, Caesennia took possession of the estate and let it. Shortly afterwards she married Aulus Caecina. To bring my story quickly to an end, she died, after making a will in which she bequeathed twenty-three twenty-fourths of her estate to Caecina and one thirty-sixth part to M. Fulcinius, a freedman of her first husband's, throwing in a seventy-second part for Aebutius.[a] This seventy-second part she intended as an acknowledgement of his devotion to her affairs and of any trouble they might have caused him. Our friend, however, looks upon this fraction as giving him a handle for raising disputes about everything.

VII. He started by having the effrontery to say 18 that Caecina could not be Caesennia's heir, since he

teriore iure esset quam ceteri cives, propter incommodum Volaterranorum calamitatemque civilem.
Itaque homo timidus imperitusque qui neque animi
neque consilii satis haberet, non putavit esse tanti
hereditatem ut de civitate in dubium veniret ; concessit, credo, Aebutio quantum vellet de Caesenniae
bonis ut haberet : immo, ut viro forti ac sapienti
dignum fuit, ita calumniam stultitiamque eius
19 obtrivit ac contudit. In possessione bonorum quum
esset, et quum iste[1] sextulam suam nimium exagge-
raret, nomine heredis arbitrum familiae herciscundae
postulavit. Atque illis paucis diebus, posteaquam
videt nihil se ab A. Caecina posse litium terrore
abradere, homini Romae in foro denuntiat fundum
illum, de quo ante dixi, cuius istum emptorem de-
monstravi fuisse mandatu Caesenniae, suum esse
seque sibi emisse. Quid ais ? istius ille fundus est,
quem sine ulla controversia quadriennium, hoc est,
ex quo tempore fundus veniit, quoad vixit, possedit
Caesennia ? Usus enim, inquit, eius fundi et
fructus, testamento viri, fuerat Caesenniae.

20 Quum hoc novae litis genus tam malitiose in-
tenderet, placuit Caecinae de amicorum sententia
constituere, quo die in rem praesentem veniretur et
de fundo Caecina moribus deduceretur. Colloquun-
tur. Dies ex utriusque commodo sumitur. Caecina
cum amicis ad diem venit in castellum Axiam ; ex
quo loco fundus is de quo agitur non longe abest.

<hr>

[1] iste *Schütz* : ipse *codd.*

had not full rights like other citizens by reason of the disability and the civil degradation to which the Volaterrans were subject. And so I suppose, like a timid and inexperienced man, lacking both in courage and resource, my client did not think it worth while, for the sake of the inheritance, to have any doubts cast on his rights as a citizen, and gave way to Aebutius, letting him keep whatever of Caesennia's estate he wanted! No indeed! He acted like a brave and wise man, and crushed this foolish and dishonest claim. Now as he was in possession of the 19 property, and Aebutius was making out his seventy-second share to be greater than it was, he asked, in his capacity as an heir, for an arbiter to divide the inheritance. In the course of the next few days, realizing that nothing could be squeezed out of Caecina by the threat of a lawsuit, Aebutius formally notified him in the Forum at Rome that the estate of which I have already spoken and which I showed that the defendant purchased on the instructions of Caesennia, was his own, bought by him for himself. What? Is Aebutius the owner of the estate of which Caesennia was indisputably in possession for four years, that is, from the day it was sold until she died? His answer is : " Yes ; for she had been left a life interest in it under her husband's will."

While Aebutius with such evil intent was planning 20 this singular kind of lawsuit, Caecina decided on the advice of his friends to fix a day on which he should repair to the actual place and be formally ejected from the estate. A conference was held and a day chosen to suit both parties. Caecina came with his friends on the appointed day to the castle of Axia, from which the disputed estate was not far distant.

Ibi certior fit a pluribus homines permultos, liberos
atque servos, coegisse et armasse Aebutium. Quum
id partim mirarentur, partim non crederent, ecce
ipse Aebutius in castellum venit. Denuntiat Caecinae se armatos habere ; abiturum eum non esse,
si accessisset. Caecinae placuit et amicis, quoad
videretur salvo capite fieri posse, experiri tamen.
21 De castello descendunt, in fundum proficiscuntur.
Videtur temere commissum ; verum, ut opinor, hoc
fuit caussae : tam temere istum re commissurum
quam verbis minitabatur nemo putavit. VIII. Atque iste ad omnes introitus, qua adiri poterat non
modo in eum fundum, de quo controversia erat, sed
etiam in illum proximum de quo nihil ambigebatur,
armatos homines opponit. Itaque primo quum in
antiquum fundum ingredi vellet, quod ea proxime
accedi poterat, frequentes armati obstiterunt.
22 Quo loco depulsus Caecina, tamen qua potuit ad
eum fundum profectus est, in quo ex conventu vim
fieri oportebat ; eius autem fundi extremam partem
oleae directo ordine definiunt. Ad eas quum acce-
deretur, iste cum omnibus copiis praesto fuit, servum-
que suum nomine Antiochum ad se vocavit, et clara
voce imperavit ut eum qui illum olearum ordinem
intrasset occideret. Homo mea sententia prudentissimus Caecina, tamen in hac re plus mihi animi
quam consilii videtur habuisse. Nam quum et
armatorum multitudinem videret, et eam vocem
Aebutii quam commemoravi audisset, tamen accessit

There he was informed by several people that a large band of freedmen and slaves had been collected and armed by Aebutius. While some were astounded at this and others refused to believe it, behold! Aebutius himself came to the castle, gave Caecina notice that he had armed men with him and swore that if he got as far as the property he should never go away again. Caecina and his friends decided to make the attempt notwithstanding, as far as should appear possible without endangering their lives. Leaving the castle they set out for the estate. I think it was rash of them to do so, but the reason for it was, I imagine, that no one supposed that Aebutius would be as rash in his actions as in his threats. VIII. The defendant, then, stationed armed men at every possible way of approach not only to the estate under dispute but even to the adjoining one about which there was no contention. And so, in the first instance, when Caecina wanted to enter the original estate, because that was the nearest way to the other, he was confronted by a crowd of armed men.

Repulsed from this spot, Caecina none the less **22** started to make his way as best he could to the estate on which it had been agreed that he should submit to force : the boundary of this estate is marked by a straight row of olive-trees. When he reached these trees, the defendant was waiting for him with all his forces, and calling to him one of his slaves named Antiochus, he ordered him in a loud voice to kill anyone who came within the row of olive-trees. Caecina, whom I consider a cautious man, seems to have displayed in this instance more spirit than sense. For although he saw the crowd of armed men and heard the remark of Aebutius which I have quoted, he

propius, et iam ingrediens intra finem eius loci, quem
oleae terminabant, impetum armati Antiochi ceterorumque tela atque incursum refugit. Eodem tempore se in fugam conferunt una amici advocatique
eius metu perterriti quemadmodum illorum testem
23 dicere audistis. His rebus ita gestis, P. Dolabella
praetor interdixit, ut est consuetudo, DE VI HOMINIBUS
ARMATIS, sine ulla exceptione, tantum ut unde deiecisset restitueret. Restituisse se dixit. Sponsio
facta est. Hac de sponsione vobis iudicandum est.

IX. Maxime fuit optandum Caecinae, recuperatores, ut controversiae nihil haberet, secundo loco,
ut ne cum tam improbo homine, tertio, ut cum tam
stulto haberet. Etenim non minus nos stultitia
illius sublevat quam laedit improbitas. Improbus
fuit, quod homines coegit, armavit coactis armatisque
vim fecit. Laesit in eo Caecinam, sublevat ibidem.
Nam in eas ipsas res quas improbissime fecit testimonia
24 sumpsit, et eis in caussa testimoniis utitur. Itaque
mihi certum est, recuperatores, antequam ad meam
defensionem meosque testes venio, illius uti confessione et testimoniis. Quid confitetur, atque ita
libenter confitetur ut non solum fateri sed etiam
profiteri videatur, recuperatores? " Convocavi
homines : coegi : armavi : terrore mortis ac peri-

---

a See Introduction, § 7 C.
b A formal way of denying liability.
c See Introduction, § 7 A.

none the less came nearer and was actually passing within the boundary of the land delimitated by the olive-trees, when Antiochus rushed at him sword in hand : the rest threw missiles at him and charged ; and he fled before them. His friends and supporters, panic-stricken, fled simultaneously as you heard my opponent's own witnesses say. Such being the 23 facts of the case, the praetor, P. Dolabella, issued the usual injunction "concerning force through armed men," [a] ordering Aebutius, without any saving clause, merely to "restore to the place whence he had ejected." Aebutius replied that "he had restored." [b] A wager at law [c] was concluded : on that wager you have to pass judgement.

IX. What Caecina would have most desired, gentlemen, was to have no quarrel with anyone : in the next place, to have no quarrel with such a knave ; and in the last, to have his quarrel with such a fool ! For actually Aebutius's folly does us as much good as his knavery does us harm. A knave he was, in that he collected men together, armed them and "used force by means of men collected together and armed." Therein he did Caecina harm, and therein, too, he does him good ; for he procured evidence of the very deeds which his knavery perpetrated and that evidence he brings forward at this trial. And 24 so I am resolved, gentlemen, before I come to present my case and summon my own witnesses, to make use of his admissions and his witnesses. What is his admission, gentlemen—made with a readiness which suggests that he is not merely making but actually volunteering it ? "I summoned my men : I collected them together, armed them and withstood your approach with the fear of death and by threatening

culo capitis ne accederes obstiti : ferro," inquit,
" ferro," et hoc dicit in iudicio, " te reieci atque
perterrui."

Quid, testes quid aiunt ? P. Vetilius, propinquus
Aebutii, se Aebutio cum armatis servis venisse ad-
vocatum. Quid praeterea ? fuisse complures armatos. Quid aliud ? minatum esse Aebutium Caecinae.
Quid ego de hoc teste dicam nisi hoc, recuperatores,
ut ne idcirco minus ei credatis quod homo minus
idoneus habetur, sed ideo credatis quod ex illa parte
25 id dicit quod illi caussae maxime est alienum ? A.
Terentius, alter testis, non modo Aebutium sed etiam
se pessimi facinoris arguit. In Aebutium hoc dicit,
armatos homines fuisse ; de se autem hoc praedicat,
Antiocho, Aebutii servo, imperasse ut in Caecinam
advenientem cum ferro invaderet. Quid loquar
amplius de hoc homine ? In quem ego hoc dicere,
quum rogarer a Caecina, numquam volui, ne arguere
illum rei capitalis viderer ; de eo dubito nunc quomodo aut loquar aut taceam, quum ipse hoc de se
26 iuratus praedicet. Deinde L. Caelius non solum
Aebutium cum armatis dixit fuisse compluribus,
verum etiam cum advocatis perpaucis eo venisse
Caecinam. X. De hoc ego teste detraham ? cui
aeque ac meo testi ut credatis postulo. P. Memmius
secutus est, qui suum non parvum beneficium com-
memoravit in amicos Caecinae, quibus sese viam per

your life." "By the sword," says he, "by the sword," yes, and he says it in a court of law, "I drove you back and routed you."

Again, what say his witnesses? Publius Vetilius, his neighbour, says that he came on the summons of Aebutius with some armed slaves. What further? That there was a large number of armed men. What else? That Aebutius threatened Caecina. What am I to say about this witness, gentlemen, except that I hope you will not believe him the less because he is little worthy of credence, but will believe him for the very reason that his story, told in my opponent's interest, is most unfavourable to my opponent's case? The second witness, Aulus 25 Terentius, charges not only Aebutius but himself with a heinous crime. Against Aebutius he says that there were armed men there; but against himself he proclaims that it was he who gave the order to Aebutius's slave Antiochus to attack Caecina with his sword if he came on. What further am I to say about this man? I never meant to say what I have said against him, although Caecina asked me to do so, for fear of seeming to be bringing a capital charge against him; but now I am wondering how I can either speak or fail to speak about him, inasmuch as he proclaims this information about himself on his oath. Next comes Lucius Caelius, who, in addition 26 to stating that Aebutius was attended by a very large body of armed men, adds that Caecina came to the spot with a very small body of supporters. X. Am I to disparage this witness? No, I demand that you believe him equally with my own witnesses. There followed P. Memmius who recorded the considerable kindness which he had done to Caecina's

fratris sui fundum dedisse dixit qua effugere possent,
quum essent omnes metu perterriti. Huic ego testi
gratias agam, quod et in re misericordem se prae-
27 buerit et in testimonio religiosum. A. Atilius et
eius filius L. Atilius et armatos ibi fuisse et se suos
armatos adduxisse dixerunt. Etiam hoc amplius :
quum Aebutius Caecinae malum minaretur, ibi tum
Caecinam postulasse ut moribus deductio fieret.
Hoc idem P. Rutilius dixit, et eo libentius dixit, ut
aliquo in iudicio eius testimonio creditum putaretur.
Duo praeterea testes nihil de vi, sed de re ipsa atque
emptione fundi dixerunt ; P. Caesennius, auctor
fundi, non tam auctoritate gravi quam corpore, et
argentarius Sex. Clodius, cui nomen est Phormio,
nec minus niger nec minus confidens quam ille
Terentianus est Phormio, nihil de vi dixerunt, nihil
praeterea quod ad vestrum iudicium pertineret.
28   Decimo vero loco testis exspectatus et ad extremum reservatus dixit, senator populi Romani,
splendor ordinis, decus atque ornamentum iudiciorum, exemplar antiquae religionis, Fidiculanius Falcula ; qui quum ita vehemens acerque venisset ut
non modo Caecinam periurio suo laederet, sed etiam
mihi videretur irasci, ita eum placidum mollem-
que reddidi ut non auderet, sicut meministis,
iterum dicere, quot millia fundus suus abesset ab
Urbe. Nam quum dixisset minus ↀ, populus cum

---

^a The *Phormio* of Terence takes its name from its leading
character, a parasite.

friends in affording them, as he said, a way of escape
through his brother's land when they were all in a
state of panic. I will ask this witness to accept my
thanks for having shown himself merciful in his conduct and scrupulous in his evidence. Aulus Atilius 27
and his son Lucius Atilius stated both that armed
men were there and that they brought thither their
own slaves ; and they said further that when
Aebutius was threatening Caecina with hurt, Caecina
then and there demanded that his ejection should
take place formally. The same statement was made
by P. Rutilius and all the more gladly for the hope
of at last securing credence for his evidence in a
court of law ! Two more witnesses gave evidence,
though not about the use of force but only about the
original facts and the purchase of the estate. Then
came Publius Caesennius, the vendor of the estate,
a man of greater physical than moral weight ; and
Sextus Clodius, the banker, surnamed Phormio, no
less black and no less brazen than the Phormio in
Terence[a] : they gave no evidence about the use of
force—or anything else relevant to your court.

The tenth witness to give evidence, anxiously 28
awaited and reserved for the last, a member of the
Roman Senate, the glory of his order, the pride and
ornament of the law courts, the model of old-time
uprightness, was Fidiculanius Falcula ; and although
he came into court in so violent and bitter a spirit as
not only to attack Caecina with his perjuries but even
to appear enraged against myself, I so far calmed and
soothed his feelings that, as you remember, he dared
not say a second time how many yards his farm is
distant from the city. For when he said " Nearly
50,000," the people laughed and cried out, " The

risu acclamavit, "ipsa esse." Meminerant enim
29 omnes quantum in Albiano iudicio accepisset. In
eum quid dicam nisi id quod negare non possit?
venisse in consilium publicae quaestionis, quum eius
consilii iudex non esset; et in eo consilio, quum
caussam non audisset et potestas esset ampliandi,
dixisse SIBI LIQUERE; quum incognita re iudicare
voluisset, maluisse condemnare quam absolvere;
quum, si uno minus damnarent, condemnari reus
non posset, non ad cognoscendam caussam sed ad
explendam damnationem praesto fuisse. Utrum
gravius aliquid in quempiam dici potest quam ad
hominem condemnandum, quem numquam vidisset
neque audisset, adductum pretio esse? An certius
quidquam obiici potest quam quod is cui obiicitur
30 ne nutu quidem infirmare conatur? Verumtamen
is testis, ut facile intelligeretis eum non adfuisse
animo, quum ab illis caussa ageretur testesque dicerent, sed tantisper de aliquo reo cogitasse, quum
omnes ante eum dixissent testes armatos cum
Aebutio fuisse complures, solus dixit non fuisse.
Visus est mihi primo veterator intelligere praeclare
quid caussae optaret, et tantummodo errare, quod
omnes testes infirmaret, qui ante eum dixissent;
quum subito, ecce idem qui solet, duos[1] solos servos

---

[1] duos *Baiter*: suos *codd.*

---

[a] Falcula was supposed to have received 40,000 sesterces
to vote Oppianicus "not guilty" and the people were
reminded of this by his saying "nearly 50,000": his words
could be taken as referring either to yards or to sesterces.
See the *Pro Cluentio*, §§ 103, 104, and 113, where a different
view of his character is given.

[b] See the *Pro Cluentio*, § 74. There were 32 jurors, and
the voting must have been 17 to 15 for conviction: had it
been equal, the accused would have been given the benefit
of the doubt.

very sum!" *a* For everyone remembered how much
he had received at the trial of Oppianicus. As for 29
him, what am I to say against him save what he
cannot deny—that he attended the session of a
public tribunal although not one of the jurors at that
session; *b* and that, in the course of it, although he
had not heard the case, and an adjournment was
possible, he voted " guilty "; that, since he decided
to pronounce judgement on the case without having
heard it, he preferred voting " guilty " to voting
" not guilty "; and that, since the accused could not
have been convicted had there been one vote less
given against him, his purpose there was not to investigate the case but to ensure a conviction? *b* Can
anything worse be said against anyone than that he
took a bribe to condemn a man whom he had never
seen or heard? Or, again, can any allegation be
made with more certainty than one which the object
of it cannot attempt to dispute even by shaking his
head? Yet this is the witness who (as if to con- 30
vince you that he was not paying attention while my
opponent was pleading his case and his witnesses
were giving evidence but that his thoughts meanwhile were with the accused *c* at some other trial)
alone, and despite the statement of all the previous
witnesses that there were armed men with Aebutius
in large numbers, said that there were none. At
first I thought that the old villain clearly realized
where his interest lay in the case and was only making
the mistake of discrediting all the previous witnesses: but suddenly he was himself again and said
that two armed slaves were there. I ask you,

c Presumably Oppianicus, about whom he had a guilty
conscience; see the *Pro Cluentio.*

armatos fuisse dixit. Quid huic tu homini facias?
nonne concedas interdum ut excusatione summae
stultitiae summae improbitatis odium deprecetur?

31 XI. Utrum, recuperatores, his testibus non credi-
distis, quum quid liqueret non habuistis?—at controversia non erat quin verum dicerent—an in coacta
multitudine, in armis, in telis, in praesenti metu
mortis perspicuoque periculo caedis dubium vobis
fuit inesse vis aliqua videretur necne? Quibus
igitur in rebus vis intelligi potest, si in his non in-
telligetur? An vero illa defensio vobis praeclara
visa est: Non deieci, sed obstiti? Non enim te sum
passus in fundum ingredi, sed armatos homines
opposui, ut intelligeres, si in fundo pedem posuisses,
statim tibi esse pereundum. Quid ais? is qui armis
perterritus, fugatus, pulsus est, non videtur esse
32 deiectus? Posterius de verbo videbimus: nunc
rem ipsam ponamus quam illi non negant, et eius
rei ius actionemque quaeramus.

Est haec res posita, quae ab adversario non
negatur: Caecinam, quum ad constitutam diem
tempusque venisset, ut vis ac deductio moribus fieret,
pulsum prohibitumque esse vi coactis hominibus et
armatis. Quum hoc constet, ego homo imperitus

Aebutius, what are you to do with a man like that?
Must you not occasionally allow him to escape the
reproach of superlative wickedness by pleading his
superlative stupidity?

XI. Was it, gentlemen, that you did not believe 31
these witnesses on the occasion when you could not
agree on a verdict?—and yet they were indisputably
speaking the truth—or was it that you could not
make up your minds to decide whether or no the
collection of a numerous body, the presence of arms
and missiles, of an instant fear of death and a manifest danger of murder, in any way amounted to the
use of force? What circumstances may be understood to amount to force, if not these? Or was it
indeed that you were so greatly impressed by my
opponent's defence—" I did not eject you; I withstood you; for I did not allow you to enter on the
estate, but placed armed men in your way in order
to convince you that if you did set foot on it, you
must perish forthwith"? What is this you say?
A man who has been by force of arms frightened
away, put to flight and driven off—has he not, in
your opinion, been ejected? We will consider the 32
appropriate expression later on; for the moment,
let me take for granted the facts of the case which
my opponents do not deny, and examine the law and
procedure relevant to those facts.

The following fact is taken for granted and not
denied by my opponents, that Caecina, arriving on
the appointed day and at the appointed hour in
order formally to submit to forcible ejection, was
driven off and debarred from entry by force, by
means of men collected together and armed. As
this is agreed, I, unskilled as I am in the law and un-

127

iuris, ignarus negotiorum ac litium, hanc puto me
habere actionem ut per interdictum meum ius
teneam atque iniuriam tuam persequar. Fac in hoc
errare me nec ullo modo posse per hoc interdictum
id assequi quod velim ; te uti in hac re magistro volo.
33 Quaero, sitne aliqua huius rei actio an nulla. Con-
vocari homines propter possessionis controversiam
non oportet, armari multitudinem iuris retinendi
caussa non convenit, nec iuri quidquam tam inimicum
quam vis, nec aequitati quidquam tam infestum est
quam convocati homines et armati.

XII. Quod quum ita sit, resque eiusmodi sit ut in
primis a magistratibus animadvertenda esse videatur,
iterum quaero, sitne eius rei aliqua actio an nulla.
Nullam esse dices ? Audire cupio. Qui in pace et
otio, quum manum fecerit, copias pararit, multitudinem hominum coegerit, armarit, instruxerit, homines
inermos, qui ad constitutum experiundi iuris gratia
venissent, armis, viris, terrore periculoque mortis
34 reppulerit, fugarit, averterit, hoc dicat : " Feci
equidem quae dicis omnia : et ea sunt et turbulenta
et temeraria et periculosa : quid ergo est ? impune
feci : nam quid agas mecum ex iure civili ac prae-
torio non habes." Itane vero, recuperatores ; hoc
vos audietis, et apud vos dici patiemini saepius ?
Quum maiores nostri tanta diligentia prudentiaque
fuerint, ut omnia omnium non modo tantarum rerum,

ᵃ The *ius civile* was based on statute law, available only
as between citizens and administered by the *praetor urbanus*.
The *ius praetorium* was based on custom and equity and was
embodied for the benefit of non-citizens in the " perpetual
edict " administered by successive provincial governors.
Its greater readiness and adaptability caused it to be increasingly preferred even by citizens.

versed in the business of litigation, consider that there
is a legal process which enables me to maintain my
rights and to deal with the injury you have done me
by means of an injunction. Suppose that I am mistaken in this and that it is quite impossible for me
to attain my ends by this injunction—I am anxious
to be your pupil in this matter: I ask you, is there 33
any legal process available in my case or is there
none? The collecting of men together because of a
disputed ownership is not right: the arming of a
mob in order to maintain a right is inexpedient:
nothing is so inimical to private rights as force, nor
anything so hostile to public justice as that men
should be collected together and armed.

XII. This being so, and the case appearing pre-
eminently one for cognizance by the magistrates, I
ask again: " Is there any legal process in my case
or is there none? " None," will you say? I am
anxious to hear. Is one who has, in a time of peace
and quiet, raised a band, levied a force, collected a
crowd of men, armed them, drawn them up, and who,
by force of arms, by numbers, by fear and by danger
of death, has driven away, put to flight, and turned
back unarmed men who had come by agreement for
the purpose of going through a legal process—is such
an one to say: " I did indeed act in all respects as 34
you describe, and such actions are both riotous, reck-
less, and dangerous. But what of that? I acted
with impunity; for law and equity alike *a* give you
no remedy against me"? Does he indeed say that,
gentlemen? Will you listen to such a statement and
suffer it to be made in your presence more than once?
Inasmuch as our forefathers displayed such care and
foresight as to prescribe and secure every right that

sed etiam tenuissimarum iura statuerint persecuti-
que sint, ut hoc genus unum vel maximum praeter-
mitterent, ut, si qui me exire domo mea coegisset
armis, haberem actionem, si qui introire prohibuisset,
non haberem ? Nondum de Caecinae caussa disputo,
nondum de iure possessionis nostrae loquor : tantum
35 de tua defensione, C. Piso, queror. Quoniam[1] ita
dicis et ita constituis, si Caecina, quum in fundo esset,
inde deiectus esset, tum per hoc interdictum eum
restitui oportuisse ; nunc vero deiectum nullo modo
esse inde ubi non fuerit, hoc interdicto nihil nos
assecutos esse ; quaero, si te hodie domum tuam
redeuntem coacti homines et armati non modo limine
tectoque aedium tuarum sed primo aditu vestibulo-
que prohibuerint, quid acturus sis. Monet amicus
meus te, L. Calpurnius, ut idem dicas, quod ipse antea
dixit, iniuriarum. Quid ad caussam possessionis,
quid ad restituendum eum quem oportet restitui,
quid denique ad ius civile aut ad praetoris[2] notionem
atque animadversionem ? Ages iniuriarum. Plus
tibi ego largiar. Non solum egeris, verum etiam
condemnaris licet ; numquid magis possidebis ? actio
enim iniuriarum non ius possessionis assequitur, sed
dolorem imminutae libertatis iudicio poenaque
mitigat.

---

[1] quoniam *Baiter*.　　　　[2] praetoris *Faber*.

---

[a] Counsel for Aebutius.　　　[b] See note, p. 128.

everyone possesses, not only in important cases like
this, but even in the slightest matters, would they
have failed to do so in this single and most important
instance, with the result that I have a remedy against
the man who compels me to leave my house, but no
remedy against the man who prevents me from
entering it? I am not yet arguing about my
client's case, I am not yet speaking of our right to
possession; what I am objecting to now is your
defence, Gaius Piso.[a] For your speech and your 35
conclusion amount to this: that, if Caecina had been
ejected from the farm when actually on it, in that
case he would have had the right to restitution by
means of this injunction; but, as it is, he was in no
sense " ejected " from a place in which he was not;
and that we have gained nothing by this injunction: I
ask you, then, what would you proceed to do if, on
your return home to-day, you were prevented by
men collected together and armed from entering not
merely the door-way and the actual interior of your
house but even the forecourt by which it is approached? My friend Lucius Calpurnius advises
you to give the same answer as he once gave: " an
action for assault." But what has that to do with
possession or with restitution of the man who ought
to be restored or, indeed, with either the civil code
or the praetor's notice and cognizance?[b] Suppose
you bring your action for assault: nay, I will grant
you more than that, suppose you not only bring your
action but win it, you will not be any nearer, will you,
to possession? For an action for assault does not seek
to establish a right to possession: it merely consoles
a man for interference with his liberty by trying and
punishing his assailant.

36 XIII. Praetor interea, Piso, tanta de re tacebit?
quemadmodum te restituat in aedes tuas non habebit? Qui dies totos aut vim fieri vetat aut restitui
factam iubet, qui de fossis, de cloacis, de minimis
aquarum itinerumque controversiis interdicit, is
repente obmutescet; in atrocissima re quod faciat
non habebit; et, C. Pisoni[1] domo tectisque suis prohibito, prohibito, inquam, per homines coactos et
armatos, praetor quemadmodum more et exemplo
opitulari possit non habebit? Quid enim dicet, aut
quid tu tam insigni accepta iniuria postulabis?
" Unde vi prohibitus sis," nemo umquam interdixit;
novum est, non dico inusitatum, verum omnino inauditum. " Unde deiectus? " Quid proficies, quum
illi hoc respondebunt tibi quod tu nunc mihi : armatos
se tibi obstitisse ne in aedes accederes; deiici porro
37 nullo modo potuisse qui non accesserit? " Deiicior
ego," inquis, " si quis meorum deiicitur." Omnino.
Iam bene agis. A verbis enim recedis et aequitate
uteris. Nam verba ipsa si sequi volumus, quo modo
tu deiiceris, quum servus tuus deiicitur? Verum ita
est, uti dicis. Te deiectum debeo intelligere, etiamsi
tactus non fueris. Nonne? Age nunc, si ne tuorum
quidem quisquam loco motus erit atque omnes in

---

[1] Pisoni *Lambinus* : Pisone *codd.*

XIII. Will the praetor, Piso, have nothing to say 36
meanwhile about so important a matter ? Will he
have no power to restore you to your house ? Will
the praetor, who spends his whole day either in
securing that force shall not be used or in counter-
acting it if it has been, who issues his injunction in
the matter of ditches and drains and trifling disputes
over rights of water and of way—will he, I say, be
suddenly struck dumb and be found without resource
to meet so iniquitous a state of things ? Will he be
without the means to relieve Gaius Piso, according
to usage and precedent, when debarred from entering his own house and home, debarred, I say, by
means of men collected together and armed ? What
terms will he employ, or what will you, in the face
of so notable an injury, demand that he use ?
" Whencesoever you have been by force debarred "?
No such injunction has ever been issued : it is an
innovation not merely unusual but unheard of.
" Whence you have been ejected " ? How will that
help you when your opponents will give you the
same answer as you are now giving me, that they
used arms to prevent you entering the house and no
one can possibly be ejected from a place he never
entered ? " I am ejected," you say, " if a member 37
of my household is ejected." By all means. Now
this is good pleading ; for you are forsaking the
wording and appealing to the spirit of the law. For
if we choose to abide by the actual words, how is it
you who are ejected when your servant is ejected ?
But you are right—I am bound to consider you
ejected even though you were not touched, am I
not ? Come now, suppose that not even one member
of your household has been removed, but that all

aedibus asservati ac retenti, tu solus prohibitus et a
tuis aedibus vi atque armis perterritus ; utrum hanc
actionem habebis qua nos usi sumus, an aliam quam-
piam, an omnino nullam ? Nullam esse actionem
dicere in re tam insigni tamque atroci neque pru-
dentiae neque auctoritatis tuae est. Alia si qua
forte est quae nos fugerit, dic quae sit : cupio discere.
38 Haec si est qua nos usi sumus, te iudice vincamus
necesse est. Non enim vereor, ne hoc dicas, in
eadem caussa, eodem interdicto, te oportere restitui,
Caecinam non oportere. Etenim cui non perspicuum est ad incertum revocari bona, fortunas,
possessiones omnium, si ulla ex parte sententia huius
interdicti deminuta aut infirmata sit ? si auctoritate
virorum talium vis armatorum hominum iudicio
approbata videatur, in quo iudicio non de armis
dubitatum, sed de verbis quaesitum esse dicatur ?
Isne apud vos obtinebit caussam suam qui se ita
defenderit : " Reieci[1] ego te armatis hominibus,
non deieci ? " ut tantum facinus non in aequitate
defensionis, sed in una littera latuisse videatur.
39 Huiusce rei vos statuetis nullam esse actionem,
nullum experiundi ius constitutum, qui obstiterit
armatis hominibus, qui multitudine coacta non in-
troitu sed omnino aditu quempiam prohibuerit ?
    XIV. Quid ergo ? hoc quam habet vim, ut distare

---

[1] reieci *Baiter* : eieci *codd.*

---

[a] See Introduction, § 7 C, note.
[b] The difference between the letters ' r ' and ' d.'

of them have been kept safely in the house, and that you alone have been debarred and frightened away from your house by force of arms, will you be entitled to employ either the same procedure which we are now employing, or a different one or none at all ? To say that no procedure is available in so signal and scandalous a case is consistent neither with your common sense nor with your position : if there be some other which I may have failed to notice, pray inform me what it is : I am anxious to learn. But if 38 it be this same procedure which we have employed, your own judgement gives us the verdict. For I have no fear of your saying that in identical cases the same injunction should restore you but not Caecina. Who indeed can fail to see that all men's goods, fortunes and tenures are reduced to insecurity if this injunction be in any respect lessened in scope or weakened in power ; if the violence of armed men appear, on the authority of men like yourselves, to be sanctioned by a court of law, a court in which, as will be said, the question of arms was not disputed, discussion being confined to a question of words ? Shall your verdict be given to the man who defends himself by saying, " I drove you back by armed men, I did not drive you out," [a] giving the impression that so infamous a deed owed its immunity not to the equity of the defence but to a single letter [b] in the law ? Shall your decision be 39 that there is no legal process to meet this case, no right prescribed for raising the issue at law, when a man has been debarred by means of armed men, by the collecting together of a multitude, from effecting not merely an entry but even an approach ?

XIV. How now ? What force has the contention

aliquid aut ex aliqua parte differre videatur, utrum,
pedem quum intulero atque in possessione vestigium
fecero, tum expellar ac deiiciar, an eadem vi atque
iisdem armis mihi ante occurratur, ne non modo
intrare, verum aspicere aut aspirare possim ? Quid
hoc ab illo differt, ut ille cogatur restituere qui ingressum expulerit, ille qui ingredientem reppulerit
40 non cogatur ? Videte, per deos immortales, quod
ius nobis, quam conditionem vobismetipsis, quam
denique civitati legem constituere velitis. Huiusce
generis una est actio per hoc interdictum quo nos
usi sumus constituta. Ea si nihil valet, aut si ad
hanc rem non pertinet, quid negligentius aut quid
stultius maioribus nostris dici potest, qui aut tantae
rei praetermiserint actionem, aut eam constituerint
quae nequaquam satis verbis caussam et rationem
iuris amplecteretur ? Hoc est periculosum dissolvi
hoc interdictum : est captiosum omnibus rem ullam
constitui eiusmodi quae, quum armis gesta sit,
rescindi iure non possit. Verumtamen illud est turpissimum, tantae stultitiae prudentissimos homines
condemnari ut vos iudicetis huius rei atque actionis
in mentem maioribus nostris non venisse.

41   "Queramur," inquit, "licet ; tamen hoc interdicto Aebutius non tenetur." Quid ita ? " Quod

that there is any sort or kind of difference between
my being expelled and ejected after I have entered
and taken possession by setting foot inside, and my
being attacked by the same force and with the same
arms before I do so, and thus prevented from entering, nay, even from beholding or approaching my
objective ? What difference is there between the
two cases such as to enforce the restitution of a man
who has been expelled after making entry but not
to enforce that of a man who has been expelled
as he was making entry ? In Heaven's name con- 40
sider what decision you are minded to impose upon
us, what a position upon yourselves, nay, what a law
upon the Commonwealth ! One process only has
been framed to meet a case of this kind, that is,
procedure by the injunction which we are now employing. If this process be non-effective or in-
applicable to this case, then what negligence or
what stupidity could be more gross than that of our forefathers, who either failed to frame any process to
deal with so grave a matter or framed one such as to
give wholly insufficient expression to the nature of
the case or the principle of law involved ? Dangerous as it is that this injunction should be annulled ;
universal as is the peril if any set of facts be held to
preclude the undoing by law of what has been done
by arms ; even so the greatest shame of all is this—
that wise men should be found guilty of such folly
as theirs must have been if you decide that no process at law to meet this case occurred to the minds of
our forefathers.

"We may, indeed, regret it," says Piso, "but 41
none the less this injunction is not applicable to
Aebutius." How so ? "Because force was not

vis Caecinae facta non est." Dici in hac caussa
potest, ubi arma fuerint, ubi coacta hominum multitudo, ubi instructi et certis locis cum ferro homines
collocati, ubi minae, pericula terroresque mortis, ibi
vim non fuisse? "Nemo," inquit, "occisus est
neque saucius." Quid ais? quum de possessionis
controversia et de privatorum hominum contentione
iuris loquamur, tu vim negabis factam, si caedes et
occisio facta non erit? Ego exercitus maximos saepe
pulsos et fugatos esse dico terrore ipso impetuque
hostium sine cuiusquam non modo morte, verum
etiam vulnere.

42 XV. Etenim, recuperatores, non ea sola vis est
quae ad corpus nostrum vitamque pervenit, sed etiam
multo maior ea, quae periculo mortis iniecto formidine animum perterritum loco saepe et certo de
statu demovet. Itaque saucii saepe homines, quum
corpore debilitantur, animo tamen non cedunt neque
eum relinquunt locum quem statuerint defendere:
at alii pelluntur integri; ut non dubium sit quin
maior adhibita vis ei sit, cuius animus sit perterritus,
43 quam illi cuius corpus vulneratum sit. Quod si vi
pulsos dicimus exercitus esse eos, qui metu ac tenui
saepe suspicione periculi fugerunt, et si non solum
impulsu scutorum neque conflictu corporum neque
ictu cominus neque coniectione telorum, sed saepe
clamore ipso militum aut instructione aspectuque
signorum magnas copias pulsas esse et vidimus et

138

used upon Caecina." Can it be said in this case that where there were weapons, a multitude of men collected together, drawn up and stationed at definite positions under arms, where there was menace, peril and fear of death, there was no force ? " No one," he replies, " was either killed or wounded." What ? When we are dealing with a dispute over possession, a private action at law, will you say that no force was used unless murder and killing took place ? I remind you that great armies have often been routed and put to flight merely by the terror inspired by the enemy's onset without a man being killed or wounded.

XV. In truth, gentlemen, force which touches our 42 persons or our lives is not the only form of force : much more serious is the force which removes a man from a definite position or situation by exposing him to the danger of death and striking terror into his mind. Thus there are many cases of wounded men whose minds refuse to give way, though their bodies are weakened, and who do not abandon the position they are resolved to defend ; others, on the contrary, are driven back although unscathed ; which proves that a greater degree of force is brought to bear upon the man whose mind is terror-stricken than on the man whose body is wounded. But if we say of armies which have been 43 put to flight by the fear or sometimes by the vaguest suspicion of danger, that they have been driven back by force ; if we have both seen and heard tell of great armies driven back, not by the weight of the enemy's shields nor the shock of impact, not by blows struck in close combat nor missiles hurled from a distance, but often enough just by the shouting of

audivimus, quae vis in bello appellatur, ea in otio non appellabitur? et quod vehemens in re militari putatur, id leve in iure civili iudicabitur? et quod exercitus armatos movet, id advocationem togatorum non videbitur movisse? et vulnus corporis magis istam vim quam terror animi declarabit? et sauciatio quaeretur, quum fugam factam esse constabit?

44 Tuus enim testis hoc dixit, metu perterritis nostris advocatis locum se qua effugerent demonstrasse. Qui non modo ut fugerent, sed etiam ipsius fugae tutam viam quaesiverunt, his vis adhibita non videbitur? Quid igitur fugiebant? propter metum. Quid metuebant? vim videlicet. Potestis igitur principia negare, quum extrema conceditis? Fugisse perterritos confitemini: caussam fugae dicitis eandem quam omnes intelligimus, arma, multitudinem hominum, incursionem atque impetum armatorum. Haec ubi conceduntur esse facta, ibi vis facta negabitur?

45 XVI. At vero hoc quidem iam vetus est et maiorum exemplo multis in rebus usitatum, quum ad vim faciendam veniretur, si quos armatos quamvis procul conspexissent, ut statim testificati discederent, optime sponsionem facere possent, NI ADVERSUS EDICTUM PRAETORIS VIS FACTA ESSET. Itane vero? scire esse armatos satis est ut vim factam probes;

---

the foe, his battle-array and the sight of his standards, shall not that which is called " force " in war be called the same in peace ? Shall that which is termed vigour in the conduct of a soldier be adjudged as mildness under citizen law ? Shall not that which dislodges hosts arrayed in arms be held to have dislodged a concourse of citizens in the garb of peace ? Shall we consider a maimed body better evidence of force than a terror-stricken mind ? Shall we go looking for wounds when the rout is an accepted fact ? For it was one of your own witnesses who 44 stated that he pointed out a way of escape to my client's terror-stricken supporters. Shall it be held that no force was used on those who sought not merely to flee but to find a way by which to flee in safety ? Why were they fleeing ? Because they were afraid. Afraid of what ? Obviously, of force. Can you then deny the cause when you admit the effect ? You confess that they fled in terror ; the reason for their flight you state to be what we all know it was—arms, a multitude, the furious onset of armed men. When this is an admitted fact, can it be denied that force was used ?

XVI. And yet this at any rate is a time-honoured 45 principle, supported by the constant practice of our forefathers, that when there was a meeting for the exercise of force, the party which caught sight of armed men, however far away, might secure evidence of the fact and depart immediately, as being perfectly entitled to make a wager at law in the form beginning : " If no force has been used in contravention of the praetor's edict . . ." [a] Is this so ? Is it enough to be aware that armed men are present, in order to prove the use of force, but not

141

in manus eorum incidere non est satis ? Aspectus
armatorum ad vim probandam valebit ; incursus et
impetus non valebit ? qui abierit facilius sibi vim
46 factam probabit quam qui effugerit ? At ego hoc
dico : si, ut primo in castello Caecinae dixit Aebutius
se homines coegisse et armasse, neque illum si eo
accessisset abiturum, statim Caecina discessisset, dubitare vos non debuisse quin Caecinae facta vis esset :
si vero, simulac procul conspexit armatos, recessisset,
eo minus dubitaretis. Omnis enim vis est quae
periculo aut decedere nos alicunde cogit aut prohibet
accedere. Quod si aliter statuetis, videte ne hoc vos
statuatis, qui vivus discesserit, ei vim non esse factam;
ne hoc omnibus in possessionum controversiis prae-
scribatis ut confligendum sibi et armis decertandum
putent ; ne, quemadmodum in bello poena ignavis
ab imperatoribus constituitur, sic in iudiciis deterior
caussa sit eorum qui fugerint quam qui ad extremum
47 usque contenderint. Quum de iure et legitimis
hominum controversiis loquimur, et in his rebus vim
nominamus, pertenuis vis intelligi debet. Vidi armatos quamvis paucos : magna vis est. Decessi
unius hominis telo perterritus : deiectus detrususque
sum. Hoc si ita statuetis, non modo non erit cur
depugnare quisquam posthac possessionis caussa velit,
sed ne illud quidem, cur repugnare. Sin autem vim

enough to fall into their hands ? Shall the sight of armed men constitute a proof of force and shall their furious onset constitute no proof ? Shall it be easier for a man to prove that he was subjected to force if he walked away than if he ran away ? I go so far as to say that had Caecina immediately departed as soon as Aebutius told him at the castle that he had collected and armed his men and that if Caecina reached the property he would never leave it, you would have had no grounds for doubting that Caecina was subjected to force : still less doubt would you feel, had he withdrawn the moment he saw armed men in the distance. For anything constitutes force which, by the threat of danger, either compels us to leave or prevents us from reaching any place. Should you decide otherwise, beware lest your decision amount to this—that no force has been employed upon a man who goes away alive : beware lest you be directing all men engaged over a disputed right of possession to the conclusion that they must decide their quarrel by an armed conflict : beware lest the punishment meted out by generals to the cowardly in war find its counterpart in the courts, and the weaker case be theirs who have fled rather than theirs who have fought to the last. When we are speaking of rights and disputes at law and in that connexion use the word " force," a very slight degree of force should be understood. I saw armed men, however few : this is an instance of great force. I was frightened away by a missile thrown by a single man : I was ejected and expelled. If you so decide, you will remove all future motive for resorting to battle over possession ; nay more, there will be no motive even for accepting battle. But if you under-

sine caede, sine vulneratione, sine sanguine, nullam intelligetis, statuetis homines possessionis cupidiores quam vitae esse oportere.

48 XVII. Age vero, de vi te ipsum habebo iudicem, Aebuti. Responde, si tibi videtur. In fundum Caecina utrum tandem noluit an non potuit accedere ? Quum te obstitisse et reppulisse dicis, certe hunc voluisse concedis. Potes igitur dicere non ei vim fuisse impedimento, cui, quum cuperet eoque consilio venisset, per homines coactos non sit licitum accedere ? Si enim id quod maxime voluit nullo modo potuit, vis profecto quaedam obstiterit necesse est, aut tu dic, quamobrem quum vellet accedere non accesserit.

49 Iam vim factam negare non potes : deiectus quemadmodum sit qui non accesserit, id quaeritur. Demoveri enim et depelli de loco necesse est eum qui deiiciatur : id autem accidere ei qui potest, qui omnino in eo loco, unde se deiectum esse dicit, numquam fuit ? Quid si fuisset et ex eo loco metu permotus fugisset, quum armatos vidisset, diceresne esse deiectum ? Opinor. An tu qui tam diligenter et tam callide verbis controversiam non aequitate diiudicas, et iura non utilitate communi sed litteris exprimis, poterisne dicere, deiectum esse eum qui tactus non erit ? Quid, detrusum dices ? nam eo

stand by force nothing which is unaccompanied by slaughter, wounds and the shedding of blood, you will be deciding that men ought to think more of possession than of life itself.

XVII. Come now, Aebutius, you shall yourself 48 pronounce judgement on the question of force. Answer me, if you please. Was Caecina in fact unwilling to enter on the estate or was he unable? In saying that you withstood my client and drove him back you admit that he had the will to enter on it. Can you, then, say that it was not force which hindered him, when he was debarred from entering by a gathering of men although he desired to enter and had come there with that intention? For if he was absolutely unable to do what he was extremely anxious to do, then some force must inevitably have prevented him; otherwise, pray tell me why, when he desired to enter, he did not do so.

Nay, but you cannot deny that force was used: 49 the question is how, since he failed to enter, he was " driven out." For if a man is to be driven out he must needs be removed and displaced. But how can he be, if he has never once been in the place out of which he claims to have been driven? Well, suppose he had actually been there and had fled in terror at the sight of armed men, would you say that he had been driven out? I think you would. Will you, then, who show such care and skill in settling disputes by the letter and not the spirit of the law, and who interpret laws in the light rather of their wording than of the general good—will you, I say, bring yourself to state that a man has been driven out without having been touched? Or will you say that he has been " thrust out "—for that was the

verbo antea praetores in hoc interdicto uti solebant.
Quid ais ? potestne detrudi quisquam qui non
attingitur ? Nonne, si verbum sequi volumus, hoc
intelligamus necesse est, eum detrudi cui manus
afferantur ? Necesse est, inquam, si ad verbum rem
volumus adiungere, neminem statui detrusum qui
non adhibita vi manu demotus et actus praeceps in-
50 telligatur. Deiectus verbo qui potest esse quisquam,
nisi in inferiorem locum de superiore motus ? Potest
pulsus, fugatus, eiectus denique : illud vero nullo
modo potest, deiectus esse quisquam, non modo qui
tactus non sit, sed ne aequo quidem et plano loco.
Quid ergo ? hoc interdictum putamus eorum esse
caussa compositum qui se praecipitatos ex locis superioribus dicerent—eos enim vere possumus dicere
esse deiectos—an quum voluntas et consilium et
sententia interdicti intelligatur, impudentiam summam aut stultitiam singularem putabimus in verborum errore versari, rem et caussam et utilitatem
communem non relinquere solum sed etiam prodere ?
51　XVIII. An hoc dubium est quin neque verborum
tanta copia sit, non modo in nostra lingua, quae
dicitur esse inops, sed ne in alia quidem ulla, res ut
omnes suis certis ac propriis vocabulis nominentur,
neque vero quidquam opus sit verbis, quum ea res
cuius caussa verba quaesita sint intelligatur ? Quae
lex, quod senatus consultum, quod magistratus edictum, quod foedus aut pactio, quod, ut ad privatas res
redeam, testamentum, quae iudicia aut stipulationes

---

^a The point, which it seems impossible to bring out in
English, lies in the derivation of the word "*deiectus*" from
de (down) and *iectus* (thrown). See Introduction, § 7
C, note.

^b Compare Lucretius, i. 832 "patrii sermonis egestas."
Cicero always denies the "poverty of our native tongue."

word the praetors were formerly in the habit of using
in this injunction ? Well, can anyone be " thrust
out " without being touched ? Surely if we mean to
go by the words, we must understand that, for a man
to be thrust out, hands must be laid on him. I
repeat, it is impossible, if we wish to give the word
its fair value, to hold that anyone has been thrust
out, unless it be clear that he had been dislodged and
driven headlong by personal application of force.
And how can anyone be literally " ejected [a] " unless 50
he has been removed from higher to lower ground ?
He may be expelled, put to flight or evicted ; but
" ejected " he cannot be if he is not touched, or
even if the ground is flat and level. What then ?
Do we imagine that this injunction was framed for
the benefit of those who claimed to have been thrown
headlong down from a height (for they it is who can
rightly be styled " ejected ") or shall we rather, since
the intention, design and meaning of the injunction
is clear to us, reckon it a piece of consummate impudence and of unparalleled stupidity to be concerned over a verbal error while abandoning, nay
betraying, the facts of the case and the interests of
the public ?

XVIII. Can it indeed be doubted that neither our 51
own language, which is said to be deficient,[b] nor even
any other, contains so large a store of words as to
distinguish every concept by a definite and peculiar
term ; or indeed, that words are superfluous when
the concept is clear for the expression of which words
were originally invented ? What statute, what
senatorial decree, what magisterial edict, what
treaty or agreement or (to speak once more of our
private concerns) what testament, what rules of law

147

aut pacti et conventi formula non infirmari ac
convelli potest, si ad verba rem deflectere velimus,
consilium autem eorum qui scripserunt et rationem
52 et auctoritatem relinquamus? Sermo hercule et
familiaris et quotidianus non cohaerebit, si verba
inter nos aucupabimur. Denique imperium dome-
sticum nullum erit, si servulis hoc nostris concesseri-
mus ut ad verba nobis obediant, non ad id quod ex
verbis intelligi possit obtemperent. Exemplis nunc
uti videlicet mihi necesse est harum rerum omnium.
Non occurrit uni cuique vestrum aliud alii in omni
genere exemplum, quod testimonio sit, non ex verbis
aptum pendere ius, sed verba servire hominum
53 consiliis et auctoritatibus? Ornate et copiose L.
Crassus, homo longe eloquentissimus, paullo ante
quam nos in forum venimus, iudicio centumvirali hanc
sententiam defendit, et facile, quum contra eum
prudentissimus homo Q. Mucius diceret, probavit
omnibus M'. Curium, qui heres institutus esset ita,
"mortuo postumo filio," quum filius non modo non
mortuus, sed ne natus quidem esset, heredem esse
oportere. Quid, verbis satis hoc cautum erat?
minime. Quae res igitur valuit? voluntas, quae si
tacitis nobis intelligi posset, verbis omnino non
uteremur; quia non potest, verba reperta sunt, non
quae impedirent, sed quae indicarent voluntatem.

---

[a] A special court of 105 persons chosen annually for the
hearing of civil suits, especially those dealing with inheritance.

[b] Cicero was called in 93 b.c.

[c] Quintus Mucius Scaevola, the Pontifex Maximus (see
§ 67), of whom Cicero had been a devoted pupil.

[d] A posthumous son, in the Roman sense, was one born

or undertakings or formal pacts and agreements could not be invalidated and abolished, if we chose to sacrifice the meaning to the words without taking into account the design, the purport, and intention of the writer? Why, the familiar speech of every 52 day will not have a consistent meaning if we set verbal traps for one another. Even our authority at home will cease to exist if we allow our slave-boys to obey our orders to the letter only, without paying any attention to the meaning implied in our words. And now I suppose I must produce examples of all these points; as though indeed every one of you cannot think of some example, whether in one connexion or another, to support my plea that Right does not depend on words, but that words are subservient to the purpose and the intentions of men. This opinion was supported by the great orator, 53 Lucius Crassus, in an elegant and ample speech before the centumviral court [a] shortly before I was called to the bar; [b] and although the learned Quintus Mucius [c] was against him he proved to everyone, and with ease, that Manius Curius, who was to succeed to an estate " in the event of the death of a posthumous son," [d] was entitled to succeed although the son was not dead—never, in fact, having been born! Well, did the wording of the will provide adequately for this situation? Far from it. Then what was the deciding consideration? Intention; for if our intention could be made clear without our speaking, we should not use words at all; but because it cannot, words have been invented, not to conceal but to reveal intention.

after the father's will had been made, and not necessarily after his death.

54 XIX. Lex usum et auctoritatem fundi iubet esse
biennium. At utimur eodem iure in aedibus, quae
in lege non appellantur.—Si via sit immunita, iubet
qua velit agere iumentum. Potest hoc ex verbis
intelligi, licere, si via sit in Brutiis immunita, agere
si velit iumentum per M. Scauri Tusculanum.—Actio
est in auctorem praesentem his verbis: QUANDOQUE
TE IN IURE CONSPICIO. Hac actione Appius ille
Caecus uti non posset, si tam vere homines verba
consectarentur, ut rem cuius caussa verba sunt non
considerarent.—Testamento si recitatus heres esset
pupillus Cornelius, isque iam annos xx haberet, vobis
interpretibus amitteret hereditatem.

55 Veniunt in mentem mihi permulta ; vobis plura,
certo scio. Verum ne nimium multa complectamur
atque ab eo quod propositum est longius aberret
oratio, hoc ipsum interdictum de quo agitur consideremus. Intelligetis enim in eo ipso, si in verbis
ius constituamus, omnem utilitatem nos huius interdicti, dum versuti et callidi volumus esse, amissuros.
UNDE TU AUT FAMILIA AUT PROCURATOR TUUS. Si me
villicus tuus solus deiecisset, non familia deiecisset,
ut opinor, sed aliquis de familia. Recte igitur
diceres te restituisse ? Quippe : quid enim facilius
est quam probari iis, qui Latine sciant, in uno servulo

---

^a That is, through the particular estate over which he has
a right of way.
^b Appius Claudius Caecus, the famous censor in 312 B.C.,
who was blind.
^c A boy attained his majority at fourteen.
^d See note ^b on § 23.

XIX. By statute, property in land is to be deter- 54
mined by two years' possession ; but we adopt the
same principle in the case of houses, which are not
specified in the statute. By statute, if a road is impassable, a man may drive his beast by any way he
likes : [a] the actual words can be held to mean that
if a road in Bruttium is impassable, a man may, if he
likes, drive his beast through the estate of Marcus
Scaurus at Tusculum. A form of action lies against
a vendor, if present in court, beginning with the
words " whereas I see you in court . . .": this form
could not be used by old Appius Claudius [b] if people
kept strictly to the words without considering the
meaning which it is the object of words to express.
If an estate had been left by will to " Cornelius the
Minor," [c] and Cornelius were now twenty years old,
he would lose his inheritance according to your
interpretation.

A great number of instances occur to me, and still 55
more to you, I feel sure, but in order not to extend
my survey unduly and not to wander too far from
the point, let me deal with the actual injunction
with which we are concerned ; for it will be clear to
you in the case of this particular injunction, that, if
we make Right dependent upon words, we shall be
losing all benefit from it as long as we like to exercise
our ingenuity and cunning. " Whence you or your
household or your agent . . ." If your steward
alone had driven me out it would not have been your
household, surely, that had done so, but a member
of your household. Would you then be entitled to
reply, " I have restored " ? [d] Certainly, for what
is easier than to prove to anyone, provided he knows
Latin, that the word " household " does not apply

familiae nomen non valere? Si vero ne habeas
quidem servum, praeter eum qui me deiecerit, clames
videlicet : si habeo familiam, a familia mea fateor te
esse deiectum. Neque enim dubium est quin, si ad
rem iudicandam verbo ducimur, non re, familiam
intelligamus quae constet ex servis pluribus, quin
unus homo familia non sit. Verbum certe hoc non
56 modo postulat, sed etiam cogit. At vero ratio iuris
interdictique vis et praetorum voluntas et hominum
prudentium consilium et auctoritas respuat hanc
defensionem et pro nihilo putet. XX. Quid ergo?
isti homines Latine non loquuntur? immo vero
tantum loquuntur quantum est satis ad intelli-
gendam voluntatem, quum sibi hoc proposuerint, ut
sive me tu deieceris sive tuorum quispiam sive servorum sive amicorum, ut servos non numero distin-
57 guant, sed appellent uno familiae nomine; de liberis
autem quisquis est, procuratoris nomine appelletur :
non quo omnes sint aut appellentur procuratores, qui
negotii nostri aliquid gerant, sed in hac re, cognita
sententia interdicti, verba subtiliter exquiri omnia
noluerunt. Non enim alia caussa est aequitatis in
uno servo et in pluribus ; non alia ratio iuris in hoc
genere dumtaxat, utrum me tuus procurator deiecerit,
is qui legitime procurator dicitur omnium rerum eius
qui in Italia non sit absitve rei publicae caussa, quasi
quidam paene dominus, hoc est, alieni iuris vicarius,

to one single slave ? And suppose you actually had
no other slave beside the one that drove me out,
doubtless you would exclaim : " I admit that it was
my household that drove you out—if I have one ! "
It cannot be doubted that if our judgement is to
follow the letter and not the spirit of the law, we
understand a household to consist of several slaves
and that a single slave is not a household ; the actual
word not only requires but compels this interpretation ; and yet such a line of defence is rejected with 56
contumely by the principles of law, the force of the
injunction, the purpose of the praetor, the design
and intention of wise legislators. XX. What then ?
Are those I mention not speaking good Latin ? On
the contrary, their Latin is good enough to make
clear what was their intention when they resolved
that, whether it be you who drive me out or one of
your associates or slaves or friends, they would
describe the slaves collectively as your household
without specifying their number, while describing any 57
free person concerned as your agent : not that
anyone who undertakes business for us is our
agent or is so described ; but the sense in the particular case being perfectly clear, they declined to
make a minute investigation of every word. For it
makes no difference to the equity of the case whether
one slave was concerned or more than one : it makes
no difference to the legal principle—at all events in
this instance—whether I was driven out by your
agent (giving the word " agent " its legal sense of a
man practically in the position of owner of all the
property belonging to someone not in Italy or absent
on State service, that is, one who possesses the rights
of another as his representative) or whether it was

an tuus colonus aut vicinus aut cliens aut libertus
aut quivis qui illam vim deiectionemque tuo rogatu
58 aut tuo nomine fecerit.   Quare si ad eum restituendum qui vi deiectus est, eandem vim habet aequitatis
ratio, ea intellecta, certe nihil ad rem pertinet quae
verborum vis sit ac nominum.   Tam restitues, si tuus
me libertus deiecerit, nulli tuo praepositus negotio,
quam si procurator deiecerit : non quo omnes sint
procuratores qui aliquid nostri negotii gerunt, sed
quod in hac re quaeri nihil attinet.   Tam restitues, si
unus servulus quam si familia fecerit universa : non
quo idem sit servulus quod familia ; verum quia non
quibus verbis quidque dicatur quaeritur, sed quae
res agatur.   Etiam si, ut longius a verbo recedamus,
ab aequitate ne tantulum quidem, si tuus servus
nullus fuerit, sed omnes alieni ac mercenarii, tamen
et ipsi tuae familiae genere et nomine continebuntur.
59   XXI. Perge porro hoc idem interdictum sequi ;
HOMINIBUS COACTIS. Neminem coegeris : ipsi convenerint sua sponte.   Certe cogit is qui congregat
homines et convocat.   Coacti sunt ii qui ab aliquo sunt
unum in locum congregati.   Si non modo convocati
non sunt, sed ne convenerunt quidem, sed ii modo
fuerunt qui etiam antea, non vis ut fieret, verum
colendi aut pascendi caussa esse in agro consueverant,

your tenant or neighbour or client or freedman or anyone else who, at your request or in your name, effected the forcible ejectment in question. Where- 58 fore, if the principle of equity has the same force in the case of a person forcibly ejected, it is surely irrelevant, once that is established, to consider the force of words and names. You will make the same "restitution" if your freedman has ejected me, though not commissioned with any business of yours, as if your agent has: not that anyone who undertakes business for us is our agent, but that the question is in this case irrelevant. You will make the same "restitution" if it be a single slave who has done it as if it had been your entire household: not that your one slave is the same as your household, but because we are concerned, not with the wording, but with the content of each clause. And even if (to depart still further from the wording though no whit from the spirit of the law) it was no slave of your own, but all those concerned belonged to other people or were hired, even they will none the less be classed together and described as your household.

XXI. Let us proceed with our examination of this 59 same injunction. "Through men collected to-gether." Suppose you did not collect anybody but they came of their own accord. Without doubt collecting means assembling and inviting, and people are said to be collected when they have been assembled by someone into one place. Suppose that, so far from being invited to assemble, they did not assemble at all, and that the only people concerned were those who had habitually frequented the place before the occurrence for the purpose not of using force but of tillage and pasturage: you will then

defendes homines coactos non fuisse, et verbo quidem
superabis, me ipso iudice ; re autem ne consistes
quidem ullo iudice. Vim enim multitudinis restitui
voluerunt, non solum convocatae multitudinis, sed,
quia plerumque, ubi multitudine opus est, homines
cogi solent, ideo de coactis compositum interdictum
est : quod etiamsi verbo differre videbitur, re tamen
erit unum et omnibus in caussis idem valebit in
quibus perspicitur una atque eadem caussa aequitatis.

60   ARMATISVE. Quid dicemus ? Armatos, si Latine
loqui volumus, quos appellare vere possumus ? opinor
eos qui scutis telisque parati ornatique sunt. Quid
igitur ? Si glebis aut saxis aut fustibus aliquem de
fundo praecipitem egeris, iussusque sis quem hominibus armatis deieceris restituere, restituisse te dices ?
Verba si valent, si caussae non ratione sed vocibus
ponderantur, me auctore dicito : vinces profecto,
non fuisse armatos eos qui saxa iacerent, quae de
terra ipsi tollerent, non esse arma caespites neque
glebas ; non fuisse armatos eos qui praetereuntes
ramum defringerent arboris ; arma esse suis nomini-
bus, alia ad tegendum, alia ad nocendum, quae qui
61 non habuerint, eos inermos fuisse vinces. Verum
siquidem erit armorum iudicium, tum ista dicito ;

ᵃ See note ᵇ on § 23.
ᵇ *Armorum iudicium* was the title of a play by Pacuvius,
Cicero's allusion to which would have been understood by
his audience.

raise the plea that there had been no collecting together of men, and on the verbal issue you will secure the verdict though I myself be your judge; but in point of actual fact you will not even be able to stand your ground whoever your judge may be. Our legislators intended restitution in cases of force employed by a number of persons and not only when those persons had been collected together; but because it is usual to collect people when numbers are needed, the injunction was framed to deal with " men collected together." So that, even though there seems to be a verbal difference yet it will be one and the same thing, and the effect will be the same in all cases where the principle of equity is seen to be one and the same.

" Or armed." What shall we say of that? Whom, 60 if we wish to speak good Latin, can we properly style armed men? Those, I suppose, who are provided and equipped with shields and spears. Well, suppose you have used clods, or sticks, or stones to drive a man headlong from his farm and are ordered to restore " him whom you have driven out by means of armed men ": will you say, " I have restored "? [a] If it is words that count, and phrases rather than principles that carry weight in a case, then you have my leave to say it. You will doubtless establish your point that those who threw stones picked up by themselves from the ground were not armed men, that clods and turf are not arms, nor were those " armed " who broke off a branch in passing: that arms are, by their definition, some for defence, some for offence; and you will establish your point that men who had no such weapons were unarmed. If 61 " arms " form the subject of a suit,[b] then by all means

CICERO

iuris iudicium quum erit et aequitatis, cave in ista
tam frigida, tam ieiuna calumnia delitiscas ; non
enim reperies quemquam iudicem aut recupera-
torem, qui, tamquam si arma militis inspiciunda sint,
ita probet armatum sed proinde valebit quasi arma-
tissimi fuerint, si reperientur ita parati fuisse ut vim
vitae aut corpori potuerint afferre.

62 XXII. Atque ut magis intelligas quam verba nihil
valeant, si tu solus, aut quivis unus cum scuto, cum
gladio impetum in me fecisset atque ego ita deiectus
essem, auderesne dicere interdictum esse de armatis
hominibus, hic autem hominem armatum unum
fuisse ? Non, opinor, tam impudens esses. Atqui
vide ne multo nunc sis impudentior. Nam tum
quidem omnes mortales implorare posses, quod
homines in tuo negotio Latine obliviscerentur, quod
inermi armati iudicarentur, quod, quum interdictum
esset de pluribus, commissa res esset ab uno, unus
63 homo plures esse homines iudicaretur. Verum in
his caussis non verba veniunt in iudicium, sed ea res
cuius caussa verba haec in interdictum coniecta sunt.
Vim quae ad caput ac vitam pertinet restitui sine
ulla exceptione voluerunt. Ea fit plerumque per
homines coactos armatosque : si alio consilio, eodem
periculo facta sit, eodem iure esse voluerunt. Non
enim maior est iniuria, si tua familia quam si tuus

ᵃ The injunction *de vi armata* (see Introduction, § 7 C)
specifies *hominibus armatis* (armed men). Cicero imagines
his assailant pleading that, in order to make these words
applicable to him, either some other (presumably unarmed)
men were included as " armed " or his single self was
referred to as plural.

158

bring those points forward ; but where the subject of the suit is law and equity, beware of taking refuge in so poor and empty a subterfuge. For you will not find a single judge or assessor who will accept the term " an armed man " only in the sense suitable to a military arms-inspection : on the contrary, those who are found in possession of the means to cause death or physical hurt will on those grounds be held to have been armed to the teeth.

XXII. In order that you may better understand 62 how unimportant are mere words, suppose that you or anyone else had attacked me singly with sword and shield and I had been thereby driven out, would you dare to say that the injunction specifies armed men but here there was only one armed man ? I do not believe you would have the effrontery. And yet, take heed that your effrontery in the present case be not far greater. For in the imaginary case you might have appealed for pity to all the world because, in dealing with your suit, the court was forgetting its Latin and holding unarmed men to be armed men, and because, while the injunction specified more than one man, and the deed was done by one only, the court was holding one man to be more than one.[a] But in the present case the issue before the court is 63 not one of words but of the actual facts which caused these words to be employed in the injunction. It was intended that " restitution " should be made for the use of force in every case without exception affecting human life ; and this usually comes about through the collecting and arming of men : if force were used with a different intention but with the same dangerous result, the same law was intended to apply. For the wrong done is no greater whether

159

villicus ; non si tui servi quam si alieni ac mercenarii;
non si tuus procurator quam si vicinus aut libertus
tuus ; non si coactis hominibus quam si voluntariis
aut etiam assiduis ac domesticis ; non si armatis
quam si inermibus, qui vim haberent armatorum ad
nocendum ; non si pluribus quam si uno armato.
Quibus enim rebus plerumque vis fit, eiusmodi hae
res appellantur interdicto. Si per alias res eadem
facta vis est, ea tametsi verbis interdicti non con-
cluditur, tamen sententia iuris atque auctoritate
retinetur.

64 XXIII. Venio nunc ad illud tuum : " Non deieci ;
non enim sivi accedere." Puto te ipsum, Piso, perspicere quanto ista sit angustior iniquiorque defensio
quam si illa uterere : " Non fuerunt armati : cum
fustibus et cum saxis fuerunt." Si mehercule mihi
non copioso homini ad dicendum optio detur, utrum
malim defendere, non esse deiectum eum cui vi et
armis ingredienti sit occursum, an armatos non
fuisse eos qui sine scutis ac sine ferro fuerint, omnino
ad probandum utramque rem videam infirmam nuga-
toriamque esse, ad dicendum autem in altera videar
mihi aliquid reperire posse, non fuisse armatos eos
qui neque ferri quidquam neque scutum ullum
habuerint : hic vero haeream, si mihi defendendum
sit, eum qui pulsus fugatusque sit non esse deiectum.

65 Atque illud in tota defensione tua mihi maxime

it was your household or your steward, whether your
own slaves or slaves that you had borrowed or hired,
whether your agent or your neighbour or your freedman, whether it was by men collected together or by
casual helpers or even by your regular staff, whether
by armed men or by unarmed, provided that they were
as capable as armed men of inflicting hurt; whether
by one armed man or by more than one. For it is
those means which are usually employed to produce
force that are correspondingly specified in the injunction : if other means are used to produce it, even
though not included in the terms of the injunction,
they come none the less within the meaning and
purport of the law.

XXIII. I come now to that argument of yours, 64
" I did not drive him out of the farm for I never let
him reach it." I believe you realize yourself, Piso,
how much more quibbling and inequitable such an
argument is than it would be to argue " they were
not armed men : they only had sticks and stones."
I swear that if I, poor speaker that I am, were
offered the choice of maintaining either that a man is
not driven out when opposed by force of arms in the
act of entering, or that those were not armed men
who had neither shields nor swords—as for establishing it I should find either proposition weak and unsubstantial enough, but as for making a speech, I
think I could find something to support the second
proposition, that is, that those were not armed
men who had nothing by way of sword or shield ;
but I should indeed be at a loss if I had to maintain
that a man who has been put to rout and to flight is
not driven out.

Then there is that statement of yours—the most 65

mirum videbatur, te dicere iurisconsultorum auctoritati obtemperari non oportere. Quod ego tametsi
non nunc primum neque in hac caussa solum audio,
tamen admodum mirabar abs te quam ob rem diceretur. Nam ceteri tum ad istam orationem decurrunt,
quum se in caussa putant habere aequum et bonum
quod defendant. Si contra verbis et litteris, et, ut
dici solet, summo iure contenditur, solent eiusmodi
iniquitati boni et aequi nomen dignitatemque
opponent. Tum illud quod dicitur, SIVE, NIVE,
irrident, tum aucupia verborum et litterarum tendi-
culas in invidiam vocant : tum vociferantur, ex aequo
et bono non ex callido versutoque iure rem iudicari
oportere ; scriptum sequi calumniatoris esse ; boni
iudicis voluntatem scriptoris auctoritatemque de-
66 fendere. In ista vero caussa, quum tu sis is qui te
verbo litteraque defendas, quum tuae sint hae partes :
" Unde deiectus es, an inde quo prohibitus es
accedere ? eiectus es, non deiectus " ; quum tua
sit haec oratio : " Fateor me homines coegisse, fateor
armasse, fateor tibi mortem esse minitatam, fateor
hoc interdicto praetoris vindicari, si voluntas et
aequitas valeat ; sed ego invenio in interdicto
verbum unum ubi delitiscam ; non deieci te ex eo
loco quem in locum prohibui ne venires " :—in ista

---

[a] It was customary for eminent lawyers, *iuris consulti*, to
sit in the Forum and give their advice (*ius respondere*) to
those who consulted them. In imperial times qualified
persons were granted the *ius respondendi*, and their rulings
were recognized as authoritative.
[b] The saying was " Summum ius, summa iniuria."

astounding thing, I thought, in the whole of your defence—that we ought not to defer to legal authorities.[a] This is not the first occasion on which I have heard it said nor have I heard it only in this case; but why you should say it I am completely at a loss to know. Most people betake themselves to an argument of that kind when they feel that they have in their case some fair and just contention to maintain: if they are met with an appeal to the wording and the letter or, as the saying goes,[b] to " the utmost rigour of the law," they usually counter unfairness of that kind with the honourable and weighty plea of fairness and justice. Then it is that they pour scorn on the formulas with their " ifs " and " if nots," cry shame on verbal catches and the snares involved in a letter, and loudly protest that a case must be decided by what is fair and just and not by legal trickery and cunning. " A false accuser," they say, " adheres to the letter of the law, a good juror to the meaning and intention of him who framed it." But in this case of yours, when you are the one whose defence is based upon the strict letter of the law; when it is you who take the line: " Whence were you driven out? From a place which you were prevented from reaching? You were driven away, not driven out " —though it was you who said, " I admit that I collected men together; I admit I armed them; I admit I threatened you with death; I admit I am liable under this actual praetorian injunction as far as its intention and fair interpretation are concerned; but I can take shelter behind a single word which I find in the injunction: I have not driven you out of a place which I have prevented you from entering "—when that, I say, is your defence, your

defensione accusas eos qui consuluntur, quod aequitatis censeant rationem non verbi haberi oportere.
67 XXIV. Et hoc loco Scaevolam dixisti caussam apud
centumviros non tenuisse ; quem ego antea commemoravi, cum[1] idem faceret quod tu nunc, tametsi
ille in aliqua caussa faciebat, tu in nulla facis, tamen
probasse nemini quod defendit, quia verbis oppugnare
aequitatem videbatur.

Quum id miror, te hoc in hac re alieno tempore et
contra quam ista caussa postulasset defendisse, tum
illud vulgo in iudiciis et nonnumquam ab ingeniosis
hominibus defendi mihi mirum videri solet, nec iuris-
consultis concedi nec ius civile in caussis semper
68 valere oportere. Nam qui hoc disputant, si id
dicunt, non recte aliquid statuere eos qui consulantur,
non hoc debent dicere, iuri civili sed hominibus stultis
obtemperari non oportere.   Sin illos recte respondere
concedunt et aliter iudicari dicunt oportere, male
iudicari oportere dicunt.   Neque enim fieri potest,
ut aliud iudicari de iure, aliud responderi oporteat,
nec ut quisquam iuris numeretur peritus qui id
69 statuat esse ius quod non oporteat iudicari.—At est
aliquando contra iudicatum.—Primum utrum recte
an perperam ?   Si recte, id fuit ius quod iudicatum

---

[1] cum *Hotoman* : quod *codd.*

* See note on § 65.   • See § 53.

ground of complaint against the authorities [a] is the opinion they record that we should be guided by the spirit and not by the letter of the law. XXIV. And 67 in this connexion you remarked that Scaevola lost his case in the centumviral court; but I have already reminded the court [b] that when he took the same line as you (though he had some reason for doing so and you have none) he failed to commend his arguments to anybody because it appeared that he was using the letter to assail the spirit of the law.

I am indeed surprised that you should have taken this line in the present instance—at the wrong moment and against the interests of your case; and it is equally surprising to me to find the same argument, that neither should the authorities [a] be followed nor should the law invariably be allowed to decide the case, commonly maintained in trials and not infrequently by able men. For if those who maintain 68 this view assert that the authorities are wrong on some point, that is no reason for saying that no attention should be paid to the authorities, but that no attention should be paid to foolish individuals. But if they admit that the opinions given by the authorities are right and still say that judgements should be at variance with them, they are stating that wrong judgements should be given. For it cannot possibly be right that the judgement of the court and the opinion of the authority should differ on a point of law or that anyone should be accounted a legal authority if what he decides to be law ought not to be followed in the law courts. "But the 69 courts have sometimes gone against the authorities." Have they, in the first place, done so rightly or wrongly? If rightly, that was law which the court

est ; sin aliter, non dubium est utrum iudices an
iurisconsulti vituperandi sint. Deinde, si de iure
vario quidpiam iudicatum est, non[1] potius contra
iurisconsultos statuunt, si aliter pronuntiatum est
ac Mucio placuit, quam ex eorum auctoritate, si ut
Manilius statuebat, sic est iudicatum. Etenim ipse
Crassus non ita caussam apud centumviros egit ut
contra iurisconsultos diceret, sed ut hoc doceret, illud
quod Scaevola defendebat non esse iuris, et in eam
rem non solum rationes afferret, sed etiam Q. Mucio,
socero suo, multisque peritissimis hominibus auctoribus uteretur.

70   XXV. Nam qui ius civile contemnendum putat, is
vincula revellit non modo iudiciorum, sed etiam utilitatis vitaeque communis ; qui autem interpretes iuris
vituperat, si imperitos iuris esse dicit, de hominibus,
non de iure civili detrahit : sin peritis non putat esse
obtemperandum, non homines laedit, sed leges ac
iura labefactat. Quod vobis venire in mentem profecto necesse est, nihil esse in civitate tam diligenter
quam ius civile retinendum. Etenim hoc sublato
nihil est quare exploratum cuiquam possit esse, quid
suum aut quid alienum sit ; nihil est quod aequa-
bile inter omnes atque unum omnibus esse possit.

71 Itaque in ceteris controversiis atque iudiciis, quum
quaeritur, aliquid factum necne sit, verum an falsum
proferatur, et fictus testis subornari solet, et interponi

---

[1] non *suppl. Angelius.*

---

^a This is Quintus Mucius Scaevola, the Pontifex Maximus,
an eminent jurist (see note ^c on § 53).

^b Manilius was a famous jurist whom Cicero often mentions.

^c This is Quintus Mucius Scaevola, the augur, also a
famous jurist.

laid down : if otherwise, there is no doubt which deserve abuse, the jurors or the authorities. In the next place, if a court has decided some doubtful point of law, it is no more going against the authorities in giving a ruling of which Mucius[a] did not approve, than it is relying on them in deciding conformably with the view of Manilius.[b] Why, Crassus himself did not take the line he did in pleading before the centumviral court, in order to disparage the authorities, but to convince the court that the point which Scaevola[c] was maintaining was not law ; and in addition to the arguments he adduced to support his contention he went so far as to quote the authority of many learned men, including that of his father-in-law, Quintus Mucius.[c]

XXV. For he who thinks that the law is to be 70 despised is sundering the bonds which maintain not only judicial procedure but the well-being and life of the community ; while he who finds fault with the interpreters of the law by calling them bad lawyers is aspersing the individuals and not the law. But in thinking that, though good lawyers, they deserve no attention, it is not the individuals that he is injuring : he is undermining law and justice. Wherefore you must needs adopt this conclusion, that no institution in our state deserves to be so carefully preserved as the law. Abolish law and there can be no means whereby the individual can ascertain what belongs to him and what to other people : there can be no universal and invariable standard. And so it often happens in the ordinary disputes 71 that come before a court, when it is a question of whether something is or is not a fact or whether an allegation is true or false, that a false witness is

167

falsae tabulae, nonnumquam honesto ac probabili
nomine bono viro iudici error obiici, improbo facultas
dari, ut, quum sciens perperam iudicarit, testem
tamen aut tabulas secutus esse videatur. In iure
nihil est eiusmodi, recuperatores, non tabulae falsae,
non testis improbus ; denique nimia ista quae domi-
natur in civitate potentia in hoc solo genere quiescit ;
quid agat, quomodo aggrediatur iudicem, qua denique
72 digitum proferat, non habet. Illud enim potest dici
iudici ab aliquo non tam verecundo homine quam
gratioso : " Iudica hoc factum esse, aut numquam
esse factum ; crede huic testi ; has comproba
tabulas : " hoc non potest : " Cui filius agnatus
sit, eius testamentum non esse ruptum iudica ; quod
mulier sine tutore auctore promiserit, deberi." Non
est aditus ad huiusmodi res neque potentiae cuiusquam neque gratiae ; denique, quo maius hoc
sanctiusque videatur, ne pretio quidem corrumpi
73 iudex in eiusmodi caussa potest. Iste vester testis,
qui ausus est dicere, FECISSE VIDERI eum, de quo ne
cuius rei argueretur quidem scire potuisset, ipse numquam auderet iudicare, deberi viro dotem quam
mulier nullo auctore dixisset.

XXVI. O rem praeclaram vobisque ob hoc retinen-
dam, recuperatores ! Quod enim est ius civile ?
Quod neque inflecti gratia, neque perfringi potentia,

***

    a A trustee was required by Roman law for women (and
minors, etc.), whose father was dead ; his sanction was
required for any obligation which his ward wished to contract.
    b Fidiculanius Falcula, see §§ 28 and 29 and footnotes.

suborned, forged documents are put in and sometimes, under the guise of fair and honest dealing, an honest juror is deceived or a dishonest juror afforded the chance of giving the impression that his wrong verdict, which was really intentional, was the result of his having been guided by the witness or the documents. In a question of law, gentlemen, there is nothing like that — no forged document, no dishonest witness ; and even undue influence, which is all-powerful in public life, is here, and only here, inoperative ; for it has no chance of getting to work, no opportunity to tamper with a juror, no means even of raising a finger. For a man of more presumption 72 than decency may say to a juror, " Give judgement that this took place or never took place : credit this witness, admit these documents " ; but he cannot say, " Decide that a will is not invalidated by the subsequent birth of a son to the testator : give judgement that a promise is binding when made by a woman without the sanction of her trustee." [a] No man's power, or influence either, can affect the decision in such a matter ; and further—to show how exalted and inviolable the law is—not even money can corrupt a juror in such a connexion. That very 73 witness of yours [b] who dared to pronounce a man guilty when he could not possibly have known even the charge against him, even he would never dare to give judgement that, if a woman settles her dowry on her husband without proper sanction,[a] the settlement is binding.

XXVI. How splendid a thing is the law, gentlemen, and how worthy, therefore, of your protection ! How may we describe it ? The law is that which influence cannot bend, nor power break, nor wealth

neque adulterari pecunia possit ; quod si non modo oppressum, sed etiam desertum aut negligentius asservatum erit, nihil est quod quisquam sese habere certum, aut a patre accepturum, aut relicturum liberis
74 arbitretur. Quid enim refert aedes aut fundum relictum a patre, aut aliqua ratione habere bene partum, si incertum sit, quae quum omnia tua iure mancipii sint, ea possisne retinere ? si parum sit communitum ius ? si civili ac publica lege contra alicuius gratiam teneri non potest ? Quid, inquam, prodest, fundum habere, si, quae decentissime descripta a maioribus iura finium, possessionum, aquarum itinerumque sunt, haec perturbari aliqua ratione commutarique possunt ? Mihi credite, maior hereditas unicuique nostrum venit in iisdem bonis a iure et a legibus, quam ab iis a quibus illa ipsa bona relicta sunt. Nam ut perveniat ad me fundus testamento alicuius fieri potest ; ut retineam quod meum factum sit sine iure civili non potest. Fundus a patre relinqui potest : at usucapio fundi, hoc est, finis sollicitudinis ac periculi litium, non a patre relinquitur sed a legibus. Aquae ductus, haustus, iter, actus, a patre : sed rata auctoritas harum rerum omnium a
75 iure civili sumitur. Quapropter non minus diligenter ea, quae a maioribus accepistis, publica patrimonia iuris, quam privatae rei vestrae retinere debetis : non solum, quod haec iure civili saepta sunt, sed

---

a *Mancipium*, an ancient form of conveyance, for the transfer of *res mancipi*, that is, everything which in those early times was regarded as valuable (land, stock, slaves, etc.).

corrupt ; if law be overthrown, nay, if it be neglected
or insufficiently guarded, there will be nothing which
anyone can be sure either of possessing himself or of
inheriting from his father or of leaving to his children.
What does it profit you to possess a house or an 74
estate left to you by your father or legitimately
acquired in some other way, if you are not certain
of being able to keep that which the law of ownership *a* now makes yours, if the law be inadequately
safeguarded and if our public code be unable to
maintain our rights in the face of some private
interest ?   What advantage is there, I say, in having
an estate if all the rights fittingly prescribed by our
forefathers in connexion with boundaries, possession,
water, and roads can be upset or changed on any consideration ?   Believe me, the property which anyone of us enjoys is to a greater degree the legacy of
our law and constitution than of those who actually
bequeathed it to him.   For anyone can secure by
his will that an estate comes into my possession ;
but no one can secure that I keep what has become
mine without the assistance of the law.   A man can
inherit an estate from his father, but a good title to
the estate, that is, freedom from anxiety and litigation, he inherits not from his father but from the
law.   Rights of water, drawn or carried, rights of
way for man or beast, he derives from his father, but
he derives from the law his established title to all
these rights.   Wherefore you ought to hold fast 75
what you have received from your forefathers—the
public heritage of Law—with no less care than the
heritage of your private property ; and that, not
only because it is the law by which private property
is hedged about, but because the individual only is

etiam, quod patrimonium unius incommodo dimit-
titur, ius amitti non potest sine magno incommodo
civitatis.

XXVII. In hac ipsa caussa, recuperatores, si hoc
nos non obtinemus, vi armatis hominibus deiectum
esse eum, quem vi armatis hominibus pulsum fuga-
tumque esse constat, Caecina rem non amittet, quam
ipsam animo forti, si tempus ita ferret, amitteret ; in
possessionem in praesentia non restituetur ; nihil
76 amplius. Populi Romani caussa, civitatis ius, bona,
fortunae possessionesque omnium in dubium incer-
tumque revocabuntur ; vestra auctoritate hoc con-
stituetur, hoc praescribetur : " Quicum tu posthac
de possessione contendes, eum, si ingressum modo
in praedium deieceris, restituas oportebit ; sin
autem ingredienti cum armata multitudine obvius
fueris, et ita venientem reppuleris, fugaris, averteris,
non restitues." Iuris si haec vox est, esse vim non
in caede solum sed etiam in animo, libidinis, nisi
cruor appareat, vim non esse factam ; iuris deiectum
esse qui prohibitus sit, libidinis, nisi ex eo loco ubi
77 vestigium impresserit deici neminem posse ; iuris,
rem et sententiam et aequitatem plurimum valere
opportere, libidinis, verbo ac littera ius omne intor-

affected if he abandons his inheritance, while the law cannot be abandoned without seriously affecting the community.

XXVII. So in the present case, gentlemen, if we fail to establish that a man who is proved to have been repelled and routed by force through armed men, has been " driven out by force through armed men," Caecina will not lose his property, though he would bear the loss bravely if it so fell out : he will fail, for the moment, to recover possession of it, and that is all. It will be the cause of the Roman people, 76 the rights of the commonwealth, the property, the fortunes, and the claims to possession of us all which will again be brought into doubt and uncertainty. Yours will be the responsibility for a decision and an ordinance in these terms : " With whomsoever you subsequently have a dispute over possession, you will be bound to ' restore ' him only if you have driven him out after he has entered on the estate : but if, while he is in the act of entering, you meet him with an armed multitude and, while he is thus approaching, drive him away, put him to flight and turn him back, you shall not ' restore ' him." If it be the voice of law which declares that force consists not only in killing but in intention to kill, and the voice of lawlessness which declares that there is no force where no blood is seen to flow ; if it be law which claims that a man is driven out if he is debarred from entering, and lawlessness, that no one can be driven out except from a place on which he has set foot ; if it be law which deems that the 77 first consideration should be the substance, the meaning, and the spirit of the law, and lawlessness that it should be twisted round to suit the terms and the

queri ; vos statuite, recuperatores, utrae voces vobis
honestiores et utiliores esse videantur.[1]

Hoc loco percommode accidit, quod non adest is
qui paullo ante adfuit et adesse nobis frequenter in
hac caussa solet vir ornatissimus, C. Aquilius : nam
ipso praesente de virtute eius et prudentia timidius
dicerem, quod et ipse pudore quodam afficeretur ex
sua laude, et me similis ratio pudoris a praesentis
laude tardaret : cuius auctoritati dictum est ab illa
caussa concedi nimium non oportere. Non vereor
de tali viro ne plus dicam quam vos aut sentiatis, aut
78 apud vos commemorari velitis. Quapropter hoc
dicam, numquam eius auctoritatem nimium valere,
cuius prudentiam populus Romanus in cavendo, non
in decipiendo perspexerit ; qui iuris civilis rationem
numquam ab aequitate seiunxerit ; qui tot annos
ingenium, laborem, fidem suam populo Romano
promptam expositamque praebuerit ; qui ita iustus
est et bonus vir, ut natura, non disciplina consultus
esse videatur ; ita peritus ac prudens, ut ex iure
civili non scientia solum quaedam verum etiam
bonitas nata videatur ; cuius tantum est ingenium,
ita prompta fides, ut quidquid inde haurias purum te
79 liquidumque haurire sentias. Quare permagnam
initis a nobis gratiam, quum eum auctorem nostrae
defensionis esse dicitis. Illud autem miror, cur vos

---

[1] Iuris . . . videantur] *this passage is hopelessly corrupt.*
I have adopted Baiter's text.

letter; then do you, gentlemen, decide to which of these two voices belongs more of honour and of expediency.

Now it happens most conveniently at this point that there is absent from the court one who was here but recently and who has been a regular attendant throughout this case—I refer to that distinguished man, Gaius Aquilius. If he were present, I should be nervous about referring to his soundness of character and of judgement; both because he would be embarrassed at hearing his own praises and because a similar feeling of embarrassment would deter me from praising him to his face. His is the authority to which I am told by the other side that undue deference must not be paid. Of such a man I am not afraid of saying more than you yourselves feel or would like to have recorded; and so I will say this, 78 that undue weight can never be attached to the authority of one whose judgement Rome has seen to be exercized in protecting, not in deceiving, her citizens; whose conception of law has never been divorced from equity; whose ability, industry and integrity have been, through all these years, ready and accessible for the service of the Roman people; who, as a man, is so just and good that he seems to be a jurist by nature rather than by training; whose wisdom and good sense suggest that the study of law has begotten in him not only some mere knowledge but goodness also; whose ability is so great and his integrity so apparent that whatever you draw from such a source you feel to be clear and pure. Wherefore you are entitled to our profound gratitude 79 when you say that he is the authority on whom we base our defence. I am indeed astounded to hear

aliquid contra me sentire dicatis, quum eum auctorem
vos pro me appelletis, nostrum nominetis.

Verumtamen quid ait vester iste auctor? "Quibus quidque[1] verbis actum pronuntiatumque sit."
XXVIII. Conveni ego ex isto genere consultorum non
neminem, ut opinor, istum ipsum, quo vos auctore rem
istam agere et defensionem caussae constituere vos
dicitis. Qui quum istam disputationem mecum in-
gressus esset, non posse probari quemquam esse
deiectum, nisi ex eo loco in quo fuisset, rem et sententiam interdicti mecum facere fatebatur, verbo me
excludi dicebat; a verbo autem posse recedi non
80 arbitrabatur. Quum exemplis uterer multis, etiam
illa materia aequitatis, a verbo et ab scripto plurimis
saepe in rebus ius et aequi bonique rationem esse
seiunctam, semperque id valuisse plurimum, quod in
se auctoritatis habuisset aequitatisque plurimum,
consolatus est me et ostendit in hac ipsa caussa nihil
esse quod laborarem; nam verba ipsa sponsionis
facere mecum, si vellem diligenter attendere.
"Quonam," inquam, "modo?" "Quia certe, inquit, deiectus est Caecina vi hominibus armatis aliquo ex loco; si non ex eo loco quem in locum venire
voluit, at ex eo certe unde fugit." "Quid tum?"
"Praetor," inquit, "interdixit ut, unde deiectus
esset, eo restitueretur, hoc est, quicumque is locus
esset unde deiectus esset. Aebutius autem, qui

---

[1] quibus quidque *Baiter.*

you say that you deem it a point against me when you describe him as the authority on my side, a partizan of mine.

However, what says the authority you claim as yours? "In whatever terms a proposal or a pronouncement has been framed . . ." XXVIII. I have met personally one lawyer at least of that persuasion, the very man, I believe, whom you quote as the authority responsible for the arguments of your defence. He started to argue with me your contention that no one could be proved to have been driven out except from a place in which he had been, and made me the admission that the substance and the meaning of the injunction were on my side, though he held that there was no getting away from its actual terms. I quoted many instances, including 80 ancient precedent, to show that the justice and the principle of right and equity were very constantly at variance with the actual wording of a law, and that decisions had always been based on the interpretation which was the best supported and the most equitable. Whereupon he consoled me by pointing out that in this particular case I had no reason for anxiety, for the actual terms of the wager-at-law were in my favour if I would consider them carefully. "How so?" I said. "Because," said he, "Caecina was undoubtedly 'driven out by force through armed men' from some place or other: if not from the place to which he wanted to go, then assuredly from the place from which he fled." "What of that?" "The praetor," he replied, "issued an injunction ordering that he be restored 'to the place from which he had been driven out,' any place, that is, from which he had been driven out. Now since Aebutius

177

fatetur aliquo ex loco deiectum esse Caecinam, is
quum se restituisse dixit, necesse est male fecerit
81 sponsionem." Quid est, Piso ? placet tibi pugnare
verbis ? placet caussam iuris et aequitatis, et non
nostrae possessionis, sed omnino possessionum
omnium, constituere in verbo ? Ego, quid mihi
videretur, quid a maioribus factitatum, quid horum
auctoritate quibus iudicandum est dignum esset
ostendi ; id verum, id aequum, id utile omnibus esse,
spectari quo consilio et qua sententia, non quibus
quidque verbis esset actum. Tu me ad verbum
vocas ; non ante veniam quam recusaro. Nego oportere, nego obtineri posse, nego ullam rem esse quae
aut comprehendi satis aut caveri aut excipi possit, si
aut praeterito aliquo verbo aut ambigue posito, re et
sententia cognita, non id quod intelligitur, sed id quod
dicitur, valebit.

82 XXIX. Quoniam satis recusavi, veniam iam quo
vocas. Quaero abs te, simne deiectus : non de
Fulciniano fundo ; neque enim praetor, si ex eo fundo
essem deiectus, ita me restitui iussit, sed eo unde
deiectus essem : sum ex proximo vicini fundo deiectus, qua adibam ad istum fundum, sum de via,
sum certe alicunde, sive de privato, sive de publico.

admits that Caecina was driven out from some place
or other, he must inevitably have made a bad wager
in answering that he had restored him." Well, Piso, 81
does it please you to join issue with me over words ?
Does it please you to make the course of justice and
equity, the right to possession—not only my client's
but absolutely everyone's—turn upon a word ? I
showed you what my opinion was, what was the
practice of our forefathers, what course was consistent with the dignity of those who must decide
our case : how that truth, justice and the general
good combine to demand that we consider not the
exact terms in which any particular law was framed
but its purpose and its intention. You challenge me
to a discussion of the terms : I will not accept without first lodging my objection. I say that your
position is wrong : I say that it is untenable : I say
that no law can possibly be adequate either in its
terms or its provisions or its exceptions if through
some word being either omitted or used in an am-
biguous context, and despite the substance and intention of the law being obvious, it is to be interpreted according to the words which it employs and
not according to the meaning it conveys.

XXIX. Now, since I have lodged my objection 82
plainly enough, I take up your challenge. I ask
you, was I driven out ? Not indeed from the estate
of Fulcinius, for the praetor did not order that I be
restored " if I had been driven out from the estate,"
but " to that place from which I had been driven
out." I was driven out—driven from my neighbour's adjoining estate, through which I was making
my way to the estate in question ; driven from the
road ; driven out, assuredly, from some place or

Eo restitui sum iussus. Restituisse te dixti. Nego
me ex decreto praetoris restitutum esse. Quid ad
haec dicimus? Aut tuo, quemadmodum dicitur,
gladio, aut nostro defensio tua conficiatur necesse
83 est. Si ad interdicti sententiam confugis, et de quo
fundo actum sit tum quum Aebutius restituere iube-
batur, id quaerendum esse dicis, neque aequitatem
rei verbi laqueo capi putas oportere, in meis castris
praesidiisque versaris. Mea, mea est ista defensio,
ego hoc vociferor, ego omnes homines deosque testor,
quum maiores vim armatam nulla iuris defensione
texerint, non vestigium eius qui deiectus sit, sed
factum illius qui deiecerit, in iudicium venire, deiectum esse qui fugatus sit, vim esse factam cui peri-
84 culum mortis sit iniectum. Sin hunc[1] locum fugis et
reformidas, et me ex hoc, ut ita dicam, campo aequitatis ad istas verborum angustias et ad omnes litterarum angulos revocas, in iis ipsis intercludere insidiis
quas mihi conaris opponere. "Non deieci, sed
eieci." Peracutum hoc tibi videtur, hic est mucro
defensionis tuae. In eum ipsum caussa tua incurrat
necesse est. Ego enim tibi refero : Si non sum ex eo
loco deiectus quo prohibitus sum accedere, at ex eo

---

[1] sin hunc *Baiter.*

other, whether private or public. To that place the injunction has ordered that I be restored. You have asserted that you have restored me : I assert that I have not been restored in accordance with the praetor's order. What are our arguments ? Your case is doomed to fall, either by your own sword, as the saying is, or by mine. If you take refuge in the 83 meaning of the injunction and say that we must inquire which farm was meant when Aebutius was ordered to restore me ; if you think it wrong that the arm of justice should be caught in a noose of words, then you are sheltering in my camp and behind my ramparts. That line of defence is mine —mine, I say ! It is I who cry aloud, I who call Heaven and Earth to witness that since our fore-fathers made no provision under cover of which the use of armed force could be defended at law, the court is not concerned with the footprints of the man who was driven out but with the action of the man who drove him out : that a man is driven out who has been put to flight, and that a man is sub-jected to force who has been put in danger of death. But if on the other hand you abandon this position 84 and shrink from holding it : if you challenge me to exchange what I may call the open field of equity for the crooked ways of verbal subtlety and all the obscurities of the letter, you will find yourself caught in just those snares which you are trying to set in my path. " I did not drive you out, I drove you back "— you think this is very smart : it is this that gives point to your defence ; and upon this very point your case is doomed to fall ! For my answer is : " If I was not driven out from the place which I was prevented from reaching I was none the

sum deiectus, quo accessi, unde fugi : si praetor non
distinxit locum quo me restitui iuberet, et restitui
iussit, non sum ex decreto restitutus.

85   Velim, recuperatores, hoc totum, si vobis versutius
quam mea consuetudo defendendi fert videbitur, sic
existimetis ; primum alium non me excogitasse,
deinde huius rationis non modo[1] inventorem sed
ne probatorem quidem esse me, idque me non ad
meam defensionem attulisse, sed illorum defensioni
rettulisse ; me posse pro meo iure dicere, neque in
hac re quam ego protuli quaeri oportere, quibus
verbis praetor interdixerit, sed de quo loco sit actum,
quum interdixit : neque in vi armatorum spectari
oportere, in quo loco sit facta vis, verum sitne facta :
te vero nullo modo posse defendere, in qua re tu velis
verba spectari oportere, in qua re nolis non oportere.

86   XXX. Verumtamen, ecquid mihi respondetur ad
illud quod antea dixi, non solum re et sententia, sed
verbis quoque hoc interdictum ita esse compositum
ut nihil commutandum videretur ? Attendite, quaeso,
diligenter, recuperatores. Est enim vestri ingenii
non meam sed maiorum prudentiam cognoscere.
Non enim id sum dicturus quod ego invenerim, sed
quod illos non fugerit. Quum de vi interdicitur, duo
genera caussarum esse intelligebant ad quae interdictum pertineret : unum, si qui ex eo loco ubi fuisset

---

[1] non modo non *mss.*: non *del. Klotz.*

less driven out from the place which I did reach and from which I fled. If the praetor has given orders that I be restored, without specifying to what place, then I have not been restored in compliance with his order."

If, gentlemen, all this part of my argument seems 85 to you less straightforward than my pleading usually is, I hope you will take into consideration first that it was not I but someone else who devised it ; and further that, so far from having originated I do not even approve of it—I use it, not to support my plea but to answer theirs—and that I have the right to say that neither in the particular instance I quoted ought we to be asking what were the actual terms in which the praetor framed his injunction but what was the place intended when he framed it, nor in any case of " force used by armed men " should we ask where it was used but whether it was used ; but that you, Piso, on the other hand, have no sort of right to plead that the actual terms should be considered where it suits you but not where it does not suit you.

XXX. But at the same time, is there any possible 86 answer to the statement I have just made, that not only the substance and the meaning of this injunction but even the terms in which it is framed are such as to leave no alteration desirable ? Listen carefully, I beg you, gentlemen ; for men of your capacity will recognize, not my foresight, but that of our fore-fathers ; for what I am about to say is nothing that I have discovered but something that they did not fail to see. They realized that an injunction dealing with the use of force might be called for by two sets of circumstances—one being a claim by somebody

CICERO

se deiectum diceret ; alterum, si qui ab eo loco quo
venisset vi deiectus esset : et horum utrumque neque
praeterea quidquam potest accidere, recuperatores.
87 Id adeo sic considerate. Si qui meam familiam de
meo fundo deiecerit, ex eo me loco deiecerit ; si qui
mihi praesto fuerit cum armatis hominibus extra
meum fundum et me introire prohibuerit, non ex eo
sed ab eo loco me deiecerit. Ad haec duo genera
rerum unum verbum, quod satis declararet utrasque
res, invenerunt : ut, sive ex fundo sive a fundo deiectus essem, uno atque eodem interdicto restituerer :
UNDE TU. Hoc verbum, UNDE, utrumque declarat, et
ex quo loco et a quo loco. Unde deiectus est Cinna ?
ex Urbe. Unde Telesinus[1] ? ab Urbe. Unde
deiecti Galli ? a Capitolio. Unde qui cum Graccho
88 fuerunt ? ex Capitolio. Videtis igitur, hoc uno verbo
UNDE significari res duas, et ex quo et a quo loco.
Quum autem EO restitui iubet, ita iubet, ut, si Galli
a maioribus nostris postularent, ut eo restituerentur
unde deiecti essent, et aliqua vi hoc assequi possent,
non, opinor, eos in cuniculum, qua aggressi erant, sed
in Capitolium restitui oporteret. Hoc enim intelligitur : UNDE DEIECISTI, sive ex quo loco sive a quo
loco. EO RESTITUAS. Hoc iam simplex est, in eum

[1] Telesinus *Baiter* : unde deiecti * * *codd.*

---

[a] The allusions are to :

Cinna, a supporter of Marius, driven out of Rome during
his consulship in 87 B.C. by his colleague, a supporter of
Sulla.

Telesinus, leader of the Samnites, who were defeated by
Sulla outside the Colline gate of Rome in 82 B.C.

The Gauls, repulsed, according to Cicero, in 390 B.C., but
Livy's account differs.

Tiberius Gracchus and his followers, who had taken refuge
in the Capitol, whence they were dragged by the forces of
the Senate and murdered 133 B.C.

that he had been forcibly driven out from the place in
which he had been, the other, from the place to which
he was going: one or the other of these cases may
arise, gentlemen, but there is no third possibility.
Now examine this point further. If anyone drives 87
my household from my estate, he drives me out of
it ; if anyone meets me with armed men outside my
estate and prevents my entering it, he does not
drive me out of it but away from it. To cover both
these sets of circumstances, our forefathers devised
one word calculated adequately to express both, in
order that whether I be driven out of my estate or
away from it, one and the same injunction might
restore me to it, the one beginning " whence you
. . ." The word " whence " covers the two cases,
both the place out of which and the place away from
which I was driven. Whence was Cinna driven ? [a]
Out of the city. Whence Telesinus ? Away from
the City. Whence were the Gauls driven ? Away
from the Capitol. Whence the followers of Gracchus ?
Out of the Capitol. So you see that the single word 88
" whence " covers two things, the place out of which
and the place away from which. Now, in ordering
restitution " to that place," the injunction does so
in the sense that, if the Gauls had demanded of our
ancestors to be restored to the place from which
they had been driven out and had somehow had the
force to gain their point, they would, in my opinion,
have had to be restored not to the underground
passage by which they had attacked the Capitol but
to the Capitol itself. For this is plain : " whence you
have driven out " means either " out of any place "
or " away from any place." " Thither thou shalt
restore " : this too is clear—you must restore to the

locum restituas; sive ex hoc loco deiecisti, restitue
in hunc locum, sive ab hoc loco, restitue in eum
locum, non ex quo sed a quo deiectus est. Ut si qui
ex alto, quum ad patriam accessisset, tempestate
subito reiectus optaret ut, quum esset a patria deiectus, eo restitueretur, hoc, opinor, optaret, ut, a quo
loco depulsus esset, in eum se fortuna restitueret, non
in salum, sed in ipsam urbem quam petebat; sic,
quoniam verborum vim necessario similitudine rerum
aucupamur, qui postulat, ut, a quo loco deiectus est,
hoc est, unde deiectus est, eo restituatur, hoc postulat
ut in eum ipsum locum restituatur.

89   XXXI. Quum verba nos eo ducunt, tum res ipsa hoc
sentire atque intelligere cogit. Etenim, Piso, redeo
nunc ad illa principia defensionis meae, si quis te ex
aedibus tuis vi hominibus armatis deiecerit, quid ages?
Opinor, hoc interdicto quo nos usi sumus persequere.
Quid, si qui iam de foro redeuntem armatis hominibus
domum tuam te introire prohibuerit, quid ages?
Utere eodem interdicto. Quum igitur praetor interdixerit, unde deiectus es, ut eo restituaris, tu hoc
idem quod ego dico et quod perspicuum est interpre-

actual place : if you have driven a man out of this
place, restore him to this place ; or if you have
driven him away from this place, restore him to the
actual place, not out of which, but away from which
he was driven. For instance, if a man on a voyage
had come near his own country but had been suddenly driven back from it by a storm and were to
wish that since he had been driven away from his
country he might be restored to it, he would, I think,
be wishing that fortune might restore him to the place
away from which he had been driven—not indeed to
the sea, but to the actual city for which he was
making. In the same way (for we are compelled to
use analogies in order to catch the exact significance
of words) a man who demands to be restored to the
place away from which, that is, " whence " he has
been driven, is demanding to be restored to the
actual place itself.

XXXI. Not only do the words of the injunction 89
lead us to this conclusion ; the facts as well compel
us to adopt this view and this interpretation. In
truth, Piso (and here I return to the point I raised
at the beginning of my speech), if anyone drives you
out of your house by force through armed men, what
will you do ? I suppose you will proceed against
him by this same injunction which we have employed.
Well, and what will you do if someone prevents you
by means of armed men from entering your home
as you are returning to it from the Forum ? You
will employ the same injunction. When, therefore,
the praetor issues an injunction ordering that you
be restored to the place from which you have been
driven out, you will put the same interpretation on
it as I am putting and as ought manifestly to be put ;

tabere : quum illud verbum, UNDE, in utramque rem valeat, EOQUE tu restitui sis iussus, tam te in aedes restitui oportere, si e vestibulo quam si ex interiore aedium parte deiectus sis.

90 Ut vero iam, recuperatores, nulla dubitatio sit, sive rem sive verba spectare vultis, quin secundum nos iudicetis, exoritur hic iam obrutis rebus omnibus et perditis illa defensio, eum deiici posse qui tum possideat ; qui non possideat nullo modo posse : itaque si ego sim a tuis aedibus deiectus, restitui non oportere ; si ipse sis, oportere. Numera quam multa in ista defensione falsa sint, Piso. Ac primum illud attende, te iam ex illa ratione esse depulsum, quod negabas quemquam deiici posse, nisi inde ubi tum esset : iam posse concedis ; eum qui non possideat negas deiici 91 posse. Cur ergo aut in illud quotidianum interdictum UNDE ILLE ME VI DEIECIT additur QUUM EGO POSSIDEREM, si deiici nemo potest qui non possidet; aut in hoc interdictum DE HOMINIBUS ARMATIS non additur, si oportet quaeri, possederit necne ? Negas deiici nisi qui possideat. Ostendo, si sine armatis coactisve hominibus deiectus quispiam sit, eum qui fateatur se deiecisse vincere sponsionem, si ostendat eum non possedisse.

---

a See Introduction, § 7 C.   *b* See Introduction, § 7 A.

namely that, since the word " whence " covers both
sets of circumstances, and the injunction orders that
you be restored " to that place," you have just as
much right to be restored to your house if you have
been ejected from the forecourt as if you had been
ejected from the inside of the house.

And now, gentlemen, as if to remove all doubt 90
that, whether you regard the substance or the letter
of the injunction, you ought to give us the verdict,
there rises out of the wreck and ruin of my opponent's
case the argument that a man can be " driven out "
if in possession at the time but cannot possibly be so
if not in possession ; and accordingly, that if I am
driven out of your house, I have no claim to restitution, but that if you are driven out yourself, you
have. Count the flaws in that argument, Piso !
And observe first of all that you have been forced
to abandon your principle that, as you maintained,
no one can be driven out except from the place in
which he was at the time. You now admit that he
can, but say that a man cannot be driven out if he is
not in possession. Why, then, in the ordinary form 91
of the injunction *a* beginning " Whence he has
driven me out by force," are the words added, " I
being in possession at the time," if no one can be
driven out unless in possession ? And why are they
not added in the case of the present injunction
"concerning armed men," if the question of possession
is relevant ? You say " No one is driven out if he
is not in possession " : I prove that if anyone is
driven out, but not by means of men armed and
collected together, then the man who admits having
driven him out wins the wager-at-law *b* if he can prove
that the other was not in possession. You say :

Negas deiici nisi qui possideat. Ostendo ex hoc interdicto DE ARMATIS HOMINIBUS, qui possit ostendere non
possedisse eum qui deiectus sit, condemnari tamen
sponsionis necesse esse, si fateatur esse deiectum.

92 XXXII. Dupliciter homines deiiciuntur, aut sine
coactis armatisve hominibus aut per eiusmodi rationem atque vim. Ad duas dissimiles res duo diiuncta
interdicta sunt. In illa vi quotidiana non satis est
posse docere se deiectum, nisi ostendere possit quum
possideret tum deiectum. Ne id quidem satis est,
nisi docet ita se possedisse, ut nec vi nec clam nec
precario possederit. Itaque is qui se restituisse dixit,
magna voce saepe confiteri solet se vi deiecisse,
verum illud addit : Non possidebat ; vel etiam, quum
hoc ipsum concessit, vincit tamen sponsione, si planum
facit ab se illum aut vi aut clam aut precario posse-
93 disse. Videtisne quot defensionibus eum, qui sine
armis ac multitudine vim fecerit, uti posse maiores
voluerint ? hunc vero, qui ab iure, officio, bonis
moribus ad ferrum, ad arma, ad caedem confugerit,
nudum in caussa destitutum videtis, ut, qui armatus
de possessione contendisset, inermus plane de sponsione certaret. Ecquid igitur interest, Piso, inter haec

" No one is driven out if he is not in possession." I prove that under the terms of the injunction " concerning armed men," a man who can prove that the person driven out was not in possession, is none the less certain to lose his wager if he admits that the other was driven out.

XXXII. There are two ways in which people are 92 driven out, either without the employment of men collected together and armed or by the employment of force in some such way. To meet the two different cases, two separate injunctions have been framed. In the case of the ordinary employment of force, it is not enough for a claimant to show that he has been driven out unless he can prove that he was in possession at the time he was driven out. And even that is not sufficient unless he can show that his possession arose neither from force, fraud, or favour. And so it is quite usual to hear a man, who has replied to the injunction " I have restored," openly admitting that he did drive out by force but adding at the same time, " He was not in possession." And further, after admitting even the fact of possession, he still wins this wager-at-law if he makes it clear that his opponent had obtained possession from him either by force, fraud, or favour. Do you see how many 93 lines of defence our forefathers placed at the disposal of a man who uses force but without recourse to arms or a multitude ? But as for my opponent who, forgetful of law, duty and decency, betook himself to the sword, to arms, and to murder, you see that they left him to plead his cause naked and defenceless, in order to show that one who had armed himself to contend for possession must come disarmed to settle a wager-at-law. Is there, then, any difference

interdicta? ecquid interest, utrum in hoc sit additum
QUUM A. CAECINA POSSIDERET, necne? Ecquid te
ratio iuris, ecquid interdictorum dissimilitudo, ecquid
auctoritas maiorum commovet? Si esset additum,
de eo quaeri oporteret. Additum non est; tamen
oportebit?

94 Atque ego in hoc Caecinam non defendo : possedit
enim Caecina, recuperatores : et id, tametsi extra
caussam est, percurram tamen brevi, ut non minus
hominem ipsum quam ius commune defensum velitis.
Caesenniam possedisse propter usumfructum non
negas. Qui colonus habuit conductum de Caesennia
fundum, quum idem ex eadem conductione fuerit in
fundo, dubium est quin, si Caesennia tum possidebat,
quum erat colonus in fundo, post eius mortem heres
eodem iure possederit? Deinde ipse Caecina, quum
circumiret praedia, venit in istum fundum, rationes a
95 colono accepit. Sunt in eam rem testimonia. Postea
cur tu, Aebuti, de isto potius fundo quam de alio, si
quem habes, Caecinae denuntiabas, si Caecina non
possidebat? Ipse porro Caecina cur se moribus
deduci volebat, idque tibi de amicorum, etiam de
ipsius C. Aquillii sententia responderat?

XXXIII. At enim Sulla legem tulit. Ut nihil de
illo tempore, nihil de calamitate rei publicae querar,

---

a See Introduction, § 7 B.
b 82 B.C. See Historical Summary.

between these injunctions, Piso ? Does it make any difference whether or not our injunction contains the additional clause " Aulus Caecina being in possession " ? Do the principles of law, the point of difference between the injunctions, the intention of our forefathers, make any impression on you ? Had the clause been added, your point would have been a relevant one. It was not added : shall the point be relevant still ?

In this particular, I am not defending Caecina : **94** for Caecina, gentlemen, has possession ; but although it is outside my case I will briefly deal with the question in order to make you no less anxious to protect the person of my client than you are to protect the rights of the public. You, Aebutius, do not deny that Caesennia had possession by virtue of her life interest.[a] Now since the tenant who had the farm on lease from Caesennia maintained his tenure by virtue of that same lease, is there any doubt that, if Caesennia had possession during the tenure of the lessee, her heir after her death had the same title to possession ?[a] Further, when Caecina came to this estate as he was going the round of his property, he received a statement of account from this tenant ; and there is evidence to prove it. Why, subsequently, **95** did you, Aebutius, serve Caecina with notice to quit this particular farm rather than any other you may have, if Caecina had no possession ? Why, moreover, did Caecina himself consent to being formally ejected, as he had informed you in the answer which he gave on the advice of his friends and of Aquillius himself?

XXXIII. But, you may say, there is Sulla's law.[b] Without a single reflection on the days of Sulla or the calamity that then overwhelmed the country,

hoc tibi respondeo, adscripsisse eundem Sullam in eandem legem, SI QUID IUS NON ESSET ROGARIER, EIUS EA LEGE NIHILUM ROGATUM. Quid est quod ius non sit, quod populus iubere aut vetare non possit ? Ut ne longius abeam, declarat ista adscriptio esse aliquid. Nam nisi esset, hoc in omnibus legibus non adscriberetur. 96 Sed quaero abs te, putesne, si populus iusserit me tuum, aut item te meum servum esse, id iussum ratum atque firmum futurum ? Perspicis hoc nihil esse et fateris : qua in re primum illud concedis[1] non quidquid populus iusserit ratum esse oportere : deinde nihil rationis affers quamobrem, si libertas adimi nullo modo possit, civitas possit. Nam et eodem modo de utraque re traditum nobis est et si semel civitas adimi potest, retineri libertas non potest. Qui enim potest iure Quiritium liber esse 97 is qui in numero Quiritium non est ? Atque ego hanc adolescentulus caussam, quum agerem contra hominem disertissimum nostrae civitatis Cottam, probavi. Quum Arretinae mulieris libertatem defenderem, et Cotta decemviris religionem iniecisset, non posse nostrum sacramentum iustum iudicari, quod Arretinis adempta civitas esset, et ego vehementius contendissem civitatem adimi non potuisse, decemviri prima actione non iudicaverunt, postea re quaesita et de-

---

[1] nihil . . . concedis *suppl. Baiter*: *om. codd.*

---

[a] A special court for trying cases connected with citizenship.

[b] The *sacramentum* originally meant a sum of money paid into court by each of the parties to a suit and at its conclusion forfeited by the loser. (See note on *sponsio,* p. 91.) Here the word means the suit itself.

my answer to you is this : that there was a clause added to this same law by this same Sulla to the effect that " if this statute contain any proposal contrary to law, that proposal be null and void." What is there which it is unlawful to propose or which the people cannot command or prohibit ? Without digressing too far, this very additional clause shows that there is such a thing : for if there were not, this clause would not be appended to all statutes. But I ask you : if the people command 96 me to be your slave or you mine, do you think that command would be binding and valid ? You realize and you admit that it would be null and void. And in doing so you first of all concede that not everything which the people command ought to be valid ; and in the second place you advance no reason why, if liberty cannot possibly be taken away, citizenship can. For we have inherited the same tradition with regard to both, and if once it is possible to take away citizenship it is impossible to preserve liberty. For how can a man enjoy his rights to the freedom of a Roman citizen if he is not among the number of Roman citizens ? I established this point as quite 97 a young man when I was opposed by Gaius Cotta, the most learned man in Rome. I was defending the freedom of a woman of Arretium; and Cotta worked upon the scruples of the court,[a] telling them that they could not give us their verdict[b] because the people of Arretium had lost their citizenship ; while I argued with great vigour that it was not possible for them to lose it. The court did not come to a decision at the first hearing, but after a thorough examination and discussion of the case,

liberata sacramentum nostrum iustum iudicaverunt.
Atque hoc et contra dicente Cotta et Sulla vivo
iudicatum est. Iam vero in ceteris, ut omnes qui in
eadem caussa sunt et lege agant et suum ius perse-
quantur et omni iure civili sine cuiusquam aut magistratus aut iudicis aut periti hominis aut imperiti
dubitatione utantur, quid ego commemorem?
Dubium est nemini vestrum.

98 Certe quaeri hoc solere me non praeterit, ut ex
me ea quae tibi in mentem non veniunt audias, quemadmodum, si civitas adimi non possit, in colonias
Latinas saepe nostri cives profecti sint. Aut sua
voluntate aut legis multa profecti sunt, quam multam
si sufferre voluissent, tum manere in civitate potuissent. XXXIV. Quid, quem pater patratus dedidit,
aut suus pater populusve vendidit, quo is iure amittit
civitatem? Ut religione civitas solvatur, civis
Romanus deditur, qui quum est acceptus, est eorum
quibus est deditus; si non accipiunt, ut Mancinum
Numantini, retinet integram caussam et ius civitatis.
Si pater vendidit eum quem in suam potestatem
99 susceperat, ex potestate dimittit. Iam populus
quum eum vendidit qui miles factus non est, non

---

^a See note on § 34.
^b On joining a " Latin colony," a Roman citizen suffered
a partial loss of status (*capitis diminutio minor*), *i.e.* he lost
his citizenship but recovered, as a Latin, some of his citizen
rights : these varied from time to time.
^c The high priest of this college concluded with the enemy
(*patrare*, to conclude) under religious forms matters relating
to peace and war.
^d Mancinus was surrendered to the Numantines in 137 B.C.
in order to free Rome from the obligation of ratifying the
treaty which he had concluded with them.
^e The reference is to the formal " taking up " of a newly
born infant by the father who thus acknowledged and

they subsequently gave us their verdict ; and they gave it us though Cotta opposed it and Sulla was still alive. But why indeed should I quote you further instances of people in the same position taking legal proceedings, vindicating their rights and availing themselves of the whole body of citizen law [a] without anyone, magistrate or juror, lawyer or layman, casting doubts on their rights to do so ? Not one of you feels any doubt.

There is certainly one question which, as I am well 98 aware, is constantly asked (and here, Piso, I propose to supply the arguments which do not occur to you) : " How is it that, if citizenship cannot be lost, our citizens have often joined Latin Colonies ? " [b] They have done so either of their own free will or to avoid a penalty imposed by law : had they been willing to undergo the penalty, they could have remained within the citizen body. XXXIV. Again, when anyone is surrendered by the Chief Priest of the Fetial College, [c] or sold as a slave by his own father or by the state, what justification is there for the loss of his citizenship ? A Roman citizen is surrendered to save the honour of the state : if those to whom he is surrendered accept him, he becomes theirs ; if they refuse to accept him, as the Numantines did Mancinus, [d] he retains his original status and his rights as a citizen. A father, by selling a son of whom he has assumed control, [e] frees him from his control. So too the state, by selling a man who 99 has evaded military service, does not take away

assumed control (*potestas*) of him. The selling of a son three times by his father, which, according to the Twelve Tables, freed him from this control, developed later into a legal fiction.

adimit ei libertatem, sed iudicat non esse eum
liberum qui ut liber sit adire periculum noluit : quum
autem incensum vendit, hoc iudicat, quum ii qui in
servitute iusta fuerunt censu liberentur, eum qui,
quum liber esset, censeri noluerit, ipsum sibi libertatem abiudicavisse.

Quod si maxime hisce rebus adimi libertas aut
civitas potest, non intelligunt, qui haec commemo-
rant, si per has rationes maiores adimi posse voluerunt,
100 alio modo noluisse ? Nam ut haec ex iure civili
protulerunt, sic afferant velim, quibus lege aut roga-
tione civitas aut libertas erepta sit. Nam quod ad
exsilium attinet, perspicue intelligi potest quale sit.
Exsilium enim non supplicium est sed perfugium
portusque supplicii. Nam qui volunt poenam aliquam
subterfugere aut calamitatem, eo solum vertunt, hoc
est, sedem ac locum mutant. Itaque nulla in lege
nostra reperietur, ut apud ceteras civitates, male-
ficium ullum exsilio esse mulctatum ; sed quum homines
vincula, neces ignominiasque vitant, quae sunt legibus
constitutae, confugiunt quasi ad aram in exsilium. Qui
si in civitate legis vim subire vellent, non prius civitatem quam vitam amitterent : quia nolunt, non adimitur
iis civitas, sed ab iis relinquitur atque deponitur.

---

[a] One of the forms of legal manumission was the entry
of the slave's name on the censor's lists as a citizen.
[b] Cicero thought (probably wrongly) that the word
exilium (exile) contained the same root as *solum* (soil).

his freedom but decrees that one who has refused to face danger for his freedom's sake is not a free man. By selling a man who has evaded the census, the state decrees that, whereas those who have been slaves in the normal way gain their freedom by being included in the census, one who has refused to be included in it although free, has of his own accord repudiated his freedom.[a]

Now if these are the special grounds on which citizenship and liberty can be lost, do those who quote them fail to understand that our forefathers, by intending that loss of liberty should be possible in these circumstances, intended that it should be impossible in any others? For as they have pro- 100 duced these instances from our law, I wish they would also produce instances in which people have been deprived of their citizenship or their liberty by any statute or proposal. For the position with regard to exile is transparently clear. Exile is not a punishment : it is a harbour of refuge from punishment. Because people want to escape from some punishment or catastrophe, they " quit their native soil," [b] that is to say, they change the place of their abode. And so, in no statute of ours will you find, as you will in the laws of other states, that exile figures as the punishment for any crime at all ; but people seeking to avoid imprisonment, death, or dishonour, when imposed upon them by our laws, take refuge in exile as in a sanctuary. Should they consent to remain within the citizen body and submit to the rigour of the law, they would lose their citizenship only with their lives. But they do not consent ; and therefore their citizenship is not taken from them, but is by them abandoned and discarded. For

Nam quum ex nostro iure duarum civitatum nemo esse possit, tum amittitur haec civitas denique, quum is qui profugit receptus est in exsilium, hoc est, in aliam civitatem.

101   XXXV. Non me praeterit, recuperatores, tametsi de hoc iure permulta praetereo, tamen me longius esse prolapsum quam ratio vestri iudicii postularit. Verum id feci, non quod vos in hac caussa hanc defensionem desiderare arbitrarer, sed ut omnes intelligerent nec ademptam cuiquam civitatem esse neque adimi posse. Hoc quum eos scire volui, quibus Sulla voluit iniuriam facere, tum omnes ceteros novos veteresque cives. Neque enim ratio afferri potest cur, si cuiquam novo civi potuerit adimi civitas, non omnibus patriciis, omnibus antiquissimis civibus possit.

102 Nam ad hanc quidem caussam nihil hoc pertinuisse primum ex eo intelligi potest, quod vos ea de re iudicare non debetis, deinde quod Sulla ipse ita tulit de civitate ut non sustulerit horum nexa atque hereditates. Iubet enim eodem iure esse quo fuerint Ariminenses, quos quis ignorat duodecim coloniarum fuisse et a civibus Romanis hereditates capere potuisse ? Quod si adimi civitas A. Caecinae lege potuisset, magis illam rationem tamen omnes boni

---

a That is, those Italians included in the citizen body after the Social War 91–88 B.C.

b These were probably twelve communities which, having received the citizenship after the Social War, were deprived by Sulla of the *ius connubii*, the right of contracting a marriage valid under Roman law, while retaining the right of contract (*ius commercii*) which Cicero divides into its chief constituent elements—*nexa*, the right to acquire property, and *hereditates*, the right to inherit under a citizen's will.

as no one under our law can be a citizen of two states, citizenship of Rome is actually lost at the moment when the runaway becomes an exile, that is, a member of another state.

XXXV. Now, gentlemen, though I fail to mention 101 very many points in connexion with this right of citizenship, I do not fail to see that I have been led on to speak about it at greater length than consideration for your verdict demanded. But I have done so, not because I thought that in this case you would look for this particular defence, but in order to bring it home to everybody that citizenship has never been and can never be taken away from any man. I wished all men to know this—both those whom Sulla intended to injure and all other citizens as well, whether the old or the new.[a] For if it has been possible to take away his citizenship from any newly created citizen, no argument can be advanced to show why it should not be taken away from all patricians, all the citizens of oldest creation. How 102 irrevelant are such considerations to the present case may be understood first from the fact that this question is not the one which you are called upon to decide ; and second, from Sulla's own law dealing with the citizen rights of these communities, which was so framed as not to deprive them of their rights of contract and of inheritance. The law enacts that they are to have the same rights as the people of Ariminum, which, as everybody knows, was one of the Twelve Colonies[b] and had the right to inherit under the wills of Roman citizens. But even had it been possible to take away Aulus Caecina's citizenship by statute, it would be more natural for us to be concerned, as good citizens, in finding some way to

quaereremus, quemadmodum spectatissimum puden-
tissimumque hominem, summo consilio, summa
virtute, summa auctoritate domestica praeditum,
levatum iniuria civem retinere possemus, quam uti
nunc, quum de iure civitatis nihil potuerit deperdere,
quisquam exsistat, nisi tui, Sexte, similis et stultitia
et impudentia, qui huic civitatem ademptam esse
dicat.

103   Qui quoniam, recuperatores, suum ius non deseruit,
neque quidquam illius audaciae petulantiaeque concessit, de reliquo iam communem caussam populique
ius in vestra fide ac religione deponit.   XXXVI. Is
homo est,[1] ita se probatum vobis vestrique similibus
semper voluit, ut id non minus in hac caussa laborarit,
nec contenderit aliud quam ne ius suum dissolute
relinquere videretur, nec minus vereretur, ne con-
temnere Aebutium quam ne ab eo contemptus esse
104 existimaretur.   Quapropter si quid extra iudicium
est quod homini tribuendum sit, habetis hominem
singulari pudore, virtute cognita, et spectata fide,
amplissimo totius Etruriae nomine,[2] in utraque fortuna
cognitum multis signis et virtutis et humanitatis.   Si
quid in contraria parte in homine offendendum sit,
habetis eum, ut nihil dicam amplius, qui se homines
coegisse fateatur.   Sin hominibus remotis de caussa
quaeritis, quum iudicium de vi sit, is qui arguitur vim

[1] est *T*: *om. cett.*
[2] amplissimo . . . nomine *Baiter.*

free from injustice and retain among our number the
most estimable and respectable of men, eminent as
he is for wisdom, for goodness and for the respect
which he commands at home, than that now, when it
has proved impossible for him to be deprived of a
single one of his citizen rights, anyone should be
found, unless your match, Sextus, in folly and
effrontery, to assert that my client's citizenship has
been taken from him.

Inasmuch, gentlemen, as he has not abandoned 103
his rights nor yielded aught to the effrontery and
insolence of his opponent, henceforward he commits
his case, which is yours as well, and the rights of the
people, to your sense of honour and of duty. XXXVI.
Such is his character, such has he ever wished to be
found by you and by men like you, that his one object
in this case and his single aim has been to avoid
losing by remissness the right that is his ; and that
he is equally afraid of appearing either to treat
Aebutius with contempt or to be so treated by him.
Wherefore, if something is due to a man's merits apart 104
from those of his case, you have in him a man of
unusual moderation, of distinguished character and
approved loyalty, bearing the most honourable
name in all Etruria, and distinguished, alike in
good fortune or ill, by abundant evidence both of a
manly and a humane character. Should there be,
on the opposite side, something in the man that
causes offence, you have there one who, to say
nothing more, admits that he collected his forces
together. But if you set personalities aside and consider the case by itself, then, since you are to pass
judgement upon the question of force, since he who
is accused of it admits that he employed force by

se hominibus armatis fecisse fateatur, verbo se, non
aequitate defendere conetur, id quoque ei verbum
ipsum ereptum esse videatis, auctoritatem sapien-
tissimorum hominum facere nobiscum, in iudicium
non venire utrum A. Caecina possederit necne, tamen
doceri possedisse ; multo etiam minus quaeri A.
Caecinae fundus sit necne, me tamen id ipsum do-
cuisse, fundum esse Caecinae :—quum haec ita sint,
statuite quid vos tempora rei publicae de armatis
hominibus, quid illius confessio de vi, quid nostra
decisio de aequitate, quid ratio interdicti de iure
admoneat ut iudicetis.

means of armed men, since he endeavours to defend himself by the letter and not the spirit of the law, and since you see that the protection even of the letter has been torn from him, that the most learned authorities are on our side, that, though this case does not raise the question of Caecina's possession, possession none the less is shown to have been his, and that, though the question of Caecina's ownership is still less a relevant issue, I have established the actual fact of his ownership ; since all this, I say, is so, make up your minds what verdict you are called upon to pass by considerations of public policy upon the employment of armed men, by his own admission upon the use of force, by our conclusion upon the claims of equity, and by the spirit of the injunction upon the legal issue.

THE SPEECH OF MARCUS TULLIUS CICERO IN DEFENCE OF AULUS CLUENTIUS HABITUS

INTRODUCTION

§ 1. The chief difficulty of the *Pro Cluentio* is the complexity of its plot, and this is increased by the fact that the audience which Cicero addressed on this occasion was already familiar with it. For though he was actually defending Aulus Cluentius on a charge of poisoning brought against him by the younger Oppianicus, his speech is mainly concerned with the earlier prosecution[a] by Cluentius of Statius Albius Oppianicus, father of the present prosecutor.

The eight years which had since passed had heightened rather than abated public interest in the case, which was rendered additionally sensational by suspicions of bribery entertained in connexion with the verdict.[b] These suspicions gave to the tribune Quinctius an opportunity to excite popular indignation against the trial and, in general, against the Senate, whose members composed the juries of that time. He succeeded in getting several of those concerned put on their trial: Junius, after whom, as president of the court, the trial was known as the *iudicium Iunianum*, was found guilty of a technical offence; and Staienus, a notorious "crook" who

---

[a] In 74 B.C.: the present trial took place in 66 B.C.
[b] Oppianicus was found guilty.

was thought to have acted as go-between, was also condemned.

The prejudice thus carefully worked up against Cluentius culminated in his being charged with having poisoned the elder Oppianicus, who was by this time generally believed to have been the innocent victim of corruption. Accordingly, in defending Cluentius, Cicero devotes the greater part of his speech to showing that the elder Oppianicus was really a villain and was convicted primarily on the evidence.

§ 2. Of the speech which he produced on this occasion, the interest is indisputable and the historical value difficult to exaggerate; for its subject matter is " the most singular and interesting *cause célèbre* bequeathed to us by antiquity"; and it gives us a vivid, indeed, a lurid picture of Italian society during the last days of the Roman Republic.

The time at which this speech was delivered was, like our own, a " period of transition," and such periods have a peculiar interest and importance; for as we look back on them, we see with a special clarity both the past which made them and the future which they were to make. There must have been among Cicero's audience many who had seen the first blow struck at the Republic by Marius and Sulla, and others who would see it fall beneath the feet of Caesar. The years between form a melancholy record of the decay both of private morals and public virtue; and the brilliant light which this speech throws on life in an Italian country town, shows how idle it is to suppose that vice and corruption were confined to the Capital or that life outside it still produced the men or the morals of older and better days.

INTRODUCTION

§ 3. The *Pro Cluentio* is not, according to Froude,[a] " a favourable specimen of Cicero's oratorical power. There is no connexion in the events. There is no order of time. We are hurried from date to date, from place to place. The same person is described under different names; the same incident by different words. The result is a mass of threads so knotted, twisted and entangled, that only patient labour can sort them out into intelligent arrangement." But the average reader is unlikely to find that this speech makes too great a demand at all events upon his patience; and will be more inclined to agree with another critic [b] who assigns to it " a foremost place in oratorical literature, as representing the high-water mark of Ciceronian eloquence."

The circumstances were indeed such as to show us Cicero at his best; and, at his best, his oratory represents the highest point attainable by the Latin language when following the lines of its natural development. When he defended Cluentius, he was in the prime of life and of his intellectual powers, and nearing the summit of his influence and popularity, for which he only had those powers to thank. He had had enough experience to bring his talents to maturity and not enough to teach him to distrust them. Moreover, the moving story which he had to tell, the wrong which he was striving to right, produced in him an emotional sincerity which, while blinding him to all that told against his case, added

---

[a] J. A. Froude, *Short Studies on Great Subjects*, vol. iii. The writer's inaccurate representation even of the facts suggests that either his patience or his labour were inadequate.

[b] Sir W. Peterson, in his edition of the *Pro Cluentio*.

INTRODUCTION

an element of passion to his pleading which the mere advocate might have lacked.

And yet the *Pro Cluentio* is advocacy, as well as oratory, at its highest. It was meant to be heard, not read, and its object was to convince a jury. Of this object Cicero never loses sight, and the result is a sustained interest, a constant variety, a consummate blend of humour and pathos, of narrative and argument, of description and declamation ; while every part is subordinated to the purpose of the whole, and combines, despite its intricacy of detail, to form a dramatic and coherent unity.

§ 4. Note on the Statutes mentioned in the Speech

1. Lex Cornelia de Sicariis et Veneficiis.

Cluentius was prosecuted under this law passed by Sulla to deal with cases of assassination and poisoning. Its provisions, embodying an older law of C. Gracchus, were contained in six sections which were applicable respectively :

§§ 1-4. " To him who has cut off a man or has, for that purpose or for the purpose of robbery, been in possession of a weapon."

§ 5. " Or who, for the purpose of murder, has had poison in his possession or has prepared it or administered it."

§ 6. " Or who has given false witness to compass a man's death or has been responsible for causing it."

This sixth section, dealing with judicial murder, Sulla made operative only against Senators, who were

the only people allowed, under the then existing constitution, to act as jurors.

How came it, then, that Cluentius, who was not a senator but a knight, was accused under both sections five and six, when only section five was strictly applicable to him ? There are two theories :

(i.) That Cicero is " throwing dust in the eyes of the jury " (see note on § 1) *either* by misquoting the limitations to § 6, *or* by misquoting the charge against his client, which was under § 5 only, his alleged guilt under § 6 having been referred to as moral only.

(ii.) That Accius had actually accused Cluentius under both §§ 5 and 6, urging that § 6 should be made retrospectively applicable to all classes who were now allowed to act as jurors (see chapter liii.).

2. Lex Cornelia de Repetundis or Repetundarum[a] (§§ 104 and 148).

This statute was designed by Sulla to check mal-administration in the provinces by making it penal to take a bribe. It was applicable to " anyone who takes a bribe when acting as a magistrate, ruler, administrator, ambassador, or other officer, or to any member of his staff."

Like the preceding statute, it contained a clause dealing with judicial corruption and applicable only to senators ; for at the time it was passed, all jurors were senators. This limitation survived anomalously after the extension of judicial functions to other orders.

[a] The phrase *pecuniae repetundae*, or simply *repetundae*, signifies money which, having been illegally gotten, was recoverable.

INTRODUCTION

3. Lex Calpurnia de Ambitu (§§ 98 and 114).

This statute, embodying older legislation, was passed in 67 b.c., and punished by exclusion from the senate or any public office, or by a fine, anyone guilty of " corrupt practice " in connexion with an election. It did not apply to the taking of bribes in any circumstances or to bribery of any kind otherwise than at an election.

The *Praemia legis*, § 98, mentioned in this section, consisted in the complete restitution (except for the fine) of any person who, having himself been convicted of " corrupt practice," secured the conviction of another for the same offence.

4. Maiestas (§§ 97 and 99).

The crime of treason consisted in " diminishing, that is, detracting from, the dignity, honour, or power of the People or of those on whom the People has conferred power." It was punished by the confiscation of all property.

N.B.—It will be seen that none of the foregoing statutes (nor indeed any other) covered the giving of a bribe in a court of law by one who was not a senator. The proper procedure in such a case was for the consuls, acting on a resolution by the Senate, to propose the setting up of an " extraordinary commission " to deal with the case (see § 137).

INTRODUCTION

§ 5. GENEALOGICAL TABLES

Note : * denotes " married to Oppianicus."
† denotes " murdered by Oppianicus."

A. Family of Cluentius

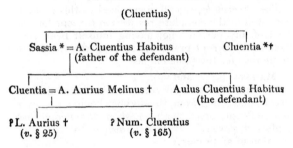

(Cluentius)

Sassia * = A. Cluentius Habitus   Cluentia *†
(father of the defendant)

Cluentia = A. Aurius Melinus †   Aulus Cluentius Habitus
(the defendant)

? L. Aurius †   ? Num. Cluentius
(*v.* § 25)   (*v.* § 165)

B. Family of Dinea

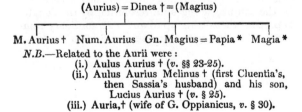

(Aurius) = Dinea † = (Magius)

M. Aurius †   Num. Aurius   Gn. Magius = Papia *   Magia *

N.B.—Related to the Aurii were :
    (i.) Aulus Aurius † (*v.* §§ 23-25).
    (ii.) Aulus Aurius Melinus † (first Cluentia's,
         then Sassia's husband) and his son,
         Lucius Aurius † (*v.* § 25).
    (iii.) Auria,† (wife of G. Oppianicus, *v.* § 30).

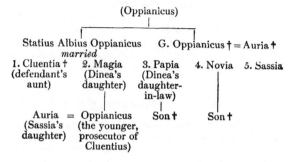

C. Family of Oppianicus

(Oppianicus)

Statius Albius Oppianicus   G. Oppianicus † = Auria †
married

1. Cluentia †   2. Magia   3. Papia   4. Novia   5. Sassia
(defendant's   (Dinea's   (Dinea's
aunt)   daughter)   daughter-
                              in-law)

Auria = Oppianicus   Son †   Son †
(Sassia's   (the younger,
daughter)   prosecutor of
            Cluentius)

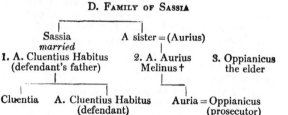

D. Family of Sassia

Sassia   A sister = (Aurius)
married

1. A. Cluentius Habitus   2. A. Aurius   3. Oppianicus
(defendant's father)   Melinus †   the elder

Cluentia   A. Cluentius Habitus   Auria = Oppianicus
            (defendant)   (prosecutor)

INTRODUCTION

Exordium (§§ 1-8)

(Chapter **i**.) Like the prosecutor, I shall divide my speech into two parts, dealing respectively with the prejudice and with the actual charges against my client. I admit that the prejudice is strong and of long standing, but (**ii**.) it should be excluded from a court of law ; (**iii**.) I ask for a fair hearing.

The Crimes of Oppianicus, §§ 9-42

(**iv**.) This prejudice is due to the idea that Cluentius bribed the court to condemn the innocent Oppianicus : I will show that neither was Oppianicus innocent nor did Cluentius bribe the court ; and will set forth the crimes of Oppianicus, father of the present prosecutor.

(**v**.) Sassia, Cluentius's mother and the villainess of the piece, conceived a passion for, and eventually married, her daughter's husband. (**vi**.) Cluentius's disapproval of such conduct first roused in her the hatred with which she has ever since pursued him. (**vii**.) As for his prosecution of Oppianicus, he was bound to bring his case and certain to win it. The crimes of Oppianicus were :

1. He attempted to poison Cluentius.

2. By the will of Dinea, his son was to inherit her fortune unless her only surviving son, M. Aurius, could be found. (**viii**.) Oppianicus had Aurius murdered before his kinsmen could trace him.

3. Driven by popular indignation to take refuge with Sulla's army he subsequently returned and put

to death several of Dinea's relations, including Sassia's husband, Aulus Aurius.

4. (ix.) He married Sassia, who demanded first the murder of two of his three sons.

5. (x.) He poisoned his first wife, (xi.) his brother's wife when pregnant, and finally his brother.

6. (xii.) He bribed the wife of his brother-in-law to procure abortion in order that her husband's money might go to Oppianicus the younger.

7. (xiii.) He murdered a wealthy youth after forging his will.

8. (xiv.) He murdered Dinea and forged her will.

These and other crimes made him universally abhorred ; but Cluentius prosecuted him only because his own life was in danger.

Oppianicus's Plot against Cluentius, §§ 43-59

(xv.) Cluentius had fallen foul of Oppianicus, whom he had opposed over municipal affairs, and who, moreover, had designs upon his money. (xvi.) Oppianicus employed a certain Fabricius who, through his freedman Scamander, attempted to poison Cluentius : the plot was discovered and Scamander caught with the poison on him.

(xvii.) Scamander was put on trial, and I, in ignorance of the nature of the case, undertook his defence. (xviii.) I did my best, but (xix.) Scamander's guilt and Oppianicus's complicity were obvious. (xx.) Scamander was convicted. (xxi.) Fabricius was tried next and convicted also.

The Trial of Oppianicus, §§ 59-87

(xxii.) Then came the trial of Oppianicus, condemned already by the verdicts against his two

accomplices. (xxiii.) Admitting that someone bribed the court, what motive had Cluentius for bribing it? (xxiv.) Oppianicus had every motive, and to this end employed (xxv.) his usual intermediary, Staienus. Staienus plotted to keep the whole bribe for himself by (xxvi.) telling the venal jurors at the last minute that no money was forthcoming from Oppianicus, whom they would therefore be sure to convict. (xxvii.) But rumours of corruption began to spread ; the hearing of the case was suddenly closed in the absence of Staienus, who was hastily recalled. (xxviii.) The venal jurors voted first, for conviction, and despite some confusion a verdict of " guilty " was finally returned. This the demagogue Quinctius proclaimed to be due to bribery by Cluentius, although Staienus was forced to confess.

(xxix.) Popular indignation, roused by Quinctius, secured the ruin of Junius, president of the court. (xxx.) At such a time the truth had no chance of a hearing, but to-day it is obvious : all the evidence points to Oppianicus as the author of the bribe. (xxxi.) To suggest that he gave the money to Staienus for any other purpose is ridiculous.

Previous Verdicts quoted against Cluentius, §§ 88-142

(xxxii.) There are said to be other verdicts which prove the guilt of Cluentius : I shall examine them : 1. (xxxiii.) Junius was convicted : yes, but for a purely technical offence ; his " trial " (xxxiv.) was a piece of mob-violence worked up by the tribune Quinctius.

2. (xxxv.) Bulbus was convicted of treason—a simple issue, unconnected with any other case.

3. (xxxvi.) Popilius and Gutta were convicted for giving, not for taking, bribes.

4. Staienus was convicted of treason : even though it was proved that he lived by bribery, it was Oppianicus, not Cluentius, who bribed him.

(5. (xxxvii.) Falcula was tried twice, and twice acquitted.

(xxxviii.) The votes cast for Oppianicus's acquittal are excusable, but the weight of character belongs rather to those who did not vote for him. (xxxix.) The prejudice against them, and particularly against Junius, was the work of Quinctius, and (xl.) you know what a conceited demagogue he was !

(xli.) But to resume, Falcula's acquittal proves nothing. Some of the jurors were tried, but on other charges ; others were not tried at all.

6. At the assessment of Scaevola's penalty, it was held that Oppianicus's trial was corrupt ; but such proceedings are irresponsible and carry no weight.

7. (xlii.) The Censors stigmatized certain of the jurors at Oppianicus's trial ; but their stigma has never had the force of a verdict : (xliii.) the courts have often disregarded it—so have the Censors themselves. (xliv.) To give it such a force would be to invest the Censors with tyrannous power. We are concerned not with opinions but with facts, and the facts are before you. (xlv.) The Censors only followed rumour and their action can be disregarded. (xlvi.) What right had they to censure certain only of the jurors ? (xlvii.) Their action was a bid for popularity and was based on inadequate knowledge : they even differed among themselves ; (xlviii.) and were induced to censure Cluentius himself only by scandal which he had no chance to refute. **8.**

Egnatius, in disinheriting his son, commented on the corruption at Oppianicus's trial; but no conclusion can be based on that.

9. (xlix.) Nor upon the Senate's resolution : they could not avoid passing one, but it was intentionally vague and non-committal.

10. (l.) My own opinion, expressed in some speech, is quoted against me. I knew no more of the case then than other people, and, in any case, spoke only as an advocate. (li.) Quotations of this kind have often been proved worthless.

The actual Charges against Cluentius

A. The Legal Issue, §§ 143-160

(lii.) I propose to rely on the merits of my case rather than on its purely legal aspect ; though, actually, the statute under which Cluentius is accused is not applicable to him. (liii.) You cannot tamper with the law, on which all our institutions rest. (liv.) Examine the statute : Cluentius, as a knight, is not among those to whom it applies, (lv.) and you cannot extend its provisions to cover his case : (lvi.) similar attempts have been defeated in the past ; (lvii.) otherwise no one would be safe. (lviii.) The jurors are bound to vote in accordance with the law as it is.

B. The Substance of the Charges, §§ 160-194

(lix.) All the trumpery scandal raked up in eight years is not enough to embarrass Cluentius.

(lx.) He is charged 1. with poisoning Cappadox : but Cappadox died a natural death. 2. With attempting to poison the present prosecutor : the

story is improbable and will not bear examination. 3. (lxi.) With poisoning Oppianicus the elder : but he had no motive for doing so, and (lxii.) the story again breaks down. Oppianicus actually died from an accident.

(lxiii.) On the death of Oppianicus Sassia tried to wring from his slaves a confession incriminating Cluentius, but in vain. (lxiv.) After three years, she secured a hold on young Oppianicus by betrothing him to her daughter, and then reopened the inquest, and this time (lxv.) she claims to have extorted the desired confession ; (lxvi.) but the records are a clumsy forgery.

What an unnatural monster Sassia must be ! She has ceaselessly plotted against her son, (lxvii.) and is here now to support the prosecution which she organized. (lxviii.) Her journey to Rome was marked by the execration of the countryside.

Peroration §§ 194-202

(lxix.) Save Cluentius from such a mother. See the enthusiasm inspired by his high character both near and far. (lxx.) All good men are eager for his safety—against him is his mother alone. (lxxi.) Banish prejudice and let justice be done at last.

M. TULLI CICERONIS PRO A. CLUENTIO HABITO ORATIO AD IUDICES

1 I. Animadverti, iudices, omnem accusatoris orationem in duas divisam esse partes, quarum altera
mihi niti et magno opere confidere videbatur invidia
iam inveterata iudicii Iuniani, altera tantum modo
consuetudinis causa timide et diffidenter attingere
rationem veneficii criminum, qua de re lege est haec
quaestio constituta. Itaque mihi certum est hanc
eandem distributionem invidiae et criminum sic in
defensione servare, ut omnes intellegant nihil me nec
subterfugere voluisse reticendo nec obscurare di-
2 cendo. Sed cum considero quo modo mihi in utraque
re sit elaborandum, altera pars et ea, quae propria
est iudicii vestri et legitimae veneficii quaestionis,
per mihi brevis et non magnae in dicendo conten-
tionis fore videtur, altera autem, quae procul ab
iudicio remota est, quae contionibus seditiose concitatis accommodatior est quam tranquillis modera-

---

See Introduction, § 1.

ᵇ Cicero afterwards boasted that he had " thrown dust in
the eyes of the judges at Cluentius's trial " (Quintilian ii.
17. 21).

THE SPEECH OF MARCUS TULLIUS CICERO IN DEFENCE OF AULUS CLUENTIUS HABITUS

I. GENTLEMEN : I noticed that the prosecutor's 1 entire speech was divided into two parts, in one of which he seemed to be relying with all confidence upon the now time-honoured prejudice felt against the trial before Junius *a* ; while in the other he seemed to make his reluctant and diffident approach, for form's sake only, to the question of the charge of poisoning, to deal with which this court has been by law established. I am, therefore, determined to imitate him in my defence, dividing my speech between the question of prejudice and the actual charges ; and hoping to make clear to all that it has been my wish neither to avoid the issue by saying too little, nor to obscure it by saying too much.*b* But when I come to consider how I am to develop 2 each of these two themes, one of them—the one which is proper to the consideration of your court and of a tribunal appointed by law to deal with poisoning cases—seems likely to demand little either of time or of effort in exposition ; whereas the other, alien as it is from a court of law and more suited to the disorderly excitement of a public meeting than to the calm deliberation of a trial, is likely to

tisque iudiciis, perspicio quantum in agendo diffi-
cultatis et quantum laboris sit habitura.

3   Sed in hac difficultate illa me res tamen, iudices,
consolatur, quod vos de criminibus sic audire con-
suestis, ut eorum omnem dissolutionem ab oratore
quaeratis, ut non existimetis plus vos ad salutem reo
largiri oportere, quam quantum defensor purgandis
criminibus consequi et dicendo probare potuerit : de
invidia autem sic inter vos disceptare debetis, ut non
quid dicatur a nobis, sed quid oporteat dici con-
sideretis. Agitur enim in criminibus A. Cluenti
proprium periculum, in invidia causa communis.
Quam ob rem alteram partem causae sic agemus, ut
vos doceamus, alteram sic, ut oremus. In altera
diligentia vestra nobis adiungenda est, in altera fides
imploranda. Nemo est enim qui invidiae sine vestro
ac sine talium virorum subsidio possit resistere.

4   Equidem quod ad me attinet, quo me vertam
nescio : negem fuisse illam infamiam iudicii corrupti ? negem esse illam rem agitatam in contionibus, iactatam in iudiciis, commemoratam in senatu ?
evellam ex animis hominum tantam opinionem, tam
penitus insitam, tam vetustam ? Non est nostri
ingenii ; vestri auxilii est, iudices, huius innocentiae
sic in hac calamitosa fama quasi in aliqua perniciosis-
sima flamma atque in communi incendio subvenire.

5 II. Etenim sicut aliis in locis parum firmamenti et

involve in its treatment a degree of toil and difficulty
of which I am well aware.

But in the face of this difficulty I console myself 3
with the reflection that whereas, in hearing a charge,
it is your custom to look wholly to the speaker for
its refutation, and not to think that it is any duty of
your own to contribute anything to the defendant's
acquittal beyond what his counsel can secure by
refuting the charge or justify by his arguments ; in
dealing on the other hand with prejudice, you ought,
as you discuss the case among yourselves, to take
into consideration the pleas that should be, rather
than those that are, advanced by counsel. For in
the actual charges against him only my client's
interests are at stake, but the question of prejudice
involves the interest of us all. And so, in one part
of my speech I shall use the language of demonstra-
tion, in the other, that of entreaty : in one I need
your careful attention, in the other I must implore
your goodwill : for no man can hope to withstand
prejudice without your support and that of men like
you.

For my part, I confess I know not where to turn : 4
am I to say that there never was a scandal over the
corruption of that court ; or that it never was discussed at the street-corners, bandied about in the
law courts, commented on in the Senate ? Am I to
expunge from public opinion such firm impressions,
so deeply and so long ingrained ? That is beyond
my power. Yours, gentlemen, is the power to help
my innocent client, to come to his rescue when beset
by this disastrous calumny, as it were by some ruin-
ous fire, some conflagration threatening all alike.
II. Moreover, though elsewhere truth is all too 5

parum virium veritas habet, sic in hoc loco falsa invidia imbecilla esse debet : dominetur in contionibus, iaceat in iudiciis : valeat in opinionibus ac sermonibus imperitorum, ab ingeniis prudentium repudietur : vehementes habeat repentinos impetus, spatio interposito et causa cognita consenescat : denique illa definitio iudiciorum aequorum, quae nobis a maioribus tradita est, retineatur, ut in iudiciis et sine invidia culpa plectatur et sine culpa invidia ponatur.

6   Quam ob rem a vobis, iudices, ante quam de ipsa causa dicere incipio, haec postulo : primum id, quod aequissimum est, ut ne quid huc praeiudicati adferatis (etenim non modo auctoritatem, sed etiam nomen iudicum amittemus, nisi hic ex ipsis causis iudicabimus ac si ad causas iudicia iam facta domo deferemus) ; deinde si quam opinionem iam vestris mentibus comprehendistis, si eam ratio convellet, si oratio labefactabit, si denique veritas extorquebit, ne repugnetis eamque animis vestris aut libentibus aut aequis remittatis ; tum autem, cum ego una quaque de re dicam et diluam, ne ipsi, quae contraria sint, taciti cogitationi vestrae subiciatis, sed ad extremum exspectetis meque meum dicendi ordinem servare patiamini : cum peroraro, tum, si quid erit praeteritum, animo requiratis.

7   III. Ego me, iudices, ad eam causam accedere,

lacking in support and efficiency, in this place it is false prejudice that should display weakness : prejudice may lord it at a public meeting, but must hide its head in a court of law ; it may thrive in the minds and in the talk of laymen, but should be refused admittance by trained intellects ; it may gain strength from the suddenness of its onslaught, but should decline in vigour after a lapse of time and an examination of the case. Finally, let us stand by that prime characteristic of a fair trial, which we hold as an heritage from our forefathers—that, in courts of law, though there be no prejudice, guilt is punished ; and if there be no guilt, prejudice is put aside.

For this reason, then, before I begin to deal with 6 the case proper, I have a request to make to you, gentlemen. First, that, as is only just, you bring to this court no preconceived judgements (for indeed men will cease, not only to respect us as judges, but even to call us judges, unless in this place we base our judgements on the facts of the case, instead of applying to the facts the ready-made judgements we have brought from home). Next—supposing you already to have formed some opinion—that, if it be dislodged by reason, shaken by argument, or finally uprooted by truth itself, you dismiss it without resistance from your minds, if not gladly, at least without reluctance. And lastly, as I proceed to a detailed refutation of the charge, do not on your part make a mental note of any point against me, but wait till the end and allow me to develop the defence in my own way : the conclusion of my speech will be time enough for you to ask yourselves the reason for any omissions I may have made.

III. I can easily understand, gentlemen, that the 7

quae iam per annos octo continuos ex contraria parte
audiatur atque ipsa opinione hominum tacita prope
convicta atque damnata sit, facile intellego : sed si
qui mihi deus vestram ad me audiendum benevolentiam conciliarit, efficiam profecto, ut intellegatis nihil
esse homini tam timendum quam invidiam, nihil
innocenti suscepta invidia tam optandum quam
aequum iudicium, quod in hoc uno denique falsae
infamiae finis aliqui atque exitus reperiatur. Quam
ob rem magna me spes tenet, si quae sunt in causa
explicare atque omnia dicendo consequi potuero,
hunc locum consessumque vestrum, quem illi horribi-
lem A. Cluentio ac formidolosum fore putaverunt,
eum tandem eius fortunae miserae multumque
iactatae portum ac perfugium futurum.

8   Tametsi permulta sunt, quae mihi, ante quam de
causa dico, de communibus invidiae periculis dicenda
esse videantur, tamen, ne diutius oratione mea sus-
pensa exspectatio vestra teneatur, adgrediar ad
crimen cum illa deprecatione, iudices, qua mihi
saepius utendum esse intellego, sic ut me audiatis,
quasi hoc tempore haec causa primum dicatur, sicuti
dicitur, non quasi saepe iam dicta et numquam probata sit. Hodierno enim die primum ipsius[1] criminis
diluendi potestas est data ; ante hoc tempus error in
hac causa atque invidia versata est. Quam ob rem
dum multorum annorum accusationi breviter di-

----

[1] *Omitting* veteris, *bracketed by F as a gloss.*

case which I am undertaking is one which, for all these eight long years, you have heard stated from the opposite point of view, and in which public opinion itself has practically given its unspoken verdict and passed sentence against my client. But if Heaven grant me a favourable hearing from you, I will assuredly convince you that a man has nothing to fear so much as prejudice, and innocence—once prejudice is afoot—nothing to hope for so much as a fair trial, wherein alone there may be found at last some means to still the calumnies of falsehood for ever. And so I greatly hope that, if I can bring out in detail and in entirety the various points of my case, this court and bench, so far from being, as his enemies imagined, a source of terror and of dread to my client, will prove at last a haven of refuge to the storm-tossed bark of his unhappy fortunes.

And now, though there is much that I might say, **8** before coming to the case itself, about the far-reaching and dangerous consequences of prejudice, I will not keep your expectation in suspense by dwelling longer on the point; but will come to the actual charge, appealing to you at the same time, gentlemen, as I realize I may have to do somewhat frequently, to accord me the hearing which I might expect if this case were now being argued for the first time—as indeed it is—and had not often before been argued but never established. For this day is the first on which any refutation of the actual charge has been possible: before to-day, the whole case has been involved in misconception and prejudice. So while I shortly and clearly reply to an accusation of so many years' standing, I crave a

lucideque respondeo, quaeso, ut me, iudices, sicut facere instituistis, benigne attenteque audiatis.

9 IV. Corrupisse dicitur A. Cluentius iudicium pecunia, quo inimicum innocentem Statium Albium condemnaret. Ostendam, iudices, primum, quoniam caput illius atrocitatis atque invidiae fuit, innocentem pecunia circumventum, neminem umquam maioribus criminibus, gravioribus testibus esse in iudicium vocatum : deinde ea de eo praeiudicia esse facta ab ipsis iudicibus, a quibus condemnatus est, ut non modo ab isdem, sed ne ab aliis quidem ullis absolvi ullo modo posset. Cum haec docuero, tum illud ostendam, quod maxime requiri intellego, iudicium illud pecunia esse temptatum non a Cluentio, sed contra Cluentium, faciamque ut intellegatis in tota illa causa quid res ipsa tulerit, quid error adfinxerit, quid invidia conflarit.

10 Primum igitur illud est, ex quo intellegi possit, debuisse Cluentium magno opere causae confidere, quod certissimis criminibus et testibus fretus ad accusandum descenderit. Hoc loco faciendum mihi, iudices, est, ut vobis breviter illa, quibus Albius est condemnatus, crimina exponam. Abs te peto, Oppianice, ut me invitum de patris tui causa dicere existimes, adductum fide atque officio defensionis. Etenim tibi si in praesentia satis facere non potuero,

boon which you have already begun to grant—that of your kind and careful attention.

IV. Aulus Cluentius is charged with having bribed **9** the court in order to secure the conviction of his enemy, Statius Albius, an innocent man. I shall proceed to show, gentlemen, first—since it was the innocence of this victim of bribery which was chiefly responsible for the virulence of all this prejudice—that no one was ever placed in the dock on graver charges or on weightier evidence : and second, that the same judges who subsequently condemned him, had previously passed verdicts so compromising his case as to make it utterly impossible for them, or indeed for any others, to acquit him. After that, I will proceed to a point, on which I understand you are most anxious for enlightenment, and show that in that trial bribery was indeed attempted, though not in my client's interest but against it. And I shall enable you to judge of the composition of the whole case—how much of it is the contribution of truth, how much the importation of error and how much the concoction of prejudice.

Our first reason for supposing that Cluentius had **10** every right to have confidence in his cause is the fact that, in coming forward with his charge, the grounds of accusation and the evidence on which he relied were equally unassailable. And here I must pause, gentlemen, in order to give you a brief recital of the charges on which Albius was found guilty : you, his son, will, I trust, believe me when I say that I refer to your father's case with reluctance, and only as bound in duty to my client. If indeed I do not satisfy your claims for the moment,

tamen multae mihi ad satis faciendum reliquo tempore facultates dabuntur : Cluentio ni nunc satis fecero, postea mihi satis faciendi potestas non erit. Simul et illud quis est qui dubitare debeat, contra damnatum et mortuum pro incolumi et pro vivo dicere ? cum illi, in quem dicitur, damnatio omne ignominiae periculum iam abstulerit, mors vero etiam doloris : hic autem, pro quo dicimus, nihil possit offensionis accipere sine acerbissimo animi sensu ac molestia et sine summo dedecore vitae et turpitudine.

11 Atque ut intellegatis Cluentium non accusatorio animo, non ostentatione aliqua aut gloria adductum, sed nefariis iniuriis, cotidianis insidiis, proposito ante oculos vitae periculo, nomen Oppianici detulisse, paulo longius exordium rei demonstrandae petam : quod quaeso, iudices, ne moleste patiamini : principiis enim cognitis multo facilius extrema intellegetis.

V. A. Cluentius Habitus fuit, pater huiusce, iudices, homo non solum municipii Larinatis, ex quo erat, sed etiam regionis illius et vicinitatis virtute, existimatione, nobilitate facile princeps. Is cum esset mortuus Sulla et Pompeio consulibus, reliquit hunc annos xv natum, grandem autem et nubilem filiam, quae brevi tempore post patris mortem nupsit A. Aurio Melino, consobrino suo, adulescenti in primis, ut tum habebatur, inter suos et honesto et nobili.

12 Cum essent eae nuptiae plenae dignitatis, plenae con-

I shall still have many subsequent opportunities for making amends: but if I fail now to meet those of my client, it will never again be in my power to do so. And who, moreover, would hesitate in his pleading to sacrifice the tainted memory of a dead felon to the stainless character of a living citizen, especially when the object of such attacks need no longer fear disgrace, for he has been condemned; nor even sorrow, for he is dead; while he whom I defend is one on whom a reverse must bring the keenest sufferings of a sensitive mind, and the gravest personal dishonour and disgrace? In order then that you may under- 11 stand that Cluentius was induced to prosecute Oppianicus by no sort of desire for self-advertisement or self-glorification, by no love of litigation, but by the scandalous outrages, the daily plots, the very manifest peril to which his life was subjected, I request you, gentlemen, not to take it amiss if I open my case at a point in the somewhat distant past; for you will much more easily grasp the ultimate issues in this case if you are aware of its first beginnings.

V. Aulus Cluentius Habitus, gentlemen, father of my client, was a man who, in character, reputation, and nobility of birth was far the most eminent man, not only in the township of Larinum to which he belonged, but in that whole district and neighbourhood. He died in the consulship of Sulla and Pompeius,[a] leaving a son, my client, who was fifteen years old, and a grown-up and marriageable daughter who, shortly after her father's death, became the wife of Aulus Aurius Melinus, her mother's nephew, a young man at that time eminent among his fellows for high character and position. This marriage, highly honourable as it was, and 12

cordiae, repente est exorta mulieris importunae
nefaria libido non solum dedecore, verum etiam
scelere coniuncta. Nam Sassia, mater huius Habiti
—mater enim a me in omni causa, tametsi in hunc
hostili odio et crudelitate est, mater, inquam, appellabitur, neque umquam illa ita de suo scelere et im-
manitate audiet, ut naturae nomen amittat: quo
enim est ipsum nomen amantius indulgentiusque
maternum, hoc illius matris, quae multos iam annos
et nunc cum maxime filium interfectum cupit,
singulare scelus maiore odio dignum esse ducetis—ea
igitur mater Habiti, Melini illius adulescentis, generi
sui, contra quam fas erat, amore capta, primo, neque
id ipsum diu, quoquo modo poterat, in illa cupiditate
se continebat: deinde ita flagrare coepit amentia,
sic inflammata ferri libidine, ut eam non pudor, non
pudicitia, non pietas, non macula familiae, non
hominum fama, non filii dolor, non filiae maeror a
13 cupiditate revocaret. Animum adulescentis, nondum consilio ac ratione firmatum, pellexit eis omnibus
rebus, quibus illa aetas capi ac deliniri potest. Filia,
quae non solum illo communi dolore muliebri in eius
modi viri iniuriis angeretur, sed nefarium matris
pelicatum ferre non posset, de quo ne queri quidem
se sine scelere posse arbitraretur, ceteros sui tanti
mali ignaros esse cupiebat: in huius amantissimi sui

attended by all goodwill, suddenly aroused the outrageous passion of an unnatural woman, involving not only dishonour, but crime. For Sassia, mother of my client Habitus—yes, as a mother I must refer to her throughout this case—his mother, I say, although she behaves towards him with the hatred and the cruelty of an enemy : nor shall the recital of her monstrous crimes ever deprive her of the name which nature has bestowed upon her ; for the more of love and tenderness the very name of mother suggests, the greater will be the detestation which you will hold to befit this, the unheard of outrage of that mother who, at this very moment, as for many years past, is longing for the destruction of her son —she, then, Habitus's mother, conceived an unholy passion for the young Melinus, her son-in-law. At first, but even so not for long, she contrived somehow to restrain her passion : but soon there arose in her so fiery a madness, such transports of inflammatory lust, that her passion was undeterred by considerations of honour, of modesty or of natural feeling ; of family disgrace, or public scandal ; of a son's indignation, or a daughter's tears. The young husband's heart, which lacked as yet the strengthening influence of wisdom and understanding, she seduced with those arts by which a man of his age can be snared and captivated. Her daughter, besides being tortured by the resentment which any woman would feel at so foul a wrong on the part of her husband, being unable to endure the monstrous sight of her mother as her husband's mistress— whereof she thought it would be sinful of her even to complain—desired that no one else should know of her trouble ; and was gradually losing her youth

fratris manibus et gremio maerore et lacrimis con-
senescebat.

14 Ecce autem subitum divortium, quod solacium ma-
lorum omnium fore videbatur. Discedit a Melino
Cluentia, ut in tantis iniuriis non invita, ut a viro
non libenter. Tum vero illa egregia et praeclara
mater palam exsultare laetitia, triumphare gaudio
coepit, victrix filiae, non libidinis : diutius suspicio-
nibus obscuris laedi famam suam noluit : lectum illum
genialem, quem biennio ante filiae suae nubenti
straverat, in eadem domo sibi ornari et sterni ex-
pulsa atque exturbata filia iubet. Nubit genero
socrus, nullis auspicibus, nullis auctoribus, funestis
ominibus omnium.

15 VI. O mulieris scelus incredibile et praeter hanc
unam in omni vita inauditum ! o libidinem effrena-
tam et indomitam ! o audaciam singularem ! nonne
timuisse, si minus vim deorum hominumque famam,
at illam ipsam noctem facesque illas nuptiales ? non
limen cubiculi ? non cubile filiae ? non parietes denique ipsos, superiorum testes nuptiarum ? Perfregit
ac prostravit omnia cupiditate ac furore : vicit pudorem libido, timorem audacia, rationem amentia.

16 Tulit hoc commune dedecus familiae, cognationis,
nominis graviter filius : augebatur autem eius
molestia cotidianis querimoniis et adsiduo fletu

ª The references are to the Roman marriage customs,
which included the conveying of the bride at night by a
torch-light procession from her old to her new home, over the
threshold of which she was lifted (to avoid her stumbling over
or even touching it, which was considered unlucky).

as she wept and lamented, clasped in the arms of my client, her most devoted brother.

But lo! a sudden divorce seems likely to put an 14 end to all her troubles. Cluentia leaves Melinus, neither sorry to do so, considering what she had suffered, nor yet glad, considering that he was her husband. Then does this exemplary, this illustrious mother make open display of her delight, revelling and rejoicing in her triumph not over her lust but over her daughter. She is reluctant that her fair fame should any longer be damaged by dim and doubtful suspicion; she gives orders that the very marriage-bed which two years before she had made ready for her daughter should be adorned and made ready for her, in the self-same house from which her daughter has been driven and hounded out. And so mother-in-law marries son-in-law, with none to bless, none to sanction the union, and amid nought but general foreboding.

VI. Oh! to think of the woman's sin, unbeliev- 15 able, unheard of in all experience save for this single instance! To think of her wicked passion, unbridled, untamed! To think that she did not quail, if not before the vengeance of Heaven, or the scandal among men, at least before the night itself with its wedding torches, the threshold of the bridal chamber, her daughter's bridal bed, or even the walls themselves which had witnessed that other union.[a] The madness of passion broke through and laid low every obstacle: lust triumphed over modesty, wantonness over scruple, madness over sense. Hard indeed was 16 it for her son to bear this disgrace, affecting equally his family, his kindred, and his name; and to add to his trouble, there were his sister's daily complaints,

sororis : statuit tamen nihil sibi in tantis iniuriis ac
tanto scelere matris gravius esse faciendum, quam
ut illa matre ne uteretur, ne quae videre sine summo
animi dolore non poterat, ea, si matre uteretur, non
solum videre, verum etiam probare suo iudicio
putaretur.

17 Initium quod huic cum matre fuerit simultatis
audistis. Pertinuisse hoc ad causam tum, cum
reliqua cognoveritis, intellegetis. Nam illud me non
praeterit, cuiuscumque modi sit mater, tamen in
iudicio filii de turpitudine parentis dici vix oportere.
Non essem ad ullam causam idoneus, iudices, si hoc,
quod in communibus hominum sensibus atque in ipsa
natura positum atque infixum est, id ego, qui ad
hominum pericula defendenda adiungerer, non
viderem. Facile intellego non modo reticere homines
parentum iniurias, sed etiam animo aequo ferre
oportere. Sed ego ea, quae ferri possunt, ferenda,
quae taceri, tacenda esse arbitror.

18 Nihil in vita vidit calamitatis A. Cluentius, nullum
periculum mortis adiit, nihil mali timuit, quod non
totum a matre esset conflatum et profectum. Quae
hoc tempore sileret omnia, atque ea, si oblivione non
posset, tamen taciturnitate sua tecta esse pateretur :
sed vero sic agitur, ut prorsus reticeri nullo modo
possit. Hoc enim ipsum iudicium, hoc periculum, illa
accusatio, omnis testium copia, quae futura est, a

her ceaseless tears. However, he came to the conclusion that despite such outrageous and criminal
conduct on Sassia's part, he ought to take no stronger
steps than merely to refrain from all intercourse with
such a mother; lest the very things he could not
look upon without anguish he might be thought,
if he maintained such intercourse, not merely **to**
look upon but even to stamp with his approval.

The origin of the enmity between my client and 17
his mother, you have now heard : how closely it
bears upon the case you will understand when you
have ascertained what follows. For I am not unaware
that, whatever character his mother bears, it is
hardly becoming at the trial of a son to mention the
depravity of his parent. I should be unfit to undertake any case, gentlemen, if I, who am retained to
defend those imperilled by prosecution, were blind
to a principle deeply rooted in the common instincts
of humanity, and in the very laws of human nature.
I fully realize that a man is bound, not only to suppress all mention of a parent's offence, but even to
endure it with resignation : but I still hold that the
silent endurance of such offences is due, only where
either silence or endurance is possible.

In all my client's life he has had nought of disaster 18
to face, no peril of death to meet, no evil to fear,
save such as have been entirely due to the contrivance and direction of his mother. Not one of these
would he now be mentioning—rather would he allow
them to be covered by the veil of silence if not of
oblivion : but the issues are indeed such that silence
is an absolute impossibility. Why, this very trial,
my client's present jeopardy, the charge brought
against him, all the crowd of witnesses presently to

239

matre initio est adornata, a matre hoc tempore in-
struitur atque omnibus eius opibus et copiis comparatur. Ipsa denique nuper Larino huius op-
primendi causa Romam advolavit : praesto est mulier
audax, pecuniosa, crudelis : instituit accusatores,
instruit testes, squalore huius et sordibus laetatur,
exitium exoptat, sanguinem suum profundere omnem
cupit, dum modo profusum huius ante videat. Haec
nisi omnia perspexeritis in causa, temere a nobis illam
appellari putatote : sin erunt et aperta et nefaria,
Cluentio ignoscere debebitis, quod haec a me dici
patiatur : mihi ignoscere non deberetis, si tacerem.

19   VII. Nunc iam summatim exponam quibus criminibus Oppianicus damnatus sit, ut et constantiam A.
Cluenti et rationem accusationis perspicere possitis.
Ac primum causa accusandi quae fuerit ostendam,
ut id ipsum A. Cluentium vi ac necessitate coactum
20 fecisse videatis. Cum manifesto venenum depre-
hendisset, quod vir matris Oppianicus ei paravisset,
et res non coniectura, sed oculis ac manibus teneretur,
neque in causa ulla dubitatio posset esse, accusavit
Oppianicum : quam constanter et quam diligenter
postea dicam : nunc hoc scire vos volui, nullam huic
aliam accusandi causam fuisse, nisi uti propositum

ᵃ A customary device for exciting the compassion of the
court.

appear, were originally worked up by his mother,
and are by his mother at this moment being organized and equipped with all the wealth and resources
at her command. Only lately she herself has come
flying from Larinum to Rome to compass the ruin
of her son. And here she is—this woman, with her
effrontery, her money, and her cruel heart; she
organizes the prosecution and marshals the evidence;
she takes delight in the squalid, mourning garb of the
defendant; [a] she longs for his destruction; she is
eager to shed every drop of her blood if only she may
first see his poured out. If the course of the trial
does not clearly reveal to you all these facts, then
believe that I am but wantonly introducing her name
into it : but if they stand revealed in all their horror
you will be bound to forgive Cluentius for allowing
me to say such things : me you would be bound not
to forgive if I failed to say them.

VII. At this point I will briefly set forth the 19
charges on which Oppianicus was found guilty, in
order that you may realize the resolute attitude of
Aulus Cluentius and the motive of the prosecution :
and first I will show what was my client's reason for
prosecuting, that you may see that it was sheer
necessity which compelled him to such action. It 20
was the actual detection of the poison which his stepfather Oppianicus had prepared for him—when the
matter was not one of inference but of visible and
palpable proof, and there was no possible room for
doubt—which induced him to prosecute Oppianicus.
How resolutely and how carefully he conducted that
prosecution I shall record later : at the moment I
want you to realize that my client's one and only
motive for prosecution was his desire to escape by

vitae periculum et cotidianas capitis insidias hac una
ratione evitaret. Atque ut intellegatis eis accusatum
esse criminibus Oppianicum, ut neque accusator
timere neque reus sperare potuerit, pauca vobis
illius iudicii crimina exponam : quibus cognitis nemo
vestrum mirabitur illum diffidentem rebus suis ad
Staienum atque ad pecuniam confugisse.

21 Larinas quaedam fuit Dinaea, socrus Oppianici,
quae filios habuit M. et N. Aurios et Cn. Magium
et filiam Magiam, nuptam Oppianico. M. Aurius
adulescentulus bello Italico captus apud Asculum in
Q. Sergi senatoris, eius qui inter sicarios damnatus
est, manus incidit et apud eum in ergastulo fuit.
Numerius autem Aurius frater eius mortuus est here-
demque Cn. Magium fratrem reliquit. Postea Magia
uxor Oppianici mortua est : postremo, unus qui
reliquus erat Dinaeae filius, Cn. Magius est mortuus.
Is heredem fecit illum adulescentem Oppianicum
sororis suae filium eumque partiri cum Dinaea matre
iussit. Interim venit index ad Dinaeam neque
obscurus neque incertus, qui nuntiaret ei filium eius,
M. Aurium, vivere et in agro Gallico esse in servitute.

22 Mulier amissis liberis cum unius reciperandi filii spes
esset ostentata, omnes suos propinquos filiique sui
necessarios convocavit et ab eis flens petivit, ut
negotium susciperent, adulescentem investigarent,
sibi restituerent eum filium, quem tamen unum ex

---

[a] 91–88 B.C.: called the " Italian war," because fought
between those possessing Roman citizenship and the other
inhabitants of Italy who were excluded from it.
[b] A strip of land extending along the coast of the Adriatic
between Ariminum and Ancona.

this, the only means, from the peril that beset his life, the daily intrigues against his very existence. And in order that you may understand that the charges brought against Oppianicus were of a nature to leave the prosecutor no room to fear, nor the defendant to hope, I will set forth a few of the charges brought at that trial. When you have heard them, none of you will be surprised that the defendant's mistrust of his prospects drove him to take refuge in Staienus and in bribery.

There was a lady of Larinum called Dinea, mother-in-law of Oppianicus, who had three sons, Marcus and Numerius Aurius and Gnaeus Magius, and a daughter Magia, married to Oppianicus. Marcus Aurius, as quite a young man, had been captured at Asculum during the Social War,[a] and fell into the hands of Q. Sergius the senator—the same who was tried and condemned in the Assassination Court—and was in his slave-prison. N. Aurius, his brother, died, leaving his property to his brother Gn. Magius. After that, Oppianicus's wife, Magia, died; and last of all Gn. Magius, Dinea's sole surviving son, died also. He left his property to young Oppianicus here, his sister's son, with instructions that he should share it with the testator's mother, Dinea. Meanwhile a reputable and positive informant came to Dinea with the news that her son, M. Aurius, was alive, and was a slave in the Ager Gallicus.[b] When this lady, who had lost all her children, was offered the hope of recovering one of her sons, she called together all her relations and her son's friends and begged them with tears to take the matter up, seek out the young man, and restore to her the only one of all her sons whom Fortune had consented to

multis fortuna reliquum esse voluisset. Haec cum
agere instituisset, oppressa morbo est. Itaque testamentum fecit eius modi, ut illi filio HS cccc milia
legaret, heredem institueret eundem illum Oppianicum, nepotem suum. Atque his diebus paucis est
mortua. Propinqui tamen illi, quem ad modum viva
Dinaea instituerant, ita mortua illa ad investigandum
M. Aurium cum eodem illo indice in agrum Gallicum
profecti sunt.

23 VIII. Interim Oppianicus, ut erat, sicuti ex multis
rebus reperietis, singulari scelere et audacia, per
quendam Gallicanum, familiarem suum, primum illum
indicem pecunia corrupit : deinde ipsum M. Aurium
non magna iactura facta tollendum interficiendum-
que curavit. Illi autem, qui erant ad propinquum
investigandum et reciperandum profecti, litteras
Larinum ad Aurios illius adulescentis suosque necessarios mittunt, sibi difficilem esse investigandi rationem, quod intellegerent indicem ab Oppianico esse
corruptum. Quas litteras A. Aurius, vir fortis et
experiens et domi nobilis et M. illius Auri perpro-
pinquus, in foro, palam, multis audientibus, cum
adesset Oppianicus, recitat et clarissima voce se
nomen Oppianici, si interfectum M. Aurium esse
24 comperisset, delaturum esse testatur. Interim brevi
tempore illi, qui erant in agrum Gallicum profecti,
Larinum revertuntur : interfectum esse M. Aurium
renuntiant. Animi non solum propinquorum, sed
etiam omnium Larinatium odio Oppianici et illius
adulescentis misericordia commoventur. Itaque cum
Aurius, is qui antea denuntiarat, clamore hominem

---

^a About £4000.
^b See the Introduction, " Family of Dinea," footnote.

leave her. No sooner had the quest started, than she fell ill; accordingly she made her will, leaving 400,000 sesterces [a] to this son of hers, but making her grandson, Oppianicus the younger, the heir-in-chief. A few days after that, she died. But her relations, now that Dinea was dead, following the resolve they had made when she was alive, started for the Ager Gallicus with the original informant to seek out M. Aurius.

VIII. Oppianicus meanwhile, with that un- 23 paralleled wickedness and effrontery of his of which you will have so many instances, first bribed the informant by the help of a friend of his who was a native of the Ager Gallicus; and next succeeded, with the expenditure of a small sum, in getting M. Aurius himself removed and murdered. Those who had started out to seek for and to recover their kinsman, wrote to the Aurii at Larinum, their own and Aulus's relations, saying that they were finding the quest difficult, because the informant had to their knowledge been bribed by Oppianicus. One Aulus Aurius,[b] a man of courage, enterprise, and noble birth and a near relation of the missing man, read out this letter in the Forum before a large audience in the presence of Oppianicus, saying in a loud voice that he would prosecute Oppianicus if he found that Marcus Aurius had been murdered. Meanwhile whose who had started out to the Ager 24 Gallicus soon returned with the news that M. Aurius had been murdered, and not only his relations but all Larinum was inflamed with hatred of Oppianicus and pity for the murdered youth. And so when the Aurius who had previously given notice of his intention to prosecute, began to inveigh against him

ac minis insequi coepisset, Larino profugit et se in
25 castra clarissimi viri, Q. Metelli, contulit.   Post illam
autem fugam et sceleris et conscientiae testem numquam se iudiciis, numquam legibus, numquam iner-
mum inimicis committere ausus est, sed per illam L.
Sullae vim atque victoriam Larinum in summo timore
omnium cum armatis advolavit : quattuorviros, quos
municipes fecerant, sustulit : se a Sulla et tres praeterea factos esse dixit et ab eodem sibi esse impera-
tum, ut Aurium illum, qui sibi delationem nominis et
capitis periculum ostentarat, et alterum Aurium et
eius L. filium et Sex. Vibium, quo sequestre in illo
indice corrumpendo dicebatur esse usus, proscribendos interficiendosque curaret.   Itaque illis crudelissime interfectis non mediocri ab eo ceteri proscriptionis et mortis metu tenebantur.   His rebus
in causa iudicioque patefactis quis est qui illum
absolvi potuisse arbitretur ?

   IX. Atque haec parva sunt : cognoscite reliqua,
ut non aliquando condemnatum esse Oppianicum,
sed aliquam diu incolumem fuisse miremini.
26   Primum videte hominis audaciam.   Sassiam in
matrimonium ducere, Habiti matrem, illam, cuius
virum A. Aurium occiderat, concupivit.   Utrum impudentior hic, qui postulet, an crudelior illa, si nubat,
difficile dictu est : sed tamen utriusque humanitatem

       ᵃ The chief magistrates of a provincial town.

with loud threats, he fled from Larinum and took refuge in the camp of the distinguished general Quintus Metellus. Never after this flight, which 25 bore witness alike to his guilt and to his guilty conscience, did he expose himself to the judgement of the law, or, unless he was armed, of his enemies : but taking advantage of the victory of violence under Sulla, he swooped down upon Larinum with an armed following to the utmost consternation of everybody. The Council of Four,[a] appointed by the townsfolk, he deposed, and announced that he and three others had been appointed by Sulla, who had also given him orders to secure the proscription and execution of the Aurius who had threatened to denounce him on a capital charge, together with a second Aurius, his son Lucius, and Sextus Vibius, whom he was alleged to have used as a go-between in bribing the informant. Accordingly they were put to a cruel death, leaving the rest of the townsfolk in no small dread of proscription and death at his hands. Who could imagine that, after the exposure of these facts to the court in the course of his trial, there was any possibility of his acquittal ?

IX. Yet these are mere trifles : hear the rest, and you will be surprised not that Oppianicus was at length convicted, but that he should have remained for any length of time a free man.

Behold first the insolence of the fellow ! He 26 conceived the desire of marrying Sassia, Habitus's mother, her whose husband, Aulus Aurius, he had murdered. Whether his effrontery was the greater in proposing to her, or her heartlessness should she accept him, it is difficult to say : but let me, none the less, describe to you the delicacy and resolution

27 constantiamque cognoscite. Petit Oppianicus, ut sibi Sassia nubat, et id magno opere contendit. Illa autem non admiratur audaciam, non impudentiam aspernatur, non denique illam Oppianici domum viri sui sanguine redundantem reformidat, sed quod haberet ille tres filios, idcirco se ab eis nuptiis abhorrere respondit. Oppianicus, qui pecuniam Sassiae concupivisset, domo sibi quaerendum remedium existimavit ad eam moram, quae nuptiis adferebatur. Nam cum haberet ex Novia infantem filium, alter autem eius filius, Papia natus, Teani Apuli, quod abest a Larino xviii milia passuum, apud matrem educaretur, arcessit subito sine causa puerum Teano : quod facere nisi ludis aut festis diebus antea non solebat. Mater misera nihil mali suspicans mittit. Ille se Tarentum proficisci cum simulasset, eo ipso die puer, hora undecima cum valens in publico visus esset, ante noctem mortuus et postridie ante quam 28 luceret combustus est. Atque hunc tantum maerorem matri prius hominum rumor quam quisquam ex Oppianici familia nuntiavit. Illa cum uno tempore audisset sibi non solum filium, sed etiam exsequiarum munus ereptum, Larinum confestim exanimata venit et ibi de integro funus iam sepulto filio fecit. Dies nondum decem intercesserant, cum ille alter filius infans necatur. Itaque nubit Oppianico continuo Sassia, laetanti iam animo et spe optime confirmata.

---

a He had actually a third son, the younger Oppianicus. See the Introduction, " Family of Oppianicus."
b *i.e.* one hour before sunset.

of them both! Oppianicus asked Sassia to marry 27
him, and pressed his suit : but she, without feeling
surprise at his insolence, or contempt for his effrontery, or even repulsion at the thought of his house,
which reeked with the blood of her husband, gave
as her reason for shrinking from such a marriage
the fact that he had three sons. Oppianicus, who
had conceived a desire for Sassia's wealth, thought
he need not look outside his own house to find a way
of surmounting this impediment to his marriage.
He had with him his infant son by Novia, but his
other son,ᵃ by Papia, was being brought up under
his mother's care at Teanum in Apulia, which is
18 miles from Larinum. Without giving any
reason, he suddenly sent for this boy from Teanum,
an unusual thing for him to do except at the games
or other occasions of holiday. His poor mother sent
him without a suspicion of harm ; and that same day
—Oppianicus having started on a pretended journey
to Tarentum—the boy, who had been seen in
perfect health at the eleventh hour,ᵇ was dead before
nightfall, and was placed on the pyre next day before
the light could dawn. And the first news of this 28
terrible bereavement was conveyed to his mother
by common gossip earlier than by anyone of Oppianicus's household. She, on hearing at one and the same
moment that she had lost both her son and her part
in his funeral, came instantly to Larinum dazed with
grief, and there celebrated his funeral afresh, though
he was already in the grave. Not ten days had
passed before his other son, the infant, was murdered. And so, without waiting, Sassia married
Oppianicus in high spirits and with the realization
of all her hopes : small wonder, when she saw her-

Nec mirum, quae se non nuptialibus donis, sed filiorum funeribus esse delinitam videret. Ita quod ceteri propter liberos pecuniae cupidiores solent esse, ille propter pecuniam liberos amittere iucundum esse duxit.

29 X. Sentio, iudices, vos pro vestra humanitate his tantis sceleribus breviter a me demonstratis vehementer esse commotos. Quo tandem igitur animo fuisse illos arbitramini, quibus his de rebus non modo audiendum fuit, verum etiam iudicandum ? Vos auditis de eo, in quem iudices non estis, de eo, quem non videtis, de eo, quem odisse iam non potestis, de eo, qui et naturae et legibus satis fecit, quem leges exsilio, natura morte multavit : auditis non ab inimico, auditis sine testibus, auditis, cum ea, quae copiosissime dici possunt, breviter a me strictimque dicuntur. Illi audiebant de eo, de quo iurati sententias ferre debebant, de eo, cuius praesentis nefarium et consceleratum voltum intuebantur, de eo, quem omnes oderant propter audaciam, de eo, quem omni supplicio dignum esse ducebant : audiebant ab accusatoribus, audiebant verba multorum testium, audiebant, cum una quaque de re a P. Cannutio, homine eloquentissimo, graviter et diu diceretur.

30 Et est quisquam qui cum haec cognoverit, suspicari possit Oppianicum iudicio oppressum et circumventum esse innocentem ?

Acervatim iam reliqua, iudices, dicam, ut ad ea, quae propiora huiusce causae et adiunctiora sunt, per-

self wooed, not by the wedding gifts of her betrothed, but by the murder of his children! And Oppianicus, on his part, far from coveting money for his children's sake, as most men do, found a pleasure in sacrificing his children for the sake of money.

X. I realize, gentlemen, that your human hearts 29 are wrung by this, my brief recital of his foul crimes. What then do you suppose their feelings were who had not only to listen to such a story, but to pass judgement on it? You are hearing the story of a man whom you are not set to judge, whom your eyes do not behold, who is beyond the reach of your hatred; who has paid his debt to nature and to the law, and has been punished, by the law with exile, by nature with death. You are hearing that story not from the lips of his enemy or on the evidence of witnesses; you are hearing my short and compendious version of events which might be narrated at length. But his judges were hearing the story of a man on whom they were bound by oath to give their verdict, a man whose wicked and guilt-stained countenance they beheld as he stood before them, a man whose effrontery commanded universal hatred and the universal opinion that he was worthy of the severest penalties: they were hearing it as told by his accusers, as supported by the testimony of many witnesses; they were hearing the grave and lengthy recital of each several point by the eloquence of P. Cannutius. Is there anyone who, with such facts 30 before him, could possibly imagine Oppianicus to be the innocent victim of judicial corruption?

Now, gentlemen, I will give you a general review of what remains to be told, bringing my narrative to those events which belong more properly to my

veniam: vos, quaeso, memoria teneatis non mihi hoc
esse propositum, ut accusem Oppianicum mortuum,
sed cum hoc persuadere vobis velim, iudicium ab
hoc non esse corruptum, hoc uti initio ac fundamento
defensionis, Oppianicum hominem sceleratissimum
et nocentissimum esse damnatum. Qui uxori suae
Cluentiae, quae amita huius Habiti fuit, cum ipse
poculum dedisset, subito illa in media potione ex-
clamavit se maximo cum dolore emori: nec diutius
vixit quam locuta est: nam in ipso sermone hoc et
vociferatione mortua est. Et ad hanc mortem re-
pentinam vocesque morientis omnia praeterea, quae
solent esse indicia et vestigia veneni, in illius mortuae
corpore fuerunt. Eodemque veneno C. Oppianicum
fratrem necavit.

31   XI. Neque est hoc satis: tametsi in ipso fraterno
parricidio nullum scelus praetermissum videtur,
tamen, ut ad hoc nefarium facinus accederet, aditum
sibi aliis sceleribus ante munivit. Nam cum esset
gravida Auria, fratris uxor, et iam appropinquare
partus putaretur, mulierem veneno interfecit, ut una
illud, quod erat ex fratre conceptum, necaretur. Post
fratrem adgressus est: qui sero iam exhausto illo
poculo mortis cum et de suo et de uxoris interitu
clamaret testamentumque mutare cuperet, in ipsa
significatione huius voluntatis est mortuus. Ita
mulierem, ne partu eius ab hereditate fraterna ex-
cluderetur, necavit: fratris autem liberos prius vita
privavit quam illi hanc a natura lucem accipere potuerunt: ut omnes intellegerent nihil ei clausum, nihil
sanctum esse posse, a cuius audacia fratris liberos ne
materni quidem corporis custodiae tegere potuissent.

client's case. Pray bear in mind that though it is not
my task to accuse the dead Oppianicus, none the
less, in my attempt to persuade you that my client
did not bribe the court, I primarily base my defence
on the fact that Oppianicus whom it condemned was
a thorough-paced and guilty scoundrel. Why, when
Oppianicus with his own hands had given a cup to
his wife, Cluentia, my client Habitus's aunt, suddenly
in the act of drinking she cried out that she was
dying in dreadful pain : she lived no longer than she
took to speak and died with the cry on her lips.
Besides the suddenness of her death and her dying
utterance, all the usual indications and traces of
poison were afterwards found on her body. And he
used poison, too, to murder his brother, G. Oppianicus.

XI. But neither was he satisfied with that : 31
although in the murder of a brother by itself every
form of guilt is comprehended, yet he previously prepared his means of approach to this monstrous deed
by yet other crimes. His brother's wife Auria was
pregnant, and was thought to be approaching her
delivery ; therefore he poisoned her in order that
his brother's seed might perish with her. He next
turned his attention to his brother who, too late,
the cup of death already drained, when crying out
upon his own death and his wife's, and wanting to
alter his will, died in the very act of expressing his
intentions. The wife, then, he murdered, to prevent
her bearing a child who would bar his inheritance of
his brother's property, and robbed the offspring of
life before they could receive nature's gift, the light
of day ; thereby making it known to all that nothing
was barred, nothing sacred to a man from whose
ruthlessness not even the protection of their mother's

32 Memoria teneo Milesiam quandam mulierem, cum essem in Asia, quod ab heredibus secundis accepta pecunia partum sibi ipsa medicamentis abegisset, rei capitalis esse damnatam : nec iniuria, quae spem parentis, memoriam nominis, subsidium generis, heredem familiae, designatum rei publicae civem sustulisset. Quanto est Oppianicus in eadem iniuria maiore supplicio dignus ! si quidem illa, cum suo corpori vim attulisset, se ipsa cruciavit, hic autem idem illud effecit per alieni corporis mortem atque cruciatum. Ceteri non videntur in singulis hominibus multa parricidia suscipere posse, Oppianicus inventus est qui in uno corpore plures necaret.

33 XII. Itaque, cum hanc eius consuetudinem audaciamque cognosset avunculus illius adulescentis Oppianici, Cn. Magius, isque, cum gravi morbo adfectus esset, heredem illum sororis suae filium faceret, adhibitis amicis, praesente matre sua, Dinaea, uxorem suam interrogavit, essetne praegnans. Quae cum se esse respondisset, ab ea petivit, ut se mortuo apud Dinaeam, quae tum ei mulieri socrus erat, quoad pareret, habitaret diligentiamque adhiberet, ut id, quod conceperat, servare et salvum parere posset. Itaque ei testamento legat grandem pecuniam a filio, si qui natus erit : ab secundo herede nihil legat.

34 Quid de Oppianico suspicatus sit videtis : quid iudicarit obscurum non est. Nam cuius filium faceret heredem, eum tutorem liberis non adscripsit. Quid Oppianicus fecerit cognoscite, ut illum Magium in-

---

^a See pp. 214, 215.
^b *i.e.* if she had a son the son would be "heir" and she would receive a large legacy. If she had no son, someone else would be "heir" and she would get nothing. See note ^a on § 13 of the *Pro Caecina*.

womb could save his brother's children. I remember 32
a case which occurred when I was in Asia : how a
certain woman of Miletus, who had accepted a bribe
from the alternative heirs and procured her own abortion by drugs, was condemned to death : and rightly,
for she had cheated the father of his hopes, his name
of continuity, his family of its support, his house of
an heir, and the Republic of a citizen-to-be. How
much more severely did the same crime deserve to
be punished in Oppianicus ; for she in doing
violence to her body brought pain upon herself, but
he produced the same result as she by the painful
death of another. Most men seem unequal to the
task of murdering a succession of victims one at a
time : Oppianicus came as a discovery—the murderer,
in a single victim, of more than one person.

XII. Now young Oppianicus's uncle, Gn. Magius, 33
had come to realize his habitual ruthlessness ; and
so, on the approach of a dangerous illness, when
making his sister's son, young Oppianicus here, his
heir, he called together his friends and asked his
wife, in the presence of his mother, Dinea, whether
she was expecting a child, and on her replying that
she was, he asked her to reside after his death with
Dinea, who was then her mother-in-law,[a] until her
confinement ; and to take every care that the child
she had conceived should come safely to the birth.
And then by his will he left her a large sum as a
charge on his son's expectation, should a son be born
to him, but nothing at all in the event of alternative
inheritance.[b] You see his suspicions of Oppianicus : 34
his estimate of the man is no less obvious ; for he
did not appoint the father of his heir trustee to his
own children. See now what Oppianicus did, and

tellegatis non longe animo prospexisse morientem.
Quae pecunia mulieri legata erat a filio, si qui natus
erit, eam praesentem Oppianicus non debitam mulieri
solvit, si haec solutio legatorum et non merces abor-
tionis appellanda est.   Quo illa pretio accepto multisque praeterea muneribus, quae tum ex tabulis Oppianici recitabantur, spem illam, quam in alvo com-
mendatam a viro continebat, victa avaritia sceleri
35 Oppianici vendidit.   Nihil posse iam ad hanc improbitatem addi videtur : attendite exitum.   Quae
mulier obtestatione viri decem illis mensibus ne
domum quidem ullam nisi socrus suae nosse debuit,
haec quinto mense post viri mortem ipsi Oppianico
nupsit.   Quae nuptiae non diuturnae fuerunt.   Erant
enim non matrimonii dignitate, sed sceleris societate
coniunctae.

36   XIII. Quid? illa caedes Asuvi Larinatis adulescentis pecuniosi, quam clara tum recenti re fuit,
quam omnium sermone celebrata !   Fuit Avillius
quidam Larino perdita nequitia et summa egestate,
arte quadam praeditus ad libidines adulescentulorum
excitandas accommodata, qui ut se blanditiis et
adsentationibus in Asuvi consuetudinem penitus
immersit, Oppianicus continuo sperare coepit, hoc se
Avillio tamquam aliqua machina admota capere
Asuvi adulescentiam et fortunas eius patrias expug-
nare posse.   Ratio excogitata Larini est, res translata

---

[a] That is to say, ten lunar months, which, according to
the unrevised Roman calendar, were regarded as the regular
period of gestation, and also as the proper time of a widow's
mourning for her husband.

you will realize that Magius's foresight on his death-
bed did not extend far enough into the future. The
legacy of money which had been made to the woman
as a charge on her son in the event of his birth,
Oppianicus discharged to her in ready money though
it was not due—if indeed such a transaction can be
called the discharge of her legacy and not the price
of her abortion. She took this fee—as well as many
other presents which at his trial were quoted from
his accounts—and, yielding to avarice, sold to the
abandoned Oppianicus the promise of her womb,
the special object of her husband's trust. You 35
would think that nothing could surpass such wickedness ; but wait to hear the end : the woman whose
duty it was, as her husband had conjured her, not
to venture inside any home but her mother-in-law's
for the next ten months,[a] married Oppianicus within
five months after her husband's death ! Their
union was not of long duration, for the bond between
them was not the holy estate of matrimony, but
companionship in crime.

XIII. Again, take the murder of Asuvius, the 36
wealthy young man of Larinum. How notorious it
was at the actual time when it occurred, and how
widely discussed ! There was at Larinum a certain
Avillius, a profligate and penurious rogue, who had
a talent of a kind for playing upon the weaknesses of
his youthful dupes. By flattery and obsequious
attentions he succeeded in worming himself into the
confidence of Asuvius ; and Oppianicus now began
to hope that he might use this Avillius as a weapon
of assault against Asuvius, and through him lay
successful siege to the young man and carry his
ancestral fortunes by storm. Larinum saw the con-

Romam. Iniri enim consilium facilius in solitudine, perficere rem eius modi commodius in turba posse arbitrati sunt. Asuvius cum Avillio Romam est profectus : hos vestigiis Oppianicus consecutus est. Iam ut Romae vixerint, quibus conviviis, quibus flagitiis, quantis et quam profusis sumptibus, non modo conscio, sed etiam conviva et adiutore Oppianico, longum est dicere mihi, praesertim ad alia properanti. Exitum huius adsimulatae familiaritatis cognoscite.

37 Cum esset adulescens apud mulierculam quandam atque, ubi pernoctaret, ibi diem posterum commoraretur, Avillius, ut erat constitutum, simulat se aegrotare et testamentum facere velle. Oppianicus obsignatores ad eum, qui neque Asuvium neque Avillium nossent, adducit et illum Asuvium appellat ipse. Testamento Asuvi nomine obsignato disceditur. Avillius ilico convalescit. Asuvius autem brevi illo tempore, quasi in hortulos iret, in harenarias quasdam extra portam Esquilinam perductus occiditur.

38 Qui cum unum iam et alterum diem desideraretur neque in his locis, ubi ex consuetudine quaerebatur, inveniretur, et Oppianicus in foro Larinatium dictitaret nuper se et suos amicos testamentum eius obsignasse, liberti Asuvi et non nulli amici, quod eo die, quo postremum Asuvius visus erat, Avillium cum

---

[a] The word *hortus* or its diminutive is regularly used to express a public pleasure-garden.

trivance of the scheme ; the scene was transferred to Rome ; for they thought that solitude was preferable for the hatching of the plot, whereas the crowded city lent itself better to the accomplishment of such a deed. Asuvius and Avillius started for Rome together ; Oppianicus followed closely in their footsteps. Their ensuing life in Rome—with all its banquetings, its wantonness, all its extravagant profligacy, not merely known but personally shared and abetted by Oppianicus—it would be tedious to relate, especially as I am anxious to pass on to other topics : but let me tell you how this false friendship ended.

While the young man was at the house of some 37 mistress, and stayed on for the following day where he was spending the night, Avillius, as had been decided, pretended that he was ill and wanted to make his will. As witnesses to seal this will, Oppianicus introduced to him persons calculated to know neither Asuvius nor Avillius, himself addressing Avillius by Asuvius's name. The will was signed and sealed as if it were that of Asuvius, and the witnesses went away. Avillius got better on the spot. A short time after that, Asuvius was taken for a walk, seemingly to the Gardens,[a] but actually further on to some sand-pits outside the Esquiline gate, and was there murdered. He had been missing for a 38 day or two and could not be found in any of the resorts where his habits led people to look for him, and Oppianicus was giving it out in the Forum of Larinum that he and some friends of his had recently sealed his will as witnesses, when his freedmen, and a few of his friends, coming to know that on the last day he had been seen alive he had been in Avillius's

eo fuisse et a multis visum esse constabat, in eum
invadunt et hominem ante pedes Q. Manli, qui tum
erat triumvir, constituunt : atque ille continuo, nullo
teste, nullo indice, recentis maleficii conscientia perterritus, omnia, ut a me paullo ante dicta sunt, ex-
ponit Asuviumque a sese consilio Oppianici inter-
39 fectum fatetur. Extrahitur domo latitans Oppianicus a Manlio : index Avillius ex altera parte coram
tenetur. Hic quid iam reliqua quaeritis ? Manlium
plerique noratis : non ille honorem a pueritia, non
studia virtutis, non ullum existimationis bonae fructum umquam cogitarat : ex petulanti atque improbo
scurra in discordiis civitatis ad eam columnam, ad
quam multorum saepe conviciis perductus erat, tum
suffragiis populi pervenerat. Itaque rem cum Oppianico transigit, pecuniam ab eo accipit, causam et
susceptam et tam manifestam relinquit. Ac tum in
Oppianici causa crimen hoc Asuvianum cum testibus
multis tum vero indicio Avilli comprobabatur : in
quo adligatum Oppianici nomen primum esse constabat, eius, quem vos miserum atque innocentem
falso iudicio circumventum esse dicitis.
40   XIV. Quid ? aviam tuam, Oppianice, Dinaeam,
cui tu es heres, pater tuus non manifesto necavit ?
ad quam cum adduxisset medicum illum suum, iam

ᵃ The words *eam columnam* in the text refer to the Columna
Maenia in the Forum, near which the Commissioners of
Police (*triumviri capitales*) had their tribunal.

company, and that many people had seen them together, broke in upon Avillius and haled him before the judgement-seat of Q. Manlius, who at that time was one of the three Commissioners of Police. Whereupon, without anyone to give evidence, or lay information against him, the recent memory of his crimes frightened him into disclosing the whole story which I have just told you, and confessing that he had murdered Asuvius on the instigation of Oppianicus. Manlius dragged the 39 skulking Oppianicus from his house, and the informer Avillius was made to confront him. What more would you have me tell you ? You knew Manlius, most of you ; from boyhood up he had never given a thought to the path of honour, the formation of character, or anything that comes as the reward of a good name : from being a brazen and reprobate hanger-on, he had been raised by the votes of the populace at the time of the Civil War to a seat on that tribunal,[a] before which he had often been haled amid the vituperation of the crowd. And so he came to an understanding with Oppianicus, accepted a bribe from him, and abandoned a perfectly clear case of which he had already taken cognizance. It was not until the trial of Oppianicus that this charge in the matter of Asuvius was brought home by numerous witnesses, as well as by the confession of Avillius, a confession which established that the person primarily implicated was Oppianicus, he whom the prosecution describes as the poor innocent victim of a corrupt trial !

XIV. Again, is it not patent, Oppianicus, that 40 your father murdered your grandmother, Dinea, whose heir you are ? For when he introduced to

cognitum et saepe victorem [per quem interfecerat
plurimos],[1] mulier exclamat se ab eo nullo modo curari
velle, quo curante omnes suos perdidisset. Tum
repente Anconitanum quemdam, L. Clodium, phar-
macopolam circumforaneum, qui casu tum Larinum
venisset, adgreditur et cum eo duobus milibus HS,
id quod ipsius tabulis est demonstratum, transigit.
L. Clodius, cum properaret, cui fora multa restarent,
simul atque introductus est, rem confecit : prima
potione mulierem sustulit, neque postea Larini
punctum est temporis commoratus.

41 Eadem hac Dinaea testamentum faciente, cum
tabulas prehendisset Oppianicus, qui gener eius
fuisset, digito legata delevit et cum id multis locis
fecisset, post mortem eius, ne lituris coargui posset,
testamentum in alias tabulas transscriptum signis
adulterinis obsignavit.

Multa praetereo consulto : etenim vereor ne haec
ipsa nimium multa esse videantur : vos tamen
similem sui eum fuisse in ceteris quoque vitae partibus
existimare debetis. Illum tabulas publicas Larini
censorias corrupisse decuriones universi iudicaverunt.
Cum illo nemo iam rationem, nemo rem ullam con-
trahebat : nemo illum ex tam multis cognatis et
adfinibus tutorem umquam liberis suis scripsit : nemo
illum aditu, nemo congressione, nemo sermone, nemo
convivio dignum iudicavit : omnes aspernabantur,
omnes abhorrebant, omnes ut aliquam immanem ac

---

[1] *These words have been generally regarded as a gloss.*

---

[a] See pp. 214, 215.
[b] The will was written with a stilus on waxed tablets.

her that doctor of his, so notorious and so often
" successful," the poor lady cried out that she
absolutely declined to be attended by one whose
attentions had lost her all her children. Thereupon
he at once approached one Lucius Clodius of
Ancona, a travelling quack, who happened to be
visiting Larinum, and came to an understanding
with him for 2000 sesterces, as is shown in his own
accounts. Clodius was in a hurry, having many
other market-towns to visit, so he finished his task
directly he was brought in. He killed the woman
with the first draught he gave her, and not another
moment did he linger in Larinum.

Moreover, when Dinea was making her will 41
Oppianicus used his position as her one time son-in-
law [a] to get hold of it, rubbed out the bequests with
his finger,[b] and to prevent his betrayal by the
erasures, for he had made many of them, transcribed
the will on to another document after her death,
forging the seals of the witnesses.

I am intentionally omitting many details for fear
that even those I have mentioned may seem all too
many : you must, however, understand that Oppianicus was ever himself, at other periods of his life
as at this. He it was whom the Town Council of
Larinum adjudged by a unanimous finding to have
falsified the public records of their censors, with
whom no one would have any pecuniary transactions,
nor any dealings whatsoever, whom not one of all his
kinsmen and connexions ever appointed by will as
trustee to his children. No one thought that it was
decent to call upon him, to meet him in society, to
converse with him, or to ask him to dinner. Everyone shrank from him, everyone loathed him, everyone

263

42 perniciosam bestiam pestemque fugiebant. Hunc
tamen hominem tam audacem, tam nefarium, tam
nocentem numquam accusasset Habitus, iudices, si
id praetermittere suo salvo capite potuisset. Erat
huic inimicus Oppianicus : erat, sed tamen erat
vitricus : crudelis et huic infesta mater, at mater.
Postremo nihil tam remotum ab accusatione quam
Cluentius et natura et voluntate et instituta ratione
vitae. Sed cum esset haec ei proposita condicio, ut
aut iuste pieque accusaret aut acerbe indigneque
moreretur, accusare, quoquo modo posset, quam illo
modo emori maluit.

43 Atque ut hoc ita esse perspicere possitis, exponam
vobis Oppianici facinus manifesto compertum atque
deprehensum : ex quo simul utrumque, et huic
accusare et illi condemnari, necesse fuisse intellegetis.

XV. Martiales quidam Larini appellabantur,
ministri publici Martis atque ei deo veteribus in-
stitutis religionibusque Larinatium consecrati : quorum cum satis magnus numerus esset, cumque item,
ut in Sicilia permulti Venerii sunt, sic illi Larini in
Martis familia numerarentur, repente Oppianicus
eos omnes liberos esse civesque Romanos coepit defendere. Graviter id decuriones Larinatium cuncti-
que municipes tulerunt. Itaque ab Habito petive-

ᵃ *i.e.* they were little better than slaves.

avoided him as a savage and dangerous brute, a very
scourge. And yet, for all his effrontery, his wicked- 42
ness, and his guilt, Habitus would never have undertaken to accuse him, gentlemen, had any other course
been consistent with his own safety. Oppianicus was
indeed my client's enemy ; yes, but his stepfather
as well : his mother was an unfeeling woman and
she hated him, but still she was his mother ; and,
finally, no one could be more averse from prosecution
than Cluentius, whether from his disposition, his
sympathies, or his settled manner of life. But when
he was confronted with the alternatives, either to
undertake a just and dutiful prosecution or to die a
premature and shameful death, he chose rather to
prosecute as best he could than to succumb to such
an end.

And now to convince you of the truth of what I 43
say, I will relate to you a crime which was completely discovered and brought home to Oppianicus :
the story will convince you that my client's charge
and Oppianicus's condemnation were equally and
alike inevitable.

XV. There were at Larinum certain persons
called Martiales, the official priests of Mars, dedicated
to the service of the god by local regulations and
religious ordinances of great antiquity. Their
number was considerable : moreover, as is the case
with the numerous priests of Venus in Sicily, these
priests of Mars at Larinum were regarded as belonging to the household of the god.[a] But despite this
Oppianicus suddenly began to maintain the plea
that they were free men and Roman citizens. This
was a great blow to the Town Council of Larinum
and all the townspeople ; so they asked Habitus to

runt, ut eam causam susciperet publiceque defenderet.
Habitus cum se ab omni eius modi negotio removisset,
tamen pro loco, pro antiquitate generis sui, pro eo,
quod se non suis commodis, sed etiam suorum municipum ceterorumque necessariorum natum esse
arbitrabatur, tantae voluntati universorum Larina-
44 tium deesse noluit. Suscepta causa Romamque delata magnae cotidie contentiones inter Habitum et
Oppianicum ex utriusque studio defensionis excita-
bantur. Erat ipse immani acerbaque natura Oppianicus : incendebat eius amentiam infesta atque
inimica filio mater Habiti. Magni autem illi sua
interesse arbitrabantur hunc a causa Martialium
removeri. Suberat etiam alia causa maior, quae
Oppianici hominis avarissimi mentem maxime com-
45 movebat. Nam Habitus usque ad illius iudicii
tempus nullum testamentum umquam fecerat.
Neque legare eius modi matri poterat animum in-
ducere, neque testamento nomen omnino praetermittere parentis. Id cum Oppianicus sciret—neque
enim erat obscurum—intellegebat Habito mortuo
bona eius omnia ad matrem esse ventura : quae ab
sese postea aucta pecunia maiore praemio, orbata
filio minore periculo necaretur. Itaque his rebus
incensus, qua ratione Habitum veneno tollere conatus
sit cognoscite.

46   XVI. C. et L. Fabricii fratres gemini fuerunt ex
municipio Alatrinati, homines inter se cum forma tum

take up the case and contest it in the public interest :
and although he had kept aloof from all such matters,
still he was unwilling to disappoint the strong and
unanimous wish of Larinum, in consideration of his
position, the antiquity of his family and his feeling
that he had not come into the world to serve his own
interests but also those of his fellow townspeople and
other friends. The case came into court and was 44
taken up to Rome, and there was a great disputation
every day between Habitus and Oppianicus, so keen
was each to make good his cause. It was Oppianicus's nature to be ungovernable and violent, and his
madness was further inflamed by the hatred and
enmity of Habitus's mother against her son. They,
then, thought it indispensable to their interests to
detach my client from the case of the Martiales. But
behind this there was another and a more cogent
reason, appealing strongly to Oppianicus's great love
of money ; for up to the time of Oppianicus's trial, 45
Habitus had never made a will, being unable to
bring himself either to leave anything to such a
mother as his, or entirely to pass over a parent's
name in his will. When Oppianicus knew this (for
there was no secrecy about it), he realized that on
Habitus's death all his property would pass to his
mother, who could afterwards be put to death with
greater advantage to himself, through the addition
to her fortune, and with less risk, through the loss
of her son. With these motives then to urge him
on, hear how he endeavoured to get rid of Habitus
by poison.

XVI. There were twin brothers, Gaius and 46
Lucius Fabricius, of the town of Alatrium, who were
much alike both in appearance and character,

moribus similes, municipum autem suorum dissimil-
limi, in quibus quantus splendor sit, quam prope
aequabilis, quam fere omnium constans et moderata
ratio vitae, nemo vestrum, ut mea fert opinio, ignorat.
His Fabriciis semper est usus Oppianicus familiarissime. Iam hoc fere scitis omnes, quantam vim
habeat ad coniungendas amicitias studiorum ac
naturae similitudo. Cum illi ita viverent, ut nullum
quaestum turpem esse arbitrarentur, cum omnis ab
eis fraus, omnes insidiae circumscriptionesque adu-
lescentium nascerentur, cumque essent vitiis atque
improbitate omnibus noti, studiose, ut dixi, ad eorum
se familiaritatem multis iam ante annis Oppianicus
47 applicarat. Itaque tum sic statuit, per C. Fabricium
—nam L. erat mortuus—insidias Habito comparare.
    Erat illo tempore infirma valetudine Habitus.
Utebatur autem medico non ignobili, sed spectato
homine, Cleophanto : cuius servum Diogenem Fabricius ad venenum Habito dandum spe et pretio sol-
licitare coepit. Servus non incallidus et, ut res ipsa
declaravit, frugi atque integer, sermonem Fabricii
non est aspernatus : rem ad dominum detulit : Cleophantus autem cum Habito est collocutus. Habitus
statim cum M. Baebio senatore, familiarissimo suo,
communicavit : qui qua fide, qua prudentia, qua
diligentia fuerit meminisse vos arbitror. Ei placuit
ut Diogenem Habitus emeret a Cleophanto, quo
facilius aut comprehenderetur res eius indicio aut
falsa esse cognosceretur. Ne multa : Diogenes

though most unlike their fellow townspeople, who are, as I suppose not one of you is ignorant, conspicuously and uniformly distinguished by the consistency and moderation of their mode of life : with these two men Oppianicus was always on most intimate terms. Now you are aware, I take it, how much can be done by a similarity of tastes and character to cement a friendship. Their lives were lived on the assumption that no source of profit was dishonourable ; they originated every form of deceit and trickery, every means of defrauding minors ; their vices and their profligacy were widely notorious : wherefore, as I have already said, Oppianicus had been anxiously devoting himself for many years past to the cultivation of their friendship. And 47 so, at this particular time, he decided to employ Gaius Fabricius—for Lucius had died—in maturing his plot against Habitus.

Habitus was at that time in poor health, and was employing as his doctor one Cleophantus, not unknown in his profession, and personally a man of repute : his slave, Diogenes Fabricius now began to tempt with promises and bribes to poison Habitus. The slave, who was no fool, but, as the event proved, honest and upright, did not reject Fabricius's overtures, but reported the matter to his master, and Cleophantus talked it over with Habitus. Habitus immediately confided in his friend, M Baebius, the senator, and I think that you remember the honour, foresight, and care which characterized him. His advice was that Habitus should purchase Diogenes from Cleophantus in order to make it easier either to bring home the charge on his information, or to prove it false. To cut the story short, Diogenes was

emitur : venenum diebus paucis comparatur : multi
viri boni cum ex occulto intervenissent, pecunia
obsignata, quae ob eam rem dabatur, in manibus
Scamandri liberti Fabriciorum deprehenditur.

48   Pro di immortales ! Oppianicum quisquam his
rebus cognitis circumventum esse dicet ? XVII.
Quis umquam audacior ? quis nocentior ? quis aper-
tior in iudicium adductus est ?   Quod ingenium, quae
facultas dicendi, quae a quoquam excogitata defensio
huic uni crimini potuit obsistere ?   Simul et illud
quis est qui dubitet quin hac re comperta manifeste-
que deprehensa aut obeunda mors Cluentio aut sus-
cipienda accusatio fuerit ?

49   Satis esse arbitror demonstratum, iudices, eis
criminibus accusatum esse Oppianicum, uti honeste
absolvi nullo modo potuerit. Cognoscite nunc ita
reum citatum esse illum, ut re semel atque iterum
praeiudicata condemnatus in iudicium venerit.   Nam
Cluentius, iudices, primum nomen eius detulit, cuius
in manibus venenum deprehenderat.   Is erat libertus
Fabriciorum Scamander.   Integrum consilium, iudicii
corrupti nulla suspicio : simplex in iudicium causa,
certa res, unum crimen adlatum est. Hic tum C.
Fabricius, is, de quo ante dixi, qui liberto damnato
sibi illud impendere periculum videret, quod mihi
cum Alatrinatibus vicinitatem et cum plerisque eorum

<hr>

a See § 46.

purchased : in a few days the poison was prepared : several reliable men, emerging from their concealment, found in the hands of Scamander, the Fabricii's freedman, a sealed packet containing the money that was being offered as consideration for the deed.

Who, in Heaven's name, after hearing these facts, 48 will say that Oppianicus was the victim of corruption ? XVII. Who was ever put on trial for such effrontery, such wickedness, such manifest guilt ? What talent, what eloquence, what defence by whomsoever elaborated, could have availed against this one charge ? And further, who could possibly doubt, with these facts before him, this actual discovery of the crime, that Cluentius was bound either to face death or to prosecute ?

I imagine, gentlemen, that I have adequately 49 proved that the charges against Oppianicus were such as to make his acquittal by honest means an impossibility : so let me now show you that he was arraigned in circumstances which, as his case had already been decided not once but twice, made him a condemned criminal before he came into court. For the first person to be indicted by Cluentius, gentlemen, was the man in whose hands the poison had actually been found—Scamander, the freedman of the Fabricii. There was no bias on the part of the jury, no suspicion that the court had been bribed. There was placed before the court a straightforward issue, an established fact, a single charge. At this juncture G. Fabricius—the same to whom I have referred before [a]—realizing that if his freedman were convicted he would be in considerable danger of being convicted too, brought to my house a deputation of the Alatrians : for he knew that I

magnum usum esse sciebat, frequentes eos ad me domum adduxit. Qui quamquam de homine, sicut necesse erat, existimabant, tamen, quod erat ex eodem municipio, suae dignitatis esse arbitrabantur eum quibus rebus possent defendere : idque a me ut facerem et ut causam Scamandri susciperem petebant, in qua causa patroni omne periculum contine-
50 batur. Ego, qui neque illis talibus viris ac tam amantibus mei rem possem ullam negare neque illud crimen tantum ac tam manifestum esse arbitrarer, sicut ne illi quidem ipsi, qui mihi tum illam causam commendabant, arbitrabantur, pollicitus eis sum me omnia quae vellent esse facturum.

XVIII. Res agi coepta est : citatus est Scamander reus. Accusabat P. Cannutius, homo in primis ingeniosus et in dicendo exercitatus : accusabat autem ille quidem Scamandrum verbis tribus : Venenum esse deprehensum : omnia tela totius accusationis in Oppianicum coniciebantur, aperiebatur causa insidiarum, Fabriciorum familiaritas commemorabatur, hominis vita et audacia proferebatur, denique omnis accusatio varie graviterque tractata, ad extremum
51 manifesta veneni deprehensione conclusa est. Hic ego tum ad respondendum surrexi : qua cura, di immortales ! qua sollicitudine animi ! quo timore ! Semper equidem magno cum metu incipio dicere : quotienscumque dico, totiens mihi videor in iudicium venire non ingenii solum, sed etiam virtutis atque officii, ne aut id profiteri videar, quod non possim, quod est impudentiae, aut non id efficere, quod possim, quod est aut perfidiae aut neglegentiae.

---

was a neighbour of theirs,[a] and on intimate terms with most of them. And although their opinion of Fabricius was what it could not help being, still, because he was their fellow-townsman, they felt that they owed it to their self-respect to do what they could for his defence. Accordingly they asked me to defend him, and undertake Scamander's case, involving also, as it did, his patron's liability to conviction. I then, being unable to refuse anything to 50 these, my good and honourable friends, and having no more idea than the actual people who sought to place it in my hands, that the case was so serious or so well established, promised them all they wanted.

XVIII. The trial began : Scamander was put in the dock. The counsel for the prosecution was P. Cannutius, a man of distinguished ability and an experienced pleader. While he confined his charge against Scamander to three words : " Poison was detected," it was against Oppianicus that he aimed every weapon of his attack, exposing the motives for his plots, recalling his friendship with the Fabricii, urging his career of effrontery ; and finally, after a diversified and telling review, bringing the whole indictment to its culmination in the overt discovery of the poison. And then I rose to reply, 51 and Heaven knows how anxious I was, how uneasy, how apprehensive ! Personally, I am always very nervous when I begin to speak. Every time I make a speech I feel I am submitting to judgement, not only my ability but even my character and honour, and am afraid of seeming either to promise more than I can perform, which suggests shamelessness, or to perform less than I can, which suggests bad faith and indifference. On this particular occasion

Tum vero ita sum perturbatus, ut omnia timerem:
si nihil dixissem, ne infantissimus: si multa in eius
modi causa dixissem, ne impudentissimus existi-
marer.

XIX. Collegi me aliquando et ita constitui, fortiter
esse agendum; illi aetati, qua tum eram, solere laudi
dari, etiam si in minus firmis causis hominum periculis non defuissem. Itaque feci: sic pugnavi, sic
omni ratione contendi, sic ad omnia confugi, quantum
ego adsequi potui, remedia ac perfugia causarum, ut
hoc, quod timide dicam, consecutus sim, ne quis illi
52 causae patronum defuisse arbitraretur. Sed ut
quicquid ego apprehenderam, statim accusator ex-
torquebat e manibus. Si quaesiveram quae inimicitiae Scamandro cum Habito, fatebatur nullas fuisse,
sed Oppianicum, cuius ille minister fuisset, huic in-
imicissimum fuisse atque esse dicebat. Sin autem
illud egeram, nullum ad Scamandrum morte Habiti
venturum emolumentum fuisse, concedebat, sed ad
uxorem Oppianici, hominis in uxoribus necandis exercitati, omnia bona Habiti ventura fuisse dicebat.
Cum illa defensione usus essem, quae in libertinorum
causis honestissima semper existimata est, Scamandrum patrono esse probatum, fatebatur, sed quaerebat
53 cui probatus esset ipse patronus. Cum ego pluribus
verbis in eo commoratus essem, Scamandro insidias
factas esse per Diogenem constitutumque inter eos
alia de re fuisse, ut medicamentum, non venenum
Diogenes adferret, hoc cuivis usu venire posse, quaere-

I was a prey to every form of nervousness, afraid of seeming tongue-tied if I said nothing, or shameless if I said much, with so weak a case.

XIX. At last I recovered my self-possession, and made up my mind that I must take a strong line, reflecting that it was generally considered creditable in a young pleader as I was then, not to fail a man on his trial even if his case were somewhat weak. And so I did ; I put forth all my resources, I availed myself, in so far as I could, of every legal nostrum and evasion, with the result that, though I hardly like to say so, no one could possibly imagine that the advocate had not done justice to his case. But as 52 fast as I laid hold on any argument, the prosecution wrenched it from my grasp. Did I call on my opponent to show any enmity between Scamander and Habitus? He admitted that there had been none, but said that Oppianicus, whose agent the accused was, had been, and still was, Cluentius's bitterest foe. Or if I took the line that Scamander did not stand to gain anything by Habitus's death, he conceded the point, but said that in that event all Habitus's property was to go to the wife of Oppianicus, a past master in the art of wife-murder. When I put forward the defence which has always been held perfectly decent at the trial of a freedman, namely, that he bore a good character with his patron, he admitted it, but asked who would give the patron a good character. When I dwelt at some length on the point that 53 Diogenes had been employed to set a trap for Scamander, and that they had arranged, in a different connexion, that Diogenes should bring medicine, not poison—adding that it was a thing that might happen to anyone—he asked why Scamander came

bat cur in eius modi locum, tam abditum, cur solus,
cur cum obsignata pecunia venisset. Denique hoc
loco causa testibus honestissimis hominibus preme-
batur. M. Baebius de suo consilio Diogenem emptum,
se praesente Scamandrum cum veneno pecuniaque
deprehensum esse dicebat. P. Quintilius Varus,
homo summa religione et summa auctoritate praeditus, de insidiis, quae fierent Habito, et de sollici-
tatione Diogenis recenti re secum Cleophantum col-
54 locutum esse dicebat. Atque in illo iudicio cum
Scamandrum nos defendere videremur, verbo ille
reus erat, re quidem vera et periculo tota accusatione
Oppianicus. Neque id obscure ferebat nec dissimu-
lare ullo modo poterat : aderat frequens, advocabat,
omni studio gratiaque pugnabat : postremo, id quod
maximo malo illi causae fuit, hoc ipso in loco, quasi
reus ipse esset, sedebat. Oculi omnium iudicum
non in Scamandrum, sed in Oppianicum coniciebantur : timor eius, perturbatio, suspensus incertus-
que voltus, crebra coloris mutatio, quae erant antea
suspiciosa, haec aperta et manifesta faciebant.

55 XX. Cum in consilium iri oporteret, quaesivit ab
reo C. Iunius quaesitor ex lege illa Cornelia, quae tum
erat, clam an palam de se sententiam ferri vellet. De
Oppianici sententia responsum est, quod is Habiti

---

^a That is, those reserved for the defence.
^b In 137 B.C. the use of the ballot was made compulsory;
Sulla, in 80 B.C., made it optional, but his law had been
repealed shortly before Cluentius's trial.

to such a lonely spot, and alone ; why with a sealed packet of money   At this point my case broke down under the weight of unimpeachable testimony. M. Baebius deposed that he had suggested the purchase of Diogenes, and had been present when Scamander was caught with the poison and the money.   Publius Quintus Varus, a scrupulous witness, whose word carried great weight, deposed to the plot against Habitus, and to a conversation which Cleophantus had had with him just after the accident, about his having tried to tamper with Diogenes. And in this trial, in which I appeared to be defending 54 Scamander, he was only nominally the accused person : the real accused, the real person in danger of conviction, was, throughout the whole prosecution, Oppianicus.   This he was at no pains to conceal, nor could he by any means disguise it : he put in a regular attendance in court ; kept beating up his supporters, and throwing all his efforts, all his influence into the struggle : and ended by taking his seat—an act which Scamander had no small cause to regret—on these very benches,[a] as if he were himself on trial.   The eyes of all the jurors were turned, not upon Scamander, but upon Oppianicus, whose fear and agitation, whose restless and anxious expression, whose frequent changes of colour, made clear and open what before had been a matter only of suspicion.

XX. When the time came for the jurors to con- 55 sider their verdict, the President of the court, G. Junius, in accordance with the law of Sulla, which was then in force, asked the accused whether he wished the voting on his case to be secret or open [b]   As Oppianicus said that Junius was Habitus's friend,

familiarem Iunium esse dicebat, clam velle ferri.
Itum est in consilium. Omnibus sententiis praeter
unam, quam suam Staienus esse dicebat, Scamander
prima actione condemnatus est. Quis tum erat
omnium qui Scamandro condemnato non iudicium
de Oppianico factum esse arbitraretur? quid est illa
damnatione iudicatum, nisi venenum id, quod Habito
daretur, esse quaesitum? Quae porro tenuissima
suspicio collata in Scamandrum est aut conferri
potuit, ut is sua sponte necare voluisse Habitum
putaretur?

56 Atque hoc tum iudicio facto et Oppianico re et existimatione iam, lege et pronuntiatione nondum condemnato, tamen Habitus Oppianicum reum statim
non fecit. Voluit cognoscere utrum iudices in eos
solos essent severi, quos venenum habuisse ipsos
comperissent, an etiam consilia conscientiasque eius
modi facinorum supplicio dignas iudicarent. Itaque
C. Fabricium, quem propter familiaritatem Oppianici
conscium illi facinori fuisse arbitrabatur, reum statim
fecit : utique ei locus primus constitueretur propter
causae coniunctionem impetravit. Hic tum Fabricius non modo ad me meos vicinos et amicos Alatri-
nates non adduxit, sed ipse eis neque defensoribus
57 uti postea neque laudatoribus potuit. Rem enim
integram hominis non alieni quamvis suspiciosam de-

Scamander acted on his suggestion and replied that he wished it to be secret. The jurors considered their verdict. By every vote but one, which Staienus admitted to be his, and at the first hearing of the case, Scamander was found guilty. Was there a man in the court at the time, who failed to realize that the conviction of Scamander amounted also to a judgement on Oppianicus? What finding was involved in that conviction unless that the poison which had been procured, was intended for Habitus? Nay, what shadow of suspicion was, or could have been thrown on Scamander of having conceived a wish to murder Habitus without any instigation?

Despite the issue of this trial, which left Oppianicus 56 virtually convicted already by public opinion, though he had yet to be expressly convicted by a court of law, Habitus did not at once have him put on trial: he wanted to find out whether juries dealt severely only with the actual persons whom they understood to have had poison in their possession, or whether they thought the abettors and accessories of such crimes no less worthy of punishment. And so he at once put on trial G. Fabricius, whom, on account of his friendship with Oppianicus, he thought to have been an accessory to the crime in question, and succeeded in securing that his case be placed first on the list, owing to its connexion with the previous case. On this occasion, not only did Fabricius fail to bring to me my neighbours and friends from Alatrium, but found himself unable any longer to secure their support, either for his case or for his character. For while it was still undecided we thought it only 57 considerate to undertake the case, however unsatisfactory, of one with whom we were not uncon-

fendere humanitatis esse putabamus, iudicatam labefactare conari impudentiae. Itaque tum ille inopia
et necessitate coactus in causa eius modi ad Caepasios
fratres confugit, homines industrios atque eo animo,
ut quaecumque dicendi potestas esset data, in honore
atque in beneficio ponerent.

XXI. Iam hoc prope iniquissime comparatum est,
quod in morbis corporis, ut quisque est difficillimus,
ita medicus nobilissimus atque optimus quaeritur, in
periculis capitis, ut quaeque causa difficillima est, ita
deterrimus obscurissimusque patronus adhibetur :
nisi forte hoc causae est, quod medici nihil praeter
artificium, oratores etiam auctoritatem praestare
debent.

58   Citatur reus, [agitur causa :][1] paucis verbis accusat,
ut de re iudicata, Cannutius : incipit longo et
alte petito prooemio respondere maior Caepasius.
Primo attente auditur eius oratio ; erigebat animum
iam demissum et oppressum Oppianicus ; gaudebat
ipse Fabricius : non intellegebat animos iudicum non
illius eloquentia, sed defensionis impudentia com-
moveri. Postea quam de re coepit dicere, ad ea,
quae erant in causa, addebat etiam ipse nova quaedam vulnera, ut quamquam sedulo faciebat, tamen
interdum non defendere, sed praevaricari accusationi
videretur. Itaque cum callidissime se dicere putaret
et cum illa verba gravissima ex intimo artificio de-
prompsisset : " Respicite, iudices, hominum fortunas, respicite dubios variosque casus, respicite C.

---

[1] *These words are suspect and are bracketed by Baiter.*

---

[a] It seems impossible to express in English the double
meaning of *respice* which, as used by Caecennius, has the
sense of " have some regard for."

nected; but we felt that any attempt to upset
the judgement, once it was passed, would be outrageous. Fabricius, consequently, was driven by his
defenceless condition to resort in desperation to the
brothers Caepasii, hard-working pleaders, disposed
to regard any chance which they were given to plead
as a compliment and a favour.

XXI. Now a somewhat unjust inference has been
drawn from the fact that in a case of physical disease,
the worse it is, the more distinguished and superior
is the doctor who is called in ; whereas in the case of
criminal trials, the worse the cause, the more obscure
and inferior is the advocate who is briefed. But perhaps the reason is this, that the doctor only lends his
skill, a pleader lends also his good name.

Well, Fabricius was summoned ; Cannutius opened 58
the prosecution with a short speech, for he held the
case prejudged. The elder Caepasius embarked on
a long and far-fetched exordium. At first his speech
had an attentive hearing : Oppianicus began to
raise his drooping and dejected spirits : Fabricius
began to feel happy : he did not realize that what
was impressing the judges was not the eloquence of
the pleader but the effrontery of the plea. Coming
to the defence proper, Caepasius gratuitously inflicted fresh wounds on a case which was maimed at
the outset, until, though he was doing his best, he
seemed at times not to be defending his client but
to be acting in collusion with the prosecutor. For
instance, he thought he was pleading very cleverly,
and produced from the secrets of his stock-in-trade
these weighty words : " Look back,ᵃ gentlemen, upon
the lot of mortal man ; look back upon its changes
and chances ; look back upon the old age of G.

Fabrici senectutem " : cum hoc " respicite " ornan-
dae orationis causa saepe dixisset, respexit ipse. At
C. Fabricius a subselliis demisso capite discesserat.
59 Hic iudices ridere, stomachari atque acerbe ferre
patronus, causam sibi eripi et se cetera de illo loco
" Respicite, iudices," non posse dicere : nec quicquam
propius est factum, quam ut illum persequeretur et
collo obtorto ad subsellia reduceret, ut reliqua posset
perorare. Ita tum Fabricius primum suo iudicio,
quod est gravissimum, deinde legis vi et sententiis
iudicum est condemnatus.

XXII. Quid est quod iam de Oppianici persona
causaque plura dicamus ? Apud eosdem iudices reus
est factus, cum his duobus praeiudiciis iam damnatus
esset : ab isdem autem iudicibus, qui Fabriciorum
damnatione de Oppianico iudicarant, locus ei primus
est constitutus : accusatus est criminibus gravissimis
et eis, quae a me breviter dicta sunt, et praeterea
multis, quae ego omnia nunc omitto : accusatus
est apud eos, qui Scamandrum ministrum Oppianici,
C. Fabricium conscium maleficii condemnarant.
60 Utrum, per deos immortales ! magis est mirandum,
quod is condemnatus est, an quod omnino respondere
ausus est ? Quid enim illi iudices facere potuerunt ?
qui si innocentes Fabricios condemnassent, tamen in
Oppianico sibi constare et superioribus consentire
iudiciis debuerunt. An vero illi sua per se ipsi iudicia

Fabricius!" After frequent repetitions of the phrase "Look back," by way of ornamenting his speech, he finally looked back himself: and lo! C. Fabricius had left his seat with hanging head. Thereupon the court burst out laughing; counsel 59 lost his temper, in annoyance that his case was slipping through his fingers, and that he could not complete his stock passage beginning "Look back": and he was as near as possible to pursuing his client and dragging him back to his seat by the scruff of his neck, so that he could conclude his peroration. And so Fabricius was found guilty, first by the very significant verdict of his own conscience, and then by the operation of law and the verdict of the court.

XXII. After this, what more am I to say of the character and trial of Oppianicus? He was put on his trial before the same judges, convicted already by their two previous verdicts. The same judges who, in convicting Fabricius and his accomplice, had already passed sentence on Oppianicus, placed his trial first on the list: he was charged with the most heinous crimes—those which I have already narrated and many others besides, all of which I now pass over: he was charged before men who had already convicted Scamander, his agent, and G. Fabricius, the accessory to his evil deed. Which in 60 Heaven's name is the more surprising—that he was convicted, or that he dared to contest the case at all? What possible course was there for judges who, had they been mistaken in convicting Fabricius and Scamander, were obliged to be consistent in the case of Oppianicus and to stand by their former verdicts? Or were they to take it on themselves to quash their own verdicts, whereas most men take

rescinderent, cum ceteri soleant in iudicando ne ab aliorum iudiciis discrepent providere? et ei, qui Fabrici libertum, quia minister in maleficio fuerat, patronum, quia conscius, condemnassent, ipsum principem atque architectum sceleris absolverent? et qui ceteros nullo praeiudicio facto tamen ex ipsa causa condemnassent, hunc, quem bis iam condem-

61 natum acceperant, liberarent? Tum vero illa iudicia senatoria non falsa invidia, sed vera atque insigni turpitudine notata atque operta dedecore et infamia defensioni locum nullum reliquissent. Quid enim tandem illi iudices responderent, si qui ab eis quaereret: "Condemnastis Scamandrum: quo crimine?" "Nempe, quod Habitum per servum medici veneno necare voluisset." "Quid Habiti morte Scamander consequebatur?" "Nihil, sed administer erat Oppianici." "Et condemnastis C. Fabricium: quid ita?" "Quia, cum ipse familiarissime Oppianico usus, libertus autem eius in maleficio deprehensus esset, illum expertem eius consilii fuisse non probabatur." Si igitur ipsum Oppianicum bis suis iudiciis condemnatum absolvissent, quis tantam turpitudinem iudiciorum, quis tantam inconstantiam rerum iudicatarum, quis tantam libidinem iudicum ferre potuisset?

62 Quod si hoc videtis, quod iam hac omni oratione patefactum est, illo iudicio reum condemnari, prae-

---

[a] This senatorial privilege, restored by Sulla in 81, was abolished in 70 B.C. See Historical Summary.

care to see when they give a verdict that they are
not at variance with the verdicts given by others ?
And were those who had convicted Fabricius's freedman, as Oppianicus's agent in the evil deed, and
Fabricius himself as accessory to it, to acquit the
actual contriver of the crime ? Were those who,
without any previous verdict to prejudice the case,
had none the less convicted others on the bare evidence before them, to set at liberty this fellow who
had been twice convicted before he came into court ?
That would indeed have been to brand the senatorial 61
juries of the day,[a] not with the false stigma of prejudice, but with real and conspicuous ignominy, and
to load them with such disgrace and dishonour as
would make it impossible to defend them. What
answer indeed were those judges to give to the
question : " You found Scamander guilty : on what
charge ? " " Why, on the charge of intending to
poison Habitus through the agency of the doctor's
slave." " What was Scamander seeking to gain by
Habitus's death ? " " Nothing : but he was the tool
of Oppianicus." " G. Fabricius, too, you found
guilty : why ? " " Because, while he was an intimate friend of Oppianicus, and his freedman was
caught in the act of evil-doing, we could not take the
view that Fabricius was not privy to it." If, then,
they had acquitted Oppianicus, though twice convicted by their own verdicts, who could have tolerated
such a disgrace to the court, such inconsistency in
judicial decisions, such caprice on the part of the
judges ?

If you now perceive what my whole speech has 62
gone to establish—that it was inevitable at Oppianicus's trial that the accused should be found guilty, all

sertim ab isdem iudicibus, qui duo praeiudicia fecissent, necesse fuisse, simul illud videatis necesse est, nullam accusatoris esse causam potuisse cur iudicium vellet corrumpere.

XXIII. Quaero enim de te, T. Acci, relictis iam ceteris argumentis omnibus, num Fabricios quoque innocentes condemnatos existimes, num etiam illa iudicia pecunia corrupta esse dicas, quibus in iudiciis alter a Staieno solo absolutus est, alter etiam ipse se condemnavit. Age, si nocentes, cuius maleficii? num quid praeter venenum quaesitum, quo Habitus necaretur, obiectum est? num quid aliud in illis iudiciis versatum est praeter hasce insidias Habito ab Oppianico per Fabricium factas? Nihil, nihil, inquam, aliud, iudices, reperietis. Exstat memoria: sunt tabulae publicae: redargue me, si mentior: testium dicta recita: doce in illorum iudiciis quid praeter hoc venenum Oppianici non modo in criminis,
63 sed in maledicti loco sit obiectum. Multa dici possunt quare ita necesse fuerit iudicari, sed ego occurram exspectationi vestrae, iudices. Nam etsi a vobis sic audior, ut numquam benignius neque attentius quemquam auditum putem, tamen vocat me alio iam dudum tacita vestra exspectatio, quae mihi obloqui videtur: " quid ergo? negasne illud iudicium corruptum esse?" Non nego, sed ab hoc corruptum non esse confirmo. " A quo igitur est corruptum?" Opinor, primum, si incertum fuisset quisnam exitus

---

ᵃ Counsel for the prosecution.

the more as his judges were the same who had given verdicts prejudicial to his case, you must needs perceive this further point, that the accuser could have no sort of motive for bribing the court.

XXIII. Now putting aside all other arguments, I ask you, Titus Accius,[a] whether you think that Fabricius and Scamander, too, were wrongly convicted, whether you say that at their trials, too, the court was bribed, trials in which the latter found only Staienus to vote for his acquittal, and the former actually convicted himself. Come, if they were rightly convicted, what was their crime ? Was anything alleged against them other than the procuring of poison to murder Habitus ? Was anything under discussion at their trials other than these very plots made by Oppianicus against Habitus through the agency of Fabricius ? Nothing, gentlemen ; I repeat, you will find nothing. There is living memory to appeal to, there are the public records ; contradict me if I am wrong, read out the record of the evidence : inform the court what allegation was made at their trials—even by way of an aspersion apart from a definite charge—other than Oppianicus's attempt to poison ? Much might be said as to why 63 those verdicts were inevitable ; but I will meet your impatience half way, gentlemen. For although I conceive that no one has ever had a kinder or more attentive hearing than you are granting to me, still your impatience, though inexpressed, has long been calling me to other topics, seeming to interrupt me with—" Come, now, do you deny that the court was bribed ? " I do not, but maintain that it was not my client who bribed it. " Who did bribe it, then ? " I consider, first, that had there been any

illius iudicii futurus esset, veri similius tamen esset,
eum potius corrupisse, qui metuisset ne ipse condemnaretur, quam illum, qui veritus esset ne alter absolveretur : deinde cum esset non dubium quid
iudicari necesse esset, eum certe potius, qui sibi alia
ratione diffideret, quam eum, qui omni ratione con-
fideret : postremo certe potius illum, qui bis apud
eos iudices offendisset, quam eum, qui bis eis causam
64 probavisset.   Unum quidem certe nemo erit tam
inimicus Cluentio qui mihi non concedat : si constet
corruptum illud iudicium esse, aut ab Habito aut ab
Oppianico esse corruptum.   Si doceo non ab Habito,
vinco ab Oppianico : si ostendo ab Oppianico, purgo
Habitum.   Quare, etsi satis docui rationem nullam
huic corrumpendi iudicii fuisse, ex quo intellegitur
ab Oppianico esse corruptum, tamen de illo ipso
separatim cognoscite.

XXIV. Atque ego illa non argumentabor, quae
sunt gravia vehementer : eum corrupisse, qui in
periculo fuerit : eum, qui metuerit : eum, qui spem
salutis in alia ratione non habuerit : eum, qui semper
singulari fuerit audacia.   Multa sunt eius modi :
verum cum habeam rem non dubiam, sed apertam
atque manifestam, enumeratio singulorum argu-
65 mentorum non est necessaria.   Dico C. Aelio Staieno
iudici pecuniam grandem Statium Albium ad corrumpendum iudicium dedisse.   Num quis negat ?

---

[a] Cicero ignores the third and most probable hypothesis,
that bribery was used by both parties. His speech against
Verres indicates that he was well aware of this. See also
note [b] on § 1.

uncertainty as to what the issue of that trial would be, the balance of probability would still be in favour of the court having been bribed by the man who was afraid that it would convict himself, and not by the man whose fear was that it would acquit his adversary : second, that, inasmuch as there was no doubt what the verdict must be, it was much more likely to have been he who had no other ground of confidence than he who had every ground : and last, that it was much more likely to have been he who had twice failed before these judges, than he who had twice won his case before them. There is assuredly 64 one point which no one, however hostile to Cluentius, could fail to concede me : if it be agreed that bribery was used in that case, it was used either by Habitus or by Oppianicus.[a] If I show you that it was not used by Habitus I gain my point that it was used by Oppianicus. If I demonstrate that it was used by Oppianicus, I clear Habitus. And so, although I have adequately shown you that my client had no reason for bribing the court, from which it follows that Oppianicus did bribe it, still let me give you a separate proof of this latter point.

XXIV. There are arguments which, though weighty indeed, I will not stress : as that the guilt of bribery must belong to the man who was in danger of conviction, the man who could hope to escape by no other recourse, the man who had always displayed an unparalleled effrontery. There are many such arguments ; but when my case is not a doubtful one but clear and obvious, I do not need to rehearse my proofs one by one. I assert that Statius Albius gave 65 a large sum of money to G. Aelius Staienus, one of the jurors, for the purpose of bribing the court. Does

Te, Oppianice, appello; te, Acci; quorum alter eloquentia damnationem illam, alter tacita pietate de-
plorat. Audete negare ab Oppianico Staieno iudici
pecuniam datam : negate, inquam, meo loco. Quid
tacetis ? an negare non potestis, quod repetistis,
quod confessi estis, quod abstulistis ? Quo tandem
igitur ore mentionem corrupti iudicii facitis, cum ab
ista parte iudici pecuniam ante iudicium datam, post
66 iudicium ereptam esse fateamini ? Quonam igitur
haec modo gesta sunt ? Repetam paullo altius,
iudices, et omnia, quae in diuturna obscuritate
latuerunt, sic aperiam, ut ea cernere oculis videamini.
Vos quaeso, ut adhuc me attente audistis, ut item,
quae reliqua sunt, audiatis : profecto nihil a me
dicetur, quod non dignum hoc conventu et silentio,
dignum vestris studiis atque auribus esse videatur.

Nam ut primum Oppianicus ex eo, quod Scamander
reus erat factus, quid sibi impenderet coepit suspicari, statim se ad hominis egentis, audacis, in
iudiciis corrumpendis exercitati, tum autem iudicis,
Staieni familiaritatem se applicavit. Ac primum
Scamandro reo tantum donis datis muneribusque
perfecerat, ut eo fautore uteretur cupidiore, quam
67 fides iudicis postulabat. Post autem cum esset
Scamander unius Staieni sententia absolutus,
patronus autem Scamandri ne sua quidem sententia

anyone deny it? I challenge you, Oppianicus, and you, Accius, who both deplore his conviction, one with the eloquence of an advocate, the other with the mute loyalty of a son. Deny if you dare that Oppianicus gave money to Staienus. Deny it, I say, though it is now my turn to speak. What! are you speechless? Or are you rather bound to admit what you brought an action to recover, what you acknowledged, what you carried off? How have you the face to speak of bribery when it was by your side, as you acknowledge, that money was given to one of the jurors before the trial, and wrested from him after it? But how in the world 66 did this come about? I shall go back a little in my narrative, gentlemen, and shall make all the events which have long lain in obscurity so clear, that you will imagine that you have seen them with your own eyes. I beg you will continue to attend as carefully to what follows as you have attended hitherto. I assure you that I shall say nothing which you will think unworthy of this hushed assembly, unworthy of a sympathetic hearing from yourselves.

As soon as Oppianicus began to suspect, from the fact of Scamander's being put on trial, what was hanging over his own head, he set himself to gain the friendship of one who was penniless, brazen, and a past master in the art of judicial corruption and, moreover, himself a juror at the time—namely Staienus. In the first instance, at Scamander's trial he had so far succeeded with his presents and largesses as to secure in him a more zealous partizan than was consistent with the honour of a juror. But 67 afterwards, when Scamander had gained none but Staienus's vote for his acquittal, and Scamander's

liberatus, acrioribus saluti suae remediis subvenien-
dum putavit. Tum ab Staieno, sicut ab homine ad
excogitandum acutissimo, ad audendum impuden-
tissimo, ad efficiendum acerrimo—haec enim ille et
aliqua ex parte habebat et maiore ex parte se habere
simulabat—auxilium capiti ac fortunis suis petere
coepit.

XXV. Iam hoc non ignoratis, iudices, ut etiam
bestiae fame monitae plerumque ad eum locum, ubi
68 pastae sunt aliquando, revertantur. Staienus ille
biennio ante, cum causam bonorum Safini Atellae
recepisset, sescentis milibus nummum se iudicium
corrupturum esse dixerat : quae cum accepisset a
pupillo, suppressit : iudicioque facto nec Safinio nec
bonorum emptoribus reddidit. Quam cum pecuniam
profudisset et sibi nihil non modo ad cupiditates suas,
sed ne ad necessitatem quidem reliquisset, statuit ad
easdem esse sibi praedas ac suppressiones iudiciales
revertendum. Itaque cum Oppianicum iam perditum
et duobus iugulatum praeiudiciis videret, promissis
suis eum excitavit abiectum et simul saluti desperare
vetuit. Oppianicus autem orare hominem coepit, ut
sibi rationem ostenderet iudicii corrumpendi.

69 Ille autem, quem ad modum ex ipso Oppianico
postea est auditum, negavit quemquam esse in civitate praeter se qui id efficere possit. Sed primo
gravari coepit, quod aedilitatem se petere cum
hominibus nobilissimis et invidiam atque offensionem
timere dicebat. Post exoratus initio permagnam
pecuniam poposcit : deinde ad id pervenit, quod con-

----

^a The case of Safinius was a *cause célèbre* of the day,
of which the details are not known.   ^b About £5360.
  ^c Literally, " with his throat cut by two previous verdicts."

patron not even his own, he felt the need of more drastic measures to save the situation, and so it was Staienus whose help he began to implore, for himself and for his fortunes, since he thought him a man both subtle in scheming, brazen in contrivance, and swift in execution :—and so he was to some extent, but not as much as he pretended.

XXV. Now you are not unaware, gentlemen, that even brute beasts, when prompted by hunger, generally return to the place where they have at some time previously found food. Two years before 68 this, our friend Staienus, in undertaking the case of Safinius Atella's estate,[a] had promised to bribe the court with a sum of 600,000 sesterces [b] ; this sum he received from the minor and kept to himself, returning it after the verdict neither to Safinius nor to the purchasers of the estate. When he had squandered the money and had nothing left to satisfy his needs, to say nothing of his pleasures, he made up his mind to return to the same practice of embezzlement in the courts which had yielded him spoils before. And so, seeing Oppianicus already lost and with two previous verdicts like millstones round his neck,[c] he raised his drooping spirits, bidding him not despair of success. And Oppianicus began to implore the fellow to show him some means of bribing the court.

Staienus—so at least we had the story later on 69 from Oppianicus himself—said that he was the only man in the country who could do it. But at first he began to make difficulties, saying that he was standing for the aedileship against men of noble family and was afraid of courting unpopularity and failure. After renewed entreaties, he at first demanded a colossal sum ; but finally came down to a practical

fici potuit : HS sescenta quadraginta milia deferri ad
se domum iussit. Quae pecunia simul atque ad eum
delata est, homo impurissimus statim coepit in eius
modi mente et cogitatione versari, nihil esse suis
rationibus utilius quam Oppianicum condemnari :
illo absoluto pecuniam illam aut iudicibus dispertien-
dam aut ipsi esse reddundam : damnato repetiturum
70 esse neminem. Itaque rem excogitat singularem.
Atque haec, iudices, quae vera dicuntur a nobis,
facilius credetis, si cum animis vestris longo intervallo recordari C. Staieni vitam et naturam volueritis.
Nam perinde ut opinio est de cuiusque moribus, ita
quid ab eo factum aut non factum sit existimari
potest.

XXVI. Cum esset egens, sumptuosus, audax, calli-
dus, perfidiosus, et cum domi suae miserrimis in locis
et inanissimis tantum nummorum positum videret,
ad omnem malitiam et fraudem versare suam mentem
coepit : " ego dem iudicibus ? mihi ipsi igitur praeter
periculum et infamiam quid quaeretur ? Nihil ex-
cogitem quam ob rem Oppianicum damnari necesse
sit ? Quid tandem—nihil enim est quod non fieri
possit—si quis eum forte casus ex periculo eripuerit,
nonne reddundum est ? Praecipitantem igitur im-
pellamus," inquit, " et perditum prosternamus."
71 Capit hoc consilii, ut pecuniam quibusdam iudicibus
levissimis polliceatur, deinde eam postea supprimat :
ut, quoniam graves homines sua sponte severe iudi-
caturos putabat, eos, qui leviores erant, destitutione

ᵃ About £5730.

proposal, bidding Oppianicus bring 640,000 sesterces [a]
to his house. As soon as the money was brought to
him, the foul fellow began to turn things over in
his mind and to say to himself: " Nothing will suit
my book better than the conviction of Oppianicus:
if he is acquitted, I shall either have to distribute
the money among the judges, or pay it to him; but
if he is convicted there will be no one to ask for the
money back." So he contrived a really remarkable 70
plan. And the events which I am truthfully narrat-
ing to you you will the more readily believe if you
will consent to recollect, after all this time, the life
and character of Staienus: for we can best judge
what a particular man's conduct may, or may not
have been, in the light of our estimate of his habits.

XXVI. Needy as he was, and extravagant, brazen,
crafty, and treacherous, seeing so large a sum of
money deposited in his house, where all was misery
and squalor, he began to turn his thoughts to every
form of knavishness and fraud. " Am I to make it
over to the judges?" said he—" What shall I gain
for myself except danger and obloquy? Can't I
devise some way of making Oppianicus's conviction
inevitable? Now suppose—for there is no such
thing as impossibility—that some accident does pull
Oppianicus's case out of the fire; shan't I have to
restore the money? Well, he's on the edge of the
precipice—let's push him over: let's finish him off
now he's down." This was his plan—to promise 71
money to certain worthless judges, and then afterwards to keep it to himself, in order that while the
conscientious men would doubtless vote independently for a severe verdict, he might make the less
worthy judges angry with Oppianicus for having

iratos Oppianico redderet. Itaque, ut erat semper
praeposterus atque perversus, initium facit a Bulbo,
et eum, quod iam diu nihil quaesierat, tristem atque
oscitantem leviter impellit. " Quid tu ? " inquit,
" ecquid me adiuvas, Bulbe, ne gratis rei publicae
serviamus ? " Ille vero, simul atque hoc audivit :
" ne gratis " : " quo voles," inquit, " sequar : sed
quid adfers ? " Tum ei quadraginta milia, si esset
absolutus Oppianicus, pollicetur, et eum, ut ceteros
appellet, quibuscum loqui consuesset, rogat, atque
etiam ipse conditor totius negotii Guttam aspergit
72 huic Bulbo. Itaque minime amarus eis visus est, qui
aliquid ex eius sermone speculae degustarant. Unus
et alter dies intercesserat, cum res parum certa videbatur : sequester et confirmator pecuniae desidera-
batur. Tum appellat hilaro vultu hominem Bulbus,
ut blandissime potest : " quid tu," inquit, " Paete ? "
—hoc enim sibi Staienus cognomen ex imaginibus
Aeliorum delegerat, ne, si se Ligurem fecisset,
nationis magis quam generis uti cognomine videretur
—" qua de re mecum locutus es, quaerunt a me ubi
sit pecunia." Hic ille planus improbissimus, quaestu
iudiciario pastus, qui illi pecuniae, quam condiderat,
spe iam atque animo incubaret, contrahit frontem—
recordamini faciem atque illos eius fictos simulatosque
voltus—queritur se ab Oppianico destitutum, et, qui

---

a It seems impossible to do justice to Cicero's somewhat
laboured *jeu de mots*, which turns on the fact that
bulbus means some such vegetable as an onion, which
was eaten at the end of a Roman meal as the savoury :
gutta means a drop and suggests a dressing of sweet oil :
and *conditor*, according as the quantity of the " i " is long
or short, means either " the seasoner " (*condio*) or " the
founder " (*condo*).

left them in the lurch. And so, with his usual
reversal of the order of things he began with the
" savoury " Bulbus,[a] and finding him yawning
gloomily (for he had made nothing for some time)
gave him a gentle fillip : " Hullo, Bulbus," he said,
" What do you say to helping me, and making something out of our services to the state ? " As soon as
he heard the words " make something," Bulbus
replied : " I'll follow you anywhere you like :
but what's your idea ? " Thereupon Staienus promised him forty thousand if Oppianicus were acquitted, and asked him to make overtures besides
to his usual associates ; while he himself, as head
cook and bottle-washer, tried the effect of combining
the " sweet " Gutta with the " savoury " Bulbus, so 72
that the latter went down very well with those to
whom his promise had given a crumb of hope. A
day or two passed, and the scheme was looking far
from safe : a need was felt of a depository and a
security for the money. Then Bulbus with a smile
on his face approached Staienus and said in his most
ingratiating manner : " Hullo, Paetus ! " (for
Staienus had adopted the surname of Paetus from
the family tree of the Aelii for fear that if he styled
himself Ligur, it would be thought that his surname
came from his race and not his family [b]) " About the
matter you discussed with me—they are asking me
where the money is." Then the profligate *flâneur*,
who battened on what he could make out of the
courts, although he had this money hidden away and
was brooding over it with eager hopes, wrinkled his
forehead—you know his face and the hypocritical
expression he used to assume—and since his nature

[b] There was a barbarous tribe called Ligurians.

esset totus ex fraude et mendacio factus quique ea
vitia, quae a natura habebat, etiam studio atque
artificio quodam malitiae condisset, pulcre adseverat
sese ab Oppianico destitutum, atque hoc addit testi-
monii, sua illum sententia, cum palam omnes laturi
essent, condemnatum iri.

73 XXVII. Manarat sermo in consilio pecuniae quandam mentionem inter iudices esse versatam. Res
neque tam fuerat occulta quam erat occultanda neque
tam erat aperta quam rei publicae causa aperienda.
In ea obscuritate ac dubitatione omnium Cannutio,
perito homini, qui quodam odore suspicionis Staienum
corruptum esse sensisset neque dum rem perfectam
arbitraretur, placuit repente pronuntiari : DIXERUNT.
Hic tum Oppianicus non magno opere pertimuit : rem
74 a Staieno perfectam esse arbitrabatur. In consilium
erant ituri iudices XXXII. Sententiis XVI absolutio
confici poterat. Quadragena milia nummum in
singulos iudices distributa eum numerum sententia-
rum conficere debebant, ut ad cumulum spe maiorum
praemiorum ipsius Staieni sententia septima decima
accederet. Atque etiam casu tum, quod illud repente
erat factum, Staienus ipse non aderat. Causam
nescio quam apud iudicem defendebat. Facile hoc
Habitus patiebatur, facile Cannutius : at non Oppianicus neque patronus eius L. Quinctius : qui cum
esset illo tempore tribunus plebis, convicium C. Iunio

ᵃ If the voting were equal, the accused would be given the
benefit of the doubt.

was compounded of dishonesty and falsehood, since he had seasoned his natural faults by careful application and by making knavery his stock-in-trade, he roundly asserted that Oppianicus had left him in the lurch, adding, to support his words, that his own vote, as they were all to vote openly, would be cast for conviction.

XXVII. A rumour had leaked out in court that **73** there was a suggestion of bribery among the jurors : the whole business was neither as secret as they wanted to keep it, nor as open as, in the public interest, it should have been. In this general mystification and uncertainty Cannutius, a man of experience, who had somehow got wind of Staienus's having taken a bribe, but did not think that his plans had yet been put into effect, decided to have it suddenly announced : " The pleadings are finished." At this juncture Oppianicus did not feel any very great anxiety, for he thought Staienus had carried through his plan. Thirty-two jurors were to con- **74** sider the verdict ; acquittal could be secured by sixteen votes.[a] That number of votes should be secured by the distribution to each juror of 40,000 sesterces, with the expectation that Staienus would be led by the hope of larger profits to crown the total with the addition of his own, the seventeenth vote. Now it so fell out, because Cannutius had acted suddenly, that Staienus himself was not present in court (he was defending some suit before an arbitrator). Habitus was indifferent enough to his absence and so was Cannutius ; but not so Oppianicus nor his counsel, L. Quinctius, who, as a tribune of the people at the time, protested in the most abusive language to the president of the court,

iudici quaestionis maximum fecit, ut ne sine illo in
consilium iretur : cumque id ei per viatores consulto
neglegentius agi videretur, ipse e publico iudicio ad
privatum Staieni iudicium profectus est et illud pro
potestate dimitti iussit : Staienum ipse ad subsellia
75 adduxit. Consurgitur in consilium, cum sententias
Oppianicus, quae tum erat potestas, palam ferri velle
dixisset, ut Staienus scire posset quid cuique deberetur. Varia iudicum genera : nummarii pauci, sed
omnes irati. Ut qui accipere in Campo consuerunt,
eis candidatis, quorum nummos suppressos esse
putant, inimicissimi solent esse, sic eius modi iudices
infesti tum reo venerant : ceteri nocentissimum esse
arbitrabantur, sed exspectabant sententias eorum,
quos corruptos esse putabant, ut ex eis constituerent
a quo iudicium corruptum videretur.

XXVIII. Ecce tibi eius modi sortitio, ut in primis
Bulbo et Staieno et Guttae esset iudicandum. Summa
omnium exspectatio quidnam sententiae ferrent leves
ac nummarii iudices. Atque illi omnes sine ulla
76 dubitatione condemnant. Hic tum iniectus est hominibus scrupulus et quaedam dubitatio quidnam esset
actum. Deinde homines sapientes et ex vetere illa
disciplina iudiciorum, qui neque absolvere hominem
nocentissimum possent neque eum, de quo esset

G. Junius, against the jury considering their verdict
without Staienus ; and thinking that his absence
was due to the intentional negligence of the criers,
he left the criminal court and went to where Staienus
was in the civil court, and by virtue of his official prerogative ordered it to adjourn : Staienus he led
back to his seat himself. The jurors rose to con- 75
sider their verdict ; for Oppianicus had declared, as
the defendant was at that time able to do, that he
wished the voting to be open, in order that Staienus
might know what he ought to pay each juror. The
jurors were of different sorts : the venal ones among
them, though not numerous, were none the less all
of them incensed. Just as those who make a
practice of taking bribes at elections are usually the
bitterest enemies of those candidates whose money
they think has not been allowed to reach them, so
now those jurors, in the same circumstances, had
come to vote with a prejudice against the accused :
the honest jurors, while thinking him guilty indeed,
none the less waited for the others whom they
thought venal, to give their votes first in order that
they might thereby judge by whom it was likely
that the court had been bribed.

XXVIII. Lo and behold ! the lot decided that
Bulbus, Staienus, and Gutta should be among the
first to vote : everywhere was the keenest expect-
ancy to see what verdict these worthless and venal
jurors would record ; and they all, without the slightest hesitation, voted guilty. This made people feel 76
uneasy and somewhat doubtful as to what had
happened. After them came prudent jurors trained
in the old style of trial, who were incapable either
of acquitting a thoroughly guilty person, or of con-

orta suspicio, pecunia oppugnatum, re illa incognita primo condemnare vellent, NON LIQUERE dixerunt. Nonnulli autem severi homines, qui hoc statuerunt, quo quisque animo quid faceret spectari oportere, etsi alii pecunia accepta verum iudicarent,[1] tamen nihilo minus se superioribus suis iudiciis constare putabant oportere : itaque damnarunt. Quinque omnino fuerunt, qui illum vestrum innocentem Oppianicum sive imprudentia sive misericordia sive aliqua suspicione sive ambitione adducti absolverunt.

77 Condemnato Oppianico statim L. Quinctius, homo maxime popularis, qui omnes rumorum et contionum ventos colligere consuesset, oblatam sibi facultatem putavit, ut ex invidia senatoria posset crescere, quod eius ordinis iudicia minus iam probari populo arbitrabatur. Habetur una atque altera contio vehemens et gravis : accepisse pecuniam iudices, ut innocentem reum condemnarent, tribunus plebis clamabat : agi fortunas omnium dicebat : nulla esse iudicia : qui pecuniosum inimicum haberet, incolumem esse neminem posse. Homines totius ignari negotii, qui Oppianicum numquam vidissent, virum optimum et hominem pudentissimum pecunia oppressum esse arbitrarentur, incensi suspicione rem in medium vocare coeperunt et causam illam totam deposcere.

78 Atque illo ipso tempore in aedes T. Anni, hominis honestissimi, necessarii et amici mei, noctu Staienus

---

[1] iudicabant *F* : iudicarent *Ernesti.*

victing at the first hearing one of whom there was
any suspicion that he might be the victim of bribery,
without going into the matter : they voted " Not
proven." But some conscientious men who held
that the motive behind any action needed examination, felt that though others were returning a true
verdict only because bribed to do so, still they ought
none the less to stand by their previous verdicts :
accordingly they voted guilty. There were five
persons in all who, whether from mistaken judgement, or pity, or a suspicion of foul play, or
interested motives, voted your poor innocent
Oppianicus not guilty.

Immediately upon the conviction of Oppianicus, 77
L. Quinctius, an ardent demagogue, whose ears
were set to catch every breath of private gossip or
public harangue, felt that here was a chance of using
the unpopularity of the Senate for his own advancement, considering how poor a reputation with the
people the Senatorial courts enjoyed at the time. He
delivered several violent and impressive harangues,
loudly protesting as tribune of the people, that the
jurors had been bribed to condemn an innocent man :
" This touches every one of us," he said. " Fair
trial is a thing of the past : not a man is safe who has
a rich enemy." So people who were completely
ignorant of the case and had never seen Oppianicus
imagined that a good citizen and a thoroughly respectable person had fallen a victim to bribery : their
suspicions blazed up, and they began to call for the
case to be reconsidered, and the proceedings quashed.
And that was just the time when Staienus came by 78
night on the summons of Oppianicus to the house of
T. Annius, a man of the highest character and a con-

arcessitus ab Oppianico venit. Iam cetera nota sunt
omnibus : ut cum illo Oppianicus egerit de pecunia,
ut ille se redditurum esse dixerit, ut eum sermonem
audierint omnem viri boni, qui tum consulto propter
in occulto stetissent : ut res patefacta et in forum
prolata et pecunia omnis Staieno extorta atque erepta
sit.

XXIX. Huius Staieni persona populo iam nota
atque perspecta ab nulla turpi suspicione abhorrebat :
suppressam esse ab eo pecuniam, quam pro reo pro-
nuntiasset, qui erant in contione, non intellegebant;
neque enim docebantur. Versatam esse in iudicio
mentionem pecuniae sentiebant, innocentem reum
condemnatum audiebant : Staieni sententia condemnatum videbant : non gratis id ab eo factum esse,
quod hominem norant, iudicabant. Similis in Bulbo,
in Gutta, in aliis non nullis suspicio consistebat.
79 Itaque confiteor—licet enim iam impune hoc praesertim in loco confiteri—, quod Oppianici non modo
vita, sed etiam nomen ante illud tempus populo
ignotum fuisset, indignissimum porro videretur circumventum esse innocentem pecunia, hanc deinde
suspicionem augeret Staieni improbitas et non nul-
lorum eius similium iudicum turpitudo, causam autem
ageret L. Quinctius, homo cum summa potestate tum
ad inflammandos animos multitudinis accommodatus,
summam illi iudicio invidiam infamiamque esse con-

nexion and friend of my own. What followed is now
a matter of common knowledge—how Oppianicus
raised the question of the money and Staienus said he
would repay it : how the whole conversation was
overheard by trustworthy persons who had secreted
themselves close by for the purpose : and how the
whole plot was exposed and taken into court and
Staienus forced to let go and give up all the money.

XXIX. The character of Staienus, now so notorious and so transparent, was such as to lend itself to
every suspicion of dishonour. Those who attended the
public meetings did not realize that he had promised
to use in the interest of the accused the money which
he had kept to himself, for the simple reason that
they were not told. They perceived that there had
been talk of bribery in the case : they heard that an
innocent man had been convicted : they saw that
Staienus had voted for his conviction : they concluded from what they knew of the man that he had
not done so without being paid for it. The same
suspicion persisted in the case of Bulbus, of Gutta,
and of sundry others. And so I confess—as I may **79**
now do with impunity, especially before this honourable court—that, because the very name of Oppianicus, to say nothing of his way of life, had hitherto
been generally unknown ; because, further, it seemed
a shameful thing that an innocent man should fall
victim to bribery ; and lastly, because the suspicion
of bribery gained colour from the bad character of
Staienus and the ill reputation of some jurors like
himself ; because, moreover, the case was taken up
by L. Quinctius with all the authority of his office,
and all his skill in kindling the passions of a crowd :
for all these reasons, I say, a high degree of resent-

flatam, atque in hanc flammam recentem tum C.
Iunium, qui illi quaestioni praefuerat, esse iniectum
memini, et illum hominem aedilicium, iam praetorem
opinionibus hominum constitutum, non disceptatione
dicendi, sed clamore de foro atque adeo de civitate
esse sublatum.

80   Neque me paenitet hoc tempore potius quam illo
causam A. Cluenti defendere. Causa enim manet
eadem, quae mutari nullo modo potest, temporis
iniquitas atque invidia recessit, ut, quod in tempore
mali fuit, nihil obsit, quod in causa boni fuit, prosit.
Itaque nunc quem ad modum audiar sentio, non modo
ab eis, quorum iudicium ac potestas est, sed etiam
ab illis, quorum tantum est existimatio. At tum si
dicerem, non audirer, non quod alia res esset, immo
eadem, sed tempus aliud. XXX. Id adeo sic cognoscite. Quis tum auderet dicere nocentem condemnatum esse Oppianicum ? quis nunc audet
negare ? Quis tum posset arguere ab Oppianico
temptatum esse iudicium pecunia ? quis id hoc tempore infitiari potest ? Cui tum liceret docere Oppianicum reum factum esse tum denique, cum duobus
proximis praeiudiciis condemnatus esset ? quis est
81 qui id hoc tempore infirmare conetur ? Quare invidia remota, quam dies mitigavit, oratio mea depre-
cata est, vestra fides atque aequitas a veritatis dis-

ment and odium was worked up against that trial,
and I remember how the president of the court, G.
Junius, was flung into the still raging furnace, and
how a man who, being already an aedile, was
marked out by public opinion as a coming praetor,
was removed from his practice at the bar, aye, and
from public life as well, not by a deliberate vote of
censure, but by popular outcry.

I am not sorry to be defending Cluentius in these 80
days rather than in those, for while his case, which
is not susceptible of change, remains the same, those
days, so unfair, so prejudicial to it, are now past ;
with the result that whatever disadvantage lay in
those times can no longer harm us, whatever advantage lies in a good cause avails us still. And so I
am conscious how close is the attention now not
only of those to whom belongs the prerogative of
judgement, but of those, too, who can only form
an opinion on the case. Had I been speaking then,
I should not have had the same hearing, not because
my case would have been different—on the contrary,
it would have been the same—but because the times
were different. XXX. Let me give you an illustra-
tion of this : who would then have dared to say that
Oppianicus was rightly convicted ? Who now dares
to deny it ? Who could then have shown that it was
Oppianicus who corrupted the court ? Who in
these days can disprove it ? Who was then at
liberty to point out that Oppianicus had only been
put on trial when already found guilty by two recent
verdicts ? Who is there in these days who would
try to dispute it ? And so—now that we are rid of 81
prejudice, now that time has modified it, that my
voice has appealed against it, that your own sense

ceptatione reiecit, quid est praeterea quod in causa relinquatur ?

Versatam esse in iudicio pecuniam constat : ea quaeritur unde profecta sit, ab accusatore an ab reo. Dicit accusator haec : " Primum gravissimis criminibus accusabam, ut nihil opus esset pecunia : deinde condemnatum adducebam, ut ne eripi quidem pecunia posset : postremo, etiamsi absolutus fuisset, mearum tamen omnium fortunarum status incolumis maneret." Quid contra reus ? " Primum ipsam multitudinem criminum et atrocitatem pertimescebam : deinde Fabriciis propter conscientiam mei sceleris condemnatis me esse condemnatum sentiebam : postremo in eum casum veneram, ut omnis mearum fortunarum status unius iudicii periculo contineretur."

82 Age, quoniam corrumpendi iudicii causas ille multas et graves habuit, hic nullam, profectio ipsius pecuniae requiratur. Confecit tabulas diligentissime Cluentius. Haec autem res habet hoc certe, ut nihil possit neque additum neque detractum de re familiari latere. Anni sunt octo, cum ista causa in ista meditatione versatur, cum omnia, quae ad eam rem pertinent, et ex huius et ex aliorum tabulis agitatis, tractatis, inquiritis : cum interea Cluentianae pecuniae vestigium nullum invenitis. Quid, Albiana pecunia vestigiisne nobis odoranda est an ad ipsum

of honour and justice has banished it from an examination of the facts—what case have I still to answer?

It is agreed that bribery was at work in the trial: the only question is, from whom did it proceed? From the prosecutor, or from the accused? The prosecutor says: " First, the charges on which I was prosecuting were so grave as to preclude the need for bribery. Second, the man I was bringing into court was already convicted, so that bribery could have availed nothing—no, not even to save him. Lastly, even if he had been acquitted, the whole basis of my fortunes would remain unaffected." What says the accused, on the other hand? " First, the mere number and gravity of the charges filled me with apprehension. Second, I felt that the conviction of Fabricius and his accomplice, as accessories to my crime, implied my conviction also. Lastly, I had come to the point where the whole basis of my fortunes was involved in the issue of a single trial."

Come, then, since Oppianicus had many weighty 82 motives for bribing the court, and my client none, let us examine the question, whence came the actual sum expended? Cluentius has kept his accounts most scrupulously—a fact which assuredly has this advantage that no addition or subtraction could have been made to or from the family estate without its appearing. Yet for all these eight years you have been thinking over your case, investigating, discussing, examining every item relevant to it in his or other people's accounts, and all this time not a trace do you find of such expenditure on the part of Cluentius. Are we indeed to go sniffing along the trail of Oppianicus's money or cannot your own ad-

cubile vobis indicibus venire possumus ? Tenentur
uno in loco HS I⊃cxl : tenentur apud hominem auda-
cissimum : tenentur apud iudicem. Quid voltis
83 amplius ? At enim Staienus non fuit ab Oppianico,
sed a Cluentio ad iudicium corrumpendum constitutus. Cur eum, cum in consilium iretur, Cluentius
et Cannutius abesse patiebantur ? cur cum in consilium mittebant, Staienum iudicem qui pecuniam
dederant non requirebant ?   Oppianicus querebatur :
Quinctius flagitabat : sine Staieno ne in consilium
iretur, tribunicia potestate effectum est. At condemnavit. Hanc enim condemnationem dederat ob-
sidem Bulbo et ceteris, ut destitutus ab Oppianico
videretur. Quare si istinc causa corrumpendi iudicii,
si istinc pecunia, istinc Staienus, istinc denique omnis
fraus et audacia est, hinc pudor, honesta vita, nulla
suspicio pecuniae, nulla corrumpendi iudicii causa,
patimini veritate patefacta atque omni errore sublato
eo transire illius turpitudinis infamiam, ubi cetera
maleficia consistunt : ab eo invidiam discedere aliquando, ad quem numquam accessisse culpam videtis.
84   XXXI. At enim pecuniam Staieno dedit Oppianicus non ad corrumpendum iudicium, sed ad conciliationem gratiae. Tene hoc, Acci, dicere, tali prudentia, etiam usu atque exercitatione praeditum ?
Sapientissimum esse dicunt eum, cui quod opus sit
ipsi veniat in mentem : proxime accedere illum, qui

mission lead us straight to his lair ? We find in one
place 640,000 sesterces, and that in the hands of a
brazen scoundrel, moreover a juror. What would
you further ? " Oh," you say, " but Staienus was 83
instigated to bribe the court not by Oppianicus but
by Cluentius." Then why were Cluentius and Cannutius ready to let him be absent when the court
was to consider its verdict ? Why did not those who
had given him the money insist on his being in his
place when they were closing the proceedings ? It
was Oppianicus who insisted ; Quinctius who insisted ; it was the tribune's prerogative which prevented the consideration of the verdict without
Staienus. " But Staienus voted guilty." Yes, for
he had stipulated to Bulbus and the rest that he
would vote guilty as a pledge to them that Oppianicus
had left him in the lurch. And so, if on your side
is to be found a motive for bribing the court, the
money which bribed it, Staienus, and every species
of dishonesty and knavery ; and on our side probity,
uprightness of life, no suspicion of having bribed the
court, no motive for doing so ; then since the truth
stands revealed and all misconception is dispelled,
suffer the taint of that dishonour to be transferred
to him at whose door lie those other crimes ; suffer
it to depart at last from him on whom you see that
no guilt has ever fastened.

XXXI. But, you may say, Oppianicus gave 84
Staienus the money not to bribe the court, but to
effect a reconciliation with Cluentius. To think
that you, Accius, for all your caution, for all your
practice and experience, should say such a thing !
Wisest, they say, is he whose own mind suggests
the appropriate idea : next comes the man who

alterius bene inventis obtemperet. In stultitia
contra est. Minus enim stultus est is, cui nihil in
mentem venit, quam ille, qui, quod stulte alteri venit
in mentem, comprobat. Istam conciliationem gratiae
Staienus tum recenti re, cum faucibus premeretur,
excogitavit, sive, ut homines tum loquebantur, a P.
85 Cethego admonitus. Nam fuisse hunc tum hominum
sermonem recordari potestis : Cethegum, quod
hominem odisset et quod eius improbitatem versari
in re publica nollet et quod videret eum, qui se ab reo
pecuniam, cum iudex esset, clam atque extra ordinem accepisse confessus esset, salvum esse non posse,
minus ei fidele consilium dedisse. In hoc si improbus
Cethegus fuit, videtur mihi adversarium removere
voluisse. Sin erat eius modi causa, ut Staienus nummos se accepisse negare non posset, nihil autem erat
periculosius nec turpius quam ad quam rem accepisset confiteri, non est consilium Cethegi reprehenden-
86 dum. Verum alia causa tum Staieni fuit, alia nunc
Acci, tua est. Ille cum re premeretur, quodcumque
diceret, honestius diceret, quam si, quod erat factum,
fateretur : te vero illud idem, quod tum explosum
et eiectum est, nunc rettulisse demiror. Qui enim
poterat tum in gratiam redire cum Oppianico Cluentius ? qui cum matre ? Haerebat in tabulis publicis
reus et accusator : condemnati erant Fabricii : nec

ᵃ The reference is to Hesiod, *Op.* 293 οὗτος μὲν παν-
άριστος ὃς αὐτὸς πάντα νοήσῃ, | ἐσθλὸς δ' αὖ κἀκεῖνος ὃς εὖ
εἰπόντι πίθηται.
ᵇ It is probable that Cethegus and Staienus were at the
time rival candidates for the aedileship. See § 69.

accepts the good ideas of another.[a] With folly the
reverse is true : for he whose mind suggests to him
nothing at all is less of a fool than the man who
adopts the foolish suggestions of his neighbour.
Your story of a reconciliation was invented by
Staienus in the midst of the crisis, when he was gripped
by the throat, or perhaps as rumour had it at the
time, it was suggested to him by P. Cethegus. For 85
you remember that there was such a rumour at the
time—to the effect that as Cethegus hated the fellow,
was reluctant to see such knavery engaged in public
life, and moreover realized that there was no hope
of acquittal for a man who had admitted to having
secretly and irregularly accepted a bribe from the
accused when serving as a juror, he gave him somewhat insincere advice. If, in thus acting, Cethegus
was unprincipled, I think it was that he wished to be
rid of an opponent.[b] But if it was the case that
Staienus could not deny his acceptance of the money,
whereas nothing was so damning or disgraceful as to
confess the ends for which he had accepted it, no
fault can be found with Cethegus's advice. But your 86
present case, Accius, has no connexion with Staienus's
case in the past ; he in his desperate plight might
have said anything, and brought less shame on himself by saying it than by confessing the truth : but
as for you, I am surprised that you have now revived
that old farce which was then hissed and hooted off
the stage. How was it at that time possible for
Cluentius to be reconciled to Oppianicus ? Or how
with his mother ? Their names were down in black
and white on the public records as defendant and
prosecutor : Fabricius and his accomplice had been
convicted : Albius could not have escaped though

elabi alio accusatore poterat Albius nec sine ignominia calumniae relinquere accusationem Cluentius.

87 XXXII. An ut praevaricaretur ? Iam id quoque
ad corrumpendum iudicium pertinet. Sed quid opus
erat ad eam rem iudice sequestre ? et omnino quam
ob rem tota ista res per Staienum potius, hominem
ab utroque alienissimum, sordidissimum, turpissimum,
quam per bonum aliquem virum ageretur et amicum
necessariumque communem ? Sed quid ego haec
pluribus quasi de re obscura disputo, cum ipsa
pecunia, quae Staieno data est, numero ac summa
sua non modo quanta fuerit, sed etiam ad quam rem
fuerit ostendat ? Sedecim dico iudices, ut Oppianicus absolveretur, corrumpendos fuisse : ad Staienum
sescenta quadraginta milia nummum esse delata.
Si, ut tu dicis, gratiae conciliandae causa, quadraginta istorum accessio milium quid valet ? si, ut nos
dicimus, ut quadragena milia sedecim iudicibus da-
rentur, non Archimedes melius potuit discribere.

88 At enim iudicia facta permulta sunt a Cluentio
iudicium esse corruptum. Immo vero ante hoc
tempus omnino ista ipsa res suo nomine in iudicium
numquam est vocata. Ita multum agitata, ita diu
iactata ista res est, ut hodierno die primum causa
illa defensa sit, hodierno die primum veritas vocem
contra invidiam his iudicibus freta miserit. Verum
tamen ista multa iudicia quae sunt ? Ego enim me

---

^a *Praevaricari* literally means to walk crookedly: hence
it is used of a prosecutor who conducts his case in the
interests of the other side.

^b The great mathematician, whose tomb Cicero had dis-
covered at Syracuse, when quaestor in Sicily, 75 B.C.

another prosecuted, nor could Cluentius have relinquished the prosecution without being branded as a false accuser.

XXXII. Or was it to secure the collision[a] of Cluentius ? That too is an act of judicial corruption. But what need, for such a purpose, of a juror as go-between ? Why, indeed, should the whole alleged transaction have been conducted through the agency of Staienus, a dirty scoundrel who had nothing to do with either party, and not through some honest man, a friend and connexion of both ? But why do I labour my point as if there were any doubt about it, when the actual sum employed shows us by its figures and its total not only the amount but its purpose ? I depose that, to secure the acquittal of Oppianicus sixteen jurors would have had to be bribed : 640,000 sesterces were paid to Staienus. If, as you maintain, it was to effect a reconciliation, what is the point of the odd forty thousand ? If, as I maintain, it was to give each of the sixteen jurors forty thousand a-piece, Archimedes[b] himself could not have worked out the amount better.

But, you may say, the result of many previous trials has proved that Cluentius bribed the court. Far from it : before to-day your contention has never come before a court as a direct issue. Much as the case has been discussed, long as it has been canvassed, this is the first day on which it has been defended, the first on which truth, emboldened by this honourable court, has raised her voice to answer prejudice. But as for those many previous trials, what do they amount to ? I have fortified myself

ad omnia confirmavi et sic paravi, ut docerem, quae
facta postea iudicia de illo iudicio dicerentur, partim
ruinae similiora aut tempestati quam iudicio et dis-
ceptationi fuisse, partim nihil contra Habitum valere,
partim etiam pro hoc esse, partim esse eius modi, ut
neque appellata umquam iudicia sint neque existi-
89 mata. Hic ego magis ut consuetudinem servem,
quam quod vos non vestra hoc sponte faciatis, petam
a vobis, ut me, dum de his singulis disputo iudiciis,
attente audiatis.

XXXIII. Condemnatus est C. Iunius, qui ei quaestioni praefuerat : adde etiam illud, si placet : tum
est condemnatus cum esset iudex quaestionis. Non
modo causae, sed ne legi quidem quicquam per tribunum plebis laxamenti datum est. Quo tempore
illum a quaestione ad nullum aliud rei publicae munus
abduci licebat, eo tempore ad quaestionem ipse
abreptus est. At ad quam quaestionem ? Voltus
enim vestri, iudices, me invitant, ut, quae reticenda
90 putaram, libeat iam libere dicere. Quid ? illa tandem quaestio aut disceptatio aut iudicium fuit ?
Putabo fuisse. Dicat qui vult hodie de illo populo
concitato, cui tum populo mos gestus est, qua de re
Iunius causam dixerit : quemcumque rogaveris, hoc
respondebit : quod pecuniam acceperit, quod innocentem circumvenerit. Est haec opinio. At, si ita
esset, hac lege accusatum oportuit, qua accusatur

---

a The " indulgence due to the case " was a respite of ten
days customarily granted to the accused in order that he
might prepare his defence : that " due to the law " was the
observance of the rule that a presiding judge must not be
withdrawn from his court.

for every issue, and am prepared to show that of the trials which followed that of Oppianicus, and are said to bear upon it, some were more like a landslide or a hurricane than a trial or an investigation : some are in no wise prejudicial to Habitus, others actually support him ; while others again were never spoken or thought of as trials. At this point I ask 89 you, gentlemen, rather for form's sake than because you are not likely to do so without being asked, to give me your careful attention while I deal with these trials one by one.

XXXIII. There is the conviction of G. Junius, who had presided at the original trial ; and further, if you please, his conviction actually took place during his term of presidency. The tribune, so far from granting any special indulgency to his case, showed none even to the law.[a] Precisely at a time when it was unlawful for him to withdraw from court for any other public duty, he was himself haled away to court. To what court indeed ? I ask you because I am encouraged by the expression of your faces to hope that I may now speak freely of what I had thought I must suppress.

Was it, I ask, a court, an investigation, a trial ? I 90 shall suppose that it was. Let any member of that excited mob—and the mob was deferred to in those days—tell me on what charge Junius stood his trial. Ask whom you will, his reply will be : " On the charge of accepting a bribe and compassing the ruin of an innocent man." That is what people think. But had it been so, he ought to have been prosecuted under the same statute [b] as Habitus is now. But

---

[b] The Lex Cornelia de sicariis : see Introduction, Note on the Statutes, 1.

Habitus. At ipse ea lege quaerebat. Paucos dies
exspectasset Quinctius. At neque privatus accusare
nec sedata invidia volebat. Videtis igitur non in
causa, sed in tempore ac potestate spem omnem
91 accusatoris fuisse. Multam petivit. Qua lege ?
quod in legem non iurasset, quae res nemini umquam
fraudi fuit, et quod C. Verres, praetor urbanus, homo
sanctus et diligens, subsortitionem eius in eo codice
non haberet, qui tum interlitus proferebatur. His
de causis C. Iunius condemnatus est, iudices, levissimis et infirmissimis, quas omnino in iudicium adferri
non oportuit. Itaque oppressus est, non causa, sed
tempore.
92 XXXIV. Hoc vos Cluentio iudicium putatis obesse
oportere ? Quam ob causam ? Si ex lege subsortitus non erat Iunius aut si in aliquam legem aliquando
non iuraverat, idcirco illius damnatione aliquid de
Cluentio iudicabatur ? " Non," inquit : " sed ille
idcirco illis legibus condemnatus est, quod contra
aliam legem commiserat." Qui hoc confitentur,
possunt idem illud iudicium fuisse defendere ?
" Ergo," inquit, " idcirco infestus tum populus
Romanus fuit C. Iunio, quod illud iudicium corruptum
per eum putabatur." Num igitur hoc tempore causa
mutata est ? num alia res, alia ratio illius iudicii, alia

^a The object of Cicero's indictment, four years before, for
misgovernment in Sicily.
^b When a vacancy occurred among the jurors, it was
filled by the president of the court, subject to the authority
of the city praetor. As Falcula, thus appointed by Junius,
voted against Oppianicus, collusion between them and
Cluentius was suspected. Cicero himself had accused Verres
and Junius (*In Verrem*, II. i. 158) of complicity.
318

Junius presided over the court administering that statute. Quinctius should have waited a few days ; but he was anxious to conduct his prosecution before either he resigned office or the popular prejudice subsided. And so you see that the prosecutor relied entirely, not on the merits of his case, but on its circumstances, and on his own prerogative. He demanded 91 a fine—under what statute ?—because, if you please, Junius had omitted to take the official oath, though that has never been held criminal in anyone, and also because the record of the city praetor, the moral and scrupulous G. Verres,[a] which was produced, full of erasures, at the trial, contained no note of his having filled up a vacancy among the jurors.[b] Such were the reasons, gentlemen, trivial and unsubstantial as they were, which led to the conviction of G. Junius, reasons which ought never to have been admitted before the court. And his downfall was due not to the facts, but to the circumstances, of his case.

XXXIV. Ought this trial, think you, to reflect 92 on Cluentius ? Why should it ? If Junius was irregular in the filling up of vacancies, or if he had at any time omitted to take any official oath, did his conviction imply any sentence on Cluentius ? " No," says my opponent, " but the reason for his conviction under those statutes was an offence committed against another statute." Can those who admit this possibly maintain that his trial was deserving of the name ? " Well, then," he goes on, " the reason for the ill-feeling in Rome against G. Junius was the belief that the corruption of the court at Oppianicus's trial had been effected through him." Has the case, then, changed since those days ? Are the facts of the case, the motive of the trial, the nature

natura totius negotii nunc est ac tum fuit ? Non
opinor ex eis rebus, quae gestae sunt, rem ullam po-
93 tuisse mutari. Quid ergo est causae quod nunc nostra
defensio audiatur tanto silentio, tum Iunio defendendi
sui potestas erepta sit ? Quia tum in causa nihil erat
praeter invidiam, errorem, suspicionem, contiones
cotidianas seditiose ac populariter concitatas. Accusabat tribunus plebis idem in contionibus, idem ad
subsellia : ad iudicium non modo de contione, sed
etiam cum ipsa contione veniebat. Gradus 'illi
Aurelii tum novi quasi pro theatro illi iudicio aedificati
videbantur : quos ubi accusator concitatis hominibus
complerat, non modo dicendi ab reo, sed ne surgendi
94 quidem potestas erat. Nuper apud C. Orchivium,
collegam meum, locus ab iudicibus Fausto Sullae de
pecuniis residuis non est constitutus, non quo illi aut
exlegem esse Sullam aut causam pecuniae publicae
contemptam atque abiectam putarent, sed quod
accusante tribuno plebis condicione aequa disceptari
posse non putarunt. Quid conferam ? Sullamne
cum Iunio ? an hunc tribunum plebis cum Quinctio ?
an vero tempus cum tempore ? Sulla maximis opibus, cognatis, adfinibus, necessariis, clientibus plurimis : haec autem apud Iunium parva et infirma et

---

a A flight of steps in the Forum supposed to have been
built by and named after M. Aurelius Cotta, consul in 74 B.C.,
the year of Junius's trial. They led up to the Tribunal
Aurelium near the Temple of Castor at the opposite end of
the Forum from where Cicero was speaking. N.B. the
Courts were held in the open air.

b Cicero's colleague in the praetorship, 66 B.C.

c Lucius Cornelius Sulla Faustus, son of the dictator, had
inherited the vast fortune which his father was supposed
to have amassed by embezzling public funds.

320

of the whole proceeding different now from what they were then ? I hold that of the actual facts of the case no single item can have changed. Whence 93 comes it, then, that my case is being heard in such deep silence now, whereas Junius then was deprived even of the chance of defending himself ? The reason is that then the case was wholly at the mercy of prejudice, misunderstanding, suspicion, and the spirit of lawlessness and tumult which daily animated the mass meetings. The accuser was a tribune of the people : whether on the platform or before the court, a tribune still; and he came into court straight from his mass meeting—nay, he brought it with him. The Aurelian steps yonder *a*—they were new then—might have been built to serve as an auditorium for the case : and when the accuser had filled them with an excited crowd, there was no possibility of speaking for the accused ; nor even of rising to speak. Not long ago, in the court presided 94 over by my colleague, G. Orchivius,*b* the judges refused to give a place on the cause-list to the case of Faustus Sulla,*c* who was being tried for retaining surplus public funds; not that they thought Sulla above the law, or considered public funds a trifle beneath their consideration ; but because they thought that, with a tribune conducting the prosecution, both sides could not be on an equal footing in the discussion of the case. What comparison shall I draw ? Shall I compare Sulla with Junius, or that tribune with Quinctius, or indeed the one occasion with the other ? Sulla was a man of great wealth, with many relations, connexions, friends, and dependants. Junius possessed these advantages only to a small and inconsiderable extent, and it was by

ipsius labore quaesita atque collecta. Hic tribunus plebis modestus, pudens, non modo non seditiosus, sed etiam seditiosis adversarius : ille autem acerbus, criminosus, popularis homo ac turbulentus. Tempus hoc tranquillum atque placatum : illud omnibus invidiae tempestatibus concitatum. Quae cum ita essent, in Fausto tamen illi iudices statuerunt, iniqua condicione reum causam dicere, cum adversario eius ad ius accusationis summa vis potestatis accederet.

95   XXXV. Quam quidem rationem vos, iudices, diligenter pro vestra sapientia [et humanitate] cogitare et penitus perspicere debetis, quid mali, quantum periculi uni cuique nostrum inferre possit vis tribunicia conflata praesertim invidia et contionibus seditiose concitatis. Optimis hercule temporibus, tum, cum homines se non iactatione populari, sed dignitate atque innocentia tuebantur, tamen nec P. Popilius neque Q. Metellus, clarissimi viri atque amplissimi, vim tribuniciam sustinere potuerunt : nedum his temporibus, his moribus, his magistratibus, sine vestra sapientia ac sine iudiciorum remediis salvi esse possimus.

96   Non fuit illud igitur iudicium iudicii simile, iudices, non fuit, in quo non modus ullus est adhibitus, non mos consuetudoque servata, non causa defensa : vis illa fuit et, ut saepe iam dixi, ruina quaedam atque tempestas et quidvis potius quam iudicium aut disceptatio aut quaestio. Quod si quis est qui illud iudi-

---

ᵃ Both went into exile when attacked by a tribune, Popilius by Gaius Gracchus in 123 and Metellus by Saturninus in 100 B.C.

his own efforts that they had been gained and collected. The tribune in Sulla's case was a quiet, respectable man ; far from being prone to lawlessness, he was its enemy in others ; whereas in Junius's case, the tribune was a sour, scurrilous fellow, a mob-orator and a fire-brand. That occasion was quiet and peaceable, the other was disturbed by all the storms of prejudice. Despite all this, the jurors in Faustus's case decided none the less that the accused was at a disadvantage in pleading his case, because his adversary, in addition to his legal rights as an accuser, had on his side all the force of his authority as a tribune.

XXXV. To this consideration then, gentlemen, 95 it is your duty, as wise jurors, to give your careful attention, and to realize completely all the harm, all the danger to which every one of us may be exposed by the violence of the tribunate, especially in the heat of prejudice and the excitement of a lawless assembly. Why, even in the best of times, when men thought to shield themselves not by posing as popular champions, but by a life of honour and integrity, neither P. Popilius nor Q. Metellus,[a] distinguished men though they were, was able to resist a tribune's violence. How much less at a time like the present, with such morals and such magistrates, could we find safety, if it were not for your wisdom and the redress provided by your courts ?

That was no semblance of a trial, gentlemen, no 96 semblance, I say : for in it no limits were observed, no traditional usage followed, nor any defence made. It was mere violence—an avalanche, a hurricane, as I have often said before—anything, in fact, but a trial, a discussion, or a legal inquiry. But if there be

cium fuisse arbitretur et qui his rebus iudicatis standum putet, is tamen hanc causam ab illa debet seiun-
gere. Ab illo enim, sive quod in legem non iurasset
sive quod e lege subsortitus iudicem non esset, multa
petita esse dicitur. Cluenti autem ratio cum illis
legibus, quibus a Iunio multa petita est, nulla potest
ex parte esse coniuncta.

97　At enim etiam Bulbus est condemnatus. Adde
maiestatis, ut intellegas hoc iudicium cum illo non
esse coniunctum. At est hoc illi crimen obiectum.
Fateor, sed etiam legionem esse ab eo sollicitatam in
Illyrico C. Cosconi litteris et multorum testimoniis
planum factum est : quod crimen erat proprium illius
quaestionis et quae res lege maiestatis tenebatur.
At hoc obfuit ei maxime. Iam ista divinatio est :
qua si uti licet, vide ne mea coniectura multo sit
verior. Ego enim sic arbitror, Bulbum, quod homo
nequam, turpis, improbus, multis flagitiis contami-
natus in iudicium sit adductus, idcirco facilius esse
damnatum. Tu mihi ex tota causa Bulbi, quod tibi
commodum est, eligis, ut id esse secutos iudices dicas.

98　XXXVI. Quapropter hoc Bulbi iudicium non plus
huic obesse causae debet quam illa, quae comme-
morata sunt ab accusatore, duo iudicia, P. Popili et

ᵃ For *maiestas* see Introduction, p. 213, Note on the
Statutes, 4.

anyone who thinks that trial a judicial proceeding, and considers its verdict binding as a judicial decision, he ought none the less to make a distinction between that case and this. In Junius's case it was proposed that he be fined, as we are told, either for his failure to take the official oath, or for his irregularity in filling a vacancy on the jury. But the case of Cluentius can in no way be connected with those statutes under which it was proposed to fine Junius.

"But," I shall be told, "Bulbus also was con- 97 victed." Yes, and you should add, "For treason," [a] that you may realize that my client's trial has no connexion with his. "But the charge in the present case was also brought up against Bulbus." I admit it : but it was also made plain by the correspondence of G. Cosconius and the evidence of many witnesses that Bulbus had tampered with a legion in Illyricum, that being the charge that was proper to that court's jurisdiction and those the facts which brought him within the law of treason. "But it was the other point which told most heavily against him." Now you are coming to mere guess-work ; and if guessing is allowed, perhaps you will find my inference far nearer the truth. For in my opinion the reason why Bulbus was so easily condemned was that he was a worthless and iniquitous scoundrel, and was already defiled with many a crime when he came into court. Out of the whole case against Bulbus you choose to select the point that suits your case, and then say that it was that point which was responsible for the verdict.

XXXVI. And so there was no more reason to consider the trial of Bulbus as reflecting on the present case, than the trials respectively of P. Popilius and

Ti. Guttae, qui causam de ambitu dixerunt, qui
accusati sunt ab eis, qui erant ipsi ambitus condemnati : quos ego non idcirco esse arbitror in integrum restitutos, quod planum fecerint illos ob rem
iudicandam pecuniam accepisse, sed quod iudicibus
probaverint, cum in eodem genere, in quo ipsi offen-
dissent, alios reprehendissent, se ad praemia legis
venire oportere. Quapropter neminem dubitare
existimo quin illa damnatio ambitus nulla ex parte
cum causa Cluenti vestroque iudicio coniuncta esse
possit.

99　　Quid, quod Staienus est condemnatus ?　Non dico
hoc tempore, iudices, id quod nescio an dici oporteat,
illum maiestatis esse condemnatum : non recito
testimonia hominum honestissimorum, quae in
Staienum sunt dicta ab eis, qui Mam. Aemilio, clarissimo viro, legati et praefecti et tribuni militares
fuerunt : quorum testimoniis planum factum est
maxime eius opera, cum quaestor esset, in exercitu
seditionem esse conflatam.　Ne illa quidem testimonia recito, quae dicta sunt, de HS͞I͞ɔͨ, quae ille
cum accepisset nomine iudicii Safiniani, sicut in
Oppianici iudicio postea, reticuit atque suppressit.

100　　Omitto et haec et alia permulta, quae illo iudicio
in Staienum dicta sunt : hoc dico, eandem tum fuisse
P. et L. Cominiis, equitibus Romanis, honestis hominibus et disertis, controversiam cum Staieno, quem
accusabant, quae nunc mihi est cum Accio.　Cominii

---

a For *ambitus* and the *praemia legis* see Introduction,
Note on the Statutes, 3.

Ti. Gutta which were quoted by the prosecution. They were tried for corrupt practice,[a] and were accused by men who had themselves been condemned for corrupt practice. And I hold that the reason why their accusers were restored to their full rights was not that they had revealed the guilt of Popilius and Gutta in taking a bribe for their verdicts, but because they proved to the court that they were entitled to the legal reward[a] as having exposed in others the same guilt as had proved their own undoing. Wherefore I hold it indisputable that this conviction for corrupt practice can in no way be connected with the case of Cluentius, and the jurisdiction of your court.

What of the fact that Staienus was condemned? 99 I forbear to mention here, gentlemen—though I rather think I ought to mention it—that he was condemned for treason. I forbear to read out the evidence against him of trustworthy witnesses who served under the distinguished Mamilius Aemilius as generals, praefects, and military tribunes; whose evidence revealed that it was he who as quaestor was chiefly responsible for exciting the army to mutiny. I even forbear to read out the evidence which was given of the 600,000 sesterces which he took for services to be rendered at Safinius's trial, and then, as afterwards at Oppianicus's trial, quietly kept the money for himself.

This, and much more evidence against Staienus at 100 that trial, I pass over: what I do say is, that those two honourable and eloquent Roman knights, Publius and Lucius Cominius, had precisely the same contention in those days against Staienus whom they were accusing, as I have to-day against Accius. The

dicebant idem, quod ego dico : Staienum ab Oppianico pecuniam accepisse, ut iudicium corrumperet :
Staienus conciliandae gratiae causa accepisse dicebat.

101 Irridebatur haec illius reconciliatio et persona viri
boni suscepta, sicut in statuis inauratis, quas posuit
ad Iuturnae : quibus subscripsit reges a se in gratiam
esse reductos. Exagitabantur eius omnes fraudes
atque fallaciae, tota vita in eius modi ratione versata
aperiebatur, egestas domestica, quaestus forensis in
medium proferebatur, nummarius interpres pacis et
concordiae non probabatur. Itaque tum Staienus,
cum idem defenderet quod Accius, condemnatus est.

102 Cominii cum hoc agerent, quod nos in tota causa
egimus, probaverunt. Quam ob rem si Staieni
damnatione Oppianicum iudicium corrumpere voluisse, Oppianicum iudici ad emendas sententias dedisse
pecuniam iudicatum est : cum ita constitutum sit,
ut in illa culpa aut Cluentius sit aut Oppianicus,
Cluenti nummus nullus iudici datus ullo vestigio
reperietur, Oppianici pecunia post iudicium factum
ab iudice ablata est ; potest esse dubium, quin illa
damnatio Staieni non modo non sit contra Cluentium,
sed maxime nostram causam defensionemque con-
firmet ?

103 XXXVII. Ergo adhuc Iuni iudicium video esse eius
modi, ut incursionem potius seditionis, vim multitudinis, impetum tribunicium, quam iudicium appellan-
dum putem. Quod si qui illud iudicium appellet,

---

a A nymph in honour of whom there was a chapel in the
Campus Martius. Nothing appears to be known about the
incident except what Cicero tells us.

Cominii maintained, as I do now, that Staienus took
money from Oppianicus to bribe the court, while
Staienus says he took it to effect a reconciliation.
The court laughed at his talking thus of reconcilia- 101
tion, and posing as an honest man, as he had done in
the matter of the gilt statues which he erected in
the Temple of Juturna,ᵃ with an inscription at the
foot recording the kings whom he had restored to
friendship with Rome. Then were all his sharp
practices and impostures driven from cover, disclosing a whole lifetime devoted to such pursuits ; his
private lack of means was brought to light, and his
source of income from the courts ; but his pose as
the paid agent of peace and goodwill carried no conviction, with the result that Staienus, when answering the same charge as Accius is now, was found
guilty. The Cominii, taking the same line as I have 102
been taking all through the case, made good their
charge. Wherefore, if the condemnation of Staienus
amounted to a judicial decision that Oppianicus intended to bribe the court, and that he gave a bribe
to a juror for the purchase of votes ; and if (since it is
agreed that either Cluentius or Oppianicus was
guilty of so doing) no trace can be found of Cluentius
having given any money to a juror, while the money
given by Oppianicus was recovered from a juror
after the trial was over ; then what possible doubt
is there that Staienus's condemnation, so far from
telling against Cluentius, provides abundant con-
firmation of my case and of my defence ?

XXXVII. So far, then, my view of the trial of 103
Junius is this—that it should be styled an assault of
anarchy, a piece of mob-violence, a tribunician outrage rather than a trial. But should anyone style

tamen hoc confiteatur necesse est, nullo modo illam
multam, quae ab Iunio petita sit, cum Cluenti causa
posse coniungi. Illud igitur Iunianum per vim
factum est, Bulbi et Popili et Guttae contra Cluentium
non est : Staieni etiam pro Cluentio est. Videamus
ecquod aliud iudicium, quod pro Cluentio sit, proferre
possimus.

Dixitne tandem causam C. Fidiculanius Falcula,
qui Oppianicum condemnarat, cum praesertim, id
quod fuit in illo iudicio invidiosissimum, paucos dies
ex subsortitione sedisset ? Dixit et bis quidem dixit.
In summam enim L. Quinctius invidiam contionibus
eum cotidianis seditiosis et turbulentis adduxerat.
Uno iudicio multa est ab eo petita, sicut ab Iunio,
quod non suae decuriae munere neque ex lege sedisset. Paulo sedatiore tempore est accusatus, quam
Iunius, sed eadem fere lege et crimine. Quia nulla
in iudicio seditio neque vis nec turba versata est,
prima actione facillime est absolutus. Non numero
hanc absolutionem. Nihilo minus enim potest, ut
illam multam non commiserit, accepisse tamen ob
rem iudicandam. *Causam nusquam Staienus ea de
re lege dixit.[1] Proprium crimen illud quaestionis
104 eius non fuit. Fidiculanius quid fecisse dicebatur ?
accepisse a Cluentio HScccc. Cuius erat ordinis ?
senatorii. Qua lege in eo genere a senatore ratio
repeti solet, de pecuniis repetundis, ea lege accusatus

---

[1] *The mss. are corrupt. F. adopts Madvig's conjecture.*

[a] For another and different view of Falcula's conduct
see the *Pro Caecina*, §§ 28 and 29.
[b] About £3574.

it a trial, he must needs admit that the fine which
was claimed from Junius can by no manner of possibility be connected with my client's case. Junius's
case, then, was the outcome of violence : those of
Bulbus, Popilius, and Gutta do not tell against
Cluentius ; while that of Staienus positively tells
in his support. Let us see if any other case can
possibly be brought forward in support of Cluentius.

Was not G. Fidiculanius Falcula,[a] who had voted
for Oppianicus's condemnation, made to stand on his
defence, and that though he had only sat for a few
days as a substitute, a fact which excited much prejudice against him at that trial ? As a matter of
fact, he was tried twice : for L. Quinctius, with the
lawless and unruly mass-meetings which he held
daily, had excited a violent prejudice against him.
At one trial an attempt was made to get him fined,
like Junius, because he had taken his seat unlawfully
when it was not the turn of his panel to do so. He
was accused at a somewhat quieter time than was
Junius but under much the same statute and on
much the same charge ; and because no part was
played at his trial by lawlessness, violence, or dis-
order, he was easily acquitted at the first hearing.
But I waive this acquittal ; for it is still possible that
though he was not fined on that occasion, he did take
a bribe for his verdict. (On the charge of bribery
Staienus was nowhere formally tried, such a charge
not being proper to the jurisdiction of that court.)
What was Fidiculanius alleged to have done ? 104
To have accepted 400,000[b] sesterces from Cluentius.
To what order did he belong ? The senatorial. He
was accused under the statute by which a senator is
usually brought to book in such a case, the Statute of

honestissime est absolutus. Acta est enim causa
more maiorum, sine vi, sine metu, sine periculo: dicta
et exposita et demonstrata sunt omnia. Adducti
iudices sunt non modo potuisse honeste ab eo reum
condemnari, qui non perpetuo sedisset, sed, aliud si
is iudex nihil scisset, nisi quae praeiudicia de eo facta
esse constarent, audire praeterea nihil debuisse.

105 XXXVIII. Tum etiam illi quinque, qui, imperitorum hominum rumusculos aucupati tum illum absolverunt, iam suam clementiam laudari magno opere
nolebant, a quibus si qui quaereret sedissentne iudices
in C. Fabricium, sedisse se dicerent: si interroga-
rentur num quo crimine is esset accusatus praeter-
quam veneni eius, quod quaesitum Habito diceretur,
negarent: si deinde essent rogati quid iudicassent,
condemnasse se dicerent: nemo enim absolvit.
Eodem modo quaesitum si esset de Scamandro, certe
idem respondissent: tametsi ille una sententia est
absolutus, sed illam unam nemo tum istorum suam
106 dici vellet. Uter igitur facilius suae sententiae
rationem redderet: isne, qui se et sibi et rei iudicatae constitisse dicit, an ille, qui se in principem
maleficii lenem, in adiutores eius et conscios vehe-
mentissimum esse respondet? Quorum ego de
sententia non debeo disputare: neque enim dubito

---

a See Introduction, Note on the Statutes, 2.
b See § 76.

Extortion,[a] and was honourably acquitted; for the case was conducted in the good old style, without violence, intimidation, or peril; every point was set forth, argued, and proved. The court was led to conclude not only that a man who had not sat through the whole trial might have acted honourably in voting for conviction, but that this particular man, when sitting as a judge, even though he had no knowledge of anything but the previous judgements admittedly outstanding against Oppianicus, was not bound to hear any further evidence.

XXXVIII. At that time even the famous five,[b] who being out to catch the idle plaudits of the ignorant, had voted for Oppianicus's acquittal, had come to be extremely loth to hear their clemency praised. Had they been asked whether they had sat as jurors at the trial of G. Fabricius they would have said yes; if questioned as to whether any other charge was brought against him than the alleged attempt to poison Habitus, they would have said no. Had they been asked what their verdict was, they would have replied that they voted guilty; for not a vote was cast for acquittal. Had the same questions been asked them about Scamander's case, they would assuredly have given the same answers: he indeed secured a single vote for his acquittal, but this single vote none of the famous five would at that time admit to have been his own. Which, then, would find it easier to give an account of his verdict, the man who says: " I was true to myself and to my verdict," or the man who answers: " I showed clemency to the principal in a crime, but great severity to his abettors and accomplices " ? It is not my business to argue about the way they voted: in the case of men such

quin tales viri suspicione aliqua perculsi repentina de
statu suo declinarint.   Quare eorum, qui absolverunt,
misericordiam non reprehendo, eorum, qui in iudicando superiora iudicia secuti sunt sua sponte, non
Staieni fraude, constantiam comprobo, eorum vero,
qui sibi non liquere dixerunt, sapientiam laudo, qui
absolvere eum, quem nocentissimum cognorant, et
quem ipsi bis antea condemnarant, nullo modo pote-
rant : condemnare, cum tanta consilii infamia et tam
atrocis rei suspicio esset iniecta, paulo posterius
patefacta re maluerunt.

107   Ac ne ex facto solum sapientes illos iudicetis, sed
etiam ex hominibus ipsis quod hi fecerunt rectissime
ac sapientissime factum probetis, quis P. Octavio
Balbo ingenio prudentior, iure peritior, fide, religione,
officio diligentior aut sanctior commemorari potest ?
Non absolvit.   Quis Q. Considio constantior ?   quis
iudiciorum atque eius dignitatis, quae in iudiciis
publicis versari debet, peritior ?   quis virtute, consilio, auctoritate praestantior ?   Ne is quidem absolvit.   Longum est de singulorum virtute ita dicere : quae, quia cognita est ab omnibus, verborum
ornamenta non quaerit. Qualis vir M. Iuventius
Pedo fuit ex vetere illa iudicum disciplina ? qualis L.
Caulius Mergus ?   M. Basilus ?   C. Caudinus ?   qui

as they, I doubt not it was some sudden suspicion
which made them abandon their previous position.
And so, while I find no fault with the clemency of
those who voted for acquittal, I approve the con-
stancy of those who, of their own free will and
uninfluenced by Staienus, in passing judgement stood
by the judgements they had passed already ; and I
applaud the prudence of those who voted " Not
proven," who were unable to acquit a man whose
extreme guilt they knew and whom they had twice
condemned already, and preferred, considering the
scandalous plot which had been rumoured and the
horrible suspicion which had arisen, to postpone their
condemnation a little till everything should be made
clear.

And now, that you may not merely infer their 107
wisdom from what they did but may judge from
their characters also that what they did was rightly
and wisely done, whom, I ask you, can you call to
mind more gifted by nature, more versed in law,
more careful or more scrupulous in honour, faith, and
duty than P. Octavius Balbus ? He did not vote for
acquittal. Whom more consistent than Q. Considius ? Whom more experienced in trials and in
the gravity which should mark the proceedings in a
public trial ? Whose character, whose judgement,
and whose authority are more distinguished ? Not
even he was for acquittal. Time does not permit
me to describe the qualities of each of them in turn ;
these qualities, known as they are to all, need no
embellishment of words. Think of a man like M.
Juventius Peto, one of the good old school of jurors ;
think of a man like L. Caulus Mergus, or M. Basilus,
or G. Caudinus ! All of them men the day of whose

omnes in iudiciis publicis iam tum, florente re publica,
floruerunt.   Ex eodem numero L. Cassius, Cn. Heius,
pari et integritate et prudentia : quorum nullius
sententia est Oppianicus absolutus.   Atque in his
omnibus natu minimus, ingenio et diligentia et religione par eis, quos antea commemoravi, P. Saturius,
108 in eadem sententia fuit.   O innocentiam Oppianici
singularem ! quo in reo, qui absolvit ambitiosus, qui
distulit cautus, qui condemnavit constans existimatur.

XXXIX. Haec tum agente Quinctio neque in contione neque in iudicio demonstrata sunt.   Neque
enim ipse dici patiebatur nec per multitudinem con-
citatam consistere cuiquam in dicendo licebat.   Itaque ipse postquam Iunium pervertit, totam causam
reliquit.   Paucis enim diebus illis et ipse privatus est
factus et hominum studia defervisse intellegebat.
Quod si per quos dies Iunium accusavit Fidiculanium
accusare voluisset, respondendi Fidiculanio potestas
facto non esset.   Ac primo quidem omnibus illis
iudicibus, qui Oppianicum condemnarant, minabatur.
109 Iam insolentiam noratis hominis : noratis animos eius
ac spiritus tribunicios.   Quod erat odium, di immortales !   quae superbia !   quanta ignoratio sui !
quam gravis atque intolerabilis adrogantia !   qui
illud iam ipsum acerbe tulerit, ex quo illa nata sunt
omnia, non sibi ac defensioni suae condonatum esse

greatness at the bar coincided with the great days
of the Republic. To the same category belong L.
Cassius and Gn. Heius, their peers in honour and in
wisdom. Of these not one voted for Oppianicus's
acquittal. And among them too was P. Saturius,
junior to them all in years, but the equal in ability,
in earnestness, and in devotion to duty of those I
have already mentioned. A wondrous innocent 108
indeed was Oppianicus, the prisoner at whose trial
those who were for acquittal are thought interested,
those for postponing judgement, cautious, those for
conviction, consistent !

XXXIX. At the time, through the action of
Quinctius all this was not pointed out either on the
platform or in court. For Quinctius himself allowed
no mention of it, and the excitement of the mob
made it impossible for a speaker to stand his ground.
And so, the ruin of Junius accomplished, Quinctius
let the whole case drop. For a few days afterwards
he himself went out of office, and realized, moreover,
that the heat of popular feeling had abated. But
had he chosen to accuse Fidiculanius during the days
which he spent in accusing Junius, Fidiculanius
would have had no chance to make a reply : and
indeed he began by threatening all the jurors who
had voted for Oppianicus's conviction. Now you had 109
cause to know the fellow's insolence ; you knew his
pride and the airs he gave himself as a tribune.
By Heaven ! how insufferable he was, and how
haughty ! How greatly he overrated himself ; how
tedious and unendurable was his conceit ! Why,
his one grievance, from which all the rest of the story
followed, was that Oppianicus had not been acquitted
as a compliment to himself and to his conduct of the

Oppianicum : proinde quasi non satis signi esse debuerit ab omnibus eum fuisse desertum, qui se ad patronum illum contulisset. Erat enim Romae summa copia patronorum, hominum eloquentissimorum atque amplissimorum, quorum certe aliquis defendisset equitem Romanum, in municipio suo nobilem, si honeste putasset eius modi causam posse defendi.

110 XL. Nam Quinctius quidem quam causam umquam antea dixerat, cum annos ad quinquaginta natus esset ? quis eum umquam non modo in patroni, sed in laudatoris aut advocati loco viderat ? qui quod Rostra iam diu vacua locumque illum post adventum L. Sullae a tribunicia voce desertum oppresserat, multitudinemque desuefactam iam a contionibus ad veteris consuetudinis similitudinem revocarat, idcirco cuidam hominum generi paulisper iucundior fuit. Atque idem quanto in odio postea suis ipsis fuit, per quos in altiorem locum ascenderat ! neque 111 iniuria. Facite enim ut non solum mores et adrogantiam eius, sed etiam voltum atque amictum atque etiam illam usque ad talos demissam purpuram recordemini. Is, quasi non esset ullo modo ferendum se ex iudicio discessisse victum, rem a subselliis ad Rostra detulit. Et iam querimur saepe hominibus novis non satis magnos in hac civitate esse fructus ? Nego usquam umquam fuisse maiores, ubi si quis ignobili loco natus ita vivit, ut nobilitatis dignitatem virtute tueri posse videatur, usque eo pervenit, quoad

---

^a Owing to the restrictions which Sulla put on their activities in 81 B.C., and which were not completely removed till 70 B.C. See Historical Summary.

^b A *novus homo* was one who, like Cicero himself, was the first of his family to hold one of the " curule " magistracies.

defence : as if it should not have been evidence
enough that everyone had abandoned Oppianicus
when he betook himself to such an advocate. For
there were any number of advocates at Rome, men
of eloquence and standing, one of whom assuredly
would have defended a Roman knight of high position
in his native place, if he had thought the defence of
such a case consistent with his honour.

XL. For as to Quinctius, what case had he ever 110
undertaken before in the fifty years that he had
lived ? Who had ever seen him in the capacity of a
witness to character or a legal adviser, not to say a
pleader ? He had indeed, since the rostrum had
long been unoccupied, nor had a tribune's voice
been heard from that place since the coming of
Sulla,[a] seized upon it and recalled the populace, now
long unused to public meetings, to a semblance
of its former practice, thus being enabled
to win, with a certain class of people, some
measure of temporary popularity. But subsequently how he came to be hated even by his
own followers on whose backs he had climbed to a
higher place ! Nor did their hatred wrong him : 111
for do but recall his manners and his arrogance, yes,
and even his expression and his clothes, and that
purple robe he wore right down to his heels. He
then, as if it were not to be borne that he should
leave the court defeated, carried the case from the
bench to the platform. And after this, do we often
lament that our state has too little to offer to a self-
made man ?[b] Never, I maintain, has a state offered
so much as does ours, wherein if a man of humble
birth shows in his life a character such as to support
the high standing which rank confers, his advance-

112 eum industria cum innocentia prosecuta est. Si quis
autem hoc uno nititur, quod sit ignobilis, procedit
saepe longius, quam si idem ille esset cum isdem suis
vitiis nobilissimus. Ut Quinctius—nihil enim dicam
de ceteris—si fuisset homo nobilis, quis eum cum illa
superbia atque intolerantia ferre potuisset ? Quod
eo loco fuit, ita tulerunt, ut, si quid haberet a natura
boni, prodesse ei putarent oportere : superbiam
autem atque adrogantiam eius deridendam magis
arbitrarentur propter humilitatem hominis quam
pertimescendam.

XLI. Sed, ut illuc revertar, quo tempore Fidiculanius absolutus est, tu, qui iudicia facta commemoras,
quaero, quid tum esse existimas iudicatum ? certe
113 gratis iudicasse. At condemnarat : at causam totam
non audierat : at in contionibus a L. Quinctio vehementer erat et saepe vexatus. Illa igitur omnia
Quinctiana iniqua, falsa, turbulenta, popularia, sedi-
tiosa iudicia fuerunt. Esto : potuit esse innocens
Falcula. Iam ergo aliqui Oppianicum gratis condemnavit : iam non eos Iunius subsortitus est, qui
pecunia accepta condemnarent : iam putabitur aliqui
ab initio non sedisse et tamen Oppianicum gratis
condemnasse. Verum, si innocens Falcula, quaero
qui sit nocens ? si hic gratis condemnavit, quis
accepit ? Nego rem esse ullam cuiquam illorum
obiectam, quae Fidiculanio non obiecta sit, aliquid

ment is dependent only on hard work and a blameless record. Indeed a man who has nothing but 112 humble birth to support him often goes further than he would, had he the same defects though born of high degree. Suppose that Quinctius (to take no other example) had been of noble birth, who could have put up with his haughtiness, his unbearable presumption ? His birth being what it was, people did endure him to the extent of thinking that any good points with which nature might have endowed him ought to count in his favour ; while his haughtiness and conceit appeared, in a man of his humble origin, more ridiculous than dangerous.

XLI. But to resume : on the occasion of Falcula's acquittal, what do you imagine to have been proved by the verdict, you who are so fond of quoting verdicts ? " Assuredly, that he had not sold his vote." And yet he voted for conviction : and yet he had not 113 sat through the whole case ; and yet at public meetings he was assailed by Quinctius, furiously and often. Then all those trials, Quinctius's work, were the fruits of injustice, lies, violence, demagogy, and insurrection. " Very good," you say, " Falcula may have been innocent." The conclusion is then that someone voted against Oppianicus without being bribed ; that Junius did not fill up vacancies with men who would take a bribe to vote against Oppianicus ; and that we may suppose someone to have voted honestly against him without having sat through the whole case. But if Falcula is innocent, what juror, I ask, can be guilty ? If he did not take a bribe to vote guilty, who did ? I deny that a single charge was brought against any one of the jurors that was not brought against Fidiculanius, or that there existed

341

fuisse in Fidiculani causa, quod idem non esset in
114 ceterorum.   Aut hoc iudicium reprehendas tu, cuius
accusatio rebus iudicatis nitebatur, necesse est, aut,
si hoc verum esse concedis, Oppianicum gratis condemnatum esse fateare.

Quamquam satis magno argumento esse debet,
quod ex tam multis iudicibus absoluto Falcula nemo
reus factus est.   Quid enim mihi damnatos ambitus
colligitis, alia lege, certis criminibus, plurimis testibus ? cum primum illi ipsi debuerint potius accusari
de pecuniis repetundis quam ambitus.   Nam si in
ambitus iudiciis hoc eis obfuit, cum alia lege causam
dicerent, certe, si propria lege huius peccati adducti
115 essent, multo plus obfuisset.   Deinde si tanta vis
fuit istius criminis, ut, qua quisque lege ex illis iudicibus reus factus esset, tamen hac plaga periret, cur
in tanta multitudine accusatorum, tantis praemiis,
ceteri rei facti non sunt ?

Hic profertur id, quod iudicium appellari non
oportet, P. Septimio Scaevolae litem eo nomine esse
aestimatam.   Cuius rei quae consuetudo sit, quoniam
apud homines peritissimos dico, pluribus verbis docere
non debeo.   Numquam enim ea diligentia, quae solet
adhiberi in ceteris iudiciis, eadem reo damnato ad-
116 hibita est.   In litibus aestimandis fere iudices aut,

ᵃ See the Introduction, Note on the Statutes, 2 and 3.
ᵇ At the " assessment of penalty," which followed on a
conviction, evidence might be put in of offences committed
by the prisoner, other than those for which he had just been
convicted.

a single feature in Fidiculanius's case which did not exist in theirs also. You, then, who rested the case 114 for the prosecution on judicial decisions, are bound either to find fault with their decision in this case or, if you will allow that it was a right one, to admit that the conviction of Oppianicus was not due to bribery.

However, this should need no better proof than the fact that after the acquittal of Falcula, not one of his fellow-jurors was put on trial. What, I ask you, is the use of quoting their convictions for giving bribes under a different statute on a definite charge and on the evidence of many witnesses ? In the first place, those jurors should have been charged with taking, not with giving bribes.[a] For if the taking of bribes told against them when on trial for giving bribes, which comes under a different statute, it would manifestly have told against them still more if they had been put on trial under the statute proper to the offence in question. And, second, if this 115 charge of yours was so forceful that under what statute soever any of those jurors was put on trial, this was still the charge which gave the *coup de grâce*, why were not all the jurors put on trial when their accusers were so many and the inducements so great ?

At this point I am reminded that, at the assessment of penalty [b]—a proceeding which should not be termed judicial—Publius Septimius Scaevola was penalized on the score of corrupt practice. It is not for me to deal at length with the nature of this proceeding, as I am addressing gentlemen of such experience : but the care which is customary in trials generally is never displayed when once the verdict of guilty has been given. At an assessment of penalty, I 116

quod sibi eum, quem semel condemnarunt, inimicum
putant esse, si quae in eum lis capitis illata est, non
admittunt, aut, quod se perfunctos iam esse arbitrantur, cum de reo iudicarunt, neglegentius attendunt
cetera. Itaque et maiestatis absoluti sunt permulti,
quibus damnatis de pecuniis repetundis lites maiestatis essent aestimatae, et hoc cotidie fieri videmus,
ut reo damnato de pecuniis repetundis, ad quos pervenisse pecunias in litibus aestimandis statutum sit,
eos idem iudices absolvant : quod cum fit, non iudicia
rescinduntur, sed hoc statuitur, aestimationem litium
non esse iudicium. Scaevola condemnatus est aliis
criminibus, frequentissimis Apuliae testibus. Omni
contentione pugnatum est, uti lis haec capitis aesti-
maretur. Quae res si rei iudicatae pondus habuisset,
ille postea vel isdem vel aliis inimicis reus hac lege
ipsa factus esset.

117   XLII. Sequitur id, quod illi iudicium appellant,
maiores autem nostri numquam neque iudicium nomi-
narunt neque proinde ut rem iudicatam observarunt,
animadversionem atque auctoritatem censoriam.
Qua de re ante quam dicere incipio, perpauca mihi
de meo officio verba faciunda sunt, ut a me cum
huiusce periculi tum ceterorum quoque officiorum et

---

    a This introduces an example, not of leniency, but of
carelessness resulting in severity.
    b See the Introduction, Note on the Statutes, 1.
    c The Censors, as guardians of the public morals, put a
" black mark " (*nota, subscriptio, animadversio*) against the
name of anyone whom they proposed to degrade from his
position as a senator, knight, or citizen.

might almost say that jurors either refuse to sanction the demand for an assessment involving the civil status of the prisoner because they think that they have made him their personal enemy by their act in finding him guilty ; or else, imagining their duty to be over as soon as they have given their verdict, they pay a somewhat scant attention to the subsequent proceedings. Accordingly [a] many persons have been acquitted of treason whose penalty, after their conviction for corrupt practice, was assessed under the head of treason ; and again, we see as a daily occurrence the spectacle of a court acquitting the very persons to whom, in the assessment following a conviction for corrupt practice, the same court adjudged that the moneys had passed. Such occurrences amount, not to the quashing of a judicial proceeding, but to the pronouncement that an assessment of penalty is not a judicial proceeding. Scaevola was found guilty of other charges on the evidence of numerous witnesses from Apulia. The utmost effort was made to secure that his penalty be assessed at the loss of civil status : if the assessment had had the weight of a judicial proceeding, he would afterwards have been put on trial—whether through the enmity of the same persons or of others—under this very statute.[b]

XLII. Next comes what my opponents term a judicial proceeding, though our forefathers never gave it that name, nor did they respect it as such —namely, the imposition by the censors of their official stigma.[c] But before I begin to deal with this point, I must first say a few words about the claims that there are upon me, in order that you may realize that I have maintained a proper regard at

amicitiarum ratio conservata esse videatur. Nam
mihi cum viris fortibus, qui censores proxime fuerunt,
ambobus est amicitia, cum altero vero, sicuti plerique
vestrum sciunt, magnus usus et summa utriusque
118 officiis constituta necessitudo. Quare quicquid de
subscriptionibus eorum mihi dicendum erit, eo dicam
animo, ut omnem orationem meam non de illorum
facto, sed de ratione censoria habitam existimari
velim : a Lentulo autem, familiari meo, qui a me pro
eximia sua virtute summisque honoribus, quos a
populo Romano adeptus est, honoris causa nominatur,
facile hoc, iudices, impetrabo, ut, quam ipse adhibere
consuevit in amicorum periculis cum fidem et diligentiam tum vim animi libertatemque dicendi, ex hac
mihi concedat ut tantum mihi sumam, quantum sine
huius periculo praeterire non possim. A me tamen,
ut aequum est, omnia caute pedetemptimque di-
centur, ut neque fides huius defensionis relicta neque
cuiusquam aut dignitas laesa aut amicitia violata esse
videatur.

119   Video igitur, iudices, animadvertisse censores in
iudices quosdam illius consilii Iuniani, cum istam
ipsam causam subscriberent. Hic illud primum commune proponam, numquam animadversionibus cen-
soriis hanc civitatem ita contentam ut rebus iudicatis
fuisse. Neque in re nota consumam tempus. Exem-
pli causa ponam unum illud : C. Getam, cum a
L. Metello et Cn. Domitio censoribus ex senatu

---

once for the needs of my client and for the claims
involved by my friendship with others as well. For
I am on friendly terms with both those excellent
men who were our last censors, and with one of
them, as most of you know, I enjoy a friendship
and an intimacy based on our mutual good offices.
And so, whatever I may have to say about their en- 118
dorsements, I shall say it with the desire to make you
feel that my every word bears not upon their actions,
but upon the censorial system. As for Lentulus,[a] my
friend, whom I name in all honour to his noble
character and to the high offices with which he has
been invested by the Roman people, he will readily
allow me to draw upon that fund of loyalty and care,
yes, and of strong feeling and free speech with
which he is always ready to support his friends at
need, exactly as much as I cannot fail to do if I
am not to betray the needs of my client. None the
less, as is only right, I shall speak throughout with
caution and reserve that I may not be found either
to have neglected my duty to him whom I am
defending or in any instance to have wounded
reputation or violated friendship.

Now I observe, gentlemen, that the censors im- 119
posed their stigma on certain of the jurors who
served in the trial before Junius, endorsing it with
the very reason alleged by the prosecution. Here I
will first lay down the general proposition that our
state has never assigned the same weight to a censorial stigma as to a judicial decision ; and without
wasting time over a matter of common knowledge,
I will merely illustrate it with a single example. G.
Geta was himself made censor after having been
degraded from the senate by the censors L. Metellus

eiectus esset, censorem esse ipsum postea factum :
et cuius mores erant a censoribus reprehensi, hunc
postea et populi Romani et eorum, qui in ipsum
animadverterant, moribus praefuisse. Quod si illud
iudicium putaretur, ut ceteri turpi iudicio damnati
in perpetuum omni honore ac dignitate privantur, sic
hominibus ignominia notatis neque ad honorem aditus
120 neque in curiam reditus esset. Nunc si quem Cn.
Lentuli aut L. Gelli libertus furti condemnarit, is
omnibus ornamentis amissis numquam ullam honestatis suae partem reciperabit : quos autem ipse L.
Gellius et Cn. Lentulus, duo censores, clarissimi viri
sapientissimique homines, furti et captarum pecuniarum nomine notaverunt, ei non modo in senatum
redierunt, sed etiam illarum ipsarum rerum iudiciis
absoluti sunt.

XLIII. Neminem voluerunt maiores nostri non
modo de existimatione cuiusquam, sed ne pecuniaria
quidem de re minima esse iudicem, nisi qui inter adversarios convenisset. Quapropter in omnibus legibus, quibus exceptum est, de quibus causis aut magis-
stratum capere non liceat aut iudicem legi aut
alterum accusare, haec ignominiae causa praeter-
missa est. Timoris enim causam, non vitae poenam
121 in illa potestate esse voluerunt. Itaque non solum
illud ostendam, quod iam videtis, populi Romani
suffragiis saepe numero censorias subscriptiones esse

and Gn. Domitius; so that one whose morals had
been stigmatized by the censors came to supervise
the morals of the Roman people including those who
had stigmatized himself. But if the stigma were
regarded as a judicial decision then no one who had
been branded by the censors with ignominy could
hope to obtain office or be restored to the senate,
just as men who have been condemned by a judicial
decision involving infamy are debarred for all time
from office and honours. But the fact is that while 120
a man found guilty of theft at the instance of a freedman of Gn. Lentulus or L. Gellius will be deprived
of every civil privilege and will never recover his
honour in any particular, yet those whom our two
learned and distinguished censors L. Gellius and
Gn. Lentulus themselves branded by name for theft
and the acceptance of bribes were not only restored
to the senate but actually acquitted by the courts
dealing with those very offences.

XLIII. It was the intention of our forefathers that
no one should act as a judge in a question involving,
I do not say a man's reputation, but even his slightest
pecuniary interest, unless the disputants agreed to
accept him. That is why in all statutes which contain clauses specifying the reasons which disqualify a
man from holding public office, serving as a juror, or
initiating a prosecution, the reason we are discussing, namely, ignominy, is never mentioned; because
our forefathers intended to invest the censor's office
with the power of inspiring fear, not of punishing for
life. And so I will proceed to show that the en- 121
dorsements of the censors have again and again
been annulled, not merely as you already realize,
by the elections of the Roman people, but by the

349

sublatas, verum etiam iudiciis eorum, qui iurati
statuere maiore cum religione et diligentia debuerunt. Primum iudices, senatores equitesque Romani
in compluribus iam reis, quos contra leges pecunias
accepisse subscriptum est, suae potius religioni quam
censorum opinioni paruerunt. Deinde praetores
urbani, qui iurati debent optimum quemque in lectos
iudices referre, sibi nunquam ad eam rem censoriam
ignominiam impedimento esse oportere duxerunt.

122 Censores denique ipsi saepe numero superiorum censorum iudiciis, si ista iudicia appellare voltis, non
steterunt. Atque etiam ipsi inter se censores sua
iudicia tanti esse arbitrantur, ut alter alterius iudicium non modo reprehendat, sed etiam rescindat :
ut alter de senatu movere velit, alter retineat et
ordine amplissimo dignum existimet : ut alter in
aerarios referre aut tribu movere iubeat, alter vetet.
Quare qui vobis in mentem venit haec appellare
iudicia, quae a populo rescindi, ab iuratis iudicibus
repudiari, a magistratibus neglegi, ab eis, qui eandem
potestatem adepti sunt, commutari, inter collegas
discrepare videatis ?

123 XLIV. Quae cum ita sint, videamus quid tandem
censores de illo iudicio corrupto iudicasse dicantur.
Ac primum illud statuamus, utrum quia censores
subscripserint ita sit, an, quia ita fuerit, illi subscripserint. Si quia subscripserint, videte quid agatis,

---

a " To place a man among the *aerarii*," used to imply
his disfranchisement ; but since the end of the fourth
century B.C. it had meant no more than *tribu movere*, to
move a man from a (superior) " country " tribe into an
(inferior) " urban " tribe. Both phrases, therefore, as here
used by Cicero, mean to degrade him.

judicial decisions of those who, being on their oath, were bound to use the more scrupulous vigilance in their pronouncements. In the first place, both senators and knights of Rome have followed the dictates of their own conscience rather than the opinion of the censors when serving as jurors, as they have often served, at the trial of men whose names had been branded as having broken the law by accepting bribes. Next, the city praetors, who are bound by oath to place the names of the best citizens on the list of selected jurors, have never felt that the ignominy inflicted by the censors ought to limit their selection. And lastly, the censors them- 122 selves have time after time thrown over the verdicts —if you wish to call them such—of their prede- cessors. So little importance indeed do the censors themselves attach to each other's verdicts that one will not only arraign but even annul his colleague's verdict : one will propose to degrade a man from the senate, while the other keeps him there, and holds him worthy of the most honourable rank. One orders him to be degraded or expelled from his tribe,[a] the other forbids it. How then can it occur to you to give the name of verdict to decisions which you see annulled by the people, rejected by sworn jurors, passed over by magistrates, altered by suc- cessive wielders of the censor's power, a subject of variance between those who wield it jointly ?

XLIV. This being so, let us see what actual 123 " verdict " the censors are alleged to have passed on the corruption of that court. And let us first decide whether it is true because the censors so framed their endorsement, or whether they so framed it because it was true. If the former be the case,

ne in unum quemque nostrum censoribus in posterum
potestatem regiam permittatis : ne subscriptio censoria non minus calamitatis civibus quam illa acerbissima proscriptio possit adferre : ne censorium
stilum, cuius mucronem multis remediis maiores
nostri rettuderunt, aeque posthac atque illum dicta-
124 torium pertimescamus. Sin autem, quod subscriptum est, quia verum est, idcirco grave debet esse, hoc
quaeramus, verum sit an falsum : removeantur
auctoritates censoriae : tollatur id ex causa, quod in
causa non est : doce quam pecuniam Cluentius
dederit, unde dederit, quem ad modum dederit :
unum denique a Cluentio profectae pecuniae vestigium ostende. Vince deinde bonum virum fuisse
Oppianicum, hominem integrum, nihil de illo umquam secus esse existimatum, nihil denique prae-
iudicatum. Tum auctoritatem censoriam amplexato :
tum illorum iudicium coniunctum cum re esse de-
125 fendito. Dum vero eum fuisse Oppianicum constabit, qui tabulas publicas municipii manu sua corrupisse iudicatus sit, qui testamentum interleverit,
qui supposita persona falsum testamentum obsig-
nandum curaverit, qui eum, cuius nomine id obsignatum est, interfecerit, qui avunculum filii sui in
servitute ac vinculis necaverit, qui municipes suos
proscribendos occidendosque curaverit, qui eius
uxorem, quem occiderat, in matrimonium duxerit,
qui pecuniam pro abortione dederit, qui socrum, qui
uxores, qui uno tempore fratris uxorem speratosque

---

a The reference is to the proscriptions of the Dictator Sulla
in 82 B.C. and to the pen which he used in writing the lists of
the proscribed.

take heed what you are about ; or you will be en-
trusting to future censors a tyrant's power over
every one of us ; the censor's endorsement will
prove as great a source of calamity to our citizens as
those cruel proscriptions [a] ; and the censor's pencil,
whose point our forefathers took so many precautions
to blunt, will hereafter inspire us with as much terror
as did once the dictator's.   But if, on the other hand, 124
the endorsement, because it is true, ought to have
great weight, let us ask the question :   " Is it true
or false ? "   Put on one side the censorial pronouncements ; remove from the case all that does not belong
to it ; tell us what bribe Cluentius gave, where he
got it, how he used it ; show us, in fact, any trace of
bribery on Cluentius's part.   Convince us next that
Oppianicus was an honest man with not a stain upon
his character ; that no one ever thought him otherwise ; that there was no verdict outstanding against
him.   Then and not till then may you cling to the
pronouncements of the censors, and maintain that
their verdict has some connexion with the facts at
issue.   But so long as it is an established fact that 125
Oppianicus was the man who was convicted of falsify-
ing with his own hand the public records of his town,
who forged a will, who by fraudulent personation
secured the seals and signatures of witnesses to a
sham will, who murdered the man in whose name it
had been signed and sealed, who put to death his
own son's uncle when a slave and a captive, who
secured the proscription and death of his own fellow-
townsmen, who killed his brother and then married
his widow, who gave a bribe to procure abortion,
who murdered his mother-in-law, murdered his
wives, murdered at one and the same time his

liberos fratremque ipsum, qui denique suos liberos
interfecerit, qui cum venenum privigno suo dare
vellet, manifesto deprehensus sit, cuius ministris
consciisque damnatis ipse adductus in iudicium
pecuniam iudici dederit ad sententias iudicum cor-
rumpendas : dum haec, inquam, de Oppianico con-
stabunt, neque ullo argumento Cluentianae pecuniae
crimen tenebitur, quid est quod te ista censoria, sive
voluntas sive opinio fuit, adiuvare aut hunc innocentem opprimere posse videatur ?

126   XLV. Quid igitur censores secuti sunt ? ne ipsi
quidem, ut gravissime dicam, quicquam aliud dicent
praeter sermonem atque famam.   Nihil se testibus,
nihil tabulis, nihil aliquo gravi argumento comperisse,
nihil denique causa cognita statuisse dicent.   Quod
si ita fecissent, tamen id non ita fixum esse deberet,
ut convelli non liceret.   Non utar exemplorum copia,
quae summa est, non rem veterem, non hominem
potentem aliquem aut gratiosum proferam.   Nuper
hominem tenuem, scribam aedilicium, D. Matrinium,
cum defendissem apud M. Iunium Q. Publicium
praetores et M. Plaetorium C. Flaminium aediles
curules, persuasi, ut scribam iurati legerent eum,
quem idem isti censores aerarium reliquisse sub-
scripserunt.   Cum enim in homine nulla culpa inveniretur, quid ille meruisset, non quid de eo

---

brother's wife, her expected children and his brother himself, and finally murdered his own children ; who, intending to give poison to his step-son, was taken in the act, and when haled to judgement after the conviction of his abettors and accomplices bribed a juror to tamper with the jurors' votes—so long, I say, as these facts are established against Oppianicus, and the charge of corruption against Cluentius is supported by no single proof, in what conceivable way can this, the whim or the opinion of the censors, whichever it was, avail to assist you, or to work the ruin of my innocent client ?

XLV. What was it then that influenced the 126 censors ? They themselves will not say—to put the case at its strongest—that it was anything more than common talk and rumour, or that they had learned anything from oral evidence or documents or any valid proof, or that their conclusion was in fact based on any hearing of the case. And even had it been otherwise, that conclusion still ought not to be so firmly planted as not to allow of its being uprooted. I will not quote a number of cases to prove this, though a large number exists, nor will I adduce one that is out of date, nor that of some powerful person or popular favourite. Only lately I was pleading the cause of D. Matrinius, a humble aedile's clerk, before the praetors M. Junius and Q. Publicius and the curule aediles M. Plaetorius and G. Flaminius : and I finally persuaded them, on their oath as they were, to appoint as clerk a man whom those same censors of yours had stated in their endorsement that they had degraded to the lowest class.[a] For since no fault was to be found with him, it was his deserts and not any pronouncement that had been

127 statutum esset quaerendum esse duxerunt. Nam
haec quidem, quae de iudicio corrupto subscrip-
serunt, quis est qui ab illis satis cognita et diligenter
iudicata arbitretur? In M'. Aquilium et in Ti.
Guttam video esse subscriptum. Quid est hoc?
duos esse corruptos solos pecunia dicant: ceteri
videlicet gratis condemnarunt. Non est igitur circumventus, non oppressus pecunia, non, ut illae
Quinctianae contiones habebantur, omnes, qui
Oppianicum condemnarunt, in culpa sunt ac suspicione ponendi: duos solos video auctoritate censorum adfines ei turpitudini iudicari. Aut illud ad-
ferant, aliquid sese, quod de his duobus habuerint
compertum, de ceteris non[1] comperisse.

128 XLVI. Nam illud quidem minime probandum est,
ad notationes auctoritatemque censoriam exemplum
illos e consuetudine militari transtulisse. Statuerunt
enim ita maiores nostri, ut, si a multis esset flagitium
rei militaris admissum, sortito in quosdam animadverteretur, ut metus videlicet ad omnes, poena ad
paucos perveniret. Quod idem facere censores in
delectu dignitatis et in iudicio civium et in animad-
versione vitiorum qui convenit? Nam miles, qui
locum non tenuit, qui hostium impetum vimque
pertimuit, potest idem postea et miles esse melior et
vir bonus et civis utilis. Quare qui in bello propter

[1] non *om. MSS., sup. Madvig.*

* Jurors who voted " guilty " at the trial of Oppianicus. See
ch. xxxviii.

made about him, which they felt they ought to investigate. And, further, as to this "corrupt 127 judgement" mentioned in their endorsement, who believes that their own was duly considered, or based on adequate investigation? I see that the endorsement was made against M'. Aquilius and Ti. Gutta.[a] What does that tell us? Supposing they say that two jurors only were bribed, then the others, I suppose, took no bribe for their verdict of "guilty." Then Oppianicus was not the victim of intrigue and bribery; nor are all those who voted for his conviction to be looked on, as Quinctius maintained at those meetings of his, with disapproval and suspicion; for I observe that two jurors only were held by the official pronouncement of the censors to be implicated in that scandal. Or else let them allege that they had discovered against those two something which they had not discovered against the others.

XLVI. For it is utterly impossible to admit the 128 plea that in the official imposition of the stigma the censors followed the analogy of military usage. Our forefathers decided that if any gross breach of military discipline was committed by a number of persons, it should be visited on certain individuals after the drawing of lots, with the object, clearly, that the warning might be felt by all, the punishment by a few. But what justification is there for the censors doing the same, whether in elevating to high rank, or in passing judgement on a citizen or in punishing a wrongdoer? For a soldier who has deserted his post, or shown cowardice before the furious onset of the enemy, may still turn out a better soldier, an honest man, and a good citizen. And so, when a soldier had failed in his duty in war through

hostium metum deliquerat, amplior ei mortis et
supplicii metus est a maioribus constitutus : ne
autem nimium multi poenam capitis subirent, idcirco
129 illa sortitio comparata est. Hoc tu idem facies
censor in senatu legendo ? Si erunt plures, qui ob
innocentem condemnandum pecuniam acceperint,
tu non animadvertes in omnes, sed carpes, ut velis,
et paucos ex multis ad ignominiam sortiere ? Habebit igitur te sciente et vidente curia senatorem,
populus Romanus iùdicem, res publica civem sine
ignominia quemquam, qui ad perniciem innocentis
fidem suam et religionem pecunia commutarit ? et,
qui pretio adductus eripuerit patriam, fortunas,
liberos civi innocenti, is censoriae severitatis nota
non inuretur ? Tu es praefectus moribus, tu magister
veteris disciplinae ac severitatis, si aut retines quemquam sciens in senatu scelere tanto contaminatum
aut statuis, qui in eadem culpa sit, non eadem poena
adfici convenire ? Aut quam condicionem supplicii
maiores in bello timiditati militis propositam esse
voluerunt, eandem tu in pace constitues improbitati
senatoris ? Quod si hoc exemplum ex re militari
ad animadversionem censoriam transferendum fuit,
sortitione id ipsum factum esse oportuit. Sin autem
sortiri ad poenam et hominum delictum fortunae
iudicio committere minime censorium est, certe in
multorum peccato carpi paucos ad ignominiam non
oportet.
130   XLVII. Verum omnes intellegimus in istis subscriptionibus ventum quendam popularem esse quae-

fear of the enemy, a still stronger fear was put before him by our forefathers' enactment—the fear of punishment and death ; but to prevent too many paying the penalty with their lives, they devised this drawing of lots. And do you propose to do 129 the same when making up the list of the senate in your capacity as censor ? Should there be several who have taken a bribe to condemn the innocent, will you, instead of visiting the crime on all, choose at your pleasure and elect for degradation a few out of many ? Shall the senate then, to your knowledge and before your eyes, retain one single member, the Roman people a single juror, the state a single citizen who has compassed the ruin of the innocent by selling his honour and his oath, and who has not suffered ignominy for it ? And shall the man who, for money's sake, robbed an innocent citizen of his country, his fortunes, and his children, shall he, I say, not be branded with the stigma of the censor's stern displeasure ? Or shall the measure of punishment designed by our forefathers as a warning to the cowardice of a soldier in time of war, be equally applied by you to the dishonesty of a senator in time of peace ? Had this precedent, drawn from military usage, been applicable to the infliction of the censorial stigma, here too it should have been carried out by the drawing of lots. But if it is consistent with a censor's duty to ballot for punishment and to submit the conduct of criminals to the arbitrament of chance, surely it is wrong, where many have sinned, to pick and choose only a few for the infliction of ignominy.

XLVII. In point of fact we all know that these 130 endorsements amounted to an attempt to catch the

situm. Iactata res erat in contione : incognita causa probatum erat illud multitudini : nemini licitum est contra dicere : nemo denique, ut defenderet contrariam partem, laborabat. In invidiam porro magnam illa iudicia venerant. Etenim paucis postea mensibus alia vehemens erat in iudiciis ex notatione tabellarum invidia versata. Praetermitti ab censoribus et neglegi macula iudiciorum posse non videbatur. Homines, quos ceteris vitiis atque omni dedecore infames videbant, eos hac quoque subscriptione notare voluerunt, et eo magis, quod illo ipso tempore illis censoribus erant iudicia cum equestri ordine communicata, ut viderentur per hominum idoneorum ignominiam sua auctoritate illa
131 iudicia reprehendisse. Quod si hanc apud eosdem ipsos censores mihi aut alii causam agere licuisset, hominibus tali prudentia praeditis certe probavissem : res enim indicat nihil ipsos habuisse cogniti, nihil comperti : ex tota ista subscriptione rumorem quendam et plausum popularem esse quaesitum. Nam in P. Popilium, qui Oppianicum condemnarat, subscripsit L. Gellius, quod is pecuniam accepisset, quo innocentem condemnaret. Iam id ipsum quantae divinationis est scire innocentem fuisse reum, quem fortasse numquam viderat, cum homines sapientis-

---

^a The courts were a monopoly of the senate from 81 to 70 B.C. See Historical Summary.
^b The scandal referred to occurred at the trial for extortion of Terentius Varro in 73 B.C.: he was defended by his relative Hortensius, Cicero's rival, who had the voting-tablets marked in such a way that he could see whether the jurors he had bribed had earned their pay.

breeze of popular favour. The case was taken up at public meetings ; and though it had never been heard, the same view of it was taken by the populace. No one had a chance to denounce that view ; no one in fact exerted himself to urge the opposite side. Moreover, the courts of those days [a] had fallen into great unpopularity. Why, only a few months afterwards the courts further incurred extreme unpopularity over the voting-tablets having been marked.[b] It was felt to be impossible that this stain on the honour of the courts should be passed by unnoticed by the censors. Seeing these men under the odium of other misdeeds and all manner of dishonour, they wished to brand them further by their endorsement ; and the fact that, at this very date and during their tenure of office, the judicial function had been extended to the order of knights, made them the more anxious to let it appear that in degrading suitable persons, they were officially arraigning the courts as formerly constituted. Yet 131 had I or anyone else been permitted to plead the case before those very censors, judges as wise as they would certainly have given me the verdict. For the facts show that they knew nothing and had ascertained nothing for themselves : their whole action in making their endorsement had been a bid for notoriety and popular applause. For in the case of P. Popilius, who had voted for Oppianicus's condemnation, L. Gellius's endorsement was to the effect that he had taken a bribe to condemn the innocent. Now as for that, what a power of divination he must have had to know the innocence of a man whom he may never have seen, when men of great sagacity, jurors who

361

simi, iudices, ut nihil dicam de eis, qui condemnarunt, causa cognita sibi dixerunt non liquere !

132 Verum esto : condemnat Popilium Gellius : iudicat
accepisse a Cluentio pecuniam. Negat hoc Lentulus.
Nam Popilium, quod erat libertini filius, in senatum
non legit, locum quidem senatorium ludis et cetera
ornamenta reliquit et eum omni ignominia liberat.
Quod cum facit, iudicat eius sententia gratis esse
Oppianicum condemnatum. Et eundem Popilium
postea Lentulus in ambitus iudicio pro testimonio
diligentissime laudat. Quare si neque L. Gelli
iudicio stetit Lentulus neque Lentuli existimatione
contentus fuit Gellius, et si uterque censor censoris
opinione standum non putavit, quid est quam ob rem
quisquam nostrum censorias subscriptiones omnes
fixas et in perpetuum ratas putet esse oportere ?

133 XLVIII. At in ipsum Habitum animadverterunt.
Nullam quidem ob turpitudinem, nullum ob totius
vitae non dicam vitium, sed erratum. Neque enim
hoc homine sanctior neque probior neque in omnibus
officiis retinendis diligentior esse quisquam potest :
neque illi aliter dicunt, sed eandem illam famam
iudicii corrupti secuti sunt : neque ipsi secus ex-
istimant quam nos existimari volumus de huius pudore, integritate, virtute : sed putarunt praetermitti
accusatorem non posse, cum animadversum esset in
iudices. Qua de re si unum factum ex omni anti-

had heard the case, gave a verdict of "not proven"
—to say nothing of those who voted "guilty."

But let that pass : Gellius finds Popilius guilty : 132
his verdict is that he took a bribe from Cluentius.
Lentulus says he did not. His reason for refusing
to admit Popilius to the Senate was that his father
was a freedman, though he allowed him to retain a
senator's seat at the Games together with his other
insignia, besides freeing him from all ignominy. In
doing this, he gave his verdict that Popilius had been
disinterested in voting for Oppianicus's condemnation.
Moreover, Lentulus afterwards singled out this same
Popilius for praise when giving evidence at a trial
for bribery. Inasmuch, then, as Lentulus did not
abide by the judgement of Gellius, nor was Gellius
content with the opinion of Lentulus, and as neither
censor thought it necessary to abide by his colleague's
decision, what reason is there for any of us to suppose
that censorial endorsement should in every case be
unalterable and binding for all time ?

XLVIII. But I am told they censored Habitus 133
himself. Yes, but for nothing that was disgraceful,
for no act in the course of his whole life that was, I
will not say wrong, but even regrettable. For no
one could possibly be purer than my client, or more
honourable, or more scrupulous in the observance of
every duty. Nor did the censors deny this ; they
merely followed the original rumour about the corruption of the court. It was not that they held any
opinion other than we should wish concerning the
honour, the blamelessness and the high character
of my client, but they thought that they could not
pass over the accuser after censuring the jurors. I
will quote one instance from all those that the past

134 quitate protulero, plura non dicam. Non enim mihi
exemplum summi et clarissimi viri, P. Africani,
praetereundum videtur : qui cum esset censor et
in equitum censu C. Licinius Sacerdos prodisset, clara
voce, ut omnis contio audire possit, dixit se scire
illum verbis conceptis peierasse : si qui contra vellet
dicere, usurum esse eum suo testimonio : deinde cum
nemo contra diceret, iussit equum traducere. Ita is,
cuius arbitrio et populus Romanus et exterae gentes
contentae esse consuerant, ipse sua scientia ad
ignominiam alterius contentus non fuit. Quod si hoc
Habito facere licuisset, facile illis ipsis iudicibus et
falsae suspicioni et invidiae populariter excitatae
restitisset.

135   Unum etiam est, quod me maxime perturbat, cui
loco respondere vix videor posse, quod elogium
recitasti de testamento Cn. Egnati patris, hominis
honestissimi videlicet et sapientissimi : idcirco se
exheredasse filium, quod is ob Oppianici condemnationem pecuniam accepisset. De cuius hominis
levitate et inconstantia plura non dicam : hoc testamentum ipsum, quod recitas, eius modi est, ut ille,
cum eum filium exheredaret, quem oderat, ei filio
coheredes homines alienissimos adiungeret, quem
diligebat. Sed tu, Acci, consideres censeo diligenter,
utrum censorium iudicium grave velis esse an Egnati.

---

a Publius Scipio Africanus, the younger, censor in 142 B.C.
b The order of knights was originally a cavalry force who
had to lead their horses past the censors for inspection. The
censors ordered them to " lead past " or " sell " their horses
according as they were or were not satisfied with them.
These phrases continued to be used at a review of the order,
though they had long ago lost their literal significance.

supplies, and then will say no more on this point.
I feel, indeed, that I cannot fail to mention the 134
example of the great and famous P. Africanus.[a]
During his term as censor he was holding the census
of knights, when G. Licinius Sacerdos came forward ;
whereupon, in a loud voice so as to be heard by the
whole assembly, he said that he knew that Licinius
had committed deliberate perjury ; and that if anyone wished to bring an accusation against him, he
would give his evidence to support it. Then, as no
one brought an accusation, he bade Licinius " lead
past his horse." [b]   And so the man with whose judgement the Roman people and foreign nations had
always been satisfied, was not satisfied with his personal knowledge when it came to degrading another.
Could Habitus have fared thus, he would easily have
held his own, even if he had had the censors as his
judges, against the groundless suspicion and prejudice roused against him by a demagogue.

There is a further point which troubles me greatly, 135
an argument to which I find myself scarcely able to
reply ; I mean the passage which you quote from
the will of the elder Egnatius—the most honourable
and intelligent of men, I need hardly say—stating
that he disinherited his son for taking a bribe to
secure Oppianicus's conviction. On this man's worthless and unreliable character I will not dilate : the
very will which you quote has the effect of disinheriting the son whom the testator hated, and at
the same time instituting absolute strangers as heirs
conjointly with the son whom he loved. But as
for you, Accius, I advise you to consider carefully
whether you wish the judgement of the censors or
that of Egnatius to carry weight. If that of Egna-

Si Egnati, leve est, quod censores de ceteris sub-
scripserunt : ipsum enim Cn. Egnatium, quem tu
gravem esse vis, ex senatu eiecerunt : sin autem
censorum, hunc Egnatium, quem pater censoria subscriptione exheredavit, censores in senatu, cum
patrem eicerent, retinuerunt.

136   XLIX. At enim senatus universus iudicavit illud
corruptum esse iudicium. Quo modo ? Suscepit
causam.   An potuit rem delatam eius modi repudiare ? cum tribunus plebis populo concitato rem
paene ad manus revocasset, cum vir optimus et homo
innocentissimus pecunia circumventus diceretur, cum
invidia flagraret ordo senatorius, potuit nihil decerni ?
potuit illa concitatio multitudinis sine summo periculo rei publicae repudiari ?   At quid est decretum ?
quam iuste ! quam sapienter ! quam diligenter ! SI
QUI SUNT, QUORUM OPERA FACTUM SIT UT IUDICIUM
PUBLICUM CORRUMPERETUR.   Utrum videtur id senatus
factum iudicare, an, si factum sit, moleste graviterque ferre ? Si ipse A. Cluentius sententiam de
iudiciis rogaretur, aliam non diceret atque ei dixerunt, quorum sententiis Cluentium condemnatum
137 esse dicitis. Sed quaero a vobis num istam legem
ex isto senatus consulto L. Lucullus consul, homo
sapientissimus, tulerit : num anno post M. Lucullus

---

^a *i.e.* the law which should have been, but was not, pro-
posed appointing a special commission to deal with the case.
See Introduction, end of § 4.

tius, then no weight can be attached to the censors'
endorsements in other cases ; for this very Gn.
Egnatius, whose judgement you wish to carry weight,
the censors expelled from the senate. But if that
of the censors, Egnatius the younger, whose father
disinherited him in the style of a censor's endorsement, was retained in the senate by the very censors
who expelled his father !

XLIX. But it is urged that the senate as a body **136**
adjudged that there had been bribery at that trial.
How so ? "It took up the case." Could it, indeed,
have refused to take notice of a matter of that kind
when duly brought before it ? When a tribune of
the people had stirred up the populace and almost
brought things to blows, when it was being said that
a good citizen and an innocent man had been victim-
ized by bribery, when the senatorial order was involved in a blaze of unpopularity, could they possibly
avoid passing a resolution ? Could they possibly
avoid taking notice of the mob's excitement without
gravely endangering the state ? But what resolution did they pass ? With what fitness, wisdom, and
exactness it was framed. "If there have been any
who have been responsible for the corruption of a
public court of justice . . ." Does it appear that
the senate was adjudging the corruption to have taken
place, or rather expressing displeasure and concern
in the event of its having taken place ? If Aulus
Cluentius himself had been asked for his opinion on
that trial, he would have expressed the same as
those by whose opinion you say he stands condemned.
But I ask you, did this so-called decree of the senate **137**
result in the proposal of this law of yours [a] by the
learned consul L. Lucullus ? Was it proposed the

et C. Cassius, in quos tum consules designatos idem
illud senatus decreverat ? Non tulerunt : et quod
tu Habiti pecunia factum esse arguis neque id ulla
tenuissima suspicione confirmas, factum est primum
illorum aequitate et sapientia consulum, ut id, quod
senatus decreverat ad illud invidiae praesens in-
cendium restinguendum, id postea referendum ad
populum non arbitrarentur. Ipse deinde populus
Romanus, qui L. Quincti fictis querimoniis antea con-
citatus rem illam et rogationem flagitarat, idem C.
Iuni filii, pueri parvuli, lacrimis commotus, maximo
clamore et concursu totam quaestionem illam et
138 legem repudiavit. Ex quo intellegi potuit id, quod
saepe dictum est : ut mare, quod sua natura tranquillum sit, ventorum vi agitari atque turbari, sic
populum Romanum sua sponte esse placatum,
hominum seditiosorum vocibus ut violentissimis tempestatibus concitari.

L. Est etiam reliqua permagna auctoritas, quam
ego turpiter paene praeterii : mea enim esse dicitur.
Recitavit ex oratione nescio qua Accius, quam meam
esse dicebat, cohortationem quandam iudicum ad
honeste iudicandum et commemorationem cum
aliorum iudiciorum, quae probata non essent, tum
illius ipsius iudicii Iuniani : proinde quasi ego non
ab initio huius defensionis dixerim invidiosum illud
iudicium fuisse, aut, cum de infamia iudiciorum disputarem, potuerim illud, quod tam populare esset,
139 illo tempore praeterire. Ego vero, si quid eius modi

---

a Probably Cicero's first speech against Verres ; the pre-
cise reference may be to §§ 38-40.

year after by M. Lucullus and G. Cassius, to whom, as
consuls-designate at the time, the senate in passing
the decree looked for its execution? It was not.
And what you maintain was effected by Habitus
through bribery, though without the vaguest suspicion to support you, was primarily due to their
just and wise conduct as consuls; that is to say, they
decided not to proceed to lay before the people a
decree which had been passed by the senate to ex-
tinguish the momentary outbreak of popular feeling
against it. The very public which had been goaded
by the hypocritical laments of L. Quinctius into
clamouring for just such a measure to be laid before
them, afterwards, when affected by the tears of G.
Junius's little son, assembled in an uproar to disown
their desire for such an inquiry or law; and this 138
brought home the truth of what has often been
remarked—that as the sea, though naturally calm,
becomes rough and stormy beneath a strong wind,
so is it with the Roman people; peaceable enough
when left to themselves, the speech of a demagogue
can rouse them like a furious gale.

L. There still remains a very weighty expression
of opinion which to my shame I all but passed over—
for it is ascribed to myself. Accius quoted a passage
from some speech [a] which he alleged to be mine, in
which I urged the jurors to return an honest verdict,
and specially quoted, among other unsatisfactory
trials, this very trial before Junius. As if indeed I
had not opened my defence on the present occasion
by mentioning the unpopularity of that trial; or as
if on the first occasion when dealing with the scandal
attaching to the courts, I could have failed to mention
what was then on every lip! If in fact I really did 139

dixi, neque cognitum commemoravi neque pro testimonio dixi, et illa oratio potius temporis mei quam iudicii et auctoritatis fuit. Cum enim accusarem et mihi initio proposuissem, ut animos et populi Romani et iudicum commoverem, cumque omnes offensiones iudiciorum non ex mea opinione, sed ex hominum rumore proferrem, istam rem, quae tam populariter esset agitata, praeterire non potui. Sed errat vehementer, si quis in orationibus nostris, quas in iudiciis habuimus, auctoritates nostras consignatas se habere arbitratur. Omnes enim illae causarum ac temporum sunt, non hominum ipsorum aut patronorum. Nam si causae ipsae pro se loqui possent, nemo adhiberet oratorem. Nunc adhibemur, ut ea dicamus, non quae nostra auctoritate constituantur, sed quae

140 ex re ipsa causaque ducantur. Hominem ingeniosum, M. Antonium, aiunt solitum esse dicere idcirco se nullam umquam orationem scripsisse, ut, si quid aliquando non opus esset ab se esse dictum, posset negare dixisse : proinde quasi si quid a nobis dictum aut actum sit, id nisi litteris mandarimus, hominum memoria non comprehendatur.

LI. Ego vero in isto genere libentius cum multorum tum hominis eloquentissimi et sapientissimi, L. Crassi, auctoritatem sequor, qui cum Cn. Plancum defenderet, accusante M. Bruto, homine in dicendo vehementi et callido, cum Brutus duobus recitatoribus constitutis ex duabus eius orationibus capita alterna inter se contraria recitanda curasset, quod

---

[a] Nicknamed "the Prosecutor" from his love of litigation.

say anything of the kind, I was not speaking of a fact
within my personal knowledge nor did I say it in
evidence : my speech was the outcome rather of the
exigencies of the moment, than of my deliberate
judgement. In my capacity as prosecutor I had
made it my first object to work upon the feelings
both of the public and of the jurors, and I was quoting, not from my own opinion, but from current
rumour, every case that told against the courts, and
I was therefore unable to pass over the case of which
you speak, as it was then a matter of general notoriety.
But it is the greatest possible mistake to suppose that
the speeches we barristers have made in court contain
our considered and certified opinions ; all those
speeches reflect the demands of some particular
case or emergency, not the individual personality of
the advocate. For if a case could speak for itself
no one would employ a pleader. As it is, we are
employed to express, not the conclusions warranted
by our own judgement, but the deductions which
can be made from the facts of the case. There is a 140
story that the brilliant M. Antonius used to say
that his reason for never having written any speech
was that, should he have occasion to regret anything
he had said, he might be able to deny having said it :
as if indeed men do not remember anything we have
said or done unless we have committed it to writing !

LI. For myself, I should prefer, on a point of this
kind, to follow, among many other authorities, that
of the eloquent and learned L. Crassus. He was
defending Gn. Plancus against M. Brutus,[a] a forcible
and skilful speaker ; and Brutus put forward two
readers, causing them to read in turn contradictory
passages taken from two of his speeches ; in one of

in dissuasione rogationis eius, quae contra coloniam
Narbonensem ferebatur, quantum potest, de auctoritate senatus detrahit, in suasione legis Serviliae summis
ornat senatum laudibus, et multa in equites Romanos
cum ex ea oratione asperius dicta recitasset, quo
animi illorum iudicum in Crassum incenderentur, ali-
141 quantum esse commotus dicitur. Itaque in respon-
dendo primum exposuit utriusque rationem temporis,
ut oratio ex re et ex causa habita videretur, deinde
ut intellegere posset Brutus, quem hominem et non
solum qua eloquentia, verum etiam quo lepore et
quibus facetiis praeditum lacessisset, tres ipse excitavit recitatores cum singulis libellis, quos M.
Brutus, pater illius accusatoris, de iure civili reliquit.
Eorum initia cum recitarentur, ea, quae vobis nota
esse arbitror : " Forte evenit, ut ruri in Privernati
essemus ego et Brutus filius," fundum Privernatem
flagitabat : " In Albano eramus ego et Brutus filius,"
Albanum poscebat : " In Tiburti forte quum adse-
dissemus ego et Brutus filius," Tiburtem fundum
requirebat : Brutum autem, hominem sapientem,
quod filii nequitiam videret, quae praedia ei relin-
queret, testificari voluisse dicebat : quod si potuisset
honeste scribere se in balneis cum id aetatis filio
fuisse, non praeterisset : eas tamen ab eo balneas
non ex libris patris, sed ex tabulis et ex censu quae-

<hr>

ᵃ For Caepio's Lex Servilia in B.c. 106 see the General
Introduction, Historical Summary.
  ᵇ *i.e.* the knights. See footnote on § 61.
  ᶜ See note on p. 370.

which when opposing a bill introduced to prevent
the founding of a colony at Narbo, he did his utmost
to disparage the senate ; while, when supporting
the statute of Servilius,[a] he had praised that body
in the highest terms ; and then, meaning to inflame
the jurors of those days[b] against Crassus, Brutus
had a further passage from this speech read out in
which he had made many bitter attacks upon the
Roman knights. This discomforted Crassus not a
little. Accordingly in his reply, he first explained 141
the requirements of the two occasions to show that
his speech had been designed to suit the facts of
either case ; next, in order to let Brutus see what
manner of man he had provoked, and how gifted not
only with eloquence but with wit and humour, he in
his turn produced three readers each carrying one
of the treatises on law left by M. Brutus, father of
Brutus " the Prosecutor."[c] They began to read the
opening passages of these books which I suspect you
know ; and at the words, " I happened to be at my
country place at Privernum with my son Brutus,"
he asked after the estate at Privernum ; at the
words, " I was at Alba with my son Brutus," he
inquired after the one at Alba ; at the words, " I
happened to be sitting at my place at Tibur with my
son Brutus," he asked for news of the estate at
Tibur, declaring that the elder Brutus, like the wise
man that he was, seeing his son's extravagance, had
wanted to leave a record of what property he was
bequeathing to him ; and could he with propriety
have written that he had been in his baths with a
son of that age he would not have failed to do so.
" But to find these baths," said Crassus, " I must
look not in your father's books but in his accounts

rere. Crassus tum ita Brutum ultus est, ut illum recitationis suae paeniteret. Moleste enim fortasse tulerat se in eis orationibus reprehensum, quas de re publica habuisset, in quibus forsitan magis requiratur 142 constantia. Ego autem illa recitata esse non moleste fero. Neque enim ab illo tempore, quod tum erat, neque ab ea causa, quae tum agebatur, aliena fuerunt : neque mihi quicquam oneris suscepi, cum ista dixi, quo minus honeste hanc causam et libere possem defendere. Quod si velim confiteri me causam A. Cluenti nunc cognosse, antea fuisse in illa populari opinione, quis tandem id possit reprehendere ? praesertim, iudices, cum a vobis quoque ipsis hoc impetrari sit aequissimum, quod ego et ab initio petivi et nunc peto, ut, si quam huc graviorem de illo iudicio opinionem attulistis, hanc causa perspecta atque omni veritate cognita deponatis.

143 LII. Nunc, quoniam ad omnia, quae abs te dicta sunt, T. Acci, de Oppianici damnatione respondi, confiteare necesse est te opinionem multum fefellisse, quod existimaris me causam A. Cluenti non facto eius, sed lege defensurum. Nam hoc persaepe dixisti tibi sic renuntiari, me habere in animo causam hanc praesidio legis defendere. Itane est ? ab amicis imprudentes videlicet prodimur, et est nescio quis de

---

a These were public baths, built by the elder Brutus as a speculation.
b See the Introduction, § 4, 1.

and in the censor's register." [a] Thus did Crassus
on this occasion avenge himself on Brutus, to make
him sorry for what he had read out. For he may have
been annoyed at being brought to book over speeches
of public import in which consistency, perhaps, is
more to be expected. But for my part, I feel no 142
annoyance at your having read out the passages you
did, for they were inappropriate neither to their
own times nor to the case in question ; and in making
the remarks you quote, I incurred no such responsibility as to affect my honour or my freedom in
defending this case. But if I should choose to admit
that, though I have now examined the case of Aulus
Cluentius, I previously shared the popular prejudice
of the time, who, pray, could find fault with me for
that ? Especially as it is only fair that from you
also, gentlemen, I should gain the request that I
made to you at the beginning and now make to you
again—the request that, should you have come into
this court with an unfavourable impression of that
trial, you lay it aside now that you have come to
understand the case, and to know the whole truth
about it.

LII. I have now replied to every point which you 143
have made about the condemnation of Oppianicus ;
and you must admit, T. Accius, that you were
greatly mistaken in supposing that I should base my
defence of my client's case not upon its merits but
upon its legal aspect. For you claimed again and
again to have information that I meant to defend it
by the protection afforded by the statute.[b] Is that
so ? Am I indeed being betrayed by my friends

eis, quos amicos nobis arbitramur, qui nostra consilia
ad adversarios deferat? Quisnam hoc tibi renuntiavit? quis tam improbus fuit? cui ego autem nar-
ravi? Nemo, ut opinor, in culpa est: et nimirum
tibi istud lex ipsa renuntiavit. Sed num tibi ita
defendisse videor, ut tota in causa mentionem ullam
legis fecerim? num secus hanc causam defendisse
ac si lege Habitus teneretur? Certe, ut hominem
confirmare oportet, nullus est locus a me purgandi
144 istius invidiosi criminis praetermissus. Quid ergo
est? Quaeret fortassis quispiam, displiceatne mihi
legum praesidio capitis periculum propulsare? Mihi
vero, iudices, non displicet, sed utor instituto meo.
In hominis honesti prudentisque iudicio non solum
meo consilio uti consuevi, sed multum etiam eius,
quem defendo, et consilio et voluntati obtempero.
Nam ut haec ad me causa delata est, qui leges eas,
ad quas adhibemur et in quibus versamur, nosse
deberem, dixi Habito statim eo capite, QUI COISSET
QUO QUIS CONDEMNARETUR, illum esse liberum: teneri
autem nostrum ordinem. Atque ille me orare atque
obsecrare coepit, ne se lege defenderem. Cum ego
quae mihi videbantur dicerem, traduxit me ad suam
sententiam. Adfirmabat enim lacrimans non se cupi-
diorem esse civitatis retinendae quam existimationis.
145 Morem homini gessi, et tamen idcirco feci—neque

without my knowing it, and is there one of those I counted my friends capable of carrying my plans to my opponents ? Who can have given you this information ? Who can have been so dishonest ? Nay, to whom did I tell it myself ? My belief is that no one is to blame : no doubt the statute itself was your informant ; but surely you do not think that, in conducting the defence, I have in the course of it made a single allusion to the statute or that I have conducted it otherwise than on the assumption that the statute is applicable to my client ? Assuredly, so far as a man may speak with certainty, I have neglected no point which concerned the disproval of your charge so fraught with prejudice. And why so ? Perhaps I shall be asked whether I 144 disapprove of taking refuge in the legal aspect of a case to avert the danger of a criminal charge. Far from it, gentlemen, but I follow my habitual practice. When engaged in the trial of a man of honour and good sense it has not been my habit merely to be guided by my own ideas : I defer also to the ideas and wishes of my client. For when this brief was brought to me, as one whose duty it was to know the statutes which we are employed to deal with and in which our work lies, I at once told Habitus that the clause beginning : "Whosoever shall have conspired to cause a man's conviction . . ." was not applicable to him, though applicable to those of my own order. He then started to beg and beseech me not to base his defence on the letter of the law. I gave him my own views, but he brought me over to his opinion ; for he protested with tears that he was not more anxious to retain his citizenship than his reputation. I gave way to him ; and I only did so 145

enim id semper facere debemus—quod videbam per
se ipsam causam sine lege copiosissime posse defendi.
Videbam in hac defensione, qua iam sum usus, plus
dignitatis, in illa, qua me hic uti noluit, minus laboris
futurum. Quod si nihil aliud esset actum nisi ut
hanc causam obtineremus, lege recitata perorassem.

LIII. Neque me illa oratio commovet, quod ait
Accius indignum esse facinus, si senator iudicio quempiam circumvenerit, legibus eum teneri : si eques
146 Romanus hoc idem fecerit, non teneri. Ut tibi con-
cedam hoc indignum esse, quod cuius modi sit iam
videro, tu mihi concedas necesse est multo esse indignius in ea civitate, quae legibus contineatur, dis-
cedi ab legibus. Hoc enim vinculum est huius dignitatis, qua fruimur in re publica, hoc fundamentum
libertatis, hic fons aequitatis : mens et animus et
consilium et sententia civitatis posita est in legibus.
Ut corpora nostra sine mente, sic civitas sine lege suis
partibus, ut nervis et sanguine et membris, uti non
potest. Legum ministri magistratus, legum interpretes iudices, legum denique idcirco omnes servi
sumus, ut liberi esse possimus.

147 Quid est, Q. Naso, cur tu in isto loco sedeas ? quae
vis est qua abs te hi iudices tali dignitate praediti
coerceantur ? Vos autem, iudices, quam ob rem ex
tanta multitudine civium tam pauci de hominum
fortunis sententiam fertis ? quo iure Accius quae
voluit dixit ? Cur mihi tam diu potestas dicendi

---

^a Quintus Voconius Naso, president of the court and
specified as such in § 148.

(for we ought not to do so always) because I saw that the case was abundantly capable of being defended on its own merits without an appeal to the statute. I saw that the line of defence which I have actually adopted would be more dignified, the line my client wished me not to adopt less arduous. But had our only concern been to get a verdict, I should have read the statute aloud and then sat down.

LIII. Nor am I impressed by the argument employed by Accius that it is a monstrous shame that the law should be applicable to a senator who diverts the course of justice, and not applicable to a Roman knight who does the very same thing. If I am to concede to you that this is a shame—and I shall consider the point presently—you must concede to me that it is a far greater shame, in a state which rests upon law, to depart from law. For law is the bond which secures these our privileges in the commonwealth, the foundation of our liberty, the fountain - head of justice. Within the law are reposed the mind and heart, the judgement and the conviction of the state. The state without law would be like the human body without mind—unable to employ the parts which are to it as sinews, blood, and limbs. The magistrates who administer the law, the jurors who interpret it—all of us in short—obey the law to the end that we may be free.

What is the reason, Quintus Naso,[a] that you sit there in the chair? What is the power by which you control eminent men like these jurors? And you, gentlemen, wherefore are you, so few among all the great body of citizens, selected to pass sentence on men's fortunes? By what right has Accius said what he pleased? Why am I given the opportunity

datur ? Quid sibi autem illi scribae, quid lictores, quid ceteri, quos apparere huic quaestioni video, volunt ? Opinor haec omnia lege fieri totumque hoc iudicium, ut ante dixi, quasi mente quadam regi legis et administrari. Quid ergo ? haec quaestio sola ita gubernatur ? Quid M. Plaetori et C. Flamini inter sicarios ? quid C. Orchivi peculatus ? quid mea de pecuniis repetundis ? quid C. Aquili, apud quem nunc ambitus causa dicitur ? quid reliquae quaestiones ? Circumspicite omnes rei publicae partes : omnia legum imperio et praescripto fieri videbitis.
148 Si quis apud me, T. Acci, te reum velit facere, clames te lege pecuniarum repetundarum non teneri. Neque haec tua recusatio confessio sit captae pecuniae, sed laboris et periculi non legitimi declinatio.

LIV. Nunc quid agatur et quid abs te iuris constituatur vide. Iubet lex ea, qua lege haec quaestio constituta est, iudicem quaestionis, hoc est, Q. Voconium, cum eis iudicibus, qui ei obvenerint—vos appellat, iudices—quaerere de veneno. In quem quaerere ? infinitum est. Quicumque fecerit, vendiderit, emerit, habuerit, dederit. Quid eadem lex statim adiungit ? Recita. Deque eius capite quaerito. Cuius ? qui coierit ? convenerit ? non ita

---

* See the Introduction, Note on the Statutes, 2.

to speak at this length? What, indeed, is the
meaning of those clerks, of the lictors, of the other
officers whom I see in attendance at this court? I
take it that all this is the result of law, and that this
whole trial, as I said before, is under the direction
of law as of some controlling mind. Nay, more :
is this the only court that is so governed? What of
the Assassination Court of M. Plaetorius and G.
Flaminius? Or the Embezzlement Court of G.
Orchivius? Or my own, which deals with taking
bribes? Or that of G. Aquilius, before whom a trial
for giving bribes is now in progress? What of the
courts I have not mentioned? Look round on all
the departments of the commonwealth ; you will
find them every one under the rule and governance
of the laws. If anyone should propose to prosecute 148
you in my court, T. Accius, you would loudly assert
that the Statute of Bribery was not applicable to
you.*a* But this demurrer on your part would not
be an admission that you had taken a bribe, but a
way of escaping a trouble and a risk not imposed on
you by law.

LIV. Now see what we are coming to, and what
principle of law you would establish. The statute
under which this court is set up bids the president
of the court, that is, Q. Voconius, together with
those jurors who have been allotted to him (meaning
you, gentlemen) to try cases of poisoning. Try
whom? There is no distinction made : " Whosoever has made it, sold it, bought it, had it in his
possession or administered it." What does this
statute straightway go on to say? Read it : " And
shall try him on a criminal charge." Whom? Him
who has conspired or has combined? Not so. What

est. Quid ergo est? dic. QUI TRIBUNUS MILITUM
LEGIONIBUS QUATTUOR PRIMIS QUIVE QUAESTOR, TRI-
BUNUS PLEBIS. Deinceps omnes magistratus nomi-
navit. QUIVE IN SENATU SENTENTIAM DIXIT, DIXERIT.
Quid tum? QUI EORUM COIT, COIERIT, CONVENIT, CON-
VENERIT, QUO QUIS IUDICIO PUBLICO CONDEMNARETUR.
" Qui eorum." Quorum? videlicet, qui supra scripti
sunt. Quid intersit utro modo scriptum sit, etsi est
apertum, ipsa tamen lex nos docet. Ubi enim omnes
mortales adligat, ita loquitur: QUI VENENUM MALUM
FECIT, FECERIT. Omnes viri, mulieres, liberi, servi
in iudicium vocantur. Si idem de coitione voluisset,
adiunxisset: QUIVE COIERIT. Nunc ita est: DEQUE
EIUS CAPITE QUAERITO, QUI MAGISTRATUM HABUERIT INVE
SENATU SENTENTIAM DIXERIT : QUI EORUM COIT, COIERIT.
149 Num is est Cluentius? Certe non est. Quis ergo
est Cluentius? qui tamen defendi causam suam lege
noluit. Itaque abicio legem : morem Cluentio gero :
tibi tamen, Acci, pauca, quae ab huius causa seiuncta
sunt, respondebo. Est enim quiddam in hac causa
quod Cluentius ad se, est aliquid quod ego ad me
putem pertinere. Hic sua putat interesse se re ipsa
et gesto negotio, non lege defendi : ego autem mea

ᵃ These tribunes took precedence over those of the second
and third legions and ranked as magistrates.
382

does it say, then ? Tell us. " Whatsoever military
tribune of the four first legions,ᵃ whatsoever
quaestor, tribune of the people " — and then are
mentioned all the magistrates in succession — " or
whosoever in the senate has, or shall have, given his
vote." What follows ? " Whosoever of them has,
or shall have, conspired or combined to secure a conviction by a public court." " Whoever of them " —
whom ? Of those, presumably, who are specified
above. Although it is obvious how great a difference
lies between the two ways of specification, the statute
itself explains the point to us : where it is binding
on all human beings, it speaks thus : " Whosoever
has, or shall have, made a noxious drug " : men and
women, freedmen and slaves, all are haled to judgement. If the intention of the law had been the same
with regard to conspiracy, it would have added :
" Or whosoever shall have conspired." But actually
it runs as follows : " And shall try on a criminal
charge him who shall have held office as a magistrate or in the senate shall have given his vote ; whosoever of these has, or shall have, conspired." Does 149
Cluentius come under this head ? Assuredly not.
Under what head then does Cluentius come ? No
matter ; for he has refused to have his case defended
on a point of law. Accordingly I waive the legal
aspect : I give way to Cluentius. But to you,
Accius, I have an answer to make on a few points
which are distinct from my client's case. For there
is an aspect of this case which Cluentius thinks to be
his concern ; there is another aspect of it which I
think to be mine. He thinks it in his interest to
have his case defended on its merits and on its
facts, and not on a point of law : and I consider it

existimo interesse me nulla in disputatione ab Accio
videri esse superatum. Non enim mihi haec causa
sola dicenda est. Omnibus hic labor meus propositus
est, quicumque hac facultate defensionis contenti esse
possunt. Nolo quemquam eorum, qui adsunt, existimare me, quae de lege ab Accio dicta sunt, si re-
ticuerim, comprobare. Quam ob rem, Cluenti, de te
tibi obsequor, neque enim legem recito neque hoc
loco pro te dico, sed ea, quae a me desiderari arbitror,
non relinquam.

150   LV. Iniquum tibi videtur, Acci, esse non isdem
legibus omnes teneri. Primum, ut id iniquissimum
esse confitear, eius modi est, ut commutatis eis opus
sit legibus, non ut his, quae sunt, non pareamus.
Deinde quis umquam hoc senator recusavit, ne quo
altiorem gradum dignitatis beneficio populi Romani
esset consecutus, eo se putaret durioribus legum condicionibus uti oportere? Quam multa sunt commoda, quibus caremus, quam multa molesta et diffi-
cilia, quae subimus! atque haec omnia tantum honoris et amplitudinis commodo compensantur. Con-
verte nunc ad equestrem ordinem atque in ceteros
ordines easdem vitae condiciones: non perferent:
putant enim minus multos sibi laqueos legum et con-
dicionum ac iudiciorum propositos esse oportere, qui
summum locum civitatis aut non potuerunt ascendere
151 aut non petiverunt. Atque ut omittam leges alias
omnes, quibus nos tenemur, ceteri autem sunt ordines

in my interest not to be seen yielding a single disputed point to Accius. For this is not the only case
which I have to plead. These my endeavours are
placed at the disposal of all who can find satisfaction
in my powers of advocacy. I am unwilling that anyone of those present in court should imagine that
by my silence I am assenting to Accius's statement
about the statute. And so, while meeting your
wishes, Cluentius, to the extent of not reading the
statute—nor am I at this point speaking on your
behalf—I shall not, at the same time, leave unspoken the argument which I think is expected of me.

LV. You think it unfair, Accius, that all men 150
should not be bound by the same laws. Supposing,
first, that I should admit this to be a great injustice ;
even so the situation demands that the existing laws
be altered, not that we should fail to obey them as
they stand. In the second place, what senator ever
refused to consider himself bound to submit to a
greater strictness in the law's demands upon him,
proportionate to the greater dignity of the position
to which he had been raised by the favour of the
Roman people ? How many are the advantages
which we forgo, how many the inconveniences and
difficulties to which we submit ! And the compensation for all these is the great honour and dignity of
our position. Now apply the same conditions of
life to the order of knights, and to the other orders :
they will not put up with them ; for they hold that
they should be less exposed to the entanglements of
statutory restrictions and legal processes, inasmuch
as they have either been unable to reach the highest
position in the state, or have not tried to reach it.
Passing over all other laws by which we senators are 151

liberati, hanc ipsam legem : NE QUIS IUDICIO CIRCUM-
VENIRETUR, C. Gracchus tulit : eam legem pro plebe,
non in plebem tulit.   Postea L. Sulla, homo a populi
causa remotissimus, tamen, cum eius rei quaestionem hac ipsa lege constitueret, qua vos hoc tempore
iudicatis, populum Romanum, quem ab hoc genere
liberum acceperat, adligare novo quaestionis genere
ausus non est.   Quod si fieri posse existimasset, pro
illo odio, quod habuit in equestrem ordinem, nihil
fecisset libentius, quam omnem illam acerbitatem
proscriptionis suae, qua est usus in veteres iudices,
152 in hanc unam quaestionem contulisset.   Nec nunc
quicquam agitur—mihi credite, iudices, et prospicite
id, quod providendum est—nisi ut equester ordo in
huiusce legis periculum concludatur.   Neque hoc
agitur ab omnibus, sed a paucis.   Nam ei senatores,
qui se facile tuentur integritate et innocentia, quales,
ut vere dicam, vos estis, et ceteri, qui sine cupiditate
vixerunt, equites ordini senatorio dignitate proximos,
concordia coniunctissimos esse cupiunt : sed ei, qui
sese volunt posse omnia neque praeterea quicquam
esse aut in homine ullo aut in ordine, hoc uno metu se
putant equites Romanos in potestatem suam re-
dacturos, si constitutum sit, ut de eis, qui rem iudi-

---

[a] Literally "to prevent anyone being circumvented in a
court of law."   This refers to the law of Gracchus afterwards
embodied in § 6 of Sulla's *lex de sicariis et veneficiis* (see
Introduction, § 4, 1).   Presumably Gracchus, as a popular
leader, passed this law before that which transferred the
control of the courts from the senate to the order of knights.
(See Historical Summary.)

[b] Sulla reversed Gracchus's enactment dealing with the
courts (see previous note); but though § 6 of Gracchus's law
against assassins was aimed at senators in their capacity as
jurors, Sulla dared not make it (retrospectively) operative
against the order of knights, whom he had just deprived of

bound while the other orders are free from them, G.
Gracchus proposed this very law to deal with cases
of "judicial murder." [a]   And he proposed it in the
interests of the people, not against their interests.
Now L. Sulla was anything but a friend to the
popular cause ; but still, when subsequently appointing a court to deal with this matter under the very
statute which you are now administering, he did not
dare to inflict this new kind of court upon the Roman
people whom he had found free from any such
liability.   Had he thought it possible to do otherwise, nothing would have pleased him so much, considering his well-known hatred of the order of
knights, as to concentrate in this one court all
the venom of his proscription as he visited it on
the former jurors.[b]   The single aim and object of 152
this (believe me, gentlemen, and look the danger
in the face) is the extension of liability under this
statute to include the order of knights.   This aim
is not shared by all senators but only by a few.
For those who have a ready protection in their own
uprightness and innocence (as may truthfully be
said of you and of all whose lives are innocent of
party spirit) are anxious that the order of knights
should occupy a position second only to that of their
own order and most firmly allied to it by the bond
of unanimity.   But those who wish to see all power
reposed in themselves and none at all in any other
person or order think that they will bring the Roman
knights under subjection to themselves merely by
the threat involved in the decision that those who
have served as jurors are liable to a prosecution like

their judicial privileges, after proscribing 1600 of them. See
Historical Summary.

carint, huiusce modi iudicia fieri possint. Vident
enim auctoritatem huius ordinis confirmari : vident
iudicia comprobari : hoc metu proposito evellere se
153 aculeum severitatis vestrae posse confidunt. Quis
enim de homine audeat paulo maioribus opibus prae-
dito vere et fortiter iudicare, cum videat sibi de eo,
quod coierit aut consenserit, causam esse dicendam ?

LVI. O viros fortes, equites Romanos, qui homini
clarissimo ac potentissimo, M. Druso, tribuno plebis
restiterunt, cum ille nihil aliud ageret cum illa cuncta,
quae tum erat, nobilitate, nisi ut ei qui rem iudicassent, huiusce modi quaestionibus in iudicium voca-
rentur. Tunc C. Flavius Pusio, Cn. Titinius, C.
Maecenas, illa robora populi Romani ceterique eiusdem ordinis, non fecerunt idem, quod nunc Cluentius,
ut aliquid culpae suscipere se putarent recusando, sed
apertissime repugnarunt, cum haec recusarent et
palam fortissime atque honestissime dicerent se
potuisse iudicio populi Romani in amplissimum locum
pervenire, si sua studia ad honores petendos conferre
voluissent : sese vidisse, in ea vita qualis splendor
inesset, quanta ornamenta, quae dignitas : quae se
non contempsisse, sed ordine suo patrumque suorum
contentos fuisse et vitam illam tranquillam et quietam
remotam a procellis invidiarum et huiusce modi iudi-
154 ciorum sequi maluisse : aut sibi ad honores petendos
aetatem integram restitui oportere, aut, quoniam id
non posset, eam condicionem vitae, quam secuti

ᵃ For the proposals of Marcus Livius Drusus in 91 B.C.
see Historical Summary : they included the setting up of a
court to try all (equestrian) jurors who had been guilty of
corruption.

the present one. For they see that the authority of this order is gaining in strength, and its administration of the courts in popularity : by exposing you to this menace they are confident that they can take the sting out of your strictness. For who 153 would dare truly and courageously to pass sentence on a man possessed of even slightly greater resources than himself, when he saw that he must stand his trial on a charge of combination or conspiracy ?

LVI. What courage they showed, those Roman knights who resisted the distinguished and powerful tribune of the people, M. Drusus,[a] when, backed by the entire aristocracy of those days, his one aim was to bring to trial before courts of this kind those who had acted as jurors ! Then did not G. Flavius Pusio, Gn. Titinius, and G. Maecenas, the flower of the Roman people, and others of their order, suppose, as Cluentius does now, that their protest exposed them to some degree of blame : they openly fought the measures, protesting against them and saying courageously and honourably before all, that if they had chosen to concentrate all their ambition upon the pursuit of honours, they might have reached the highest position in the state by the award of the Roman people. " We have seen," they said, " the magnificence, the privilege and the distinction attaching to a senator's life. These we have not despised ; but satisfied with our own order, which was our fathers' too, we have preferred to pursue the life it offers in peace and quiet, sheltered from the storms of popular prejudice and from legal actions such as this. Either you must give us back 154 the heyday of our youth in which to pursue ambition, or, since that is impossible, leave us that position

petitionem reliquissent, manere : iniquum esse eos,
qui honorum ornamenta propter periculorum multitudinem praetermisissent, populi beneficiis esse
privatos, iudiciorum novorum periculis non carere :
senatorem hoc queri non posse, propterea quod ea
condicione proposita petere coepisset, quodque permulta essent ornamenta, quibus eam mitigare mole-
stiam posset, locus, auctoritas, domi splendor, apud
exteras nationes nomen et gratia, toga praetexta,
sella curulis, insignia, fasces, exercitus, imperia, provinciae : quibus in rebus cum summa recte factis
maiores nostri praemia tum plura peccatis pericula
proposita esse voluerunt. Illi non hoc recusabant,
ne ea lege accusarentur, qua nunc Habitus accusatur,
quae tunc erat Sempronia, nunc est Cornelia : intellegebant enim ea lege equestrem ordinem non teneri,
155 sed ne nova lege adligarentur laborabant. Habitus
ne hoc quidem umquam recusavit, quo minus vel ea
lege rationem vitae suae redderet, qua non tenetur.
Quae si vobis condicio placet, omnes id agamus, ut
haec quam primum in omnes ordines quaestio per-
feratur.

LVII. Interea quidem, per deos immortales !
quoniam omnia commoda nostra, iura, libertatem,
salutem denique legibus obtinemus, a legibus non
recedamus : simul et illud quam sit iniquum cogite-
mus, populum Romanum aliud nunc agere : vobis

---

a See Introduction, § 4, 1.

in life which we abandoned our ambition to pursue.
It is unfair that we who have renounced the privileges of office by reason of its innumerable dangers,
should be debarred from public recognition and yet
not free from the danger of prosecution in the courts.
A senator is not entitled to make this complaint,
because those are conditions under which he embarked on his career, and because he has many
privileges calculated to alleviate its drawbacks—
rank, position, magnificence at home, reputation and
influence abroad, the embroidered robe, the chair of
state, the badges of rank, the lictors' rods, armies,
commands, provinces. In all this our forefathers
intended to make the rewards of upright dealing
as high as possible but the risk to wrongdoers more
than ordinarily heavy." The objection of these
knights was not to their being accused under the
same statute under which Habitus is accused to-day
(at that time it was the Sempronian law, to-day it is
the Cornelian^a); for they realized that it was not
applicable to the order of knights : but their efforts
were directed to prevent their being brought within
the toils of a new statute. Habitus has never 155
objected even to rendering account of his life under
a law which is actually not binding on him ; and if
such a state of affairs pleases you let us all do our
best to get the jurisdiction of this court extended
over every order as soon as possible !

LVII. But in the meanwhile, in Heaven's name,
since it is the laws that give us all our advantages,
our rights, our freedom and our security—let us
abide by the laws. And further, let us reflect how
unfair this is—the Roman people are off their guard :
they have placed in your keeping their country and

rem publicam et fortunas suas commisisse : sine cura
esse : non metuere, ne lege ea, quam numquam ipse
iusserit, et quaestione, qua se solutum liberumque
156 esse arbitretur, per paucos iudices astringatur. Agit
enim sic causam T. Accius, adulescens bonus et
disertus, omnes cives legibus teneri omnibus : vos
attenditis et auditis silentio, sicut facere debetis.
A. Cluentius causam dicit eques Romanus ea lege,
qua lege senatores et ei, qui magistratum habuerunt,
soli tenentur : mihi per eum recusare et in arce legis
praesidia constituere defensionis meae non licet. Si
obtinuerit causam Cluentius, sicuti vestra aequitate
nixi confidimus, omnes existimabunt, id quod erit,
obtinuisse propter innocentiam, quoniam ita de-
fensus sit : in lege autem, quam attingere noluerit,
praesidii nihil fuisse.

157   Hic nunc est quiddam, quod ad me pertineat, de
quo ante dixi, quod ego populo Romano praestare
debeam, quoniam is vitae meae status est, ut omnis
mihi cura et opera posita sit in hominum periculis
defendendis. Video quanta et quam periculosa et
quam infinita quaestio temptetur ab accusatoribus,
cum eam legem, quae in nostrum ordinem scripta sit,
in populum Romanum transferre conentur. Qua in
lege est : QUI COIERIT, quod quam late pateat videtis :
CONVENERIT, aeque incertum et infinitum est : CONSEN-
SERIT, hoc vero cum infinitum tum obscurum et occul-
tum : FALSUMVE TESTIMONIUM DIXERIT, quis de plebe
Romana testimonium dixit umquam, cui non hoc peri-

their fortunes : they have no anxiety nor do they fear to find themselves subjected by a handful of jurors to a law which they themselves have never sanctioned and to a court from which they imagine themselves exempt and free. For my worthy and 156 fluent young friend T. Accius is basing his case on the assumption that all laws are binding on all citizens, and you, as your duty is, listen to him in attentive silence. Aulus Cluentius is being tried as a Roman knight under a statute which is only binding on senators and ex-magistrates ; and I am refused his permission to enter my protest and to set the bulwarks of my defence upon the vantage-ground of law. If Cluentius secures the verdict, as, relying on your sense of justice, I confidently expect, everyone will believe, and rightly, that he secured it by his innocence, since that was the line his defence followed ; but that the statute on which he declined to dwell afforded him no protection.

I now come to a point which, as I have said before, 157 concerns myself, and which I owe to the public to make good ; for such are the conditions of this life of mine that all my care and all my effort is expended in the defence of men in perils by the law. I see how great, how perilous and how unbounded in its jurisdiction is the court which the prosecution is bent on establishing in its effort to extend to the whole Roman people the statute which was framed against us senators. The statute runs : " Whoso shall have combined "—you see how much that covers—" or conspired "—which is equally vague and undefined, and besides, mysterious and unintelligible—" or shall have given false evidence "—what man of the whole populace of Rome who has ever given evidence

culum T. Accio auctore paratum esse videatis ? Nam
dicturum quidem certe, si hoc iudicium plebi Romanae
propositum sit, neminem umquam esse confirmo.
158 Sed hoc polliceor omnibus, si cui forte hac lege
negotium facessetur, qui lege non teneatur, si is uti
me defensore voluerit, me eius causam legis praesidio
defensurum, et vel his iudicibus vel horum similibus
facillime probaturum et omni me defensione usurum
esse legis, qua nunc ut utar, ab eo, cuius voluntati
mihi obtemperandum est, non conceditur.

LVIII. Non enim debeo dubitare, iudices, quin,
si qua ad vos causa eius modi delata sit eius, qui lege
non teneatur, etiam si is invidiosus aut multis offensus
esse videatur, etiam si eum oderitis, etiam si inviti
absoluturi sitis, tamen absolvatis et religioni potius
159 vestrae quam odio pareatis. Est enim sapientis
iudicis cogitare tantum sibi a populo Romano esse
permissum, quantum commissum sit et creditum, et
non solum sibi potestatem datam, verum etiam fidem
habitam esse meminisse : posse quem oderit absolvere, quem non oderit condemnare, et semper non
quid ipse velit, sed quid lex et religio cogat cogitare :
animadvertere qua lege reus citetur, de quo reo

is not threatened through the proposal of Accius with the peril of prosecution ? For, as for giving evidence hereafter, I can at all events assure you of this, that if the Roman people be made liable to these proceedings, no one will ever be found to do so. But I 158 promise you all that should any man on whom this statute is not binding be harassed by proceedings under it, and should he entrust his defence to me, I shall base my conduct of his case upon its legal aspect, and shall find no difficulty in commending my argument, whether to these jurors or to others like them, availing myself fully of the defence afforded by the law which the wishes of one to whom I am bound to defer do not on this occasion permit me to adopt.

LVIII. For I have no right to doubt, gentleman, that if a case of this kind comes before you in which the defendant is outside the scope of the statute, then, even though you deem him the object of prejudice, or a cause of offence to many, even though you hate him, even though you would be sorry to acquit him, you would acquit him none the less, obeying your conscience rather than your animosity. For it is the duty of a wise juror to reflect that the 159 Roman people allows him only such functions as are consistent with his commission and his mandate ; to remember that not only has power been entrusted to him, but faith reposed in him ; to bring himself to acquit a man though he hate him, or to condemn a man though he hate him not ; to study, not his own inclinations but his duty to his conscience and the law ; and to observe the statute under which the accused is indicted, the character of the accused whose case he is examining, and the facts which are

cognoscat, quae res in quaestione versetur. Cum
haec sunt videnda, tum vero illud est hominis magni,
iudices, atque sapientis, cum illam iudicandi causa
tabellam sumpserit, non se reputare solum esse neque
sibi quodcumque concupierit licere, sed habere in
consilio legem, religionem, aequitatem, fidem : libidinem autem, odium, invidiam, metum cupiditatesque
omnes amovere maximique aestimare conscientiam
mentis suae, quam ab dis immortalibus accepimus,
quae a nobis divelli non potest : quae si optimorum
consiliorum atque factorum testis in omni vita nobis
erit, sine ullo metu et summa cum honestate vivemus.
160 Haec si T. Accius aut cognovisset aut cogitasset, profecto ne conatus quidem esset dicere, id quod multis
verbis egit, iudicem, quod ei videatur, statuere et
non devinctum legibus esse oportere. Quibus de
rebus mihi pro Cluenti voluntate nimium, pro rei
dignitate parum, pro vestra prudentia satis dixisse
videor.

Reliqua perpauca sunt, quae, quia vestrae quaestionis erant, idcirco illi statuerunt fingenda esse sibi
et proferenda, ne omnium turpissimi reperirentur, si
in iudicium nihil praeter invidiam attulissent.

LIX. Atque ut existimetis me necessario de his
rebus, de quibus iam dixerim, pluribus egisse verbis,
attendite reliqua : profecto intellegetis ea, quae

at issue before the court. These points must he keep before him; but further, it is equally the duty of a wise and high-minded man, on taking up the juror's tablet to record his vote, to bethink him that he is not alone, not free to obey his whim; and rather to take as his assessors the law and his conscience, justice and honour; to put away from him caprice, malice, prejudice, fear, and every passion, and to put first the testimony of his own conscience. Conscience is God's gift to us all and cannot be wrested from us, and if conscience testifies throughout our lives to good intentions and good deeds, those lives will be wholly fearless and entirely virtuous. Had T. Accius either realized these 160 things or reflected upon them, he would not even have attempted to say what he has actually urged at length; namely, that a juror ought to decide as he thinks best without being fettered by statutes. What I have said on this point, though more than Cluentius desires and less than the importance of the subject demands, is, I think, sufficient to satisfy your good sense.

There remain but a few points which, because proper to this court, the prosecution thought fit to trump up and bring forward, but only for fear that, if they brought nothing but prejudice into court, they would be found of all men the most base.

LIX. And now, in order that you may understand that I have been absolutely compelled to speak at some length on the matters which I have dealt with hitherto, give close attention to what follows; you will realize, I am sure, that where my point could be

paucis demonstrari potuerint, brevissime esse defensa.

161 Cn. Decidio Samniti, ei, qui proscriptus est, iniuriam in calamitate eius ab huius familia factam esse dixistis. Ab nullo ille liberalius quam a Cluentio tractatus est. Huius illum opes in rebus eius incommodissimis sublevarunt, atque hoc cum ipse tum eius amici necessariique omnes cognorunt. Anchari et Paceni pastoribus huius vilicum vim et manus attulisse. Cum quaedam in callibus, ut solet, controversia pastorum esset orta, Habiti vilici rem domini et privatam possessionem defenderunt. Cum esset expostulatio facta, causa illis demonstrata, sine

162 iudicio controversiaque discessum est. P. Aeli testamento propinquus exheredatus cum esset, heres hic alienior institutus est. P. Aelius Habiti merito fecit, neque hic in testamento faciendo interfuit, idque testamentum ab huius inimico Oppianico est obsignatum. Floro legatum ex testamento infitiatum esse. Non est ita. Sed cum HS$\overline{\text{xxx}}$ scripta essent pro HS$\overline{\text{ccc}}$, neque ei cautum satis videretur, voluit eum aliquid acceptum referre liberalitati suae. Primo debere negavit : post sine controversia solvit. Cei cuiusdam Samnitis uxorem post bellum ab hoc esse repetitam. Mulierem cum emisset a sectoribus, quo tempore eam primum liberam esse audivit, sine

---

[a] The Social War, 91–88 b.c.
[b] A wholesale purchaser at a sale of the property of proscribed persons. In this particular sale the wife had been included as well as the slaves.
398

proved in a few words, my defence has been very
concise.

You have stated that Gn. Decidius the Samnite— 161
the same who was proscribed—was insulted in his
misfortune by my client's slaves. Actually he was
treated by no one more generously than by Cluentius:
it was my client's wealth that relieved him in his dire
distress, a fact of which both he and all his friends
and relations are aware. You have stated that my
client's bailiff committed assault and battery upon
the shepherds of Ancharius and Pacenus : actually
his bailiffs defended their master's property and
right of occupancy in the course of an ordinary
quarrel between shepherds on the upland pastures.
When a complaint was made, explanations were
given to the other party, and they parted without
carrying their dispute to the courts. " By the will 162
of P. Aelius his kinsman was disinherited, and the
defendant, though quite a stranger, was made heir."
P. Aelius did this in discharge of an obligation, nor
had my client any hand in the making of the will,
which was witnessed by his enemy Oppianicus. " He
refused to discharge a legacy left to Florus." On
the contrary, although 30,000 sesterces had been
written instead of 300,000, and Florus's title was, in
Cluentius's opinion, insufficient, he wanted to place
Florus under an obligation to his generosity. So he
did at first deny the obligation, but subsequently
discharged it without dispute. " One Ceius, a
Samnite, brought an action against him after the
war *a* to recover his wife." Actually, when he heard
that she was a free woman, although he had purchased her from the broker,*b* he immediately returned her to Ceius without the intervention of the

163 iudicio reddidit Ceio.   Ennium esse quendam, cuius
bona teneat Habitus.   Est hic Ennius egens quidam
calumniator, mercenarius Oppianici, qui permultos
annos quievit : deinde aliquando cum servis Habiti
furti egit : nuper ab ipso Habito petere coepit.   Hic
illo privato iudicio, mihi credite, vobis isdem fortasse
patronis, calumniam non effugiet.   Atque etiam, ut
nobis renuntiatur, hominem multorum hospitum,
Ambivium quendam, coponem de via Latina, subor-
natis, qui sibi a Cluentio servisque eius in taberna sua
manus adlatas esse dicat.   Quo de homine nihil
etiam nunc dicere nobis est necesse.   Si invitaverit,
id quod solet, sic hominem accipiemus, ut moleste
164 ferat se de via decessisse.   Habetis, iudices, quae in
totam causam[1] de moribus A. Cluenti, quem illi
invidiosum esse reum volunt, annos octo meditati
accusatores collegerunt.   Quam levia genere ipso !
quam falsa re ! quam brevia responsu !

LX. Cognoscite nunc id, quod ad vestrum ius
iurandum pertinet, quod vestri iudicii est, quod vobis
oneris imposuit ea lex, qua coacti huc convenistis, de
criminibus veneni : ut omnes intellegant quam paucis
verbis haec causa perorari potuerit et quam multa a
me dicta sint, quae ad huius voluntatem maxime, ad
vestrum iudicium minime pertinerent.

165   Obiectum est Vibium Cappadocem ab hoc A. Cluentio veneno esse sublatum.   Opportune adest homo

---

[1] *Reading* causam *STb (corr.) for* vitam *R left in F.'s*
text " *by an oversight.*"

---

[a] The plural indicates other accusers besides Accius: compare *illi* in § 160 and *dixistis* in § 168, etc.
[b] There is a play on the word *via*, which suggests the
innkeeper leaving the Latin Way to come to Rome as well as
going out of his way to invite travellers to his inn.

court. " There is one, Ennius, whose property 163
Habitus retains." This Ennius is actually a needy
individual in the pay of Oppianicus, of whom nothing
had been heard for many years, until at last he
brought an action against Habitus's slaves for theft,
and has lately begun to claim restitution from
Habitus. In this civil suit, believe me, even though
he too may chance to employ you [a] to defend him, he
will not escape conviction as a false accuser. Again,
it is reported to me that you [a] are suborning that man
of much hospitality, Ambivius, innkeeper of the
Latin Way, to say that he was assaulted in his own
inn by Cluentius and his slaves. About this fellow
it is at present unnecessary for me to speak : if he
gives us his customary invitation, we will give him
so warm a reception as to make him sorry he ever
went out of his way.[b] Here, gentlemen, you have 164
every reflexion on Aulus Cluentius's character, which,
after eight years of preparation, the prosecution
has raked together for the whole case, anxious as
they are to embarrass his trial with prejudice. How
essentially trivial they are ; how substantially false ;
how easily refutable !

LX. Pass now to what concerns your oath, what
belongs to your jurisdiction, what is laid on you as a
responsibility by the statute through whose operation you are here met together — that is, to the
charges of poisoning—and you will all realize in how
few words my case might have been concluded, and
how much I have said which, though entirely relevant
to my client's instructions, was entirely irrelevant to
your court.

My client Aulus Cluentius is charged with having 165
removed by poison Vibius Cappadox. Fortunately

summa fide et omni virtute praeditus, L. Plaetorius, senator, qui illius Vibi hospes fuit et familiaris Apud hunc ille Romae habitavit, apud hunc aegrotavit, huius domi est mortuus. Intestatum dico esse mortuum possessionemque eius bonorum, ex edicto praetoris, huic, illius sororis filio, adulescenti pudentissimo et in primis honesto, equiti Romano datam, Numerio Cluentio, quem videtis.

166 Alterum veneficii crimen Oppianico huic adulescenti, cum eius in nuptiis more Larinatium multitudo hominum pranderet, venenum Habiti consilio paratum : id cum daretur in mulso, Balbutium quendam, eius familiarem, intercepisse, bibisse statimque esse mortuum. Hoc ego si sic agerem, tamquam mihi crimen esset diluendum, haec pluribus verbis dicerem, per quae nunc paucis percurrit oratio mea.

167 Quid umquam Habitus in se admisit, ut hoc tantum ab eo facinus non abhorrere videatur ? quid autem magno opere Oppianicum metuebat, cum ille verbum omnino in hac ipsa causa nullum facere potuerit, huic autem accusatores viva matre deesse non possint ? id quod iam intellegetis. An ut de causa eius periculi nihil decederet, ad causam novum crimen accederet ? Quod autem tempus veneni dandi illo die, illa frequentia ? per quem porro datum ? unde sumptum ? quae deinde interceptio poculi ? cur non de integro autem datum ? Multa sunt, quae dici pos-

---

a Witnesses could be examined and cross-examined as in an English court; but no rule apparently decided what evidence they might give or when they might give it.
b See the Introduction, § 5 A.

there is present in court *a* a man of eminent trustworthiness and the highest character, L. Plaetorius,
the senator, the host and friend of the said Vibius.
It was in his house that Vibius lived at Rome, in his
house that he fell ill, in his house that he died. I
assert that he died intestate, and that administration of his estate was assigned under the praetors'
edict to my client's sister's son, Numerius Cluentius, *b*
whom you see here, an honourable young man of
eminent respectability, and a Roman knight.

The second charge of poisoning is that Habitus 166
instigated an attempt to poison young Oppianicus
here, at a dinner which Oppianicus, after the custom
of Larinum, gave to a large number of people on
his marriage. The poison was being offered him in
mead when a certain Balbutius, his friend, intercepted it, drank it, and instantly expired. If I were
dealing with the charge as if I really had to disprove
it, I should do so at length ; whereas I am now dis-
missing it with a brief notice. What crime has 167
Habitus ever had upon his conscience that you should
imagine such a deed to be otherwise than abhorrent
from him ? What was there, moreover, to make him
fear Oppianicus so much—a man who has not been
able to utter a single word during the whole of this
case—whereas my client could never lack accusers
while Sassia lives, as you will presently see ? Or did
he wish the case against him to remain as serious as
before, and also be reinforced by a fresh charge ?
Again, what opportunity had he of giving the poison
on such a day and in such a crowd ? Further, by
whom did he give it ? Whence did he procure it ?
What means this intercepting of the cup ? Why was
it not given over again ? There are many possible

sunt : sed non committam ut videar non dicendo
168 voluisse dicere : res enim se ipsa defendit. Nego
illum adulescentem, quem statim epoto poculo mortuum esse dixistis, omnino illo die esse mortuum.
Magnum crimen et impudens mendacium. Perspicite cetera. Dico illum, cum ad illud prandium
crudior venisset et, ut aetas illa fert, sibi tum non
pepercisset, aliquot dies aegrotasse et ita esse mortuum. Quis huic rei testis est ? Idem, qui sui luctus,
pater : pater, inquam, illius adulescentis : quem
propter animi dolorem pertenuis suspicio potuisset
ex illo loco testem in A. Cluentium constituere, is
hunc suo testimonio sublevat ; quod recita. Tu
autem, nisi molestum est, paulisper exsurge : perfer
hunc dolorem commemorationis necessariae : in qua
ego diutius non morabor, quoniam, quod fuit viri
optimi, fecisti, ut ne cui innocenti maeror tuus
calamitatem et falsum crimen adferret.

169   LXI. Unum etiam mihi reliquum eius modi crimen
est, iudices, ex quo illud perspicere possitis, quod a me
initio orationis meae dictum est : quicquid mali per
hosce annos A. Cluentius viderit, quicquid hoc tempore habuerit sollicitudinis ac negotii, id omne a
matre esse conflatum. Oppianicum veneno necatum
esse, quod ei datum sit in pane per M. Asellium quendam, familiarem illius, idque Habiti consilio factum
esse dicitis. In quo primum illud quaero, quae causa
Habito fuerit, cur interficere Oppianicum vellet.

---

[a] These words were addressed to the clerk of the court
who thereupon read out the father's deposition.
404

answers : but I would not have it thought that I meant to suggest them by my silence ; for the substance of the charge supplies the answer to it. I 168 assert that the young man who, according to you, died directly after he drank the cup, did not die on that same day at all. It is a monstrous charge, and a shameless lie ! Consider what follows : I assert that the man in question came to the dinner suffering from indigestion ; over-indulged his appetite in the course of it as young men will do, and eventually died after an illness lasting some days. Who testifies to this ? The same man who testifies to his own grief, his father—the father, I say, of the young man in question ; and he who would have been ready, if the shadow of a suspicion had crossed his anguished mind, to stand over there and give evidence against Cluentius, actually offers that evidence on his behalf. Read it.ᵃ And do you, sir, if I am not asking too much, stand up for a few moments and nerve yourself for this painful but indispensable recital : I shall not dwell long upon it, because you have determined with true nobility not to let your sorrow involve the ruin of an innocent man upon a false accusation.

LXI. There is still one charge remaining, gentle- 169 men, the nature of which may illustrate to you what I said at the beginning of my speech—that whatever misfortune has in these years befallen Aulus Cluentius, whatever anxiety and difficulty has beset him at this time, the moving spirit through it all has been his mother. You assert that Oppianicus's death was caused by poison given to him in bread by one M. Asellius his friend, and that Habitus instigated the deed. My first question here is : what motive had Habitus for wishing to murder Oppianicus ? I

Inimicitias enim fuisse confiteor, sed homines inimicos
suos morte adfici volunt, aut quod eos metuunt aut
170 quod oderunt. Quo tandem igitur Habitus metu
adductus tantum in se facinus suscipere conatus est ?
quid erat quod iam Oppianicum poena adfectum pro
maleficiis et eiectum e civitate quisquam timeret ?
quid metuebat ? ne oppugnaretur a perdito, an ne
accusaretur a damnato, an ne exsulis testimonio
laederetur ? Si autem quod oderat Habitus inimicum, idcirco illum vita frui noluit, adeone erat stultus,
ut illam, quam tum ille vivebat, vitam esse arbitraretur, damnati, exsulis, deserti ab omnibus, quem
propter animi importunitatem nemo recipere tecto,
nemo adire, nemo adloqui, nemo aspicere vellet ?
171 Huius igitur Habitus vitae invidebat ? Hunc si
acerbe et penitus oderat, non eum quam diutissime
vivere velle debebat ? huic mortem maturabat
inimicus, quod illi unum in malis erat perfugium
calamitatis ? qui si quid animi et virtutis habuisset,
ut multi saepe fortes viri in eius modi dolore, mortem
sibi ipse conscisset : huic quam ob rem id vellet
inimicus offerre, quod ipse sibi optare deberet ?   Nam
nunc quidem quid tandem illi mali mors attulit ? nisi
forte ineptis fabulis ducimur, ut existimemus illum
ad inferos impiorum supplicia perferre ac plures illic
offendisse inimicos, quam hic reliquisse : a socrus, ab

admit the existence of enmity between them ; but a man desires the death of his enemy either because he fears him, or because he hates him. What fear 170 then can possibly have induced Habitus to burden his conscience with such a crime ? What reason was there for anyone to fear Oppianicus now that he had paid the penalty for his misdeeds and been expelled from the country ? What had he to fear ? That a ruined man might assail him, a condemned criminal accuse him, or the evidence of an exile do him harm ? If, on the other hand, it was hatred of his enemy that made Habitus unwilling that he should enjoy life any longer, was he such a fool as to suppose that the life Oppianicus was then living was worth the name—the life of a felon, an exile, an outcast ; when, through the enormity of his nature, no one would receive him under his roof, no one would go near him, no one would speak to him, no one would look at him ? Would Habitus grudge a man like that his life ? If he hated him bitterly and 171 intensely, should he not have desired such a man to live as long as possible ? Was it for an enemy to be hastening his death, to whom in his misery death alone offered an escape from wretchedness ; who, if he had had any spirit of manliness would have done as many a brave man has done in a like affliction, and put an end to his own life ? Why then should his enemy wish to bestow on him what he ought to have coveted for himself ? For what harm at all has death done him, now that he is actually dead ? Unless perhaps we are led by silly stories to suppose that he is enduring the torments of the damned in the nether world, and that he has there encountered more of his enemies than he left on earth ; that the

uxorum, a fratris, a liberum Poenis actum esse praecipitem in sceleratorum sedem ac regionem. Quae
si falsa sunt, id quod omnes intellegunt, quid ei
tandem eripuit mors praeter sensum doloris ?

172 Age vero, per quem venenum datum ? Per M.
Asellium. LXII. Quid huic cum Habito? nihil: atque
adeo, quod ille Oppianico familiarissime est usus, potius
etiam simultas. Eine igitur, quem sibi offensiorem,
Oppianico familiarissimum sciebat esse, potissimum
et scelus suum et illius periculum committebat ?
Cur igitur tu, qui pietate ad accusandum excitatus
es, hunc Asellium esse inultum tam diu sinis ? cur
non Habiti exemplo usus es, ut per illum, qui at-
173 tulisset venenum, de hoc praeiudicaretur? Iam vero
illud quam non probabile, quam inusitatum, iudices,
quam novum, in pane datum venenum ! Faciliusne
potuit quam in poculo, latius potuit abditum aliqua in
parte panis, quam si totum colliquefactum in potione
esset, celerius potuit comestum quam epotum in
venas atque in omnes partes corporis permanare ?
facilius fallere in pane, si esset animadversum, quam
in poculo, cum ita confusum esset, ut secerni nullo
174 modo posset ? At repentina morte periit. Quod si
esset ita factum, tamen ea res propter multorum eius
modi casum minime firmam veneni suspicionem

---

[a] *i.e.* young Oppianicus.
[b] In prosecuting Fabricius and Scamander before Oppianicus.

avenging spirits of his mother-in-law, his wives, his brother, and his children have driven him headlong into the abiding-place of the wicked. But if these stories are false, as every one knows they are, what is it that death has taken from him except the power to feel pain ?

But come, by whom was the poison given ? By M. Asellius. LXII. What connexion had he with Habitus ? None : there was more probably actual enmity between them because Asellius was on intimate terms with Oppianicus. Was it likely then that Habitus would chose a man whom he knew to be more or less ill-disposed to himself and an intimate of Oppianicus, as agent for his own crime and the plot against his enemy ? Then why have you,[a] who were impelled to prosecute by loyalty to your father so long allowed this Asellius to go unpunished ? Why did you not follow Habitus's example,[b] and secure a verdict which, through the person who administered the poison, should reflect upon my client ? Again, what an improbable story is this—how unusual, gentlemen, and how strange—this giving of poison in bread ! Could it thus more easily permeate the veins and every part of the body, than if given in a cup, more thoroughly when stowed away somewhere in a piece of bread than if it had been completely dissolved in a draught, more speedily when taken with food than with drink ? Would it have been harder to detect in bread, if attention had been drawn to it, than when so dissolved in the contents of a cup as to be quite indistinguishable ? " But," you say, " Oppianicus died a sudden death." Supposing he did : that has been the lot of too many people to afford good ground for suspecting poison ;

172

173

174

haberet : quodsi esset suspiciosum, tamen potius ad
alios quam ad Habitum pertineret. Verum in eo
ipso homines impudentissime mentiuntur. Id ut
intellegatis, et mortem eius et quem ad modum post
mortem in Habitum sit crimen a matre quaesitum
cognoscite.

175 Cum vagus et exsul erraret atque undique exclusus
Oppianicus in Falernum se ad L. Quinctium contulisset, ibi primum in morbum incidit ac satis vehementer diuque aegrotavit. Cum esset una Sassia
eaque Sex. Albio quodam colono, homine valenti, qui
simul esse solebat, familiarius uteretur, quam vir
dissolutissimus incolumi fortuna pati posset, et ius
illud matrimonii castum atque legitimum damnatione
viri sublatum arbitraretur, Nicostratus quidam,
fidelis Oppianici servulus, percuriosus et minime
mendax, multa dicitur domino renuntiare solitus esse.
Interea Oppianicus cum iam convalesceret neque
improbitatem coloni in Falerno diutius ferre posset
et huc ad urbem profectus esset—solebat enim extra
portam aliquid habere conducti—cecidisse de equo
dicitur et homo infirma valetudine latus offendisse
vehementer, et, postea quam ad urbem cum febri
venerit, paucis diebus esse mortuus. Mortis ratio,
iudices, eius modi est, ut aut nihil habeat suspicionis
aut, si quid habet, id intra parietes in domestico
scelere versetur.

176 LXIII. Post mortem eius Sassia moliri statim

and if there were any suspicion, it would attach to others before Habitus. But actually the whole story is a bare-faced lie. To bring this home to you, let me tell you about his death and the way in which, after his death, Cluentius's mother tried to find a charge against her son.

Wandering about, a vagabond and an exile, and 175 finding all doors shut against him, Oppianicus betook himself to L. Quinctius in the Falernian district. It was there that he first fell sick; and he had a long and serious illness. Sassia was with him, and was on terms of greater intimacy with one Sextus Albius, a lusty yeoman who was usually in her company, than the most dissolute of husbands could tolerate had his fortunes been unimpaired; for she was of the opinion that the bonds of that chaste, that lawful wedlock had been removed by the condemnation of her husband. And it is said that a favourite slave of Oppianicus called Nicostratus, a faithful fellow, very inquisitive and no liar, used to bring many tales of this to his master. Meanwhile Oppianicus was beginning to get better, and could endure no longer the misconduct of the Falernian yeoman; so he started to come here to the neighbourhood of Rome, where it was his custom to take some hired lodging outside the gates. But, so they say, he was thrown from his horse, and, ailing as he was, sustained a serious injury to his side; he reached the city in a fever, and died a few days afterwards. The circumstances of his death, gentlemen, are such as to admit of no suspicion; or, if any be admissible, to confine it to the four walls of his house, and to incriminate his own people.

LXIII. After his death, the unspeakable Sassia 176

nefaria mulier coepit insidias filio : quaestionem
habere de viri morte constituit.   Emit de A. Rupilio,
quo erat usus Oppianicus medico, Stratonem quendam, quasi ut idem faceret quod Habitus in emendo
Diogene fecerat.   De hoc Stratone et de Ascla quodam servo suo quaesituram esse dixit.   Praeterea
servum illum Nicostratum, quem nimium loquacem
fuisse ac nimium domino fidelem arbitrabatur, ab
hoc adulescente Oppianico in quaestionem postulavit.
Hic cum esset illo tempore puer et illa quaestio de
patris sui morte constitui diceretur, etsi illum servum
et sibi benevolum esse et patri fuisse arbitrabatur,
nihil tamen est ausus recusare.   Advocantur amici
et hospites Oppianici et ipsius mulieris multi, homines
honesti atque omnibus rebus ornati. Tormentis
omnibus vehementissime quaeritur.   Cum essent
animi servorum et spe et metu temptati, ut aliquid
in quaestione dicerent, tamen, ut arbitror, auctoritate advocatorum atque vi tormentorum adducti,[1]
in veritate manserunt neque se quicquam scire dixerunt.   Quaestio illo die de amicorum sententia dimissa
est.   Satis longo intervallo post iterum advocantur.
Habetur de integro quaestio : nulla vis tormentorum acerrimorum praetermittitur : adversari advocati et iam vix ferre posse, furere crudelis atque

177

[1] *These words are possibly corrupt.*

---

[a] See § 47.
[b] Slaves were usually tortured before being allowed to give
evidence ; otherwise, it was thought, they would be incapable of telling the truth.
[c] These words are difficult : if the sense which I have

immediately started to plot against her son, and decided to institute an inquiry into her husband's death. She purchased from Aulus Rupilius, whom Oppianicus had employed as a doctor, a certain Strato, ostensibly meaning to do the same as Habitus had done in purchasing Diogenes.[a] This Strato and a slave of her own, called Ascla, she said she was going to examine under torture,[b] and also demanded that young Oppianicus here should give up for similar examination the slave Nicostratus, whom she suspected of having been too free with his tongue and too loyal to his master. Oppianicus was a boy at the time ; and as this purported to be an inquiry into the death of his father he dared refuse her nothing, although he believed this slave to be as devoted to himself as formerly to his father. Many of her own and her husband's friends and associates were summoned, respectable men with every honourable recommendation. In the rigorous inquiry which followed, every form of torture was employed. But although both promises and threats were used to make the slaves say something under examination, they were none the less induced—as I believe, by the moral support of the witnesses, and the actual violence of the tortures [c]—to stand by the truth and deny all knowledge. The inquiry was abandoned 177 for that day, on the suggestion of the friends ; but after a considerable interval, they were summoned a second time, and the inquiry was held over again. The most exquisite tortures were rigorously employed. The witnesses protested, unable to bear the sight any longer, while that cruel, savage woman

given them (following Fausset's note) appears too much strained, it remains to take them (with Peterson) as sarcastic.

importuna mulier, sibi nequaquam ut sperasset, ea,
quae cogitasset, procedere. Cum iam tortor atque
essent tormenta ipsa defessa neque tamen illa finem
facere vellet, quidam ex advocatis, homo et honoribus populi ornatus et summa virtute praeditus, intellegere se dixit non id agi, ut verum inveniretur, sed
ut aliquid falsi dicere cogerentur. Hoc postquam
ceteri comprobarunt, ex omnium sententia consti-
178 tutum est satis videri esse quaesitum. Redditur
Oppianico Nicostratus, Larinum ipsa proficiscitur
cum suis maerens, quod iam certe incolumem filium
fore putabat, ad quem non modo verum crimen, sed
ne ficta quidem suspicio perveniret et cui non modo
aperta inimicorum oppugnatio, sed ne occultae quidem matris insidiae nocere potuissent. Larinum
postquam venit, quae a Stratone illo venenum antea
viro suo datum sibi persuasum esse simulasset, in-
structam ei continuo et ornatam Larini medicinae
exercendae causa tabernam dedit. LXIV. Unum,
alterum, tertium annum Sassia quiescebat, ut velle
atque optare aliquid calamitatis filio potius quam id
179 struere et moliri videretur. Tum interim Q. Hortensio Q. Metello consulibus, ut hunc Oppianicum
aliud agentem ac nihil eius modi cogitantem ad hanc
accusationem detraheret, invito despondit ei filiam
suam, illam, quam ex genero susceperat, ut eum
nuptiis adligatum simul et testamenti spe devinctum
possit habere in potestate.

---

was beside herself with rage to find her scheme by
no means turning out as she had hoped. At last,
when the torturer and even the instruments of
torture were wearied, and still she would not make
an end, one of the witnesses, a man of eminent public
position and high character, declared himself convinced that the object of the inquiry was not to
discover the truth, but to compel the slaves to say
something untrue. The others agreed : and everyone supported the decision that the inquiry had gone
far enough. Nicostratus was returned to Oppiani- 178
cus : Sassia went to Larinum with her people,
grieving over the thought that her son must now be
safe, seeing that no genuine charge, no, nor even a
trumped up suspicion could touch him; and that
not only the open assaults of his enemies but even
the secret plots of his mother had been unable to
harm him. On reaching Larinum she proceeded to
bestow on Strato a shop, furnished and stocked, so
that he might set up as a doctor at Larinum ; and
that though she had pretended to be convinced that
this same Strato had formerly poisoned her husband.
LXIV. A year passed, a second, then a third ; and
Sassia made no move ; till it looked as if she were
content to hope and long for some disaster to befall
her son without actually doing anything to contrive
it. Meanwhile, when Q. Hortensius and Q. Metellus 179
were consuls,[a] in order to force the young Oppianicus
to undertake this prosecution, though his interests were
elsewhere and no such idea had occurred to him, she
betrothed him against his will to her daughter—the
one she had borne to her son-in-law—hoping that
the ties of marriage, added to the hold she had on him
through his expectations, would put him in her power.

Hoc ipso fere tempore Strato ille medicus domi
furtum fecit et caedem eius modi. Cum esset in
aedibus armarium, in quo sciret esse nummorum
aliquantum et auri, noctu duos conservos dormientes
occidit in piscinamque deiecit : ipse armarii fundum
exsecuit, et HS . . . et auri quinque pondo abstulit,
180 uno ex servis puero non grandi conscio. Furto
postridie cognito omnis suspicio in eos servos, qui non
comparebant, commovebatur. Cum exsectio illa
fundi in armario animadverteretur, quaerebant
homines quonam modo fieri potuisset. Quidam ex
amicis Sassiae recordatus est se nuper in auctione
quadam vidisse in rebus minutis aduncam ex omni
parte dentatam et tortuosam venire serrulam, qua
illud potuisse ita circumsecari videretur. Ne multa ;
perquiritur a coactoribus : invenitur ea serrula ad
Stratonem pervenisse. Hoc initio suspicionis orto
et aperte insimulato Stratone puer ille conscius pertimuit : rem omnem dominae indicavit, homines in
piscina inventi sunt, Strato in vincula coniectus est
atque etiam in taberna eius nummi, nequaquam
181 omnes reperiuntur. Constituitur quaestio de furto.
Nam quid quisquam suspicari aliud potest ? An hoc
dicitis ? armario expilato, pecunia ablata, non omni
reciperata, occisis hominibus, institutam esse quaestionem de morte Oppianici ? cui probatis ? quid est
quod minus veri simile proferre possitis ? Deinde,

---

a The figures are missing from the mss.
b Those sent round by the auctioneer after a sale to collect
the money from the purchasers.

About that very time, this Strato, the doctor, committed theft and murder at her house in the following circumstances. There was a safe in the house which he knew to contain a quantity of cash and of gold; so one night he killed two of his fellow-slaves as they slept, threw them into the fish-pond, and himself cut out the bottom of the safe, abstracting . . .[a] sesterces and five pounds weight of gold, with the connivance of one of the slaves, quite a young lad. The theft was discovered next day, and the entire 180 suspicion fell on the two slaves who were not forthcoming. Then they noticed the cutting out of the bottom of the safe, and people began to wonder how it could have been done. One of Sassia's friends recalled having recently seen among the odds and ends for sale at some auction a small curved saw with teeth all round and crooked, by which it seemed that this circular cut might have been made. To put it shortly, inquiries were made from the auctioneer's agents,[b] and it was discovered that the saw went to Strato. This roused suspicion against Strato; and when he was openly taxed with the crime, the boy, his accomplice, took fright and told the whole story to his mistress: the bodies were found in the fish-pond, Strato was put in irons, and the coins, though by no means all of them, were actually found in his shop. An inquiry was held to investigate the theft. 181 For what else but theft could anyone suspect? Or do you assert that after the robbery of the safe, the removal and only partial discovery of the money and the murder of the slaves, the inquiry was held to investigate the death of Oppianicus? Who will believe you? What less probable suggestion could you advance? Besides, apart from anything else,

ut omittam cetera, triennio post mortem Oppianici de eius morte quaerebatur ? Atque etiam incensa odio pristino Nicostratum eundem illum tum sine causa in quaestionem postulavit. Oppianicus primo recusavit. Postea, cum illa abducturam se filiam, mutaturam esse testamentum minaretur, mulieri crudelissimae servum fidelissimum non in quaestionem tulit, sed plane ad supplicium dedidit.

182 LXV. Post triennium igitur agitata denuo quaestio de viri morte habebatur, et de quibus servis habebatur ? Nova, credo, res obiecta, novi quidam homines in suspicionem vocati sunt ? De Stratone et de Nicostrato. Quid ? Romae quaesitum de istis hominibus non erat ? Itane tandem ? mulier iam non morbo, sed scelere furiosa, cum quaestionem habuisset[1] Romae, cum de T. Anni, L. Rutili, P. Saturi, ceterorum honestissimorum virorum sententia constitutum esset satis quaesitum videri, eadem de re triennio post, isdem de hominibus, nullo adhibito non dicam viro, ne colonum forte adfuisse dicatis, sed bono viro, in filii caput quaestionem habere conata est ?

183 An hoc dicitis—mihi enim venit in mentem quid dici possit, tametsi ab hoc non esse hoc dictum mementote—cum haberetur de furto quaestio, Stratonem aliquid de veneno esse confessum ? Hoc uno modo, iudices, saepe multorum improbitate depressa veritas emergit et innocentiae defensio inter-

---

[1] *Reading* habuisset *Madvig*: habuisses *ST.*

was an inquiry likely to be investigating Oppianicus's death, three years after it occurred ? Yes, and more than this, inflamed by her former hatred, she now, without any reason, demanded that Nicostratus be examined once again. Oppianicus at first refused ; but later on when she threatened to take her daughter from him, and to alter her will, he surrendered his faithful slave to this cruel woman, not for examination but simply for execution.

LXV. And so the question of her husband's death 182 was revived after three years and a fresh inquiry held : and who were the slaves examined ? Some new fact, I suppose, was alleged, some new persons implicated ? Strato and Nicostratus were the men. What ? Had not these two been examined at Rome ? Is it possible ? Did this woman—beside herself now, not with madness, but with wickedness—although she had held an inquiry at Rome, although in the view of T. Annius, L. Rutilius, P. Saturus and other honourable men that inquiry was considered to have gone far enough, did she still—without securing the presence, I will not say of anyone at all in case you should say that the yeoman was there, but of anyone respectable—attempt to strike at her son's liberty by an inquiry into the same facts and an examination of the same people after a lapse of three years ?

Or do you say—for I am thinking of what might 183 be said though it must be remembered that my friend has not said it—that during the inquiry about the theft, Strato confessed something about the poison ? Gentlemen, there is only one way by which truth, though overwhelmed by a mass of villainy, often comes to light and the defence of innocence, though half stifled, recovers breath—and

419

clusa respirat, quod aut ei, qui ad fraudem callidi
sunt, non tantum audent, quantum excogitant, aut
ei, quorum eminet audacia atque proiecta est, a consiliis malitiae deseruntur. Quod si aut confidens
astutia aut callida esset audacia, vix ullo eis obsisti
modo posset. Utrum furtum factum non est? At
nihil clarius Larini. An ad Stratonem suspicio non
pertinuit? At is et ex serrula insimulatus et a puero
conscio est indicatus. An id actum non est in quae-
rendo? Quae fuit igitur alia causa quaerendi? an,
id quod vobis dicendum est et quod tum Sassia dicti-
tavit, cum de furto quaereretur, tum Stratonem isdem
184 in tormentis dixisse de veneno? En hoc illud est,
quod ante dixi: mulier abundat audacia, consilio
et ratione deficitur. Nam tabellae quaestionis plures
proferuntur, quae recitatae vobisque editae sunt,
illae ipsae, quas tum obsignatas esse dixit: in quibus
tabellis de furto nulla littera invenitur. Non venit
in mentem, primum orationem Stratonis conscribere
de furto, post aliquod dictum adiungere de veneno,
quod non percontatione quaesitum, sed per dolorem
expressum videretur. Quaestio de furto est, veneni
iam suspicio superiore quaestione sublata: quod
ipsum haec eadem mulier iudicarat, quae ut Romae
de amicorum sententia statuerat satis esse quaesitum,
postea per triennium maxime ex omnibus servis

that is because either those who are skilled in fraud
lack daring to match their designs, or because
those who in daring are conspicuous and pro-
minent, find that their rascally devices fail for
lack of contrivance ; whereas, if either the cunning
were bold, or the daring crafty, resistance to
them would be almost impossible. Was theft
not committed ? But nothing was more notorious
at Larinum. Or did suspicion not attach to Strato ?
But he was incriminated by the saw and denounced
by the boy, his accomplice. Or was this not the
issue at the inquiry ? What other reason was there
for holding it ? Or did Strato—and this is what you
ought to say and what Sassia said so often at the
time—did Strato, when being examined about the
theft, say something, while then under torture,
about the poison ? And there you have exactly what 184
I told you : the woman has daring in abundance,
but her judgement and common sense are failing
her. For numerous memoranda of the inquiry are
produced in court, which have been read out and laid
before you, the very ones which she has stated to
have been witnessed and sealed there and then.
And in these memoranda there is not a syllable about
theft ; it did not occur to her first to record the
deposition of Strato about the theft, and then afterwards put in some remark about the poison, to look
as if it had been wrung from him by torture, and not
elicited by questioning. The inquiry dealt with
theft : any suspicion of poisoning had been removed
by the previous inquiry, and that had been the
woman's own verdict ; for at Rome she had decided
on the advice of her friends that the inquiry had gone
far enough ; and during the three following years

Stratonem illum dilexerat, in honore habuerat, com-
185 modis omnibus adfecerat. Cum igitur de furto
quaereretur et eo furto, quod ille sine controversia
fecerat, tum ille de eo, quod quaerebatur, verbum
nullum fecit ? De veneno statim dixit ? de furto si
non eo loco, quo debuit, ne in extrema quidem aut
media aut aliqua denique parte quaestionis verbum
fecit ullum ?

LXVI. Iam videtis illam nefariam mulierem,
iudices, eadem manu, qua, si detur potestas, interficere filium cupiat, hanc fictam quaestionem con-
scripsisse. Atque istam ipsam quaestionem dicite
qui obsignarit unum aliquem nominatim : neminem
reperietis, nisi forte eius modi hominem, quem ego
186 proferri malim quam neminem nominari. Quid ais,
T. Acci ? tu periculum capitis, tu indicium sceleris,
tu fortunas alterius litteris conscriptas in iudicium
adferas ; neque earum auctorem litterarum neque
obsignatorem neque testem ullum nominabis ? et
quam tu pestem innocentissimo filio de matris sinu
deprompseris, hanc hi tales viri comprobabunt ?
Esto : in tabellis nihil est auctoritatis : quid, ipsa
quaestio iudicibus, quid, amicis hospitibusque Oppianici, quos adhibuerat antea, quid, huic tandem ipsi
tempori cur non servata est ? Quid istis hominibus
187 factum est, Stratone et Nicostrato ? Quaero abs te,
Oppianice, servo tuo Nicostrato quid factum esse
dicas : quem tu, cum hunc brevi tempore accusaturus

she had shown a greater fondness for this Strato than for all her other slaves, held him in special honour, and shown him every favour. Are we to suppose 185 that, during the inquiry into the theft—a theft, moreover, of which he was admittedly guilty—Strato said not a word about the matter under inquiry? Did he at once speak about the poison? Did he not so much as mention the theft, if not in its proper place, then at least at the end or in the middle or at some point in the examination?

LXVI. You see now, gentlemen, that this wicked woman, with the same hand with which she would fain kill her son if she had the power, forged this record of the inquiry. And as for this alleged record, tell me the name of one single witness who signed it: you will not find one except perhaps that of the kind of man whose character makes me glad to have his name produced rather than no one's. How now, T. Accius? Are you to bring into court 186 a capital charge, a criminal indictment, and an attack based on documentary evidence upon the fortunes of another, without naming anyone to vouch for that document, or anyone who sealed or witnessed it? Do you expect to commend to a court like this the instrument which you have drawn from his mother's bosom to work the ruin of her innocent son? Enough: the memoranda have no weight. Why was not the complete record kept for the jurors? Why not for the friends and associates of Oppianicus whom she had summoned in the first instance? Why not indeed for the present occasion? What was done with those two, Strato and Nicostratus? I ask you, 187 Oppianicus, to say what was done with your slave Nicostratus: in view of your intention shortly to

esses, Romam deducere, dare potestatem indicandi, incolumem denique servare quaestioni, servare his iudicibus, servare huic tempori debuisti. Nam Stratonem quidem, iudices, in crucem esse actum exsecta scitote lingua : quod nemo Larinatium est qui nesciat. Timuit mulier amens non suam conscientiam, non odium municipum, non famam omnium, sed quasi non omnes eius sceleris testes essent futuri, sic metuit, ne condemnaretur extrema servuli voce morientis.

188 Quod hoc portentum, di immortales ! quod tantum monstrum in ullis locis, quod tam infestum scelus et immane aut unde natum esse dicamus ? Iam enim videtis profecto, iudices, non sine necessariis me ac maximis causis principio orationis meae de matre dixisse. Nihil est enim mali, nihil sceleris, quod illa non ab initio filio voluerit, optaverit, cogitaverit, effecerit. Mitto illam primam libidinis iniuriam, mitto nefarias generi nuptias, mitto cupiditate matris expulsam ex matrimonio filiam : quae nondum ad huiusce vitae periculum, sed ad commune familiae dedecus pertinebant. Nihil de alteris Oppianici nuptiis queror : quarum illa cum obsides filios ab eo mortuos accepisset, tum denique in familiae luctum atque in privignorum funus nupsit. Praetereo, quod A. Aurium, cuius illa quondam socrus, paulo ante uxor fuisset, cum Oppianici esse opera proscriptum occisumque cognosset, eam sibi domum sedemque delegit

---

accuse my client, you ought to have brought him to
Rome, enabled him to give information, and kept him
safe for examination, for this court and for this
occasion. As for Strato, gentlemen, I have to inform you that he was crucified, after first having had
his tongue cut out, as everyone at Larinum knows.
This frenzied woman feared not her own conscience,
not the hatred of her neighbours, nor the general
scandal ; she forgot that all men would be witnesses
to her crime, and dreaded only that she might be denounced by the last utterances of a poor, dying slave.

Great heavens, what a monstrosity is this ! In all **188**
the world could there be named aught so unnatural,
so hateful, so inhuman an abomination ? If so, what
gave it birth ? For now, gentlemen, you surely see
that it was not without the best and most compelling
reasons that I mentioned my client's mother at the
beginning of my speech ; for there is no evil, no
wickedness which from the first she has not wished
for, longed for, plotted and executed against her son.
I say nothing of the first outrage of her passion ;
nothing of her infamous marriage with her step-son,
nothing of the mother's lust that drove the daughter
from her husband's arms. These things constituted
a dishonour to her family as a whole, but not as yet
a peril to my client's life. I make no complaint of
her second [a] marriage with Oppianicus, which, con-
tracted only after receiving as security from his
hands the murder of his sons, was fraught with
mourning to his household and death to her step-
children. I pass over the fact that when she learned
that Aulus Aurius, once her daughter's husband, now
her own, had been by the contrivance of Oppianicus
proscribed and murdered, she chose as her own resid-

in qua cotidie superioris viri mortis indicia et spolia
189 fortunarum viderit. Illud primum queror de illo scelere, quod nunc denique patefactum est, Fabriciani
veneni—quod iam tum recens suspiciosum ceteris,
huic incredibile, nunc vero apertum iam omnibus ac
manifestum videtur—non est profecto de illo veneno
celata mater : nihil est ab Oppianico sine consilio
mulieris cogitatum : quod si esset, certe postea,
deprehensa re, non illa ut a viro improbo discessisset,
sed ut a crudelissimo hoste fugisset domumque illam
in perpetuum scelerum omnium adfluentem reli-
190 quisset. Non modo id non fecit, sed ab illo tempore
nullum locum praetermisit, in quo non strueret
insidias aliquas ac dies omnes atque noctes tota
mente mater de pernicie filii cogitaret. Quae primum ut illum confirmaret Oppianicum accusatorem
filio suo, donis muneribus, collocatione filiae, spe
hereditatis obstrinxit.

LXVII. Ita quod apud ceteros novis inter propinquos susceptis inimicitiis saepe fieri divortia atque
adfinitatum discidia vidimus, haec mulier satis firmum
accusatorem filio suo fore neminem putavit, nisi qui
in matrimonium sororem eius antea duxisset. Ceteri
novis adfinitatibus adducti veteres inimicitias saepe
deponunt : illa sibi ad confirmandas inimicitias ad-
191 finitatis coniunctionem pignori fore putavit. Neque

---

* See ch. xvi.

ence and home the very house in which she might
every day behold the traces of her former husband's
death, and the spoils of his estate. My first com- 189
plaint deals with that crime which has now at last
been brought to light, the attempt to poison through
Fabricius *ᵃ*—an attempt which, at the time of its
occurrence, people generally only suspected, and
my client refused to believe, though it is now clear
and obvious to all. Of that attempt his mother,
assuredly, was not kept in ignorance ; for Oppianicus
devised nothing without her advice. Had it been
otherwise, it is certain that afterwards, when the
plot was detected, she would not have left him as a
wicked husband ; she would rather have fled from
him as from a cruel foe, and would have abandoned
for ever a house that was a very sink of iniquity. So 190
far from acting thus, there was no place in which she
did not contrive some pitfall, while day and night
this mother gave her whole mind to plotting the
destruction of her son. And in the first place, in
order to have Oppianicus there for the prosecution
of her son, she bound him to her by gifts and dona-
tions, by his marriage to her daughter, and his expectations from her estate.

LXVII. And so, while we have noticed as a
general rule that divorce and the sundering of
family ties follow the outbreak of a quarrel between relations, this woman considered that no one
could be sufficiently relied on to prosecute her son
except he first married that son's sister. Most
people are induced by the contraction of new relation-
ships to lay aside old quarrels ; but she believed that
the bond of relationship would serve her as a guarantee for the perpetuation of her quarrel. Nor did 191

in eo solum diligens fuit, ut accusatorem filio suo
compararet, sed etiam cogitavit, quibus eum rebus
armaret. Hinc enim illae sollicitationes servorum
et minis et promissis, hinc illae infinitae crudelissimae-
que de morte Oppianici quaestiones : quibus finem
aliquando non mulieris modus, sed amicorum auctoritas fecit. Ab eodem scelere illae triennio post
habitae Larini quaestiones : eiusdem amentiae falsae
conscriptiones quaestionum : ex eodem furore etiam
illa conscelerata exsectio linguae : totius denique
huius ab illa est et inventa et adornata comparatio
192 criminis. Atque his rebus cum instructum accusatorem filio suo Romam misisset, ipsa paulisper con-
quirendorum et conducendorum testium causa Larini
est commorata : postea autem quam appropinquare
huius iudicium ei nuntiatum est, confestim huc advolavit, ne aut accusatoribus diligentia aut pecunia
testibus deesset aut ne forte mater hoc sibi optatissi-
mum spectaculum huius sordium atque luctus et
tanti squaloris amitteret.

LXVIII. Iam vero quod iter Romam eius mulieris
fuisse existimatis ? quod ego propter vicinitatem
Aquinatium et Fabraternorum ex multis audivi et
comperi : quos concursus in his oppidis ? quantos et
virorum et mulierum gemitus esse factos ? mulierem
quandam Larinatem illim usque a mari supero
Romam proficisci cum magno comitatu et pecunia,
quo facilius circumvenire iudicio capitis atque oppri-
193 mere filium posset. Nemo erat illorum, paene dicam,
quin expiandum illum locum esse arbitraretur, qua-

---

a See footnote to § 18.
b These places were near Arpinum where Cicero was born.

428

she bestow her pains only on procuring an accuser
for her son ; she considered also wherewith to equip
him : hence her overtures to slaves, alike by threats
and promises ; hence these inquiries, so far-reaching
and so cruel, into the death of Oppianicus, which
were brought to an end not by any moderation
on her part but by the interposition of her friends.
The same criminal design resulted in those inquiries
at Larinum three years after the event ; the same
frenzy inspired her to forge the records of those
inquiries ; the same madness was responsible for
her dastardly act in cutting out the slave's tongue ;
the whole elaborate charge is, in fact, hers both in
conception and presentation. Her son's accuser, 192
thus fortified, she dispatched to Rome, while she
herself waited a short time at Larinum to collect and
engage witnesses ; but on receipt of the news that
my client's trial was approaching, she came flying
hither with all speed in case the prosecution might
need her vigilance, or the witnesses her money ; or
perhaps it was that she might not lose a spectacle
that her mother's heart so craved—the squalid
mourning and unkempt attire of her son.[a]

LXVIII. But what manner of journey, think you,
did this woman make to Rome ? I have heard and
learnt of it from many, living as I do near Aquinum
and Fabrateria.[b] How they flocked together in
those towns ! What groans went up from men and
women alike to think that a woman of Larinum was
starting thence to go all the way from the Adriatic
coast to Rome with a great retinue and large funds,
the better to contrive the ruin, on a capital charge,
of her own son ! I will go so far as to say that there 193
was not one of them but thought that every place

cumque illa iter fecisset : nemo quin terram ipsam
violari, quae mater est omnium, vestigiis conscele-
ratae matris putaret. Itaque nullo in oppido con-
sistendi potestas ei fuit : nemo ex tot hospitibus
inventus est qui non contagionem aspectus fugeret.
Nocti se potius ac solitudini quam ulli aut urbi aut
194 hospiti committebat. Nunc vero quid agat, quid
moliatur, quid denique cotidie cogitet quem ignorare
nostrorum putat? Quos appellarit, quibus pecuniam promiserit, quorum fidem pretio labefactare
conata sit tenemus. Quin etiam nocturna sacrificia,
quae putat occultiora esse, sceleratasque eius preces
et nefaria vota cognovimus : quibus illa etiam deos
immortales de suo scelere testatur neque intellegit
pietate et religione et iustis precibus deorum mentes,
non contaminata superstitione neque ad scelus per-
ficiendum caesis hostiis posse placari. Cuius ego
furorem atque crudelitatem deos immortales a suis
aris atque templis aspernatos esse confido.

195 LXIX. Vos iudices, quos huic A. Cluentio quasi
aliquos deos ad omne vitae tempus fortuna esse voluit,
huius importunitatem matris a filii capite depellite.
Multi saepe in iudicando peccata liberum parentum
misericordiae concesserunt : vos ne huius honestissime actam vitam matris crudelitati condonetis
rogamus, praesertim cum ex altera parte totum

by which she passed needed to be purified ; not one
but felt that the earth itself, the common mother of
us all, was suffering pollution from the feet of that
accursed mother.   And so in no town was she
allowed to halt ; of all those many inns she found not
one whose host did not flee before her baleful glance :
she was fain to entrust herself to night and solitude
rather than to any city or hostelry.   And of her 194
present intentions, designs, and daily plottings, which
of us does she imagine to be ignorant ? We are well
aware whom she has approached, to whom she has
promised money, whose loyalty she has tried to
undermine with a bribe : nay more, we have found
out about her midnight sacrifices which she thinks
so secret, her infamous prayers, and her unholy vows
by which she calls even Almighty God to witness
her crime ; not realizing that the favour of Heaven
may be gained by duty done to God and man,
and by righteous prayers, not by base superstition
and victims offered for the success of crime.   But
well I know that Almighty God has spurned from
his altars and his temples this woman's rage and
cruelty.

LXIX. Gentlemen, chance has made you as gods, 195
to sway for all time the destiny of my client, Aulus
Cluentius : do you shield from this unnatural mother
the life of her son. Many a judge, ere now, has
allowed his pity for the parents to cover the sin of
their children : you I entreat not to sacrifice to his
mother's cruelty my client's honourable past, especially when you may see a whole township ranged

municipium videre possitis. Omnes scitote, iudices
—incredibile dictu est, sed a me verissime dicetur—
omnes Larinates, qui valuerunt, venisse Romam, ut
hunc studio frequentiaque sua quantum possent in
tanto eius periculo sublevarent. Pueris illud hoc
tempore et mulieribus oppidum scitote esse traditum,
idque in praesentia communi Italiae pace, non
domesticis copiis, esse tutum. Quos tamen ipsos
aeque et eos, quos praesentes videtis, huius exspec-
196 tatio iudicii dies noctesque sollicitat. Non illi vos de
unius municipis fortunis arbitrantur, sed de totius
municipii statu, dignitate commodisque omnibus
sententias esse laturos. Summa est enim, iudices,
hominis in communem municipii rem diligentia, in
singulos municipes benignitas, in omnes homines
iustitia et fides. Praeterea nobilitatem illam inter
suos locumque a maioribus traditum sic tuetur, ut
maiorum gravitatem, constantiam, gratiam, liberali-
tatem adsequatur. Itaque eis eum verbis publice
laudant, ut non solum testimonium suum iudicium-
que significent, verum etiam curam animi ac dolorem.
Quae dum laudatio recitatur, vos quaeso, qui eam
197 detulistis, adsurgite. Ex lacrimis horum, iudices,
existimare potestis omnes haec decuriones decre-
visse lacrimantes. Age vero, vicinorum quantum
studium, quam incredibilis benevolentia, quanta cura
est ! Non illi in libellis laudationem decretam mise-

against her. Be it known to all of you, gentlemen (and, unbelievable as the statement is, I shall make it in all truth), that all the able-bodied men in Larinum have come to Rome to give my client in his hour of great peril all the assistance in their power by their enthusiasm and their numbers. To women and children, be it known to you, is committed at this time the protection of their town, whose safety lies at present in the general peace of Italy, and not in any resources of its own. Yet those that are left, equally with those whom you see before you, are racked day and night with suspense to know the issue of this trial. They feel that the sentence you 196 are about to pass will touch not merely the fortunes of one fellow-townsman, but the standing of the whole township, its honour and all its privileges. For nothing, gentlemen, can exceed my client's devotion to the general good of his town, his kindness to its individual members, his uprightness and sincerity to all men. Moreover, he in such wise supports the distinction of his birth and the high position which his forefathers bequeathed to him, as not to be behind them in dignity, steadfastness, popularity, or generosity. And their testimonial to him on behalf of their community is couched in such terms as to express not merely their evidence and their opinion but also their heartfelt anxiety and sorrow. While this testimonial is being read aloud, you who have presented it will kindly stand up. You may judge 197 by their tears, gentlemen, that all the town-councillors wept, as these do, when passing this resolution. Furthermore, what real enthusiasm is displayed by his neighbours, what extraordinary goodwill, what deep anxiety ! So far from merely forwarding in

runt, sed homines honestissimos, quos nossemus omnes,
huc frequentes adesse et hunc praesentes laudare
voluerunt.   Adsunt Ferentani, homines nobilissimi,
Marrucini item pari dignitate : Teano Apulo atque
Luceria equites Romanos, homines honestissimos,
laudatores videtis : Boviano totoque ex Samnio cum
laudationes honestissimae missae sunt tum homines
198 amplissimi nobilissimique venerunt.   Iam qui in agro
Larinati praedia, qui negotia, qui res pecuarias
habent, honesti homines et summo splendore praediti, difficile dictu est quam sint solliciti, quam labo-
rent.   Non multi mihi ab uno sic diligi videntur, ut
hic ab his universis.

LXX. Quam doleo abesse ab huius iudicio L.
Volusienum, summo splendore hominem ac virtute
praeditum.   Vellem praesentem possem P. Helvi-
dium Rufum, equitem Romanum omnium ornatissi-
mum, nominare ! qui cum huius causa dies noctesque
vigilaret et cum me hanc causam doceret, in morbum
gravem periculosumque incidit : in quo tamen non
minus de capite huius quam de sua vita laborat.   Cn.
Tudici senatoris, viri optimi et honestissimi, par
studium ex testimonio et laudatione cognoscetis.
Eadem spe, sed maiore verecundia de te, P. Volumni,
quoniam iudex es in A. Cluentium, dicimus.   Et, ne
longum sit, omnium vicinorum summam esse in hunc

writing the testimonial they had decreed, they preferred that many honourable men, likely to be known to you all, should come into court in large numbers and give their testimonial in person. There are in court many from the best families of Ferentum, and others equally distinguished from the Marrucini: you see honourable Roman knights from Teanum in Apulia and from Luceria supporting this testimonial; from Bovianum and the whole of Samnium have been sent honourable testimonials, accompanied, moreover, by men of distinction and high birth. As for 198 those who have estates, business interests, or stock in the district of Larinum—all of them honourable men of eminent distinction—I find it hard to express their anxiety and solicitude. Few men, I think, are so much beloved by a single individual as my client is by this entire community.

LXX. How much I regret, gentlemen, the absence from my client's trial of the eminent and virtuous L. Volusienus! Would that I could name as present in court that most highly gifted Roman knight, P. Helvidius Rufus! For while spending days and nights of watchfulness in the defendant's interest and instructing me in the case, he fell seriously and dangerously ill; but even so, he is as much concerned for my client's liberties as for his own life. You will perceive no less enthusiasm on the part of that excellent and honourable man, Gn. Tudicus, the senator, from his evidence both as to fact and as to character. To you, P. Volumnius, I hope I may refer in the same terms, though with greater reserve, as you are a juror in the case of Aulus Cluentius. To be brief, I assert that his entire neighbourhood displays the utmost goodwill towards my

199 benevolentiam confirmamus. Horum omnium studium, curam, diligentiam meumque una laborem, qui
totam hanc causam vetere instituto solus peroravi,
vestramque simul, iudices, aequitatem et mansuetudinem una mater oppugnat. At quae mater? Quam
caecam crudelitate et scelere ferri videtis, cuius
cupiditatem nulla umquam turpitudo retardavit,
quae vitiis animi in deterrimas partes iura hominum
convertit omnia, cuius ea stultitia est, ut eam nemo
hominem, ea vis, ut nemo feminam, ea crudelitas, ut
nemo matrem appellare possit. Atque etiam nomina
necessitudinum, non solum naturae nomen et iura
mutavit: uxor generi, noverca filii, filiae pelex: eo
iam denique adducta est, uti sibi praeter formam
200 nihil ad similitudinem hominis reservarit. Quare,
iudices, si scelus odistis, prohibete aditum matris a
filii sanguine: date parenti hunc incredibilem dolorem
ex salute, ex victoria liberum: patimini matrem, ne
orbata filio laetetur, victam potius vestra aequitate
discedere. Sin autem, id quod vestra natura postulat, pudorem, veritatem virtutemque diligitis,
levate hunc aliquando supplicem vestrum, iudices,
tot annos in falsa invidia periculisque versatum, qui
nunc primum post illam flammam aliorum facto et
cupiditate excitatam spe vestrae aequitatis erigere
animum et paulum respirare a metu coepit, cui

ᵃ The older practice was for one advocate to undertake the
whole of the defence: in Cicero's time as many as twelve
might be employed.

client. The enthusiasm, the trouble, and the pains 199
of all these people, conjointly with my own endeavours (for in accordance with ancient practice I
have performed the entire conduct of this case single-
handed *a*), and withal your own spirit of justice and of
mercy, gentlemen—all are assailed by one person
only, his mother. But what a mother! You see
her, swept along by the blind impulses of cruelty and
crime ; her lust has never stopped short of any dishonour ; her moral obliquity has prostituted every
institution of mankind ; she is too demented to be
called a human being, too ruthless to be called a
woman, too savage to be called a mother. Nay,
more ; as the wife of her son-in-law, the step-mother
of her son, the rival of her daughter, she has changed
not merely the names and the ordinances which
nature gives, but even the name we give to relation-
ships ; and she is come at last to such a pass that she
has lost all semblance of humanity save only her out-
ward form. Wherefore, gentlemen, if you hate 200
wickedness, forbid a mother to come at the blood
of her son : grant to a parent the unutterable grief
involved in the safety, the triumph of her offspring :
permit a mother, lest she be overjoyed at being
bereft of her son, rather to go hence defeated by your
sense of justice. If, on the other hand, as your
nature demands, you love honour, truth, and goodness,
raise up this your suppliant at the last, gentlemen,
who for all these years has been beset by false prejudice and peril ; who, for the first time since the
criminal avarice of others fanned prejudice into
flame, has begun in reliance on your sense of justice
to take heart again and enjoy a short breathing-
space from his fears ; whose all lies in your hands ;

437

posita sunt in vobis omnia, quem servatum esse
201 plurimi cupiunt, servare soli vos potestis. Orat vos
Habitus, iudices, et flens obsecrat, ne se invidiae,
quae in iudiciis valere non debet, ne matri, cuius vota
et preces a vestris mentibus repudiare debetis, ne
Oppianico, homini nefario, condemnato iam et
mortuo, condonetis.

LXXI. Quod si qua calamitas hunc in hoc iudicio
adflixerit innocentem, ne iste miser, si, id quod
difficile factu est, in vita remanebit, saepe et multum
quereretur deprehensum esse illud quondam Fabri-
cianum venenum. Quod si tum indicatum non esset,
non huic aerumnosissimo venenum illud fuisset, sed
multorum medicamentum maerorum : postremo
etiam fortassis mater exsequias illius funeris prosecuta mortem se filii lugere simulasset. Nunc vero
quid erit profectum, nisi ut huius ex mediis mortis
insidiis vita ad luctum conservata, mors sepulcro
202 patris privata esse videatur. Satis diu fuit in
miseriis, iudices : satis multos annos ex invidia labora-
vit. Nemo huic tam iniquus praeter parentem fuit,
cuius non animum iam expletum esse putemus. Vos,
qui aequi estis omnibus, qui, ut quisque crudelissime
oppugnatur, eum lenissime sublevatis, conservate A.
Cluentium : restituite incolumem municipio : amicis,
vicinis, hospitibus, quorum studia videtis, reddite :
vobis in perpetuum liberisque vestris obstringite.
Vestrum est hoc, iudices, vestrae dignitatis, vestrae

whom so many would, but only you can, save. Habitus implores you, gentlemen, and beseeches 201 you with tears to sacrifice him neither to prejudice, which should have no weight in the court of law; nor to his mother, whose vows and prayers you ought to banish from your minds; nor to the infamous Oppianicus, now condemned and dead.

LXXI. But if a disaster overwhelms my client in this trial, then verily that hapless man, if (though 'twere hard for him) he continue to live, will ofttimes and bitterly regret that the attempt to poison him through Fabricius was ever discovered. For if it had not then come to light it would have been to my suffering client no poison but the healing balm of many woes. Aye, and it may be that even his mother, as she followed in that funeral train, would have feigned to mourn the death of her son. But as it is, what will have been achieved, save that he will seem to have been saved alive from out the snares of death only for mourning, and in death to have been robbed of the sepulchre of his fathers? Long 202 enough, gentlemen, has he been in misery, long years enough has he laboured under prejudice. No one save her who bore him has been so malignant against him but that we may feel that his resentment is now satisfied. Do you, who are benignant to all men, who grant your gentlest succour to those most cruelly assailed, deliver Aulus Cluentius, restore him still a citizen to his town: give him back to his friends, his neighbours and his associates, whose enthusiasm you behold: make him a debtor for all time to you and to your children. Yours, gentlemen, is this duty; yours as men of honour and

clementiae : recte hoc repetitur a vobis, ut virum optimum atque innocentissimum plurimisque mortalibus carissimum atque iucundissimum his aliquando calamitatibus liberetis, ut omnes intellegant in contionibus esse invidiae locum, in iudiciis veritati.

humanity ; and rightly do we require you to free at last from these disasters a good and innocent man, beloved and cherished by so many of mankind ; that thereby all men may know that public meetings are the place for prejudice, courts of law for truth.

THE SPEECH OF MARCUS TULLIUS CICERO IN DEFENCE OF GAIUS RABIRIUS CHARGED WITH HIGH TREASON

INTRODUCTION

1 THE trial for high treason of Gaius Rabirius may appear at first sight a trivial and even a ridiculous proceeding. The defendant, an aged senator, was solemnly impeached for the murder, no less than thirty-six years before, of the demagogue Saturninus. Whether he was actually guilty no one probably knew and few cared. Yet the occasion was a momentous one; for the issues were not personal but political, and Cicero makes it clear that in this speech he is defending not the insignificant senator but the foundations of senatorial government; and that he has to face not merely the spite of the tribune Labienus but the deliberately planned attack of the democratic party under the leadership, and almost in the person, of Julius Caesar.

2 Comparatively few among Cicero's audience could have had a clear recollection of the event which nominally occasioned the trial: it belonged to an earlier chapter in the "decline and fall" of the Roman Republic. In the year 100 B.C., which saw the birth of Julius Caesar and the sixth consulship of his uncle, Gaius Marius, the tribune Lucius Saturninus brought forward proposals [a] which aimed, like those of Gaius Gracchus before him, at nothing less than at destroying the power of the senatorial

[a] Known as the *Leges Appuleiae.*

oligarchy : behind them was the reputation of Marius and behind him the power of his reconstituted army. Violence overcame the desperate resistance of the senate, and not only were the proposals carried but the senate was compelled to take an oath to observe them faithfully.

But success was fatal to the alliance between Marius and Saturninus, and dissension soon broke out between them ; for Marius had all the parvenu's sneaking admiration for the aristocracy, and Saturninus was, like most demagogues, a revolutionary at heart : each began increasingly to distrust the other. Meanwhile the middle classes drew nearer to the patricians for mutual protection ; and eventually Saturninus found himself isolated. He, therefore, made a bid to seize the supreme power and determined to secure the highest offices for the coming year for himself and his associates. He himself and a rogue who masqueraded as a son of Gaius Gracchus were actually elected tribunes, but his candidate for the consulship, the praetor Gaius Glaucia, found a strong opponent in the senator, Gaius Memmius. Memmius was therefore murdered.

This gave the Senate the desired opportunity to use force ; they issued the *senatus consultum ultimum* calling on the consuls to protect the Republic ; and Marius obeyed the call. The supporters of law and order rallied round him and the " popular " party, more numerous than Cicero would have us suppose, was driven from the Forum into the Capitol, where they were besieged and their water supply cut off. They had no choice but surrender ; and though Marius would have wished to save the lives of his prisoners and former associates, no one waited for

his orders, and Saturninus, Glaucia, and nearly all their following were ignominiously done to death.

3   A generation passed, and brought small encouragement to the supporters of democracy. In 91 B.C. Livius Drusus tried to reform the Senate from within and was murdered for his pains. Marius died in 86 B.C. amid an orgy of bloodshed, and in 81 B.C. the last hopes of democracy were crushed by Sulla who, as dictator, openly abolished the chief safeguards of liberty, nor was any substantial recovery made till the passing of the Lex Aurelia of Cotta in 75 B.C Thenceforward till 63 B.C., the year of Rabirius's trial, a succession of wars left the Romans little time for setting their own house in order.

But the power of the Senate, so long and so flagrantly abused, was ripe for dissolution, though few as yet could have foretold who was to be its destroyer. For Julius Caesar, though now thirty-seven years old, had given but faint indications of his political programme and still less of his ability to carry it through. He was, however, already recognized as a friend of democracy : the time had now come for him to show himself an enemy of the senate.

4   It was Caesar, therefore, and the democratic party who originated this attack on Rabirius ; and they did so not from any hostility to the senator but because, through him, they could strike a blow at the Senate and assert the sovereignty of the People. Rabirius had been a party to the death of Saturninus [a] in obedience to the summons of the consuls,

---

[a] An unknown writer of the fourth century A.D., in a work entitled *De viribus illustribus*, tells us that " a certain senator called Rabirius carried the head of Saturninus round the dinner table as a joke."

who were themselves obeying the *senatus consultum ultimum* and claimed immunity thereby. It was precisely this claim that was now challenged.

The *senatus consultum ultimum* was a proclamation by the Senate, issued in a time of emergency, ordering the magistrates, and especially the consuls to " see to it that no ill befall the Republic " *a* : it was roughly equivalent to proclaiming a state of siege ; and by freeing them from responsibility for any illegal acts which they might commit in the execution of their duty, it placed in the hands of the Senate a dictatorial power which could be used as a weapon for the suppression of demagogues and revolutionaries when they became dangerous. The origin of this power is not known : it was certainly not conferred by law ; but centuries of use had made it constitutional. By the year 63 B.C., it was defended by Cicero and attacked by the democrats as the very foundation, the ultimate sanction, of senatorial prerogative.

The first step on the part of the democrats was to procure an accuser in the person of the tribune Titus Labienus, who had a personal motive for attacking Rabirius, as his uncle had been among the associates of Saturninus who had perished with him. He, therefore, secured the passing into law of a resolution which instituted, in general terms, an inquiry into the death of Saturninus and appointed a board of two *b* to try any case of high treason that

---

a "Videant consules ne quid respublica detrimenti capiat." This phrase was always embodied in the *senatus consultum ultimum* of which the wording might otherwise vary.

b The *duumviri* constituted an antiquated form of judicial commission dating from the time of the kings.

might result from its findings. The Senate, unable
to prevent this, had to be content with securing, at
the instance of Cicero, that the penalty of exile be
substituted for the statutory one of crucifixion,[a] and
the popular party found compensation in the appointment of Julius Caesar and his uncle Lucius to the
board. They promptly found Rabirius guilty, whereupon he appealed to the People. Dion Cassius[b]
records that the People, too, would have condemned
him despite the eloquence of Cicero (though it is not
certain at what particular stage in the trial this
speech was delivered). But the praetor, Metellus
Celer, availed himself of an ancient custom and
stopped the proceedings by hauling down the red
flag which was flown from the Janiculum during
meetings of the Assembly.[c]

No opposition was offered, for the trial had gone
far enough to satisfy the democratic leaders : the
principle of popular sovereignty in judicial as well as
political matters had been asserted ; and the Senate
henceforward would hesitate to employ the *senatus
consultum ultimum* as a means to suppress a tribune
acting in the popular interest.

[a] The crime of *perduellio* included any offence against
the State: as in the case of high treason to-day, both the
procedure and the penalty proper to it were cumbrous and
obsolete.

[b] Dion Cassius, *History of Rome*, xxxvii. 27.

[c] *i.e.* the Comitia Centuriata, of which the military origin
is reflected by this custom, the original purpose of the red
flag having been to signify that a watch was being kept from
the top of the Janiculum while the army was deliberating on
the Campus Martius outside the City.

INTRODUCTION

ANALYSIS OF THE SPEECH

§§ 1-5. The speech which I am about to make is more than an advocate's defence of his client : it is a consul's defence of the community ; for this attack on Rabirius masks a revolutionary conspiracy against the Republic. I implore the favour both of the gods and of the court.

§§ 6-9. Labienus has limited the time at my disposal to half an hour, so I must deal shortly with the subsidiary charges against Rabirius : not one of them bears the stamp of probability, or is consistent with the respect in which my client is held.

§§ 10-17. It is alleged that I have attempted to abolish the procedure for high treason. That is irrelevant as against Rabirius and a compliment to me. What claim has Labienus, who seeks to revive this barbarous procedure, to be considered a truer democrat than I, who seek to abolish it ? His very language, borrowed from the worst of the kings, is offensive to a free people. Gracchus, though he had a better motive for employing this procedure, would have none of it ; and Gracchus was a better democrat than Labienus. It is foreign to our conception of citizenship, and I am proud of having opposed it.

§§ 18-19. The real charge against Rabirius is the killing of Saturninus. Rabirius did not kill him—I only wish he had !—but he did take up arms with intent to kill him.

[Here occurs a *lacuna* : some account was probably given of the revolutionary conduct of Saturninus.]

INTRODUCTION

§§ 20-23. The Senate called on all good citizens to defend the Republic, provided them with arms and assembled them, under the orders of the consuls, in the Forum. Now I put it to you, Labienus : in the Forum were the consuls, followed by every citizen of distinction from every order in the state. What, then, ought Rabirius to have done ? What would you have done yourself ? Your uncle's example was not one to follow, least of all for Rabirius, who had no alternative but to join the consuls.

§§ 24-25. Labienus, I see, is parading a portrait of Saturninus. He should be warned by the punishment meted out by the courts to Titius and Decianus merely for having such a thing in their possession.

§§ 26-30. But this accusation affects many more than my client : it is tantamount to bringing a charge of murder against the best men of the time, including the great Marius, who was far more responsible for the death of Saturninus than Rabirius was. Though Marius is dead, I believe his immortal spirit would deeply feel this attack upon his honour. Indeed, every man who was alive at the time is equally involved.

§§ 31-32. The actual slayer of Saturninus has been recognized and publicly rewarded.

[Here occurs a *lacuna* : Cicero probably defended the policy of the Senate and urged the court to support it now as on previous occasions.]

§§ 33-34. No danger from outside can now trouble our Empire : against internal dangers the greatest safeguard is the Senate's power to call on all citizens to defend the Republic.

§ 35. If the same situation arose to-day, I should

do as Marius did; but for the moment, the Republic needs only your votes.

§§ 36-38. Behold the aged Rabirius! As a soldier he has never shunned danger in the cause of the Republic: all he now asks of you is to let him die a citizen of the Republic still!

M. TULLI CICERONIS PRO C. RABIRIO PERDUELLIONIS REO AD QUIRITES ORATIO

1 I. Etsi, Quirites, non est meae consuetudinis initio dicendi rationem reddere qua de causa quemque defendam, propterea quod cum omnibus civibus in eorum periculis semper satis iustam mihi causam necessitudinis esse duxi, tamen in hac defensione capitis, famae fortunarumque omnium C. Rabiri proponenda ratio videtur esse offici mei, propterea quod, quae iustissima mihi causa ad hunc defendendum esse visa est, eadem vobis ad absolvendum debet 2 videri. Nam me cum amicitiae vetustas, cum dignitas hominis, cum ratio humanitatis, cum meae vitae perpetua consuetudo ad C. Rabirium defendendum est adhortata, tum vero, ut id studiosissime facerem, salus rei publicae, consulare officium, consulatus denique ipse mihi una a vobis cum salute rei publicae commendatus coegit. Non enim C. Rabirium culpa delicti, non invidia vitae, Quirites, non denique veteres iustae gravesque inimicitiae civium in dis-

---

THE SPEECH ADDRESSED TO HIS FELLOW CITIZENS ^a BY MARCUS TULLIUS CICERO IN DEFENCE OF GAIUS RABIRIUS CHARGED WITH HIGH TREASON

I. Although it is not my habit, fellow-citizens, to **1** begin a speech by explaining the reason why I am defending a particular individual—for I have felt that, in the case of any citizen, the peril in which he stands is enough to constitute a true bond between us—none the less, in defending, as I now am, the life, the honour and the fortunes of Gaius Rabirius, I consider it my duty to lay before you an explanation of my services to him; because the reasons which make me feel it my duty to defend him ought also to make you feel it yours to acquit him. For my part, then, while the friendship which I have **2** long enjoyed with my client, the high position which he occupies ^b and the practice which I have followed all my life incline me to defend him, considerations of the public welfare, my duty as a consul,^c nay, the very office of consul which, together with the public welfare, you have committed to my charge, compel me to exert in his defence the utmost zeal. For it is not guilt attaching to his misdemeanour nor odium incurred by his life nor even a deep and natural resentment long felt against him by private

---

^a Cicero was consul in the year of this trial, 63 B.C.

crimen capitis vocaverunt, sed ut illud summum auxilium maiestatis atque imperi quod nobis a maioribus est traditum de re publica tolleretur, ut nihil posthac auctoritas senatus, nihil consulare imperium, nihil consensio bonorum contra pestem ac perniciem civitatis valeret, idcirco in his rebus evertendis unius hominis senectus, infirmitas solitudoque temptata est.

3 Quam ob rem si est boni consulis, cum cuncta auxilia rei publicae labefactari convellique videat, ferre opem patriae, succurrere saluti fortunisque communibus, implorare civium fidem, suam salutem posteriorem salute communi ducere, est etiam bonorum et fortium civium, quales vos omnibus rei publicae temporibus exstitistis, intercludere omnis seditionum vias, munire praesidia rei publicae, summum in consulibus imperium, summum in senatu consilium putare ; ea qui secutus sit, laude potius et honore quam poena et 4 supplicio dignum iudicare. Quam ob rem labor in hoc defendendo praecipue meus est, studium vero conservandi hominis commune mihi vobiscum esse debebit.

II. Sic enim existimare debetis, Quirites, post hominum memoriam rem nullam maiorem, magis periculosam, magis ab omnibus vobis providendam neque a tribuno pl. susceptam neque a consule defensam neque ad populum Romanum esse delatam. Agitur enim nihil aliud in hac causa, Quirites, nisi ut nullum

---

[a] This may refer merely to the resentment felt against him by Labienus owing to the death of his uncle (see Introduction, paragraph 5) or, as Mommsen thinks, to other deeds of violence committed by Rabirius. (Compare §§ 7 and 8 below.)

[b] See Introduction, paragraph 5.

citizens[a] which have brought Gaius Rabirius to trial
for his life : it is rather an attempt to abolish from
the constitution that chief support of our imperial
dignity handed down to us by our forefathers, to
make the authority of the Senate, the power of the
consuls, the concerted action of good citizens im-
potent henceforward to combat the curse and bane of
our country, which, in the process of overturning
those institutions, has prompted this attack upon
my client—old, infirm, and friendless as he is.   Where-   3
fore if it is the duty of a good consul, when he sees
everything on which the state depends being shaken
and uprooted, to come to the rescue of the country,
to aid in securing the welfare and the fortunes of the
public, to plead for the loyal support of the citizens,
and to set the public welfare before his own ; it is
also the duty of good and courageous citizens, such as
you have shown yourselves to be at every crisis in
our history, to block all the approaches of revolution,
to strengthen the bulwarks of the Republic and to
hold supreme the executive power of the consuls, the
deliberative power of the Senate, and by your verdict
to declare that he who has followed their guidance
deserves praise and honour rather than condemnation and punishment.   Therefore, while the task of   4
defending Rabirius falls primarily to me, an earnest
desire to save him will be your duty as much as mine.

II. For you should realize, gentlemen, that never
within the memory of man has any project more
important, more dangerous, more in need that all
of you should guard against it, been undertaken by
a tribune of the people, resisted by a consul, and
referred to the Roman people.[b]   For this case,
gentlemen, is nothing less than an attempt to secure

sit posthac in re publica publicum consilium, nulla
bonorum consensio contra improborum furorem et
audaciam, nullum extremis rei publicae temporibus
5 perfugium et praesidium salutis. Quae cum ita sint,
primum, quod in tanta dimicatione capitis, famae
fortunarumque omnium fieri necesse est, ab Iove
Optimo Maximo ceterisque dis deabusque immortalibus, quorum ope et auxilio multo magis haec res
publica quam ratione hominum et consilio gubernatur, pacem ac veniam peto precorque ab eis ut
hodiernum diem et ad huius salutem conservandam
et ad rem publicam constituendam inluxisse patian-
tur. Deinde vos, Quirites, quorum potestas proxime
ad deorum immortalium numen accedit, oro atque
obsecro, quoniam uno tempore vita C. Rabiri, hominis
miserrimi atque innocentissimi, salus rei publicae
vestris manibus suffragiisque permittitur, adhibeatis
in hominis fortunis misericordiam, in rei publicae
salute sapientiam quam soletis.

6 Nunc quoniam, T. Labiene, diligentiae meae
temporis angustiis obstitisti meque ex comparato et
constituto spatio defensionis in semihorae articulum
coegisti, parebitur et, quod iniquissimum est, accusatoris condicioni et, quod miserrimum, inimici potestati.
Quamquam in hac praescriptione semihorae patroni
mihi partis reliquisti, consulis ademisti, propterea
quod ad defendendum prope modum satis erit hoc
7 mihi temporis, ad conquerendum vero parum. Nisi

---

* Labienus could do this through his right as a tribune
to veto any public proceeding.

that there be henceforward no general council in the
state, no concerted action of good citizens against
the frenzy and audacity of wicked men, no refuge
for the Republic in emergencies, no security for its
welfare. Since this is so, I, as in duty bound where 5
a man's life and honour and all his fortunes are at
stake, first beg of most high and mighty Jupiter and
all the other immortal gods and goddesses by whose
help and assistance the Republic is directed rather
than by the counsel and deliberation of man, to grant
me their grace and favour ; and I pray that by their
will this day that has dawned may see the salvation
of my client and the establishment of our constitution.
And next I beg and beseech you, gentlemen, whose
power is second only to that of divine Providence, to
remember that to your hands and to your votes are
committed at one and the same time the life of the
hapless and innocent Gaius Rabirius and the welfare
of the Republic ; and accordingly to display your
usual clemency in dealing with the fortunes of the
prisoner, your usual wisdom in securing the well-
being of the Republic.

And now, Titus Labienus, since you have put a 6
check on my industry by shortening the time at my
disposal and have cut down the appropriate and
customary period for the defence to the narrow
limits of a single half-hour,[a] I must submit to injustice
in yielding to the terms of the prosecution and to misfortune in deferring to the prerogative of an enemy.
In thus confining me to half an hour, you have left
me my part as an advocate but have robbed me of my
part as a consul ; for the time at my disposal, though
almost long enough for my defence, will be too short
for my protest. Or perhaps you expect me to reply 7

forte de locis religiosis ac de lucis quos ab hoc
violatos esse dixisti pluribus verbis tibi respondendum
putas ; quo in crimine nihil est umquam abs te
dictum, nisi a C. Macro obiectum esse crimen id
C. Rabirio. In quo ego demiror meminisse te quid
obiecerit C. Rabirio Macer inimicus, oblitum esse
8 quid aequi et iurati iudices iudicarint. III. An de
peculatu facto aut de tabulario incenso longa oratio
est expromenda ? quo in crimine propinquus C. Rabiri
iudicio clarissimo, C. Curtius, pro virtute sua est
honestissime liberatus, ipse vero Rabirius non modo
in iudicium horum criminum, sed ne in tenuissimam
quidem suspicionem verbo est umquam vocatus.
An de sororis filio diligentius respondendum est ?
quem ab hoc necatum esse dixisti, cum ad iudici
moram familiaris funeris excusatio quaereretur.
Quid enim est tam veri simile quam cariorem huic
sororis maritum quam sororis filium fuisse, atque
ita cariorem ut alter vita crudelissime privaretur,
cum alteri ad prolationem iudici biduum quaereretur ? An de servis alienis contra legem Fabiam
retentis, aut de civibus Romanis contra legem
Porciam verberatis aut necatis plura dicenda sunt,
cum tanto studio C. Rabirius totius Apuliae, singulari
voluntate Campaniae ornetur, cumque ad eius pro-
pulsandum periculum non modo homines sed prope
regiones ipsae convenerint, aliquanto etiam latius

---

a It was still held by Ulpian (third century A.D.) that this
circumstance excused a man from performing any public
act.
b *i.e.* the Curtius mentioned above : it is not possible to
say what this trial was about.
c It is probable that Rabirius had estates in both districts.
458

at length to the charge of violating holy places and
groves which you have brought against my client;
though you had not a word to say in support of it
except that this charge was brought against him by
Gaius Macer. And in this connexion I am amazed
that you should have remembered the charge which
his enemy Gaius Macer brought against my client
and forgotten the verdict which impartial judges
returned upon their oath. III. Or am I to produce 8
a long speech upon the charge of peculation or of
the burning of public records? Of this charge
Gaius Curtius, a relative of Gaius Rabirius, was, by
an illustrious bench of judges and as was to
be expected from his character, most honourably
acquitted; while as for Rabirius himself, so far
from his having been brought to trial on these
charges, not a word has ever been said to cause the
slightest suspicion to attach to him. Or must I be
careful to reply about his sister's son, whom you say
my client murdered with a view to using the death
of a member of the family as a plea for the stay of
proceedings? [a] What? Is it likely that he would
have been fonder of his sister's husband [b] than of her
son, and so much fonder that he would have cruelly
murdered the son in order to provide the husband
with a postponement of his trial merely for two days?
Or is there much left for me to say about his having
infringed the law of Fabius by detaining another
man's slaves, or the law of Porcius by scourging or
killing Roman citizens, when all Apulia honours him
with so much enthusiasm and Campania with such
remarkable goodwill [c]; when, to avert his peril, not
only individuals but whole districts, almost, have
assembled, actuated by an interest too widespread

excitatae quam ipsius vicinitatis nomen ac termini
postulabant ? Nam quid ego ad id longam orationem
comparem quod est in eadem multae inrogatione
praescriptum, hunc nec suae nec alienae pudicitiae
9 pepercisse ? Quin etiam suspicor eo mihi semihoram
ab Labieno praestitutam esse ut ne plura de pudicitia
dicerem. Ergo ad haec crimina quae patroni diligentiam desiderant intellegis mihi semihoram istam
nimium longam fuisse. Illam alteram partem de
nece Saturnini nimis exiguam atque angustam esse
voluisti ; quae non oratoris ingenium sed consulis
auxilium implorat et flagitat.

10 Nam de perduellionis iudicio, quod a me sublatu n
esse criminari soles, meum crimen est, non Rabiri.
Quod utinam, Quirites, ego id aut primus aut
solus ex hac re publica sustulissem ! utinam hoc,
quod ille crimen esse volt, proprium testimonium
meae laudis esset. Quid enim optari potest quod
ego mallem quam me in consulatu meo carnificem
de foro, crucem de campo sustulisse ? Sed ista laus
primum est maiorum nostrorum, Quirites, qui expulsis
regibus nullum in libero populo vestigium crudelitatis
regiae retinuerunt, deinde multorum virorum fortium
qui vestram libertatem non acerbitate suppliciorum
infestam sed lenitate legum munitam esse voluerunt.

---

a A tribune could hale an offender before the Assembly
(*Comitia Tributa*), whose judicial powers were, however,
limited to the infliction of a fine.

b See Introduction, paragraph 5 and footnote.

c Crucifixion always took place outside the City on the
Campus Martius.

to be attributed to mere neighbourly feeling? Or why should I prepare a long speech in answer to the point which was laboured on that same occasion when it was proposed to fine Rabirius [a]—I mean the statement that he had respected neither his own chastity nor that of others? Actually, I suspect that the 9 reason why Labienus cut down my time to half an hour was to prevent my enlarging on the topic of chastity! And so, as for the charges which demand my labours as an advocate, you realize that the half hour which you have allowed me has proved more than long enough: it was the other part of my speech dealing with the death of Saturninus, that you desired should be reduced and curtailed; and that part stands in crying need, not of a pleader's skill but of a consul's intervention.

Now as for your constant allegation that I have 10 abolished the procedure for High Treason,[b] that is a charge against me, not against Rabirius. Nay, gentlemen, would that it were I who was either the first or the only man to have abolished it from our country! I would that, though Labienus makes it a charge against me, I might appropriate it as evidence of my glory. For what is so greatly to be desired that I should prefer it to the claim of having in my consulship abolished the executioner from the Forum, the cross from the Campus [c]? But that glory, gentlemen, belongs in the first place to our forefathers who, when they drove out the kings, retained among a free people no trace of their cruel ways; and in the second place to many brave men who intended that your liberty should not be made offensive by savage punishments but safeguarded only by mild laws.

11 IV. Quam ob rem uter nostrum tandem, Labiene,
popularis est, tune qui civibus Romanis in contione
ipsa carnificem, qui vincla adhiberi putas oportere,
qui in campo Martio comitiis centuriatis auspicato in
loco crucem ad civium supplicium defigi et constitui
iubes, an ego qui funestari contionem contagione
carnificis veto, qui expiandum forum populi Romani
ab illis nefarii sceleris vestigiis esse dico, qui castam
contionem, sanctum campum, inviolatum corpus
omnium civium Romanorum, integrum ius libertatis
12 defendo servari oportere? Popularis vero tribunus
pl. custos defensorque iuris et libertatis! Porcia lex
virgas ab omnium civium Romanorum corpore amovit,
hic misericors flagella rettulit; Porcia lex libertatem
civium lictori eripuit, Labienus, homo popularis,
carnifici tradidit; C. Gracchus legem tulit ne de
capite civium Romanorum iniussu vestro iudicaretur,
hic popularis a iiviris iniussu vestro non iudicari de
cive Romano sed indicta causa civem Romanum
13 capitis condemnari coegit. Tu mihi etiam legis
Porciae, tu C. Gracchi, tu horum libertatis, tu cuiusquam denique hominis popularis mentionem facis,
qui non modo suppliciis inusitatis sed etiam verborum
crudelitate inaudita violare libertatem huius populi,
temptare mansuetudinem, commutare disciplinam

---

[a] See Introduction, footnote [c] to paragraph 5.

[b] The *Comitia Centuriata*, owing to its military origin,
met on the Campus Martius: compare Introduction, footnote [c] to paragraph 5.

[c] See Introduction, footnote [b] to paragraph 5.

[d] Gaius Gracchus, one of the greatest of Roman democrats, was killed in 121 B.C. owing to his attempt to carry out
the reforms proposed by his brother, Tiberius, who had been
killed in similar circumstances twelve years earlier.

IV. Which, then, of us two, Labienus, is the 11
people's friend ? You, who think it right to threaten
Roman citizens even in the midst of their assembly
with the executioner and with bonds ; who, on the
Campus Martius,*a* at the Assembly of the Centuries,*b*
in that holy place, give orders for the construction
and erection of a cross for the punishment of
citizens ; or I, who refuse to allow the assembly to
be defiled by contact with the executioner ; who
assert that the Forum of the Roman people must be
purified from those traces of hideous crime, who urge
against you the need to keep the assembly undefiled,
the Campus holy, the person of every Roman citizen
inviolable, the rights of a free people unimpaired ?
What a friend of the people is our tribune, what a 12
guardian and defender of its rights and liberties !
The law of Porcius forbade the rod to be used on
the person of any Roman citizen : this merciful man
has reintroduced the scourge. The law of Porcius
wrested the liberty of the citizens from the lictor :
Labienus, the friend of the people, has handed it
over to the executioner. Gaius Gracchus carried a
law forbidding sentence to be passed on the life of a
Roman citizen without your consent : this friend of
the people has illegally secured without your consent,
not indeed that the Duumvirs *c* should put a Roman
citizen on trial, but actually that they should condemn
him to death without his case being heard. Do you 13
really dare to talk to me of the law of Porcius or of
Gaius Gracchus *d* or of any other friend of the people,
after having attempted, not merely by the use of
unwonted punishments but by the unparalleled
cruelty of your language, to violate the liberty of
this people, to put their clemency to the test, to alter

conatus es ? Namque haec tua, quae te, hominem
clementem popularemque, delectant, " I, lictor,
conliga manvs," non modo huius libertatis mansue-
tudinisque non sunt sed ne Romuli quidem aut
Numae Pompili ; Tarquini, superbissimi atque cru-
delissimi regis, ista sunt cruciatus carmina quae tu,
homo lenis ac popularis, libentissime commemoras :
" Capvt obnvbito, arbori infelici svspendito," quae
verba, Quirites, iam pridem in hac re publica non
solum tenebris vetustatis verum etiam luce libertatis
oppressa sunt.

14   V. An vero, si actio ista popularis esset et si ullam
partem aequitatis haberet aut iuris, C. Gracchus eam
reliquisset ? Scilicet tibi graviorem dolorem patrui
tui mors attulit quam C. Graccho fratris, et tibi
acerbior eius patrui mors est quem numquam vidisti
quam illi eius fratris quicum concordissime vixerat,
et simili iure tu ulcisceris patrui mortem atque ille
persequeretur fratris, si ista ratione agere voluisset, et
par desiderium sui reliquit apud populum Romanum
Labienus iste, patruus vester, quisquis fuit, ac Ti.
Gracchus reliquerat. An pietas tua maior quam
C. Gracchi, an animus, an consilium, an opes, an
auctoritas, an eloquentia ? quae si in illo minima
fuissent, tamen prae tuis facultatibus maxima puta-

---

a Romulus and Numa Pompilius were the first two kings of
Rome and were regarded as the founders respectively of the
City and of its religious institutions. Tarquinius, the last,
was surnamed Superbus and finally expelled in 510 B.C. for
his tyranny.

b *i.e.* Quintus Labienus; see Introduction, paragraph 5.
The word *vester* suggests that T. Labienus was supported in
the prosecution by one or more of his cousins : *vester* was
not used for *tuus* till long after Cicero's time.

their traditions ? For those phrases of yours which,
being a merciful man and a friend of the people, you
are so fond of, such as " Lictor, go bind his hands,"
are foreign not only to Roman liberty and clemency
but even to Romulus *a* or Numa Pompilius : Tarquin,
haughtiest and most cruel of tyrants, provides your
torture-chamber with those mottoes which, like the
gentle soul, the people's friend that you are, you
delight to record, such as " Veil his head, hang him
to the tree of shame." Such phrases, I say, have
long since disappeared from our state, overwhelmed
not only by the shadows of antiquity but by the light
of Liberty.

V. Again, if your favourite procedure were in the 14
people's interest, if it contained any measure of
justice or of right, would Gaius Gracchus have
neglected it ? Doubtless you felt a deeper grief
at the death of your uncle *b* than Gaius Gracchus
at that of his brother ; *c* and to you the death of this
uncle whom you had never seen was more painful
than was to Gracchus the death of the brother with
whom he had lived on such affectionate terms ; and
you are avenging your uncle in the same way as he
would have sought to requite the death of his brother
if he had consented to act on your principles ; and
this uncle of yours, this Labienus, whoever he was,
left behind him among the Roman people a regret
no less deep than Tiberius Gracchus had left. Or had
you a greater sense of duty than Gracchus ? Or
greater courage ? Or greater resource ? Or greater
wealth ? Or a greater position ? Or greater eloquence ? Had these attributes been found in him
only to a very slight degree, they would pass as great

a *i.e.* Tiberius Gracchus : see footnote to § 13.

15 rentur. Cum vero his rebus omnibus C. Gracchus
omnis vicerit, quantum intervallum tandem inter te
atque illum intericctum putas ? Sed moreretur prius
acerbissima morte miliens C. Gracchus quam in eius
contione carnifex consisteret ; quem non modo foro
sed etiam caelo hoc ac spiritu censoriae leges atque
urbis domicilio carere voluerunt. Hic se popularem
dicere audet, me alienum a commodis vestris, cum
iste omnis et suppliciorum et verborum acerbitates
non ex memoria vestra ac patrum vestrorum sed ex
annalium monumentis atque ex regum commentariis
conquisierit, ego omnibus meis opibus, omnibus consiliis, omnibus dictis atque factis repugnarim et
restiterim crudelitati ? nisi forte hanc condicionem
vobis esse voltis quam servi, si libertatis spem
propositam non haberent, ferre nullo modo possent.
16 Misera est ignominia iudiciorum publicorum, misera
multatio bonorum, miserum exsilium ; sed tamen in
omni calamitate retinetur aliquod vestigium libertatis. Mors denique si proponitur, in libertate
moriamur, carnifex vero et obductio capitis et nomen
ipsum crucis absit non modo a corpore civium
Romanorum sed etiam a cogitatione, oculis, auribus.
Harum enim omnium rerum non solum eventus
atque perpessio sed etiam condicio, exspectatio,
mentio ipsa denique indigna cive Romano atque

ᵃ The censors, as superintendents of the Public Works, assigned quarters to the " public slaves," who included the executioners.

ᵇ It is impossible to say what "Chronicles" are referred to: the "Archives" must have been forgeries.

indeed when compared with your abilities! But 15
inasmuch as Gaius Gracchus possessed all those attributes to a greater degree than any other man, how
great a gulf do you then suppose to be fixed between
you and him? And yet Gaius Gracchus would have
died a thousand cruel deaths rather than that the
executioner should stand in an assembly of his;
while the censors' regulations [a] are so framed as to
cut off such a man not merely from using the Forum
but from beholding our horizon, breathing our air or
living in our city. Is this the man who dares to
style himself a friend of the people and me an enemy
of your interests, though he has hunted out all these
cruel punishments, this cruel language, not from
what you and your fathers can remember but from
the records of the Chronicles, the Archives of the
Kings; [b] while I, with all my resources, by all my
counsels, by my every word and deed, have combated
and resisted his savagery? Unless perchance you
wish your prospect to be one which would be utterly
intolerable to slaves if some hope of liberty were not
held out to them. How grievous a thing it is to be 16
disgraced by a public court; how grievous to suffer
a fine, how grievous to suffer banishment; and yet
in the midst of any such disaster some trace of
liberty is left to us. Even if we are threatened with
death, we may die free men. But the executioner,
the veiling of the head, and the very word "cross"
should be far removed not only from the person of a
Roman citizen but from his thoughts, his eyes and
his ears. For it is not only the actual occurrence of
these things or the endurance of them, but liability
to them, the expectation, nay, the mere mention of
them, that is unworthy of a Roman citizen and a free

homine libero est. An vero servos nostros horum
suppliciorum omnium metu dominorum benignitas
vindicta una liberat ; nos a verberibus, ab unco, a
crucis denique terrore neque res gestae neque acta
17 aetas neque vestri honores vindicabunt ? Quam ob
rem fateor atque etiam, Labiene, profiteor et prae
me fero te ex illa crudeli, importuna, non tribunicia
actione sed regia, meo consilio, virtute, auctoritate
esse depulsum. Qua tu in actione quamquam omnia
exempla maiorum, omnis leges, omnem auctoritatem
senatus, omnis religiones atque auspiciorum publica
iura neglexisti, tamen a me haec in hoc tam exiguo
meo tempore non audies ; liberum tempus nobis
dabitur ad istam disceptationem.
18　VI. Nunc de Saturnini crimine ac de clarissimi patrui
tui morte dicemus. Arguis occisum esse a C. Rabirio
L. Saturninum. At id C. Rabirius multorum testimoniis, Q. Hortensio copiosissime defendente, antea
falsum esse docuit ; ego autem, si mihi esset integrum, susciperem hoc crimen, agnoscerem, confiterer.
Vtinam hanc mihi facultatem causa concederet ut
possem hoc praedicare, C. Rabiri manu L. Saturninum, hostem populi Romani, interfectum !—Nihil
me clamor iste commovet sed consolatur, cum indicat
esse quosdam civis imperitos sed non multos. Numquam, mihi credite, populus Romanus hic qui silet

---

ᵃ It was fastened in the necks of condemned criminals in
order to drag them along.
ᵇ This may hint either at a further hearing of Rabirius's
case or at Cicero's intention to bring Labienus to trial
subsequently.
ᶜ See Introduction, paragraph 2.

man. Or shall it be said that while a kind master, by a single act of manumission, frees a slave from the fear of all these punishments, we are not to be freed from scourgings, from the executioner's hook,[a] nor even from the dread of the cross by our achievements, by the lives we have led or even by the honours you have bestowed upon us? So, then, I 17 admit, nay, Labienus, I avow and I boast, that it is by my counsel, my determination, my influence that you have been forced to abandon a procedure which is cruel, savage, and more suited to a tyrant than a tribune. And although in seeking to impose this procedure you have set aside all precedent, all laws, all the authority of the Senate, all scruples imposed by religion, all constitutional observance of the auspices, still not a word of all that shall you hear from me in the short time that is at my disposal. We shall have an unrestricted opportunity later for discussing those points.[b]

VI. For the present let me deal with the charge 18 relating to Saturninus and the death of your illustrious uncle.[c] You maintain that Gaius Rabirius killed Lucius Saturninus, a charge which Gaius Rabirius has previously, on the evidence of many witnesses in the course of his most ample defence by Quintus Hortensius, proved to be false. But for my part, if I were undertaking his defence anew, I would brave this charge : I would admit it, I would plead guilty to it ! Would that my case gave me the chance to proclaim that my client's was the hand that struck down that public enemy, Saturninus ! The outcry that I hear does not perturb me, nay, it consoles me ; for it shows there are some uninstructed citizens but not many. Never, believe me, would the Roman people,

consulem me fecisset, si vestro clamore perturbatum
iri arbitraretur. Quanto iam levior est acclamatio!
Quin continetis vocem indicem stultitiae vestrae,
19 testem paucitatis!—Libenter, inquam, confiterer, si
vere possem aut etiam si mihi esset integrum, C.
Rabiri manu L. Saturninum esse occisum, et id
facinus pulcherrimum esse arbitrarer; sed, quoniam
id facere non possum, confitebor id quod ad laudem
minus valebit, ad crimen non minus. Confiteor inter-
ficiendi Saturnini causa C. Rabirium arma cepisse.
Quid est, Labiene? quam a me graviorem confes-
sionem aut quod in hunc maius crimen exspectas?
nisi vero interesse aliquid putas inter eum qui
hominem occidit, et eum qui cum telo occidendi
hominis causa fuit. Si interfici Saturninum nefas
fuit, arma sumpta esse contra Saturninum sine scelere
non possunt; si arma iure sumpta concedis, interfectum iure concedas necesse est.

* * * * * *

20 VII. Fit senatus consultum ut C. Marius L. Valerius
consules adhiberent tribunos pl. et praetores, quos
eis videretur, operamque darent ut imperium populi
Romani maiestasque conservaretur. Adhibent omnis
tribunos pl. praeter Saturninum, praetores praeter
Glauciam; qui rem publicam salvam esse vellent,
arma capere et se sequi iubent. Parent omnes; ex
aedificiis armamentariisque publicis arma populo

---

a See the Analysis of the Speech, §§ 18-19.
b *i.e.* the *senatus consultum ultimum*; see Introduction,
paragraph 4.

who stand here in silence, have made me consul, did
they suppose that I should be disconcerted by your
outcry. How much diminished is your clamour now !
Nay, you repress the murmurs which would denounce
your folly and reveal your isolation. Gladly, I say, **19**
would I admit—if I could do so with truth or even if
I were opening the defence anew—that it was my
client's hand which struck down Saturninus, and I
should consider it a most glorious achievement; but
since I am debarred from so doing, I will admit what
is less relevant to his credit but equally relevant to
the charge against him. I admit that Gaius Rabirius
took arms for the purpose of killing Saturninus.
Well, Labienus, what more important admission on
my part, what weightier charge against my client
are you expecting me to make, unless, perhaps, you
imagine that there is some difference between him
who killed a man and him who was armed for the
purpose of killing a man ? If the killing of Saturninus was a crime, the taking of arms against Saturninus cannot but have been a wrongful act : if you
agree that the taking of arms was lawful, you must
also agree that the killing was lawful.

[*One page is lacking in the oldest manuscript.*] [a]

VII. The Senate passed a decree [b] that the **20**
consuls, Gaius Marius and Lucius Valerius, should
summon such tribunes of the people and praetors as
they thought fit, and should take measures to preserve the imperial majesty of the Roman people.
They summoned all the tribunes except Saturninus,
all the praetors except Glaucia : those who desired
the safety of the Republic they ordered to take arms
and follow them. Everyone obeyed. Arms were
taken from the public buildings and arsenals and,

Romano C. Mario consule distribuente dantur. Hic
iam, ut omittam cetera, de te ipso, Labiene, quaero.
Cum Saturninus Capitolium teneret armatus, esset
una C. Glaucia, C. Saufeius, etiam ille ex compedibus
atque ergastulo Gracchus ; addam, quoniam ita vis,
eodem Q. Labienum, patruum tuum ; in foro autem
C. Marius et L. Valerius Flaccus consules, post
cunctus senatus, atque ille senatus quem etiam
vos ipsi, quo facilius de hoc senatu detrahere
possitis, laudare consuevistis ; cum equester ordo—at
quorum equitum, di immortales ! patrum nostrorum
atque eius aetatis, qui tum magnam partem rei
publicae atque omnem dignitatem iudiciorum tene-
bant,—cum omnes omnium ordinum homines qui in
salute rei publicae salutem suam repositam esse
arbitrabantur arma cepissent ; quid tandem C.
21 Rabirio faciendum fuit ? De te ipso, inquam,
Labiene, quaero. Cum ad arma consules ex senatus
consulto vocavissent, cum armatus M. Aemilius,
princeps senatus, in comitio constitisset, qui cum
ingredi vix posset, non ad insequendum sibi tardi-
tatem pedum sed ad fugiendum impedimento fore
putabat, cum denique Q. Scaevola confectus senec-
tute, perditus morbo, mancus et membris omnibus
captus ac debilis, hastili nixus et animi vim et in-

ª It is probable that private citizens were not allowed to
keep arms.
ᵇ His real name was Equitius ; see Introduction, para. 2.
ᶜ The Order of Knights was given this privilege by Gaius
Gracchus in 123 B.C. and deprived of it by Sulla in 81 B.C.
ᵈ Marcus Aemilius Scaurus, a leader of the senatorial
party much admired by Cicero, is said to have supplanted
Saturninus in some government appointment and thereby
to have thrown him into the arms of the extremists.
ᵉ Quintus Mucius Scaevola, surnamed the augur, to dis-

under the direction of the consul, Gaius Marius, distributed to the Roman people.[a] Now, at this point I confine myself to putting to you personally, Labienus, one question : seeing that Saturninus was in armed possession of the Capitol and with him Gaius Glaucia, Gaius Saufeius, yes, and the ex-convict and gaol-bird Gracchus,[b] and, as you insist upon it, I will add that your uncle Quintus Labienus was there too ; while in the Forum were the consuls, Gaius Marius and Lucius Valerius Flaccus, followed by the entire Senate (such a Senate, moreover, as even you, in order to increase your chance of slandering the present Senate, are wont to praise) seeing that the order of Knights—and what Knights they were, by Heaven !—which in those days played an important part in politics and was invested with the entire dignity of the law courts,[c] had taken up arms, and so indeed had all men of every order who held that their own well-being was bound up with the well-being of the Republic ; what, I ask you, was Rabirius to do ?   Once again, I ask you personally, Labienus : 21 seeing that it was the consuls who, acting on a decree of the Senate, had issued the call to arms ; that Marcus Aemilius,[d] the president of the Senate, had taken his stand in the Assembly with arms in his hand (for though he could hardly set foot to the ground, he thought that his lameness would be no hindrance to him in pursuit but only in flight) and that Quintus Scaevola,[e] hampered though he was by old age, incurably ill, disabled, crippled, and infirm in every limb, was displaying as he leaned upon his spear at once his mental vigour and his bodily weak-

tinguish him from his kinsman the pontifex maximus. Both were great jurists.

firmitatem corporis ostenderet, cum L. Metellus,
Ser. Galba, C. Serranus, P. Rutilius, C. Fimbria,
Q. Catulus omnesque qui tum erant consulares pro
salute communi arma cepissent, cum omnes prae-
tores, cuncta nobilitas ac iuventus accurreret, Cn. et
L. Domitii, L. Crassus, Q. Mucius, C. Claudius, M.
Drusus, cum omnes Octavii, Metelli, Iulii, Cassii,
Catones, Pompeii, cum L. Philippus, L. Scipio, cum
M. Lepidus, cum D. Brutus, cum hic ipse, P. Servilius,
quo tu imperatore, Labiene, meruisti, cum hic Q.
Catulus, admodum tum adulescens, cum hic C. Curio,
cum denique omnes clarissimi viri cum consulibus
essent ; quid tandem C. Rabirium facere convenit ?
utrum inclusum atque abditum latere in occulto atque
ignaviam suam tenebrarum ac parietum custodiis
tegere, an in Capitolium pergere atque ibi se cum
tuo patruo et ceteris ad mortem propter vitae turpitudinem confugientibus congregare, an cum Mario,
Scauro, Catulo, Metello, Scaevola, cum bonis denique
omnibus coire non modo salutis verum etiam periculi
societatem ?

22   VIII. Tu denique, Labiene, quid faceres tali in
re ac tempore ? Cum ignaviae ratio te in fugam
atque in latebras impelleret, improbitas et furor
L. Saturnini in Capitolium arcesseret, consules ad
patriae salutem ac libertatem vocarent, quam tandem

---

a In a campaign against the pirates of the south-west
coasts of Asia Minor.

ness: seeing that Lucius Metellus, Servius Galba, Gaius Serranus, Publius Rutilius, Gaius Fimbria, Quintus Catulus and all the men at that time of consular rank had taken arms to defend the common safety : seeing that all the praetors and all the nobles of military age were hastening to join them, including Gnaeus and Lucius Domitius, Lucius Crassus, Quintus Mucius, Gaius Claudius and Marcus Drusus : seeing that all who bore the names of Octavius, Metellus, Julius, Cassius, Cato, or Pompeius ; that Lucius Philippus and Lucius Scipio ; that Marcus Lepidus and Decius Brutus ; that Publius Servilius, here, the very man under whose command you served, Labienus ;[a] that Quintus Catulus, here, who was then quite a young man ; that Gaius Curio, here, and indeed every man of distinction, was with the consuls ; what, I ask you, was the right course for Gaius Rabirius ? Was he to remain hidden in close concealment, shielding his cowardice behind the protecting walls of his house or the darkness of night ? Was he to make his way into the Capitol and there herd with your uncle and others who were seeking to find in death a refuge from the dishonour of their lives ? Or was he to unite with Marius, Scaurus, Catulus, Metellus, and Scaevola, in fact with all good citizens, in a communion not only of safety but also of peril ?

VIII. And you, yourself, Labienus—what should 22 you have been doing in such a time of crisis ? When the promptings of indolence were driving you to flight and concealment, when the wickedness and madness of Lucius Saturninus were inviting you to the Capitol, when the consuls were calling you to the defence of your country and to freedom, whose

CICERO

auctoritatem, quam vocem, cuius sectam sequi, cuius
imperio parere potissimum velles? " Patruus," inquit, " meus cum Saturnino fuit." Quid? pater
quicum? quid? propinqui vestri, equites Romani?
quid? omnis praefectura, regio, vicinitas vestra?
quid? ager Picenus universus utrum tribunicium
furorem, an consularem auctoritatem secutus est?
23 Equidem hoc adfirmo, quod tu nunc de tuo patruo
praedicas neminem umquam adhuc de se esse confessum; nemo est, inquam, inventus tam profligatus,
tam perditus, tam ab omni non modo honestate sed
etiam simulatione honestatis relictus, qui se in
Capitolio fuisse cum Saturnino fateretur. At fuit
vester patruus. Fuerit, et fuerit nulla vi, nulla
desperatione rerum suarum, nullis domesticis volneri-
bus coactus; induxerit eum L. Saturnini familiaritas
ut amicitiam patriae praeponeret; idcircone oportuit
C. Rabirium desciscere a re publica, non comparere
in illa armata multitudine bonorum, consulum voci
24 atque imperio non oboedire? Atqui videmus haec
in rerum natura tria fuisse, ut aut cum Saturnino
esset, aut cum bonis, aut lateret. Latere mortis erat
instar turpissimae, cum Saturnino esse furoris et
sceleris; virtus et honestas et pudor cum consulibus
esse cogebat. Hoc tu igitur in crimen vocas, quod
cum eis fuerit C. Rabirius quos amentissimus fuisset
si oppugnasset, turpissimus si reliquisset?

IX. At C. Decianus, de quo tu saepe commemoras,
quia, cum hominem omnibus insignem notis turpi-

ᵃ Nothing else is known of him save that Valerius
Maximus describes him as well known for his integrity:
perhaps that was why Labienus so often quoted him as an
authority.

authority, whose voice, whose party should you have preferred to follow, whose orders to obey? "My uncle," he says, "was with Saturninus." Well, and with whom was your father? What of the Knights, your kinsmen? What of all the men of your prefecture, your district, your neighbourhood? Did the whole of Picenum follow the madness of a tribune or the authority of the Senate? For my part I 23 maintain that what you are now proclaiming about your uncle, no one has ever yet admitted about himself: no one, I say, has yet been found so worthless, so abandoned, so bereft of decent feeling, nay, of any pretence to such feeling, as to admit that he was in the Capitol with Saturninus. But you say, your uncle was there. Well, suppose he was; and suppose he was there, not because his ruined fortunes and his private calamities left him no choice, but because his intimacy with Saturninus led him to put his friend before his country—was that therefore a reason why Gaius Rabirius should desert the Republic, why he should not take his place in that host of good citizens assembled under arms, why he should not obey the command and the authority of the consuls? As a matter of fact, the circumstances 24 clearly gave him three choices: either to join Saturninus, or to join the good citizens or to hide. To hide was as bad as to die a shameful death: to join Saturninus was an act of madness and of crime: virtue and honour and decency demanded that he should join the consuls. Do you then make it a charge against Rabirius that he joined those whom he would have been mad to oppose, infamous to abandon?

IX. But take the case of Gaius Decianus, whom you are so fond of quoting:[a] he was condemned because

tudinis, P. Furium, accusaret summo studio bonorum
omnium, queri est ausus in contione de morte
Saturnini, condemnatus est, et Sex. Titius, quod
habuit imaginem L. Saturnini domi suae, condemnatus
est. Statuerunt equites Romani illo iudicio improbum
civem esse et non retinendum in civitate, qui hominis
hostilem in modum seditiosi imagine aut mortem eius
honestaret, aut desideria imperitorum misericordia
commoveret, aut suam significaret imitandae improbi-
25 tatis voluntatem. Itaque mihi mirum videtur unde
hanc tu, Labiene, imaginem quam habes inveneris;
nam Sex. Titio damnato qui istam habere auderet
inventus est nemo. Quod tu si audisses aut si per
aetatem scire potuisses, numquam profecto istam
imaginem quae domi posita pestem atque exsilium
Sex. Titio attulisset in rostra atque in contionem
attulisses, nec tuas umquam ratis ad eos scopulos
appulisses ad quos Sex. Titi adflictam navem et in
quibus C. Deciani naufragium fortunarum videres.

Sed in his rebus omnibus imprudentia laberis.
Causam enim suscepisti antiquiorem memoria tua,
quae causa ante mortua est quam tu natus es; et
qua in causa tute profecto fuisses, si per aetatem
26 esse potuisses eam causam in iudicium vocas. An
non intellegis, primum quos homines et qualis viros
mortuos summi sceleris arguas, deinde quot ex his

---

^a An *imago* was, properly speaking, the cast of a man's
face, his death-mask.

478

—while with the entire approval of all good citizens he was accusing Publius Furius, a man notorious for every kind of infamy—he dared to lament in the course of his speech the death of Saturninus. And Sextus Titius also was condemned for having a portrait of Saturninus in his house. The Roman Knights by their verdict on that occasion branded as a worthless citizen, unfit to remain in the citizen body, anyone who, by keeping the portrait *a* of a man whose sedition made him a public enemy, either did honour to his death or, by exciting the pity of the uninstructed, caused them to regret him or showed an inclination on his own part to imitate such villainy. And so I find it difficult to imagine where you, 25 Labienus, found the portrait which you have here. For since the condemnation of Sextus Titius no one has been found with the courage to have such a thing in his possession. Had you been told of this incident or been old enough to know about it, I am sure you would never have paraded on the platform of a public assembly a portrait like that, which, when merely placed in his house, brought ruin and exile on Sextus Titius, and you would never have driven your bark upon those rocks on which you had seen the ship of Sextus Titius dashed in pieces and the fortunes of Gaius Decianus completely wrecked.

But throughout this whole case, ignorance is your stumbling-block. For in bringing into court a cause which was dead before you were born, a cause in which you would certainly have been involved if you had been old enough, do you not realize in the first 26 place who are the men, how distinguished the citizens, whom you are accusing, now that they are dead, of a monstrous crime ; and again, how many still alive

479

qui vivunt eodem crimine in summum periculum
capitis arcessas ? Nam si C. Rabirius fraudem
capitalem admisit quod arma contra L. Saturninum
tulit, huic quidem adferet aliquam deprecationem
periculi aetas illa qua tum fuit ; Q. vero Catulum,
patrem huius, in quo summa sapientia, eximia virtus,
singularis humanitas fuit, M. Scaurum, illa gravitate,
illo consilio, illa prudentia, duos Mucios, L. Crassum,
M. Antonium, qui tum extra urbem cum praesidio
fuit, quorum in hac civitate longe maxima consilia
atque ingenia fuerunt, ceteros pari dignitate praeditos
custodes gubernatoresque rei publicae quem ad
27 modum mortuos defendemus ? Quid de illis honestissimis viris atque optimis civibus, equitibus Romanis,
dicemus qui tum una cum senatu salutem rei publicae
defenderunt ? quid de tribunis aerariis ceterorumque
ordinum omnium hominibus qui tum arma pro communi libertate ceperunt ?

X. Sed quid ego de eis omnibus qui consulari
imperio paruerunt loquor ? de ipsorum consulum
fama quid futurum est ? L. Flaccum, hominem
cum semper in re publica, tum in magistratibus
gerendis, in sacerdotio caerimoniisque quibus
praeerat diligentissimum, nefarii sceleris ac parricidi mortuum condemnabimus ? adiungemus ad
hanc labem ignominiamque mortis etiam C. Mari
nomen ? C. Marium, quem vere patrem patriae,

ᵃ See footnotes to § 21.

ᵇ Marcus Antonius, a famous orator, was stationed outside the city to prevent the country people coming to the
rescue of Saturninus.

ᶜ Who they were or how they came to constitute an *ordo*
is not known : under the law of Cotta, 70 B.C., they shared
with senators and knights the right to sit on juries.

you are bringing by this same charge into the utmost
peril of their lives ?   For if Gaius Rabirius incurred
the guilt of a capital crime in taking up arms against
Lucius Saturninus, yet he at all events might hope
to urge in extenuation his youth at the time ; but as
for Quintus Catulus, the father of our Catulus, in
whom were combined great wisdom, high character,
and unequalled humanity ; as for Marcus Scaurus,
whose dignity, judgement, and far-sightedness were
famous ; as for the two Scaevolas,[a] as for Lucius
Crassus and Marcus Antonius who at the time was
stationed on guard outside the city,[b] all of them pre-
eminently the leading men in the country both in
judgement and ability ; and as for other men of equal
eminence, the guardians and the rulers of the state—
how shall we defend them now that they are dead ?
What shall we say of the Roman Knights, most 27
honourable men and best of citizens, who on that
occasion combined with the Senate in defence of the
Republic ; or of the *Tribuni Aerarii* [c] and the men of
all other classes who on that occasion took up arms
to defend the common liberty ?

X. But why do I speak of all those who obeyed the
authority of the consuls ?   What will befall the
reputation of the consuls themselves ?   Shall Lucius
Flaccus,[d] who always showed the most scrupulous care
both in his political career and in the conduct of the
civil and religious offices of which he was in charge,
be condemned, now that he is dead, as guilty of the
hideous crime of murder ?   Shall the name of Gaius
Marius also be branded with the infamy of that killing ?   Shall Gaius Marius whom we may in very
truth entitle the father of his country, the parent, I

---

[d] The colleague of Marius in the consulship for 100 B.C.

parentem, inquam, vestrae libertatis atque huiusce
rei publicae possumus dicere, sceleris ac parricidi
28 nefarii mortuum condemnabimus? Etenim si C.
Rabirio, quod iit ad arma, crucem T. Labienus in
campo Martio defigendam putavit, quod tandem
excogitabitur in eum supplicium qui vocavit? Ac si
fides Saturnino data est, quod abs te saepissime
dicitur, non eam C. Rabirius sed C. Marius dedit,
idemque violavit, si in fide non stetit. Quae fides,
Labiene, qui potuit sine senatus consulto dari?[a]
Adeone hospes es huiusce urbis, adeone ignarus disciplinae consuetudinisque nostrae ut haec nescias, ut
peregrinari in aliena civitate, non in tua magistra-
29 tum gerere videare? " Quid iam ista C. Mario,"
inquit, " nocere possunt, quoniam sensu et vita
caret? " Itane vero? tantis in laboribus C. Marius
periculisque vixisset, si nihil longius quam vitae
termini postulabant spe atque animo de se et gloria
sua cogitasset? At, credo, cum innumerabilis hostium copias in Italia fudisset atque obsidione rem
publicam liberasset,[b] omnia sua secum una moritura
arbitrabatur. Non est ita, Quirites; neque quisquam nostrum in rei publicae periculis cum laude ac
virtute versatur quin spe posteritatis fructuque
ducatur. Itaque cum multis aliis de causis virorum bonorum mentes divinae mihi atque aeternae videntur
esse, tum maxime quod optimi et sapientissimi
cuiusque animus ita praesentit in posterum ut nihil
30 nisi sempiternum spectare videatur. Quapropter

---

[a] No such decree would have been necessary, as all such
powers were already bestowed on the consuls by the *senatus
consultum ultimum*, for which see Introduction, paragraph 4.
[b] Refers to the defeat of the Cimbri by Marius at Vercellae,
101 B.C.

say, of your liberties and of our state, be condemned
by us, now that he is dead, as guilty of the hideous
crime of murder ?

Indeed, if Titus Labienus has thought fit to erect a 28
cross on the Campus Martius for Gaius Rabirius
because he took up arms, what punishment shall be
devised for the man who summoned him to arms ?
And if, as you are so fond of asserting, a promise of
safety was given to Saturninus, it was not Rabirius
but Marius who gave it ; and Marius, too, who broke
it if it was not kept.   How could such a promise have
been given, Labienus, without a decree of the Senate?*
Are you such a stranger to this city, so ignorant of
our traditions and our custom, as not to know this,
till we get the impression that you are a visitor in
a foreign country, not a magistrate in your own ?
" What harm," says he, " can all this do to Gaius 29
Marius now, since he is dead and cannot feel ? "
But is that true ?   Would Gaius Marius have lived
a life of so much toil and danger if he had had no
hope, no thought, of winning for himself a glory more
lasting than his mortal life ? Nay, I suppose that
when, on the soil of Italy,* he had routed the countless hosts of the enemy and delivered the city from
a siege, he imagined that all his achievements would
perish with himself ! It is not true, gentlemen :
there is not one of us who, in the hours of his country's
peril, is led to play his part with credit and with
valour save by the hope that posterity will reward
him.   And so among the many reasons which lead
us to think that the souls of good men are divine and
immortal, the chief is this, that the spirits of our best
and wisest men look forward to the future with a gaze
fixed only on eternity.   Therefore do I call to 30

equidem et C. Mari et ceterorum virorum sapien-
tissimorum ac fortissimorum civium mentis, quae
mihi videntur ex hominum vita ad deorum religionem
et sanctimoniam demigrasse, testor me pro illorum
fama, gloria, memoria non secus ac pro patriis fanis
atque delubris propugnandum putare, ac, si pro
illorum laude mihi arma capienda essent, non minus
strenue caperem, quam illi pro communi salute
ceperunt. Etenim, Quirites, exiguum nobis vitae
curriculum natura circumscripsit, immensum gloriae.
XI. Qua re, si eos qui iam de vita decesserunt ornabi-
mus, iustiorem nobis mortis condicionem relinquemus.

Sed si illos, Labiene, quos iam videre non possumus
neglegis, ne his quidem quos vides consuli putas
31 oportere ? Neminem esse dico ex his omnibus, qui
illo die Romae fuerit, quem tu diem in iudicium
vocas, pubesque tum fuerit, quin arma ceperit, quin
consules secutus sit. Omnes ei quorum tu ex aetate
coniecturam facere potes quid tum fecerint abs te
capitis C. Rabiri nomine citantur. At occidit Saturninum Rabirius. Vtinam fecisset! non supplicium
deprecarer sed praemium postularem. Etenim, si
Scaevae, servo Q. Crotonis, qui occidit L. Saturninum,
libertas data est, quod equiti Romano praemium dari
par fuisset ? et, si C. Marius, quod fistulas quibus
aqua suppeditabatur Iovis Optimi Maximi templis

witness the souls of Gaius Marius and all other wise
and good citizens, whom I believe to have left behind
the life of men and passed to the holy and sacred
estate of the gods, that I feel it my duty to contend
no less in defence of their honour, their glory and their
memory than I would for the temples and shrines of
my country ; and that if I needed to take arms to
defend their renown, I would do so not less vigor-
ously than they did when they took up arms to
defend the common liberty. Narrow indeed, gentlemen, are the bounds within which Nature has confined our lives, but those of our glory are infinite.
XI. And so it follows that in doing honour to those
who have passed away, we shall thereby be making
our own prospect in death more favourable.

But even if you are regardless, Labienus, of those
whom we can see no longer, do you hold that nothing
should be done for those whom you do see ? I 31
declare that of all those who were in Rome on that
day—the day that you are now haling to judgement
—not one who was of age failed to take arms and
follow the consuls. Every one of those at whose
conduct on that occasion you can arrive by a com-
putation of their age, is, in the person of Gaius
Rabirius, by you impeached upon a capital charge.
You say that Gaius Rabirius killed Saturninus.
Would that he had ! I should not then be trying to
save him from punishment but should be claiming
his reward. Indeed, if Scaeva, the slave of Quintus
Croton, who did kill Lucius Saturninus, was granted
his freedom, what reward could have been fittingly
bestowed upon a Roman Knight ? And if Gaius
Marius, for having given orders to cut the pipes
which supplied water to the Temple and shrine of

CICERO

ac sedibus praecidi imperarat, quod in clivo Capitolino
improborum civium ***

FRAGMENTA

a Niebuhrio e cod. Vaticano palimpsesto primum edita

32 XII. *** aret. Itaque non senatus in ea causa
cognoscenda me agente diligentior aut inclementior
fuit quam vos universi, cum orbis terrae distributionem
atque illum ipsum agrum Campanum animis, manibus,
vocibus repudiavistis.

33 Idem ego quod is qui auctor huius iudicii est
clamo, praedico, denuntio. Nullus est reliquus rex,
nulla gens, nulla natio quam pertimescatis ; nullum
adventicium, nullum extraneum malum est quod
insinuare in hanc rem publicam possit. Si immortalem
hanc civitatem esse voltis, si aeternum hoc imperium,
si gloriam sempiternam manere, nobis a nostris
cupiditatibus, a turbulentis hominibus atque novarum
rerum cupidis, ab intestinis malis, a domesticis consiliis
34 est cavendum. Hisce autem malis magnum praesidium vobis maiores vestri reliquerunt, vocem illam
consulis : " qui rem publicam salvam esse vellent."
Huic voci favete, Quirites, neque vestro iudicio abstu-
leritis mihi . . . . . . neque eripueritis rei publicae spem

---

^a Here occurs a lacuna: see Analysis of the Speech, §§ 31-
32, and Introduction, paragraph 2.
^b This refers to the recent proposal of Rullus to invest a
commission of ten (from whose number Pompeius was expressly excluded) with extraordinary powers to purchase
land in Italy, and particularly in Campania, for the settlement of colonies, the money to be provided by the recent
conquests in Asia. The opposition of the Senate, voiced by
Cicero, had resulted in its withdrawal.

most High and Mighty Juppiter, and for having, on
the Capitoline Hill . . .*a*

*(The following Fragments were first published by
Niebuhr, who discovered them in a palimpsest* MS. *in
the Vatican Library)*

XII. . . . And so, in its handling of that case at my 32
instance, the Senate was not more particular or more
severe than were all of you when by your attitude,
your hands, and your voices you refused to accept the
proposal to divide the world, nay, you refused to
accept the actual territory of Campania.*b* . . .

That which I cry aloud, I proclaim, I publish 33
abroad is the same as does he who is responsible for
this trial : *c* no king is left, no nation, no tribe to
cause you fear : there is no evil from outside, of
other's causing, that can make its way into our
country : if you desire that country to be immortal,
if you desire our empire to be eternal and our glory
everlasting, it is against our own passions that we
must be on our guard, against men of violence and
revolutionaries, against evils from within, against
plots devised at home. But against these evils your 34
forefathers have left you a great protection in the
consul's power to pronounce the words " Let those
who desire the safety of the Republic. . . ." *d*
Cherish this pronouncement, gentlemen, and never
by a verdict of yours take from me . . . nor snatch

c This may mean either Labienus or Caesar ; see Introduction, paragraph 4.
d This power was based on the *senatus consultum ultimum* ;
see Introduction, paragraph 4.

35 libertatis, spem salutis, spem dignitatis. Quid facerem,
si T. Labienus caedem civium fecisset ut L. Saturninus,
si carcerem refregisset, si Capitolium cum armatis
occupavisset? Facerem idem quod C. Marius fecit,
ad senatum referrem, vos ad rem publicam defenden-
dam cohortarer, armatus ipse vobiscum armato ob-
sisterem. Nunc quoniam armorum suspicio nulla est,
tela non video, non vis, non caedes, non Capitoli
atque arcis obsessio est, sed accusatio perniciosa,
iudicium acerbum, res tota a tribuno pl. suscepta
contra rem publicam, non vos ad arma vocandos esse,
verum ad suffragia cohortandos contra oppugnationem
vestrae maiestatis putavi. Itaque nunc vos omnis
oro atque obtestor hortorque. Non ita mos est,
consulem cum es . . .

36 XIII. *** timet; qui hasce ore adverso pro re publica
cicatrices ac notas virtutis accepit, is ne quod accipiat
famae volnus perhorrescit; quem numquam in-
cursiones hostium loco movere potuerunt, is nunc
impetum civium, cui necessario cedendum est, per-

37 horrescit. Neque a vobis iam bene vivendi sed
honeste moriendi facultatem petit, neque tam ut
domo sua fruatur quam ne patrio sepulcro privetur
laborat. Nihil aliud iam vos orat atque obsecrat
nisi uti ne se legitimo funere et domestica morte pri-
vetis, ut eum qui pro patria nullum umquam mortis
periculum fugit in patria mori patiamini.

---

* This may be a reference to the pseudo-Gracchus (see
Introduction, paragraph 2), who was imprisoned by Marius
but released by the mob.

from the Republic its hopes of freedom, of safety, and of honour.

What should I do if Titus Labienus, like Lucius 35 Saturninus, caused a massacre of the citizens, broke from prison,[a] seized the Capitol with an armed force ? I should do as Gaius Marius did. I should bring a motion before the Senate, exhort you to defend the Republic and take arms myself to oppose, with your help, an armed enemy. But as it is, since there is no thought of arms, no weapon to be seen, no violence, no slaughter, no siege of the fortress of the Capitol, but a baleful prosecution, an envenomed trial—the whole amounting to an attack upon the Republic by a tribune—I felt my duty to lie not in summoning you to take up arms but in exhorting you to give your votes against this assault upon your sovereign majesty. And so I now beg you, beseech you, and exhort you all : not thus is it our custom, when . . .

XIII. . . . is afraid : he who, facing the foe, has 36 received these scars, these marks of valour, in his country's cause, trembles lest he receive any wound upon his honour. He whom the assaults of the enemy have never succeeded in dislodging from his post, now trembles at the onset of his fellow-citizens before which he cannot but give way. Nor does he 37 ask you now to grant him a happy life but only an honourable death : his endeavour is less to secure that he may enjoy his home, than that he may not be deprived of burial with his fathers. That is now his one petition, his sole prayer, save also this, that you do not deprive him of lawful obsequies and the right to die at home : that you suffer him to die within that country for whose sake he has never shunned any peril of death.

CICERO

38   Dixi ad id tempus q*uod* mihi a tribuno pl. prae*sti*-
tutum est ; a vob*is peto* quaesoque ut ha*nc me*am
defension*em* pro amici pericu*lo fi*delem, pro rei publicae salu*te* consularem pu*tetis.*

I have now spoken as long as I am allowed by the 38 tribune. I hope and pray that you will regard this my speech for the defence as having fulfilled my duty both as an advocate to the requirements of my friend and as a consul to the welfare of my country.

INDEX OF PROPER NAMES

(The references throughout are to the pages.)

Accius, Titus, 206-441 *passim*
Achaean League, 24
Aebutius, Sextus, 84-205 *passim*
Aeetes, 35
Aegean Sea, 67
Aelius, Publius, 399
Aemilius, Mamercus, 327
Aemilius, Marcus, Scaurus, 151, 472, 473, 481
Aetolian League, 27
Africa, 8, 41, 43, 47, 73
Ager Gallicus, 243, 245
Alatrium, 267, 279
Alba, 373
Albius, Sextus, 411
Albius, Statius. See Oppianicus
Ambivius, 401
Amisus, 33
Ancharius, 399
Ancona, 263
Annius, Titus, 303
Antiochus, 119, 121
Antiochus III. of Syria, 27, 65
Antium, 66
Antonius, Marcus, 44, 371, 481
Appian Way, 67
Apulia, 249, 345, 459
Aquilius, Gaius, 175, 193, 381
Aquilius, Manius, 5, 22
Aquilius, Marcus, 357
Aquinum, 429
Archimedes, 315
Ariminum, 201
Ariobarzanes, 5, 19, 25
Armenia, 6, 7, 35
Arpinum, 428
Arretium, 195
Artaxata, 7
Ascla, 413

Asculum, 243
Asellius, Marcus, 405, 409
Asia, 1-88 *passim*
Asuvius, 257, 259, 261
Atella, Safinius, 293, 327
Athens, 65
Atilius, Aulus and Lucius, 123
Auria, 253
Aurius, Aulus, 245, 247
Aurius, Aulus, Melinus, 233, 235, 247, 425
Aurius, Lucius, 247
Aurius, Marcus, 243, 245
Aurius, Numerius, 243
Aurius, Titus, 419
Avillius, 257, 259, 261
Axia, castle of, 115

Baebius, Marcus, 269
Balbus, Publius Octavius, 335
Basilus, Marcus, 335
Bithynia, 6, 19
Bosphorus, the, 21
Bovianum, 435
Brundisium, 45, 47
Brutus, Marcus, 373, 375
Brutus, M. ("the Prosecutor"), 371, 373
Brutus, Decius, 475

Cabira, 6
Caecina, Aulus, 84-205 *passim*
Caelius, Lucius, 121
Caelius, Quintus, Latiensis, 69
Caepasius (the brothers), 281
Caepio, Quintus Servilius, 372
Caesar, Gaius Julius, 209, 444, 446, 448, 487

INDEX OF PROPER NAMES

Caesar, Lucius, 448
Caesennia, 86, 87, 107-113, 193
Caesennius, Publius, 86, 109, 123
Caieta, 45
Calpurnius, Lucius, 131
Campania, 459, 486, 487
Campus Martius, the, 328, 460-463, 483
Cannutius, Publius, 251, 273, 281, 299, 309
Cappadocia, 5, 21, 33
Cappadox, Vibius, 401
Carbo, Gaius Papirius, 42
Carthage, 2, 58, 65, 71
Cassius, Gaius, 81, 369
Castor, temple of, 320
Catulus, Quintus, 63, 71-77, 475, 481
Catulus, Quintus (son of the above), 481
Caudinus, Gaius, 335
Ceius, 399
Cethegus, Publius, 312, 318
Cilicia, 5, 9, 47, 77
Cimbrians, the, 58, 71, 482
Cinna, Lucius Cornelius, 181, 185
Claudius, Appius, "Caecus," 150,151
Claudius, Gaius, 475
Cleophantus, 269, 277
Clodius, Lucius, 263
Clodius, Sextus, " Phormio," 123
Cluentia (Habitus's aunt), 253
Cluentia (Habitus's sister), 237
Cluentius, Aulus, Habitus, 206-441 *passim*
Cluentius, Numerius, 403
Cnidus, 45
Colophon, 45
Columna Maenia, 260
Cominius, Lucius and Publius, 327, 329
Considius, Quintus, 335
Corinth, 23, 66
Cosconius, Gaius, 325
Cotta, Gaius, 195, 197
Cotta, Marcus Aurelius, 320, 446
Crassus, Lucius, 149, 167, 371-375, 475, 481
Crassus, Marcus Licinius, 8
Crete, 49, 57, 59
Croton, Quintus, 485
Curio, Gaius, 81, 475
Curius, Manius, 149
Curtius, Gaius, 458, 459
Cyzicus, 6, 33

Decianus, Gaius, 477, 479
Decidius, Gnaeus, 399
Delos, 66, 67
Dinea, 243, 245, 255, 261, 263
Diogenes, 269, 275, 277, 413
Dolabella, Publius, 119
Domitius, Gaius and Lucius, 475
Domitius, Gnaeus, 349
Drusus, Marcus Livius, 388, 389, 446, 475

Egnatius, Gaius and his son, 365, 367
Ennius, 401
Equitius, 472
Esquiline Gate, 259
Euphrates, 7

Fabius, Quintus, Maximus, 58, 59
Fabrateria, 429
Fabricius, Gaius, 267, 269, 271, 279-287, 309, 313, 333, 408, 427
Fabricius, Lucius, 267, 269
Falcidius, Gaius, 69
Falcula, Fidiculanius, 123, 124, 318, 331, 337, 341, 343
Falernum, 411
Ferentum, 435
Fidiculanius. See Falcula
Fimbria, Gaius, 475
Flaccus, L. Valerius. See Valerius
Flaminius, Gaius, 355, 381
Florus, 399
Fulcinius, Marcus, 86, 107-113
Furius, Publius, 479

Gabinius, Aulus, 63, 67, 69
Galba, Servius, 475
Gaul, 41, 43, 47
Gellius, Lucius, 349, 361, 363
Geta, Gaius, 347
Glabrio, Manius Acilius, 7, 24, 39
Glaucia, 445, 446, 471, 473
Gracchus, Gaius, 2, 211, 386, 444, 445, 462-467, 472
Gracchus, Tiberius, 184, 185, 465
Gutta, Tiberius, 297, 301, 305, 327, 331, 357

Habitus. See Cluentius
Hannibal, 58
Heius, Gnaeus, 337
Helvidius, Publius, Rufus, 435

494

INDEX OF PROPER NAMES

Hortensius, Quintus, 62, 63, 67, 77, 360, 415

ILLYRIAN SEA, the, 47
Illyricum, 825

JANICULUM, the, 448
Jugurtha, 58, 71
Julius Caesar. See Caesar
Junius, Gaius, 206-441 passim
Junius, Marcus, 355
Jupiter, 457
Juturna, 329

LABIENUS, Quintus, 464, 465, 473
Labienus, Titus, 442-491 passim
Larinum, 442-491 passim
Latiensis. See Caelius
Latin Way, the, 400, 401
Lentulus, Gnaeus, 69, 347, 349, 363
Lepidus, Marcus Aemilius, 8, 475
Lex Aurelia, 446
Lex Calpurnia, 212
Lex Cornelia de repetundis, 212
Lex Cornelia de sicariis, 211, 391
Lex Fabia, 459 ;
Lex Gabinia, 9, 65, 66, 69.
Lex Manilia, 9, 66
Lex Porcia, 459, 463
Lex Sempronia, 391
Lex Servilia, 372, 373
Ligurians, the, 297
Livius Drusus. See Drusus
Luceria, 435
Lucullus, Lucius, 1-83 passim, 367
Lydia, 16

MACER, Gaius, 459
Maecenas, Gaius, 389
Magia, 243
Magius, Gnaeus, 243, 255, 257
Mancinus, 196, 197
Manilius, Gaius, 9, 81
Manlius, Quintus, 261
Marcellus, Marcus Claudius, 58, 59
Marius, Gaius, 59, 71, 184, 209, 442-491 passim
Marrucini, the, 435
Mars, 265
Marsian War, the, 40
Martiales, the, 265, 267
Matrinius, Decius, 355
Medea, 34, 35
Melinus. See Aurius, Aulus

Memmius, Gaius, 445
Mergus, Lucius Caulus, 335
Metellus, Lucius Caecilius (Dalmaticus), 347, 475
Metellus, Quintus Caec. (Celer), 448
Metellus, Q. Caec. (Creticus), 56, 69, 415
Metellus, Q. Caec. (Numidicus), 322, 323
Metellus, Q. Caec. (Pius), 247
Milesia, 255
Misenum, 45
Mithridates VI., of Pontus, 1-83 passim
Mucius, Quintus. See Scaevola
Mummius, Publius, 121
Murena, Lucius, 6, 21
Mutina, 8

NARBO, 373
Naso, Quintus Voconius, 379, 381
Nicostratus, 411-415, 419, 423
Novia, 249
Numa Pompilius, 464, 465
Numantia, 58, 71
Numidia, 42

OCEAN, 47
Oppianicus, Statius Albius, 124, 125, 206-441 passim
Oppianicus, son of the above, 231, 243, 245, 261, 408, 415, 419, 423
Oppianicus, Gaius, 253
Orchivius, Gaius, 321, 381
Ostium, 47

PACENUS, 399
Pacuvius, 156
Pamphylia, 49
Papia, 249
Pedo, Marcus Juventius, 335
Perses, 65
Picenum, 477
Philip V. of Macedonia, 27
Philippus, Lucius, 73, 475
Phormio. See Clodius
Phormio, the, of Terence, 122
Phrygia, 16
Piso, Gaius, 84-205 passim
Plaetorius, Lucius, 403
Plaetorius, Marcus, 355, 381
Plancus, Gnaeus, 371
Pompeius, Gnaeus Magnus, 1-83 passim

INDEX OF PROPER NAMES

Pompeius, Quintus Rufus, 233
Pontus, 4, 6, 7, 21, 33, 35
Popilius, Publius, 322-327, 331, 361, 363
Privernum, 373
Publicius, Quintus, 355
Punic War, the first, 26
Pusio, Gaius Flavius, 389

Quinctius, Lucius, 206-441 *passim*
Quirites, 14 (note) and *passim*

Rabirius, Gaius, 442-491 *passim*
Recoverers, 87, 93
Rhodes, 65
Romulus, 464, 465
Rufus, Publius Helvidius. See Helvidius
Rullus, Publius Servilius, 486
Rupilius, Aulus, 413
Rutilius, Lucius, 419
Rutilius, Publius, 123
Rutilius, Publius Rufus, 475

Sacerdos, Gaius Licinius, 365
Safinius. See Atella
Samnium, 435
Samos, 45
Sardinia, 47
Sassia, 206-441 *passim*
Saturius, Publius, 337, 419
Saturninus, 442-491 *passim*
Saufeius, Gaius, 473
Scaeva, 485
Scaevola, Quintus Mucius, the Augur, 166, 167, 472, 473, 481
Scaevola, Q. Mucius, the Pontifex Maximus, 148, 149, 166, 167, 481
Scaevola, Publius Septimius, 343, 345
Scamander, 206-441 *passim*
Scaurus, Marcus. See Aemilius, Marcus
Scipio, Lucius Cornelius (Asiaticus), 475
Scipio, Publius Aemilianus (Africanus, minor), 58, 59, 71, 364, 365
Sergius, Quintus, 243
Serranus, Gaius, 475
Sertorius, Quintus, 6, 8, 23, 33, 42
Servilius, Publius, 81, 475
Servilius, Quintus. See Caepio

Sicily, 3, 8, 42, 43, 47, 73, 265, 314
Sinope, 33
Spain, 6, 8, 21, 23, 41, 43, 47, 59, 71
Spartacus, 43
Staienus, Gaius, 206-331 *passim*
Statius Albius. See Oppianicus
Sulla, Lucius Cornelius, 1-83 *passim*, 88, 184, 193-197, 200, 201, 209, 233, 276, 277, 338, 339, 386, 387, 446, 472
Sulla, L. Cornelius Faustus, 320-323
Syracuse, 58, 314
Syria, 77

Tarentum, 249
Tarquinii, 107
Tarquinius Superbus, 464, 465
Teanum, 249, 435
Telesinus, 184, 185
Terentius, Aulus, 121
Teutons, the, 58, 71
Tiber, 47
Tibur, 373
Tigranes, 6, 7, 35, 37, 57
Tigranocerta, 7
Titinius, Gnaeus, 389
Titius, Sextus, 479
Tribunal Aurelium, 320
Tribuni aerarii, 481
Tudicus, Gnaeus, 435
Tusculum, 151

Utica, 42

Valerius Flaccus Lucius, 471, 473, 481
Varro, Terentius, 360
Varus, Publius Quintilius, 277
Venus, 265
Vercellae, 482
Verres, Gaius, 3, 62, 319
Vetilius, Publius, 121
Vibius Cappadox. See Cappadox
Vibius, Sextus, 247
Voconius, Quintus. See Naso
Volaterrae, 88, 115
Voluminius, Publius, 435
Volusienus, Lucius, 435

Ziela, 7